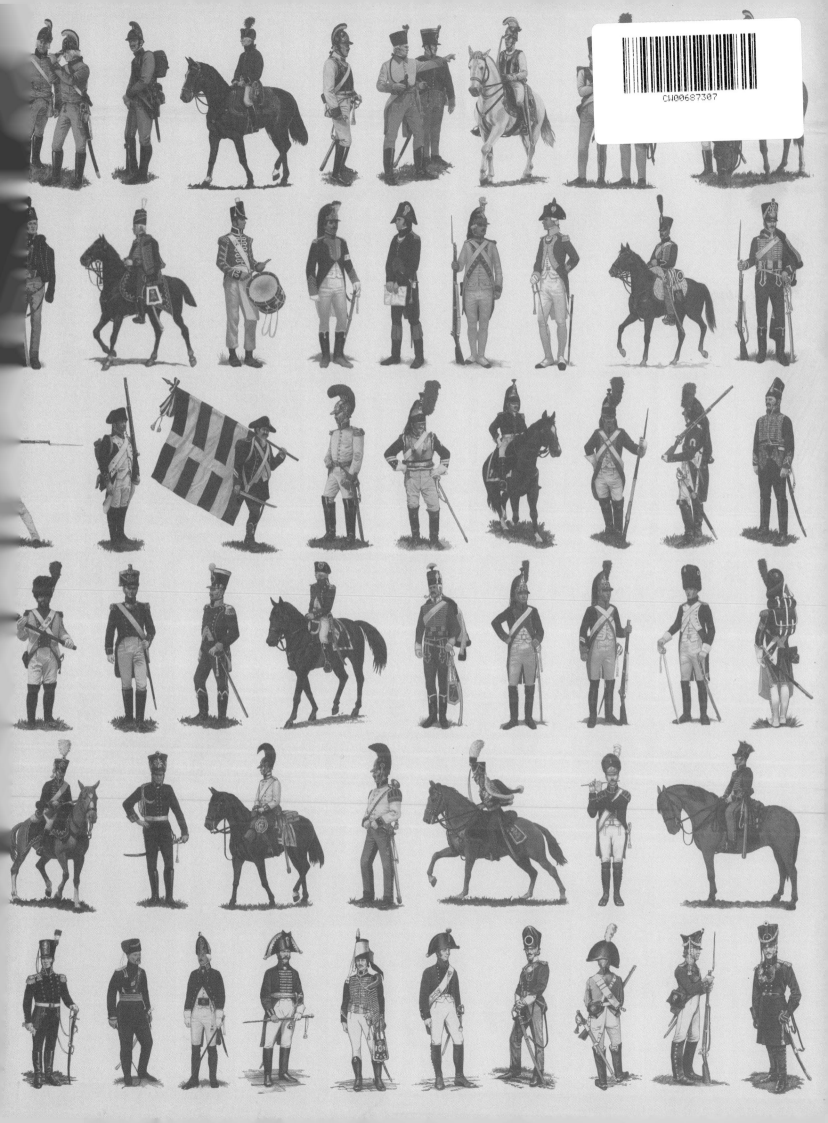

CW00687307

AN ILLUSTRATED ENCYCLOPEDIA OF
UNIFORMS OF THE NAPOLEONIC WARS

AN ILLUSTRATED ENCYCLOPEDIA OF
UNIFORMS OF THE NAPOLEONIC WARS

An expert, in-depth guide to the officers and soldiers
of the Revolutionary and Napoleonic period, 1792–1815

AUTHOR DIGBY SMITH • CONSULTANT JEREMY BLACK

LORENZ BOOKS

This edition is published by Lorenz Books
an imprint of Anness Publishing Ltd
Hermes House, 88–89 Blackfriars Road, London SE1 8HA
tel. 020 7401 2077; fax 020 7633 9499
www.lorenzbooks.com; www.annesspublishing.com

If you like the images in this book and would like to investigate using them
for publishing, promotions or advertising, please visit our website
www.practicalpictures.com for more information.

UK agent: The Manning Partnership Ltd; tel. 01225 478444;
fax 01225 478440; sales@manning-partnership.co.uk

UK distributor: Grantham Book Services Ltd;
tel. 01476 541080; fax 01476 541061; orders@gbs.tbs-ltd.co.uk

North American agent/distributor: National Book Network;
tel. 301 459 3366; fax 301 429 5746; www.nbnbooks.com

Australian agent/distributor: Pan Macmillan Australia;
tel. 1300 135 113; fax 1300 135 103; customer.service@macmillan.com.au

New Zealand agent/distributor: David Bateman Ltd;
tel. (09) 415 7664; fax (09) 415 8892

Publisher: Joanna Lorenz
Editorial Director: Helen Sudell
Executive Editor: Joanne Rippin
Copy Editor: Jonathan North
Illustration: figures: Rob McCaig, Simon Smith, Nick Spender, Peter Denis,
  maps: Peter Bull Studio
Designer: Nigel Partridge
Editorial Reader: Lindsay Zamponi
Production Controller: Steve Lang

ETHICAL TRADING POLICY
Because of our ongoing ecological investment programme, you, as our
customer, can have the pleasure and reassurance of knowing that a tree is
being cultivated on your behalf to naturally replace the materials used to make
the book you are holding. For further information about this scheme, go to
www.annesspublishing.com/trees

© Anness Publishing Ltd 2006, 2008

All rights reserved. No part of this publication may be reproduced, stored in a
retrieval system, or transmitted in any way or by any means, electronic,
mechanical, photocopying, recording or otherwise, without the prior written
permission of the copyright holder.

A CIP catalogue record for this book is available from the British Library.

CONTENTS

INTRODUCTION

This book has a broad scope, with information included from the Revolutionary period (1789–1804), which is usually excluded from most publications. Without this early background, the Napoleonic era (1805–15) is sometimes difficult to place in the right context. The first part of this book sets the scene for the reader, giving brief explanations of the political climate and systems of the period, the social structures and the effects upon them of the French Revolution, which rocked the foundations of all the thrones in Europe. Parallel to this political whirlwind, the Industrial Revolution was already transforming commerce and society in Britain, in particular. The book then covers the campaigns throughout the period, with analytical comments providing the background to events in the field. The world in which soldiers of that time lived is also examined, with examples drawn from various European armies to illustrate the conditions under which they lived, fought and died. The main body of the work examines in great detail the uniforms and organization of the armies of the period 1792 to 1815. France, with the largest army in Europe – including Russia until 1812 – and the second largest navy, was the leading continental power in 1789.

Social and Military Upheaval

Although there can be little doubt that there were many justifiable grounds for radical social change in pre-Revolutionary France, the upheavals of the revolution itself and the Terror that followed (July 1793–July 1794) did great damage to the fabric of the nation, and to the armed services, which lost over half of its officers. Some of these ended up on the guillotine, but most fled the country to avoid that fate, abandoning their estates and in many cases their fortunes. This period of turbulence

▲ *Napoleon, dressed in regal splendour as Emperor of France, with all the symbols of his imperial office displayed.*

allowed many opportunists to elbow their way on to the world stage, the most remarkable of whom was Napoleon Bonaparte.

In the traditional monarchies, such social mobility was extremely rare, but in the army it was possible. In Russia there were 32 former peasants in the officer corps in 1812. In Britain, until the reforms instituted by the Duke of York in 1797–1802, it was customary for rich schoolboys to have commissions bought for them by their parents, so that when they eventually joined their regiment – years later – they had already worked, or bought, their way up the promotion ladder without having the slightest idea of the requirements of their jobs. Other ranks might win commissions on the field, but their subsequent careers were extremely limited.

It is no exaggeration to say that, prior to about 1800, the British had merely been playing at being soldiers. Another peculiarity of the British army

was that it was relatively small and was scattered around the globe in small pockets. While the use of divisions and corps was being developed in the major continental armies, there was no similar trend in the British Army. The only place where such experiences in handling large-scale formations could be gathered was in India. It was here that Arthur Wellesley, the Sepoy General, learned his craft, which was to stand him in such good stead in both Portugal and Spain from 1808.

The other great change that was to burst upon the armies of Europe was the replacement of small armies of ageing, long-service professional soldiers, by larger armies, fleshed out with rapidly trained young conscripts, selected for limited military service by ballot. Captain Lazare-Nicolas-Marguerite Carnot (an officer of engineers) had saved France from her enemies with this measure in 1792; by 1813 conscription was common on mainland Europe.

Uniforms and Badges of Rank

Military uniforms underwent considerable change during this period, change that extended across nations in many cases, and which reflected alterations in civilian fashion as well. Hairstyles altered dramatically: the old, unsanitary powdered, curled and queued fashion, which took hours to prepare, gave way to almost modern cuts, the exception being the Electorate of Hessen-Kassel (re-established in late 1813), where the old style of 1806 was rigorously reintroduced, powder and all. In 1792 most of the small German states copied the Prussian style, with brass or tin grenadier caps and elaborate gold or silver lace decoration to officers' coats.

While officer status was clearly expressed by the quality and expense of the uniform, and by the wearing of voluminous waist sashes, gorgets and silver or gold sword knots, individual

ranks were much less emphasized. Catholic countries tended to dress their troops in white coats; Protestant states generally favoured dark blue or red. The French infantry`s change from white to dark blue coats in the early 1790's was a dramatic step.

The French Revolution, with its egalitarian guiding principles, led the way in the abolition of officers' embroidery. The new system of expressing officers' ranks through the use of various types of epaulettes was widely copied, particularly as, after the formation of the Confederation of the Rhine in 1806, a sort of "Warsaw Pact" emerged, with the German states following the French military sartorial lead. Following the end of the Napoleonic wars, military fashion throughout Europe went overboard as peacetime soldiering fostered all sorts of expensive frivolities and eccentricities, such as bell-topped shakoes and ultra-tight jackets with padded chests.

▲ *Europe, as it was before Napoleon made his mark on its old boundaries, kingdoms, states and principalities.*

▼ *Uniforms became more tight-fitting in the Napoleonic era. Coat skirts reduced in volume and length, and standing collars appeared.*

Europe's New Order

Europe after the Napoleonic era was markedly different, and foundations were laid for its modern manifestation. France was one of the leaders in the development of permanent formation structures. There is a school of thought that holds that Napoleon`s field command headquarters was the model for that of the modern North Atlantic Treaty Organization (NATO). This is hotly disputed, as Napoleon`s staff was entirely built around his needs to rule his empire and command his army simultaneously in his inimitable style. It failed to work as soon as the Emperor was removed from its centre. It would seem that the Prussian and Austrian staff systems of the Napoleonic age have equally valid claims to have fathered the NATO staff organization. It is against this dynamic background that we shall come to learn about the armies that fought and died in, lost and won the many battles of the period.

EUROPE IN THE LATE EIGHTEENTH CENTURY

At this time, Europe was a melting pot of political ideas. The *ancien régime* of Bourbon France was the epicentre of radical concepts made manifest by the Revolution of 1789. This spark – initially a moderate plea for greater power-sharing – ignited a pan-European war destined to last for 23 years. The era, therefore, was a time of dynamic change, as the ideals of liberty, equality and fraternity challenged the crowned heads of Europe to face the power of the people. The result of this clash of ideologies was the demise of the old political order – symbolized by the decrepit Holy Roman Empire – and the emergence of the modern era.

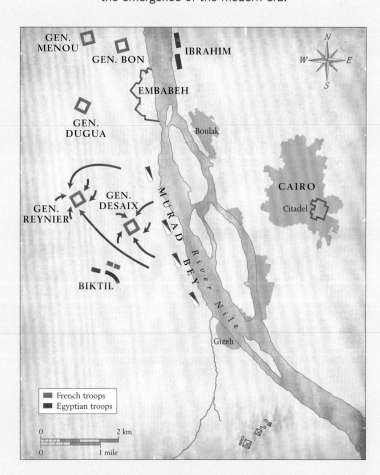

▲ *The Battle of the Pyramids, which took place on 21 July 1798, demonstrated the formidable military power of the French Army.*

◄ *The meeting of the Allies on the banks of the River Danube on 6 July 1809, at the Battle of Wagram.*

THE POLITICAL AND SOCIAL POSITION OF EUROPEAN STATES

At the time of the Revolutionary and Napoleonic Wars, Europe was largely made up of a patchwork of independent kingdoms, dukedoms and city states. Much of Europe was controlled by Vienna, in the name of the Holy Roman Empire: this included most of Germany, still to be unified by Bismarck. The only real superpower was Great Britain, whose head start in the Industrial Revolution – matched with supremacy at sea – had created the potential for considerable wealth. And yet, the nation that lay at the centre of political and military events was France: birthplace of revolution, and surrogate mother to the "Corsican ogre" Napoleon Bonaparte.

Pre-Revolutionary France

France was an absolutist monarchy at the end of the eighteenth century with the king as the unchallenged power in the realm. Since 1774 that had been Louis XVI. Tension evolved out of the serious state of France's finances and Louis did nothing to prevent the headlong rush into crisis. The body politic consisted of three "Estates" of

▼ British ships dominated the European seas and facilitated her huge national wealth.

clergy, aristocracy and the rest. The First and Second Estates were the major landowners in the country, and were free from taxation. Only the Third Estate was liable for taxation, and most of the peasantry lived on the verge of starvation. The system was ripe for uprising and revolution.

Causes of the French Revolution

In 1788–89 France's harvest was only 25 per cent of the normal level because of bad weather. In Paris there were food riots. Louis called the Estates General together in May 1789, for the populace to express their grievances. Needless to say, the aristocracy wanted to protect its privileges, but on 17 June the representatives of the Third Estate, joined by many clergymen, declared themselves the "National Assembly", swearing to remain in session until they had given France a constitution.

Louis backed down but began gathering troops to crush the revolt. The National Assembly asked him to disperse them but he refused. The National Assembly launched a massive popular mobilization to oppose what they saw as a plot. On 13 July, in Paris, mobs ransacked gunsmiths' shops for weapons, and the day after stormed the

▲ Louis XVI of France, a weak king led by his extravagant Austrian wife, Marie Antoinette.

Bastille, which supposedly contained political prisoners. The garrison was massacred and two senior royal officials were lynched in Paris the same day. The rebels then declared the royal government of Paris defunct, forming a republican one in its place. On 27 August 1789 the National Assembly published "The Declaration of the Rights of Man and of the Citizen", sealing the fate of the old order.

The National Assembly acted as the interim government of France during 1789–91. However, France's financial crisis continued, with the government printing more and more paper money and only increasing inflation. The political climate began to polarize between the moderates and the extremists. A new constitution was completed on 30 September 1791, and the National Assembly dissolved itself so elections could be held for a new legislative body. This convened in October 1791; the extremists, or Jacobins, were the pro-war party, while the moderates, or *Feuillants*, were for peace. In April 1792 France declared

war on Austria, the Holy Roman Empire, Prussia and the *émigrés*, noble families who had fled the country. The latter included many Army officers. About 50 per cent of Army officers and a crippling 75 per cent of naval officers had emigrated.

On 10 August 1792 the Legislative Assembly declared the king to be "suspended", the mob stormed the royal palace, the Swiss Guard was slaughtered and the royal family imprisoned. Many deputies fled Paris; leaving radical revolutionaries at the controls of the state. They ordered new elections to a "National Convention". Maximilien Robespierre argued that the state must become the instrument of the people's punitive will.

The Fall of the King

An Allied invasion of Champagne, intended to reinstate the king, had wilted at Valmy on 20 September 1792. The next day the National Convention abolished the monarchy, and in January 1793 they tried the king for treason. He was found guilty and died, as "Citizen Capet", on the guillotine on 21 January. Marie Antoinette followed him on 16 October. The National Convention now had a firm grip on political power, with the ten-member Committee of Public Safety enlisting the Jacobin Clubs across the nation to monitor local officials. On 19

November 1792, the French National Convention directed that it would "grant fraternity and succour to all people who should wish to recover their liberty" and would "give orders to their republican generals to aid all such efforts". The French resolved to forcefully export revolution to their European neighbours.

The Terror

On 27 July 1793 Robespierre set about eliminating his political foes. First he

▲ *The dramatic arrest of Robespierre marked a radical political change in France.*

turned on the extreme left, then on the moderates under Georges Danton. On 5 September 1793 Parisian militants expelled the remaining moderates from the city's Communes and took them over to "use terror against the enemies of the Revolution".

Robespierre embraced the Terror as a necessary means of preserving a nation menaced from abroad and sliding into civil war at home. In 1793–94 well over 200,000 citizens, many of them aristocracy, were arrested: some 10,000 died in the jails and 17,000 were condemned to death. By June 1794 the Jacobin dictatorship had secured the frontiers against foreign invasion and calm was restored. Robespierre then made another speech on 26 July 1794 denouncing another group as traitors. The Committee of Public Safety had had enough; Robespierre was arrested the next day and executed the day after.

◄ *Battle plan of Jemappes, 6 November 1792, a victory for the French that broke the Austrian will to hold Belgium; Revolutionary France went wild with joy.*

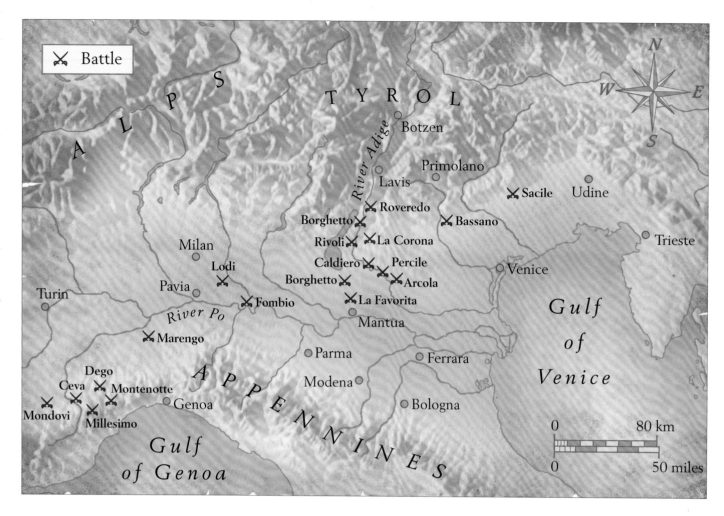

Battle

The Directory

In October 1795, the Committee of Public Safety was replaced by the Directory. Disaffected royalists tried to stage a coup in Paris on 5 October 1795, and the task of suppressing it was given to Napoleon Bonaparte, who quickly set up an ambush of 40 cannon and killed about 200 of the rebels. This was his famous "whiff of grapeshot". Even so, by 1797, public support for the Directory was waning.

The Rise of Napoleon

Following his suppression of the royalist coup, Napoleon was eager for action, fame and glory. After marrying Josephine de Beauharnais on 9 March 1796, he left Paris, having been assigned to command France's threadbare Army of Italy. His ability soon carried him forward through north Italy defeating the Austrian and Sardinian armies. The action began on 10 April at Voltri; 12 days later the Sardinians sued for peace. The whirlwind rushed eastward, scattering

the Austrians. A clash at Lodi became immortalized in Napoleonic legend; Milan fell on 29 June, but Napoleon was already besieging Mantua. He also looted the liberated regions, sending the assets back to Paris. Mantua surrendered on 2 February 1797, and the subsequent Treaty of Campo Formio on 17 October destroyed Austrian rule in much of north Italy.

Now one of the leading figures in France, Napoleon's ambitions grew and crystallized day by day. In August 1797, Napoleon convinced the Directory to mount an expedition to Egypt to threaten Britain's possessions in India. The Directory agreed and the expedition sailed in May 1798, captured Malta on 12 June, and on 3 July landed just west of Alexandria. Despite easy victories against the native Mamelukes, Napoleon was trapped following Nelson's defeat of the French fleet at the Battle of the Nile on 1 August 1798. He invaded Syria in 1799, but failed to take Acre and was forced to withdraw. That year Britain

▲ *Napoleon's campaign in northern Italy, so critical in his career, was fought from Turin in the west across to Venice, and from Innsbruck south to Genoa.*

financed the Second Coalition against France; Austro-Russian armies retook northern Italy and fighting took place in southern Germany and Holland. The defeated Directory grew more unpopular. Believing he might benefit, Napoleon abandoned his army and sailed for France, landing at Fréjus on 9 October. He raced for Paris, where he was greeted as a returning hero.

The *Coup d'État*

Napoleon was appointed Commander-in-Chief of all troops in the Paris region on 7 November. Three days later he entered the Chamber of the Five Hundred at St Cloud with a force of grenadiers to throw the representatives out. Following the coup, Napoleon wrote a new constitution in which he was elevated to First Consul, supported by two other consuls, Sièyes and Pierre-

Roger Ducos. Victory over the Austrians at Marengo, consolidated by the Peace of Luneville, enhanced his power. On 27 March 1802, Britain and France signed the Treaty of Amiens. Napoleon was voted First Consul for life on 2 August 1802, and on 18 May 1804 an empire was established, with Napoleon as emperor.

Georgian Britain

In contrast to continental kingdoms, Britain was a constitutional monarchy: the ruler's power was limited by Parliament and financial power rested in the hands of the House of Commons. King George III suffered from porphyria and the doctors thought him insane for certain periods. At such times, his eldest son, George, the unpopular Prince of Wales, was pronounced regent and ruled in his stead. The loss of the American colonies had been a personal blow to George III but, despite such political setbacks, he remained a relatively popular ruler. There were, of course, many defects in the British political system, but for its time it was benign and democratic. Political activity, however, was the preserve of the rich, landed gentry, and the government was as fearful of unrest by the masses – who were downtrodden – as of threats of foreign invasion. It was a time when political corruption was the norm.

▼ *A portrait of the dashing young Napoleon at the start of his military successes in 1796.*

The Industrial Revolution

In Britain, industrial change began relatively early on. Mechanical advancements were accompanied by great improvements in agricultural techniques and output. From around 1760 there was a great increase in the enclosure of common land, which increased agricultural efficiency and output levels. Small farms were increasingly bought up and absorbed into larger units, leading to a decrease in the agricultural labour force.

Population growth in England increased; before 1751 it was about 3 per cent per annum. During 1781–91 it was running at 9 per cent per annum. Crops from the new world, such as potatoes, were introduced, which provided plentiful, cheap food enabling larger populations to be sustained. In 1803–13 agricultural produce in England increased by 25 per cent. Open competition among producers was introduced and accelerated levels of output. Between 1769 and 1792 significant mechanical advances were made, culminating in steam engines, which were quickly developed for many purposes.

The result of this revolution was that expensive items could be rapidly and cheaply produced. With Indian cotton imports, Britain became the supplier of the world's clothing. This triggered social change on a large scale. Improved public health and cheaper

▲ *Bustling Billingsgate Market, London, with all the signs of a prosperous trading nation.*

food supplies led to a fast increase in the population and developments in political matters. Britain's international trade increased, and a new, wealthy middle class appeared; populations were urbanized, and a new, working class was created in the growing cities. Governments of the day recognized the advantages of an increased landless, penniless layer of society – among them a ready supply of cannon fodder.

The European Alliances

It was always Britain's aim to ensure that no single mainland European power achieved complete supremacy, thus she followed a policy of allying herself with several of the underdogs at any one time. As France was usually the dominant continental power, the two nations were often at odds.

France at first enjoyed support among the British, mainly in the lower classes, but also from thinkers and politicians. But even before the Terror of 1793–94, there was a change in public opinion, caused by the French declaration of war on her mainland European rivals. During this period the treaty constellations changed radically. Even the old enemy, Spain, was to be Britain's ally from 1808. There was but one constant: Britain and France were always on opposing sides.

The Reconfiguration of the Holy Roman Empire

The Treaty of Luneville, of 9 February 1801, had ceded to France all German territories on the left bank of the Rhine. These amounted to 37,284 square miles (60,000 square km) and 3.5 million inhabitants. They included the defunct electorates of Cologne, Mainz and Trier. This dispossession of many rulers caused much unrest and Napoleon suggested the remaining major states of the old Holy Roman Empire should compensate themselves by seizing the imperial-free cities and ecclesiastical properties that were left. In 1803 the Parliament of the Empire was convened. In the wings, Russia and France successfully supported the demands and aims of Baden, Bavaria, Hesse and Württemberg against Austria and Prussia.

▼ *Napoleon's victories in the campaign of 1807 relegated Prussia to a third-rate power, established the Grand Duchy of Warsaw and saw the birth of a Franco-Russian alliance.*

The *Reichsdeputationshauptschluss* of 25 February 1803 secularized all ecclesiastical states except that of the Teutonic Order. All free cities were absorbed into larger states except the Hanseatic towns of Hamburg, Bremen and Lübeck – which are still independent states within modern Germany today – and Frankfurt, Augsburg and Nuremburg.

Although the fortress of Mainz was now in French hands, the Prince-Archbishop of Mainz, Dalberg, was allowed to continue in office in Frankfurt and was awarded the territories of Regensburg, Wetzlar and Aschaffenburg. This state later became the Grand Duchy of Frankfurt.

The Peace of Pressburg of 26 December 1805, following the Battle of Austerlitz, saw the Austrian empire cede Venice to the Kingdom of Italy; and the Tyrol, Vorarlberg and other territories to Bavaria. Kaiser Franz II laid down the crown of the Holy Roman Empire and became Kaiser Franz I of Austria.

The Confederation of the Rhine

As the edifice of the Holy Roman Empire crumbled, an opportunity presented itself for the remoulding of the entire geography of central Europe. Napoleon knew at once how he would employ the political rubble left after the defeat and dismantling of the old imperial structure. He would reshape it into a new fortification, which would be of benefit to him against other potential enemies. The patchwork of tiny, fragmented states that had constituted the Holy Roman Empire would be moulded by Napoleon into a coalition of more viable kingdoms and duchies, all firmly under the influence of France. States that refused to co-operate with Napoleon and his new order were simply erased from the map: Brunswick, Hessen–Kassel and Hanover vanished, to become parts of the newly created Kingdom of Westphalia. Other territorial juggling produced the Grand Duchy of Kleve-Berg and the kingdoms of Bavaria and Württemberg. In 1807, to the east, the

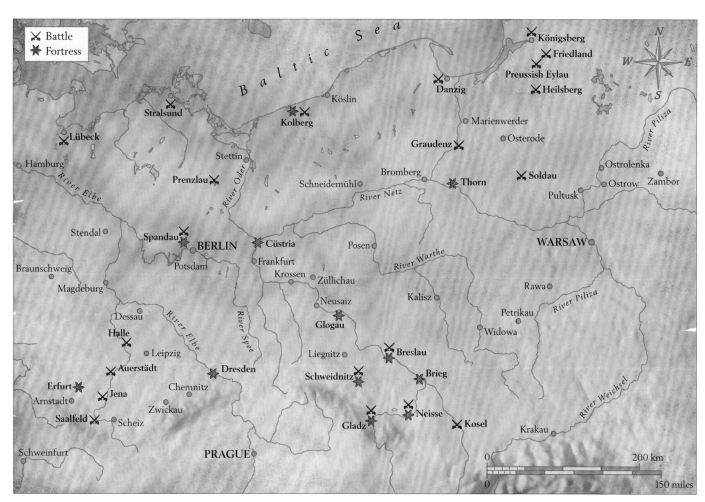

Grand Duchy of Warsaw arose from the ashes of the defunct Kingdom of Poland that had disappeared in 1795.

In the old Holy Roman Empire, each member state had to provide a military contribution towards common defence. This contribution was in proportion to the population of the state concerned. Napoleon took over this principle practically unchanged. The new contribution seems to have been fixed at 0.75 per cent of the population. Contributions of many of the small states were not viable on their own and were grouped on a geographical basis to form composite "Confederation Regiments". Some of the tiniest remaining states in south-western Germany entered contracts with larger neighbouring states, whereby they paid them to provide the manpower contribution on their behalf. Most of these states adopted French-style badges of rank and intercompany distinctions, as well as French organization and drill.

By the end of 1806 the balance of power on mainland Europe had lurched markedly in France's favour. Her enemies had lost 150,000 troops and she had gained them. The same had happened with all the economic resources and markets of the territories concerned. The Confederation of the Rhine was to be France's main export market for the rest of the period. In 1816, France paid reparations to the states of the Confederation, in ratio to the men they had lost in the wars under Napoleon's command. Bavaria claimed for 60,000 lives lost; while Liechtenstein claimed for 100.

Eastern Europe

If political border adjustments were frequent in western and southern Europe, they were dwarfed in scale by what had happened, and was happening, to the east. The border areas of the states along the south shores of the Baltic Sea have always been flexible. Unlike France, which had been able to lay claim to her natural borders of the sea, the Rhine, the Alps and the Pyrenees, there were no such conveniently emphatic natural

▲ *The French Marshal, Jean-Baptiste-Jules Bernadotte, became Crown Prince of Sweden in 1810. Sweden was an important Baltic power and a rival to Denmark and Russia.*

barriers on which political entities might be based in the areas towards Russia. The north-west European plain stretched away from Holland in the west to the Ural mountains, thousands of miles to the east, which were remote even to most Russians.

There were major river systems, but for most of the year these were shallow, slow-moving and ran between gently sloping banks. In winter, they froze hard enough to carry artillery and thus had no value as obstacles at all. Even today, in the northern expanses of the tundra, frozen rivers are used as roads in the winter by Russian industry.

Poland

Remarkable in its ability to expand and contract across the face of Europe throughout history, Poland first came to prominence in 1410, when King

Vladislav II Jagiello defeated the Teutonic Knights at the Battle of Tannenberg and expanded to the west. In the 15th century, Poland spread to the south and west. In 1446, West Prussia fell under Polish rule and East Prussia was a Polish vassal state. From 1490 to 1582, Poland spread from the Baltic to the Black Sea, extending to within 187 miles (300 km) of Moscow. It encompassed Lithuania, Latvia, Estonia, Belorussia and most of the Ukraine. Her inhabitants included many Muslim Tartars, from whom they adopted the lance as a cavalry weapon.

Decline began in 1697 and by 1733 Poland's power was gone and she was largely under Russia's influence. The downward slide continued in 1772, when King Frederick the Great instigated the first Partition of Poland. Internal Polish political chaos led to her being easy prey for her rapacious neighbours. In 1792 the vultures returned for the second Partition, and three years later, the hapless rump of the once-mighty state vanished from the map of Europe completely.

The Kingdom of Saxony

Saxony was a dynamic political entity during the Napoleonic era, especially as its king was also Grand Duke of Warsaw. The Saxon king, Frederick August, stuck to his alliance with Napoleon right through the fighting, culminating in the great Allied victory at Leipzig on 19 October 1813, when he was treated as a prisoner of war and whisked away by the Prussians. The Congress of Vienna took over half of his kingdom and gave it to Prussia.

Baltic Rivalries

To the north of the Polish lands, Sweden and Russia were rivals for the control of the eastern Baltic. Matters would come to a head in early 1808 when the Russians attacked and took the great fortress of Sveaborg south of Helsinki. This fortress was known as the Gibraltar of the North; its loss so demoralized the Swedes that by 18 September 1808, the great, lake-strewn tract of modern Finland passed into Russian control.

THE BALANCE OF NAVAL POWER

Between 1792 and 1815, Britain was acknowledged as the world's naval superpower, and her control of the seas often frustrated French ambition and provided Britain with the economic means of continuing the wars. The French Revolution had badly weakened the once perfectly competent French Navy. The exodus of trained officers had an impact that lasted for years and the general neglect of the French fleet led to a series of defeats before 1800. Napoleon sought to rebuild the fleet but his schemes were largely ruined at Trafalgar. From then on, his fleet was blockaded in port. The British Navy largely ruled the waves.

Some of the smaller European fleets, such as the the Dutch and Danish, were relatively effective, even after the latter was largely destroyed by the British in 1807. Spain lost most of her ships at Trafalgar and never recovered. Russia invested little in her fleet, and divided those resources between a Baltic and Black Sea fleet, and Prussia completely neglected maritime warfare. In 1790 the USA had a tiny naval force.

The Battle of Trafalgar

By the time the pivotal naval battle of Trafalgar was fought, on 21 October 1805, Napoleon had taken the Grand Army out of their camps at Boulogne

▲ *The British ship* Formidable *breaks the French line in the Battle of the Saints.*

down into the Danube valley, where, on 15 October, he forced the Austrian General Mack to surrender with 23,000 men. Trafalgar was the result of months of Admiral Nelson chasing French Admiral Villeneuve across the Atlantic and back. The tactics used by Nelson were remarkably similar to those used by Admiral Duncan at the Battle of Camperdown 1797, against the Dutch. Both fleets were damaged in the battle, Nelson was among those killed, and of the 18 ships taken by the British, only four survived: most sank in the violent storm that blew up, the next day. Britain's naval supremacy was secured for the next 100 years.

Warships of the Period

Ships of the period were essentially floating gun platforms and the most effective were those that could fire tremendous "broadsides", frequently at close range, to cripple an enemy ship or disable it by killing the crew or bringing down the rigging. Sinking, unless in a storm, was relatively rare and, most ship losses were by capture.

A ship capable of fighting in the line of battle ("ship of the line") was heavily armed. The heavier guns on a ship were mounted on the lower decks

The Relative Strength of the Navies in 1790 (*ships of the line)							
	Population	SOL*	Frigates	Sloops	SHIPS	GUNS	CREW
Britain	10.9	195	210	256	661	12,000	100,000
France	26.9	81	69	141	291	14,000	78,000
Spain	11.5	72	41	109	222	10,000	50,000
Russia	37.5	67	36	700	803	9,000	21,000
Holland	4	44	43	100	187	2,300	15,000
Denmark	0.8	38	20	60	118	3,000	12,000
Turkey	?	30	50	100	180	3,000	50,000
Sweden	2.4	27	12	40	79	3,000	13,000
Venice	?	20	10	58	88	1,000	14,000
Portugal	2.9	10	14	29	53	1,500	10,000
Naples	4.6	10	10	12	32	1,000	5,000
USA (1812)	5.3	7	2	9	18	246	5,500

Neptune

Neptuno
Scipion

Entreprenante
Pickle
Phoebe
Sirius
Britannia
Spartiate
Naiad
Agamemnon
Africa
Orion
Euryalus
Minotaur
Ajax
Conqueror

Leviathan   San Francisco
de Asis
Téméraire

Intrépide   Rayo   Cornélie
Formidable   Duguay-Trouin
Mont Blanc
San Augustino
Hortens
Heros   Santissima-   Furet
Trinidad   Neptune
San Leandro

VICTORY   BUCENTAURE
(flagship)   (flagship)

Redoubtable
Colossus
Dreadnought   Tonnant   San Justo
Prince of Wales
Defence   Mars   Royal
Swiftsure   Polyphemus   Sovereign   Indomptable
Thunderer   Defiance   Revenge   Achilles   Belle   Santa Anna
Bellerophon   Isle   Fougueux   Monarca
Pluton
Algéciras
Aigle   Bahama
Argonaute   Swiftsure
Montañez
San Juan   Berwick   Themis
Nepomuceno   Hermione

Cadiz

S P A I N

San
Ildefonso   Argonauta
Achille

PRINCIPE
DE ASTURIAS
(flagship)

Site of
Battle   Cape
Trafalgar   Gibraltar

Strait of Gibraltar

N

W   E

S

Tangiers

	British
	French
	Spanish

Argus

to help the stability of the ship. At maximum charge a 32-pounder gun could fire a ball just over 6 in (15 cm) in diameter to a range of 2,000 yd (1.8 km). At close-range, 30 yd (27.4 m), an 18-lb (8-kg) round shot would pierce four oak planks 32$^1/_2$ in (75 cm) thick, hurling splinters of wood up to 30 yd. A 32-pounder gun could inflict the same damage at a range of 300 yd (274.3 m).

Other projectiles used in naval battles were bar-shot and chain-shot: devices for damaging the sails and rigging of an enemy ship. A ship would have a marine for each gun and an officer to command them.

Apart from the conventional, long-barrelled heavy cannon, each ship would have up to ten carronades, so-called from the factory in which they were made. These were short-barrelled, mounted on the upper deck and used for short-range work, just before an

attempted boarding. They would fire solid shot or a load of musket balls. Due to their lighter construction, carronades could be mounted on higher decks. Their range was just over half that of a cannon of the same size.

▲ *The decisive Battle of Trafalgar. This map shows when Nelson's double column of attack pierced the Franco-Spanish line.*

▼ *Nelson stands on the deck of HMS* Victory *amidst the bustle of a ship at battle stations.*

THE LIFE OF A SOLDIER

In many European countries at this time military service was for life; the average ages of the officers and men in such armies were thus relatively high. This was one of the reasons why the influx of youthful French officers and conscripts of the 1790s could bounce back from their defeats, while their aged opponents could hardly drag themselves along in the cold and rain.

Recruitment

In many countries, including France until the introduction of conscription in 1793, the normal method of luring peasants to become soldiers was for a regiment to send recruiting parties out into their designated cantonment. In feudal Russia there was no such problem; the czar would decree how many recruits were needed and the landowners would be told how many serfs to deliver.

A recruiting party would usually consist of an officer, a sergeant, a drummer and several men. The officer would be supplied with cash. In the Britain of 1792, it was customary for a man – or boy – to have committed himself to being a recruit when he accepted the king's shilling. In those days, to men of the lower classes, a shilling was considerable bait. To increase the success rate, the recruiting party would set up shop in an inn on the town square on market day. A drummer would attract potential recruits, who were often decked out with flowers and treated to a few pints of ale while being regaled with tales of exciting lands far away. Many young farm lads, bored and discontented at home, fell for the sales pitch, signed the roll and took the shilling. They were then whisked off to the local barracks, where the process of making men out of them began in earnest. There was no going back, and no opportunity for second thoughts.

Life in Barracks

The shock of being torn from your home – boring as it may have been – and of being shouted at and confined within the barracks for weeks on end was less traumatic for recruits then than it is now. Alternative career prospects for most of these illiterates were not much better than the army; at least one was paid, clothed and fed regularly. Each man would be given a regimental number, by which he would be known and tracked for the rest of his service.

Life in barracks was regulated by signals given on drum or bugle; there were signals (calls) for everything from getting out of bed, falling in for parade, collecting meals and putting out lights before going bed. Barrack rooms contained several wide, wooden beds, each built for two or three men and having straw-filled mattresses and woollen blankets. In many barracks, each such large room formed a "mess" and food would be issued to them daily; they would take it in turns to cook. And then there was drill.

The purpose of drill in the armed services and other organizations was – and still is – to instil in the individual automatic responses to orders that might have to be given to them under conditions of extreme danger, when non-compliance might result in the entire regiment being destroyed or an operation miscarrying. The movements were practised and practised until each one became second nature. The recruits learned how to stand, march, turn in various directions and to stop. When all these evolutions had been mastered, muskets were issued and the whole process began again, this time carrying and handling the weapons.

After all the recruits had become proficient in these exercises, they would be formed into platoons (half companies) usually in three ranks, then in companies, then in battalions. Arms drill revolved around the tactics and use of the smooth-bore musket for the infantry, the loading and cleaning of cannon for the artillery, and the use of the sword and control of the horse for the cavalryman.

Then there was the cleaning of kit. The buttons, buckles, belt plates and shako plates had to be polished every day. The white belts had to be pipe-clayed at least twice a week; black belts,

◄ *A recruiting party made up of fifer and drummer to attract attention, and officers to entice the youths of England into the army.*

▲ *Repeated drilling in formation played a large part in the life of the Napoleonic soldier.*

shoes and boots were polished daily. Muskets had also to be cleaned. The inside and outside of the barrel (and the bayonet) had to be kept shining and free of rust; the stock was to be polished and waxed; the nooks and crannies of the lock all had to be free of rust and powder residue. British soldiers' hair (at the beginning of the period) had to be powdered, rolled over the ear and queued to regulation length at the rear. This was best done by a section of men in a circle, one behind the other, each dressing the queue of the man in front.

Life on Campaign
Where possible, armies billeted their men on the populations of the areas through which they passed. In earlier times, tents would have been carried in the regimental baggage train, but by 1800 these had largely been scrapped as being too cumbersome. If the line of march led through uninhabited regions, the soldiers would be forced to bivouac. In theory, before an army moved, the exact stages to be covered every day would have been planned by the general staff. Ideally, the men would be accommodated in houses, as this kept sickness rates down and meant the location of all units was known to the commander. The daily march distance might be modified to take advantage of the available towns.

A normal day's march was 12–15 miles (20–24 km); it began usually early and ended in the afternoon. An army would usually march for 10 days then rest for two days.

Despite aiding the speed of an operation, bivouacking had many negative effects on an army: the men soon became filthy; they dispersed in an uncontrolled manner in all directions and were difficult to recall. In order to find or make shelters, the men would often force their way into houses, barns and churches and take whatever they needed. The misery of trying to sleep in the open, in the winter, when one is cold, wet and hungry, is easy to imagine. Discipline also suffered, as the men were often tempted to steal.

Discipline
In most armies of this period, flogging was the usual form of punishment. Imprisonment was also used, and in the worst cases, offenders would be shot. This seems barbaric – and it was – but must be seen against the national criminal justice systems of the era, which were no less brutal. In Continental armies it was common for officers guilty of serious offences to be confined for months or even years. The exception to this was Revolutionary France, where flogging was abolished and its place taken by confinement, carrying a ball and chain, or being posted to a punishment battalion.

▼ *A British encampment in 1810, fortunate enough to have regulation tents.*

Rations

Napoleon is credited with saying, "An army travels on its stomach. Soup makes the soldier." French Army rations in Napoleon's day consisted of bread and soup, supplemented with wine and vinegar, as an antiscorbutic, to prevent scurvy. Theoretically all armies of the period had ration scales for the men, and most of them went to considerable lengths to supply the goods. This meant a system of supply of pre-stocked food from magazines by commissary wagons, which impeded the mobility of the army and clogged lines of communication.

But Marshal Marmont, in his memoirs, revealed the true thinking of French generals on the matter of food supplies for their men: "The only certain way of insuring the regular subsistence of the soldier, is to impose on him the duty of looking after it himself, in accordance with some arranged plan… War is generally made in inhabited countries, and where there are men there is grain to feed them with. It is in the manner of utilizing the grain which the granaries contain that the solution of the question really rests."

The general who paid the greatest attention to the supply of rations and forage to his army was the Duke of Wellington; his commissary officials were spread far and wide, with cash to

▼ *The 2nd Hussars (French) bivouacking at Austerlitz in 1805.*

buy local produce and animals at market rates. When the British landed in Portugal in July 1808 the daily rations were: 1 lb (0.4 kg) bread or biscuit and 1lb (0.4kg) meat, fresh or salted. No wine or spirits were issued if the meat was fresh; if salted then ¼ pint (142 ml) spirits or 1 pint (0.5 l) wine would be handed out. Also each man was entitled to 3 lb (1.3 kg) firewood. Women travelling with a regiment were allowed a half ration and children a quarter ration; but no wine or spirits for either. Horses had 10 lb (4.5 kg) hay and 10 lb (4.5 kg) oats each day and 10 lb (4.5 kg) straw for bedding. If oats were not available they received 14 lb (6.3 kg) maize or barley, and 10 lb (4.5 kg) straw.

▲ *Grenadiers distribute meat, cavalrymen give out wine, line troops hand out bread and hussars dispense brandy in this contemporary print of daily routines in Napoleon's army.*

Sickness and Disease

Life was tough for almost everybody back in the Napoleonic era by our standards, even the better off had so much less than we do now. It will therefore come as no surprise that soldiers on campaign either became a hardy lot, or fell sick and often died.

Diets were usually poor and gave only a fraction of the nutrition that we receive today. Hygiene was basic and soldiers on campaign often had few opportunities to wash well. Typhus was an everyday danger for all armies on campaign, particularly when they were billeted with the civilian population for long periods and overloaded the already fragile and inadequate sewage and drinking-water supply systems. Ignorance compounded the problems and thousands died needlessly.

Wide areas of Europe were then breeding grounds for mosquitoes, and malaria was an additional hazard for the soldier on campaign, as the British found to their cost in the Walcheren expedition of 1809. But if Europe was a relatively hazardous place then, the West Indies put things in perspective. We have an account of the effects of yellow fever, so feared by potential

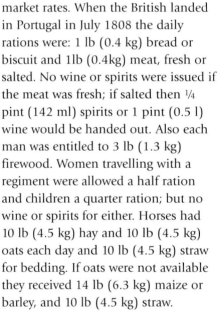

▲ *Baron Dominique-Jean Larrey, surgeon-in-chief of Napoleon's Guard, treats officers on the battlefield of Borodino, September 1812.*

volunteers, from the memoirs of Admiral George Vernon Jackson, who contracted the disease in English Harbour, Antigua, while aboard the frigate *Carysfort* in 1803. In all, 47 of the officers and men of the ship died in this brief outbreak. Thirteen of his crew, including himself, fell ill and were in hospital for several weeks. When they left the wards, they were so weak that they could scarcely stand. Sometimes, the flesh of the patients began to rot as they lay there. The Spanish name for the disease was then "the black vomits", for, once a patient had begun to emit such vomit, death was almost certain.

Treatment of Wounds

Wounds were caused by three types of weapons: muskets and pistols, sabres and bayonets and artillery (solid shot, canister, shell). All wounds could be fatal, even if small; the high fatality rates were due to two main causes: lack of hygiene and shock.

Anaesthetics were not used in the operating theatres of the day, and the "operating theatre" for the wounded soldier might be an old door in a cold, dirty barn. At the most, the unfortunate patient might be given a

swig or two of brandy, then he would be held down by two or more orderlies while his wounds were probed with anything from tweezers and scalpels to the surgeon's filthy and bloody fingers. The purpose of probing was to locate and remove (if possible) any foreign object such as musket balls, bone, canister and shell fragments, scraps of uniform or equipment. These, it was known, would cause infection, which was so often the fatal gangrene. The surgeon's tools included two saws, for cutting bones in cases of amputation, a hammer and chisel for the same purpose, and various knives, scissors, tweezers, probes and arterial forceps.

The fate of a wounded soldier, even if he was recovered from the battlefield promptly by his comrades, was bleak. Often he would have to wait for hours in the cold and wet – or in the blazing sun – before enjoying the indifferent attentions of the regimental surgeon and being dumped in some ruin or corner to recover or die. Usually a wounded soldier was bereft of his friends and of the *esprit de corps* of his regiment and might well be unable to move at all. Nurses were non-existent; medicines, bandages, clean bed linen – any bed linen, any bed – a change of soiled clothing just as rare. In Russia in 1812 there are many harrowing accounts of the plight of the wounded, particularly after Borodino.

Captain Morgenstern, an invader with the 2nd Westphalia Infantry Regiment of the VIII Corps, has left us a vivid picture of the nature of the retreat from Moscow, even in the early stages. As we follow him along parts of his desperate trek westwards across the field of Borodino, his account may be taken as being typical for thousands who were now fighting for their survival. "We saw the pitiful fear of those helpless sick and wounded as they watched the convoy passing them by, to leave them to the mercies of the vengeful Russians. We felt the bitterness of those seriously ill who now gave up all hope of being moved from their pestilential cells." Napoleon ordered that every vehicle passing the hospital at Kolotskoi should take one of the unfortunates with them. The order was followed, but the sick and wounded were dumped in the woods at the first opportunity.

All in all, the provision of medical care for the sick and wounded of all armies of the era was woefully inadequate. There was far less chance of a soldier being killed in action than there was of him dying of infected wounds, disease or starvation if he were a member of the Grand Army.

▼ *The rough, heavy wagons used to transport the wounded can hardly have increased a soldier's likelihood of survival.*

UNIFORMS AND BADGES OF RANK

Many aspects of the flamboyant military uniforms of the Napoleonic period were highly impractical: the colours, especially white; the work involved to keep them up to scratch – to pipe clay belts, polish brass buttons and cap plates; the excessive weight of the brass-fronted mitre caps of the grenadiers; and the terrible lack of adequate protection against the cold and the wet. These were all indicative of societies that were obsessed with appearance at the expense of utility and common sense. It was later in the Napoleonic period that the seeds of change were sown whereby a high degree of peacockery crept into the design of military uniform. This peaked in the 1830s with ridiculous bell-topped shakos and huge plumes. Russia's adoption of the Potemkin uniforms of 1786 were a notable exception. Their rifle battalions, with their sombre colours and black belts, were a step towards utility in military fashion, but it was not until khaki and field grey came into use at the end of the nineteenth century that common sense began to become a significant feature of military fashion. It was not until the Second World War that real practicality was introduced into uniforms in general.

Regiments were distinguished by the colour of their "facings": that is to say, the cuffs, collars and the shoulder strap on the left shoulder and by their buttons, which were of brass or tin. Further distinction was often achieved by the colour of the waistcoats and breeches (known as the "small clothes") with white, buff and yellow being the colours mostly selected. The coat turnbacks were often the same colour for all regiments, as were the belts. The latter were usually white for regiments of the line and black for light infantry, fusiliers and *Jägers*.

It quickly became evident to all armies that they needed to have some visible way of identifying the status of

▲ *All armies of the period loved their hussars, as can be seen in this French gold-encrusted colonel. Massive bearskin bonnets, and tall, metal grenadier mitre caps were* de rigeur.

commanders on and off the battlefield. Those in command had to be easily located by messengers, staff officers and superiors. Subordinates needed to be able to recognize authority. In the early days the richness of senior officers' clothing sufficed, but later a formalized system was introduced.

Badges of Rank

In the sixteenth century officers were identified by wide silk sashes, worn around the waist or over the shoulder. These were originally intended to be used as a hammock or sling, in which the officer, if wounded, would be carried from the battlefield. By the Napoleonic era the size of these sashes had dwindled. They were usually in the colours of the ruling house and ended

in heavy worsted, silk or bullion tassels, depending on the wearer's rank. Examples are Prussia – silver and black; Russia – silver with black and orange stripes; Hessen-Darmstadt – silver with red and blue stripes; Austria – yellow with black stripes. When Revolutionary France adopted the tricolour, Hessen-Darmstadt dropped the blue stripe. Officers in Britain and the United States wore crimson sashes.

Most general officers wore gold or silver lace edging and feathered trim to their bicorns, and had elaborate gold or silver brooches to hold their national cockades. The tassels of their hat cords were also of precious metal. When full armour was abandoned, officers retained the gorget (a steel collar to protect the throat) as a sign of office. This would be decorated with the ruler's crest.

Epaulettes

The French Army of the eighteenth century seems to have led the way for the general introduction of epaulettes for officers. These were usually in the button colour, and were fringed in bullion or silk according to rank. Eventually, these became a well-defined system used by most nations.

The *sous lieutenant* wore two epaulettes, each with two red stripes along the strap, that on the left having thin fringes. The lieutenant wore the same, but the straps had only one stripe; the captain's epaulettes had no stripes. A *chef d'escadron* (commander of a cavalry squadron) had a bullion fringe on the left shoulder. Field officers (battalion commanders, majors and colonels) had bullion fringes on both shoulders. Generals had heavier bullion fringes and two, three or four of the five-pointed stars in the epaulette fields. Marshals wore crossed batons in the epaulette fields. French corporals wore two diagonal bars (chevrons if the cuffs were pointed) on the forearm in the button colour and

▲ *An officer and private of the Prussian Grenadiers c.1815. The practicality of trying to march, let alone fight, in this headgear must be questioned.*

edged red; the fourrier had the same bars, plus a third bar, in the button colour and on red backing, on the upper arm. Sergeants had a single bar in the button colour, on red backing, on the forearm, and sergeant majors had two such bars. Senior NCOs also had gold threads mixed in their red or green epaulette fringes if in the élite companies. Long service was shown for non-commissioned ranks by one or two red chevrons on the left arm.

Britain used an odd system of generals' ranks in 1792, expressed by a series of chevrons on the lower arms. As troopers of the Household Cavalry also wore such stripes, confusion was a possibility. Fringed epaulettes in the button colour were worn on both shoulders by field officers and by junior officers in the grenadier and light companies; grenade or bugle horn badges would be worn on the epaulettes of the latter officers. Centre company junior officers wore one epaulette on the right shoulder. In 1798 the British non-commissioned ranks wore fringed epaulettes on the right shoulder. Corporals had a plain white one, sergeants had a silver

strap with two red stripes along it and a twisted red and silver edging; sergeant majors were as for sergeants but with a silver crescent.

This system gradually gave way from one to four large chevrons, point down, on the upper arm. Lance corporals' and corporals' chevrons were in the regimental lace, sergeants' in white and sergeant majors' in gold or silver, as for the officers. Colour-sergeants wore one chevron under crossed swords on the staff of a union jack, all under a crown; by 1815 the sergeant major also had a crown over his four chevrons. British sergeants also wore crimson serge waist sashes, with a central stripe in the regimental facing colour and crimson tassels.

Bavaria introduced a system of ranks based on silver or gold stripes and collar edging: junior officers had one to three stripes, field officers stripes with a braid edging, generals had gold edging and oak leaf embroidery.

The Austrian system was less finely graded than many others. All officers

▲ *A British private and officer, 27th Foot 1815. Compared with other armies, the uniforms of the British were modest, and far more practical for active service.*

had the gold and black sword strap and tassel. Junior officers had plain cuffs, with either two narrow or one wide gold or silver edging to the hat or shako. Field officers had a ³/₄-in (2-cm) wide edging in the button colour to their cuffs and the wider hat edging. Colonels had a 1³/₄-in (4.4-cm) wide cuff edging, major generals 2¹/₄-in (5.9-cm) wide, field marshals had a double cuff edging and the general of infantry and cavalry had three gold buttons and gold braid embroidery to the top and back of his cuff. Austrian corporals had yellow and black sabre straps, and sergeants had a gold tassel. Sergeant majors also had the golden "FI" in their black and yellow cockades.

It was not until 1808 that rank badges were introduced for Prussian junior officers. These were shoulder straps in the regimental facing colour, edged red and with one or two double black and silver laces along them for lieutenants. A Prussian captain had the black and silver lace around the edges of his shoulder straps.

◀ *The extraordinary parade dress uniform of the officers of the Prussian Leib-Husaren Regiment von Zieten, with leopard pelts worn over the top of Hungarian costume.*

MAJOR CAMPAIGNS AND BATTLES

Between 1792 and 1804 the European war was fought for or against the French Revolution. After 1804, when Napoleon proclaimed himself emperor, it became an imperial struggle. The fighting raged across the European continent from Russia to Portugal, from Scandinavia to Egypt and spilled over into India and the Americas. At first Napoleon seemed unstoppable, but when the coalition system worked the balance shifted, and Napoleon's power was broken.

▼ *The series of fortified towns and fortresses along the French border that played a major part in the campaigns of 1792 and 1814–15.*

The Campaigns of 1792–96
The opening of hostilities between France on the one side, and the Austrian-led Holy Roman Empire with Prussia on the other, began in 1792. France was the major European power with an army of 140,000 men and a navy second only in size to that of Britain. The Allies mobilized 105,000 men including several thousand French *émigrés* in various legions. As was to be the case for the next 23 years, the French had the distinct advantages of a centralized position, a homogeneous army and command system and internal lines of communication. The Allies were hampered by several

languages and command structures, external lines of communication and differing national agendas, which often provoked inter-Allied friction and frustrated their efforts against the common foe. Whenever Russia was in the coalition, there was the added complication that their Julian calendar was 12 days behind the Gregorian calendar of their western Allies.

1792 France declared war on 26 April; her initial aim was to invade the Austrian Netherlands (Belgium) and to set up an allied republic there. The Allied aim was to invade north-eastern France and march on Paris. Four

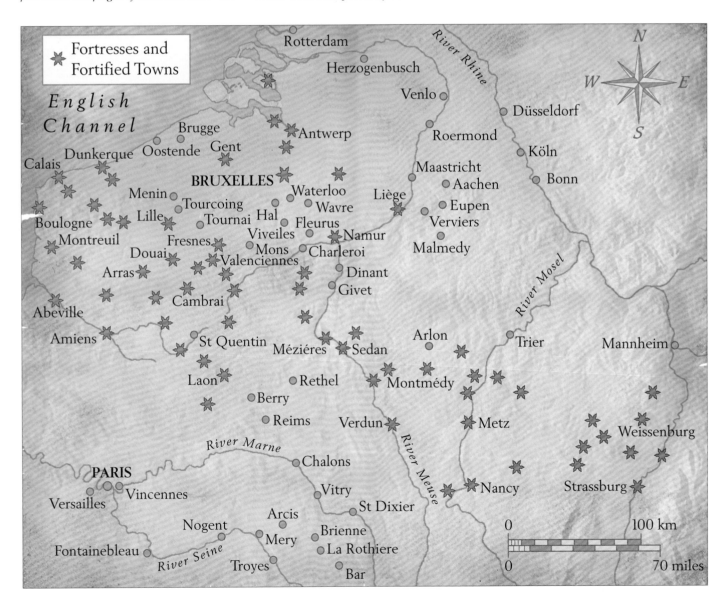

French raids into Belgium in April, May and June were easily repulsed by the Austrians there, who were separated from the Allied army around Mainz and Frankfurt by some 170 miles (275 km).

The fumbling Allied thrust at Paris was stopped at the non-battle of Valmy on 20 September. The Allies turned tail and on 21 October the French took Mainz. Frankfurt fell the next day. On 6 November, General Dumouriez defeated the Austrians at Jemappes, causing them to evacuate all Belgium. A civil war broke out in the Vendée.

1793 The French launched the famous *levée en masse*, mobilizing the entire nation in her defence. On 21 January ex-king Louis XVI was executed. Britain now entered the war against France on land and at sea. A British contingent of 6,000 troops (of dubious quality), commanded by the Duke of York, joined the Allies in Holland. In this year the conflict spilled over into northern Italy and the Pyrenees. In Holland, Dumouriez made dramatic headway against the demoralized Dutch Army, but was beaten at Neerwinden on 18 March by the Prince of Coburg, commanding the Allies. Coburg failed to exploit his victory. Britain's mistrust of her allies then

caused the failure of the thrust on Paris and the war on the upper Rhine went in France's favour.

The Allies were invited into the great French naval base of Toulon by the royalist inhabitants in August, but clever use of artillery by a certain Captain Napoleon Bonaparte forced them out again on 18 December. The Royal Navy was set to implement the well-tried policy of blockading enemy fleets in their home harbours.

1794 The French overran Holland in this year, pushing the Allies out of France and back over the Rhine. Prussia had left the coalition to concentrate on gobbling up her share of the old Kingdom of Poland. This War of the First Coalition was ended by the Peace of Basle in April 1795. With her command of the seas, Britain embarked on a campaign of snatching colonies in the East and West Indies. Martinique was taken, as were Tobago, St Domingo and Guadaloupe.

In this year there occurred the Battle of the Glorious First of June, in which Admiral Lord Howe soundly defeated Admiral Villaret-Joyeuse 400 miles (650 km) west of Ushant. Here he employed the tactic of breaking the enemy line, which was to be used to such terrible effect at Trafalgar in 1805.

▲ *The Battle of Lodi, Italy, 10 May 1796. Napoleon personally leads a bayonet charge over the bridge, against the Austrians.*

1795 In this year the action took place at sea, on the upper Rhine and northern Italy. From 16 to 20 July there was a disastrous attempted invasion of the Quiberon peninsula by French *émigré* forces in British ships. The fighting in Italy went in France's favour as did that in the Pyrenees. On the upper Rhine the Allies maintained their positions. In the West Indies, Britain took St Vincent, Jamaica and other islands, as well as the Cape of Good Hope and Ceylon. France recaptured St Lucia.

1796 Napoleon burst on to the stage in northern Italy in this year, to outwit and defeat the Austrians in his race across the plains of the Po. Archduke Charles's success against General Jourdan at Würzburg on 3 September was rendered meaningless by events in Italy. Britain retook the island of St Lucia from France in April, but lost control of the Mediterranean. In the Far East, the Dutch colony of Amboyna was captured in mid-February. The French mounted an invasion of Ireland in December, but bad seamanship and stormy weather wrecked operations.

The Campaigns of 1797–1801

Napoleon's victory over the Austrians at Rivoli led to the capitulation of Mantua, the end of the war and the Peace of Campo Formio on 18 October 1797. Austria withdrew from Italy.

1797 Naval actions were characterized by the British victories at Cape St Vincent on 14 February over the Spanish, where Admiral Sir John Jervis took four ships of the line and badly damaged ten others. At Camperdown on 11 October, Admiral Duncan defeated a Dutch fleet under Admiral De Winter, using the "Trafalgar tactics" of piercing the enemy line in two places. Trinidad was taken from Spain in February. The iron blockade of Continental navies continued.

1798 Britain was now standing alone against France; a sullen peace reigned on mainland Europe. The French government, increasingly uneasy at Napoleon's meteoric rise to prominence, hurriedly agreed to his suggestion that he should invade Egypt to strike at Britain's communications with her Far Eastern empire. Evading the Royal Navy, Napoleon's task force captured Malta on 11 June and went

on to land in Egypt. On 2 July he stormed Alexandria; on 21 July he won the Battle of the Pyramids. His victorious progress was given a sharp check on 1 August, when Rear Admiral Horatio Nelson destroyed the French fleet of Admiral Count Brueys in

▼ *Austria signs the Alexandria Convention, 15 June 1800, after Marengo. Some 14 strongholds were handed over to France.*

▲ *French troops rest by the banks of the Nile in 1799. Napoleon's Egyptian expedition included scientists whose findings began the popularization of Egyptology around Europe.*

Aboukir Bay. French losses were 11 ships of the line, two frigates, 1,700 dead (including the admiral), 1,500 wounded and 2,000 captured. Nelson lost 218 dead and 678 wounded.

1799 Relentless French expansion in Europe allowed the British Prime Minister, William Pitt the Younger, to broker the Second Coalition with Austria, Russia, Portugal, the Two Sicilies and Turkey. A Russian army under General Suvorov marched into Austria to operate with them in northern Italy. Archduke Charles led an army against France in southern Germany. Despite successful operations against French General Jourdan, the Austrians forbade him to exploit them.

In northern Italy the Austro-Russians made excellent progress, defeating the French at the Battle of Magnano on 5 April and at the Battle of Vaprio and Cassano on 28 April. Austrian General Bellegarde now joined up with the Allies from Switzerland. The French commander in

Italy was General Scherer; he was no match for Suvorov, the Russian commander. Milan fell to the Allies on 24 May and Archduke Charles defeated General André Masséna at the first Battle of Zürich on 4 June. In Italy, the Allies won the Battle of the Trebbia against General Macdonald on 20 June. The French surrendered Mantua on 28 July and the Allies were again victorious at the Battle of Novi on 15 August. The tide turned against the Allies, however, when Suvorov was ordered by the czar to take his army into Switzerland. There, a second Russian army, under General Korsakov, was heavily defeated by Masséna at Zürich on 26 September and the Allied hold on the country was smashed. With great skill and determination, Suvorov was able to extract his army and withdraw to Russia. Austria was left in command of most of Italy.

In August an Anglo-Russian force invaded Holland, but after losing the Battle of Bergen to General Brune on 19 September, they were soon forced to re-embark under the terms of the Convention of Alkmaar on 18 October. In Egypt, Napoleon invaded Syria, but was stopped by the Anglo-Turks at Acre on 21 May and was forced to retreat. On 9 October he abandoned his army and hastened back to France, where, on

▼ *At the Battle of Marengo the Austrians swept French troops off the field before victory was snatched from them by General Desaix.*

10 November, he seized political power and became First Consul. Another French invasion of Ireland was launched in September; on 12 October Captain Sir J. B. Warren's squadron intercepted their fleet, took three ships of the line and scattered the rest. In the West Indies, Britain captured Surinam.

1800 This was the year of Napoleon's legendary reconquest of northern Italy and of his lucky escape from certain defeat at Marengo on 14 June by the returning General Desaix's corps. The next day he dictated peace to the Austrian generals and Italy was his. This victory stopped any Austrian

▲ *The Consular Guard in square formation at the Battle of Marengo on 14 June 1800.*

offensive in southern Germany. In the Mediterranean the British took Malta and in the Caribbean seized Curaçao.

1801 Britain was again alone; she invaded Egypt and defeated the French at the Battle of Alexandria on 21 March. This effectively decided the campaign; by the terms of the Capitulation of 2 September, the French Army in Egypt was to be evacuated on British ships to France. To ensure naval supremacy, Britain attacked Copenhagen on 2 April and destroyed or captured the Danish fleet. Britain continued to attack French and Dutch colonies, snatching the Virgin Islands, St Bartholomew, St Eustatius and St Martin. On 6 July 1801 the naval clash at Algeciras took place. British Admiral Saumarez, with seven ships of the line, battled with Rear Admiral Linois' three ships of the line and a frigate under fire from Spanish shore batteries. The French were joined by five Spanish ships and a frigate. The combat went on for days and ended indecisively on 13 July. The Peace of Amiens secured a lull in the wars from 1802 to 1803. In June 1803 the British captured St Lucia, Tobago Barbice and Demerara. Surinam was taken in 1804.

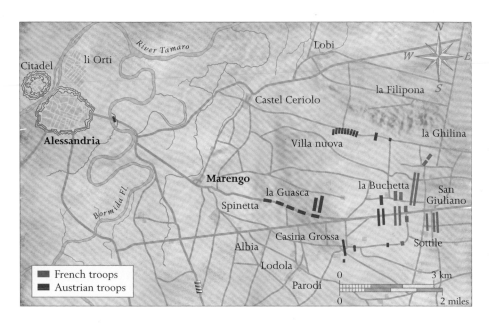

River Tamaro

Lobi

Citadel

li Orti

la Filipona

Castel Ceriolo

Alessandria

la Ghilina

Villa nuova

Marengo

la Buchetta

San Giuliano

la Guasca

Spinetta

Bormida Fl.

Casina Grossa

Sottile

Albia

Lodola

Parodi

■ French troops
■ Austrian troops

0   3 km

0   2 miles

The Campaigns of 1805–08

On 2 December 1804 Napoleon Bonaparte had crowned himself Emperor of the French. Austria was burning for revenge and joined Russia and Britain in another coalition to clip his wings. The incompetent Austrians under Archduke Ferdinand and General Mack fielded 35,000 men, and had invaded Bavaria and pushed westwards as far as Ulm on the River Danube. There they sat, waiting for a Russian army to join them.

1805 Napoleon had planned to invade Britain and had concentrated his Grand Army in the camps at Boulogne for years to train them up for this undertaking. His plan hinged upon Admiral Villeneuve leading the Royal Navy away from the Channel for four days, which was the time needed for the French Army to cross the Channel. Villeneuve failed. Bitterly disappointed, Napoleon turned his back on England and marched south-eastwards in great secrecy and at great speed to destroy the Austrians. By 17 October, Napoleon had encircled the Austrians at Ulm, where 24,000 men and 59 guns fell into his hands. His army raced on towards Vienna, reaping victories as it went, the only Allied

▼ The Battle of Austerlitz, on 2 December 1805, was the victory with which Napoleon knocked the Austrians out of the war.

bright spot being the defeat of Mortier's corps at Dürrnstein-Loiben on 11 November by a joint force under Russian General Kutusov.

On 21 October Nelson won his epic victory at Trafalgar over the Franco-Spanish fleets and ensured a century of British control of the world's seas. He died at the moment of his greatest triumph. The French lost eight ships of the line captured; of these three sank. The Spanish lost nine ships captured. No British ships were taken or sunk.

The Austrian Emperor, Francis II, abandoned his capital city, Vienna, and withdrew to the north-east, into Bohemia, to unite the remnants of his

▲ The Surrender of Ulm, 20 October 1805, in which Napoleon's ingenious flanking move won him 25,000 Austrians and 59 guns.

army with the Russians under Czar Alexander I. Napoleon followed. He was now at the end of a long line of communication, with a tired army; he needed a quick victory. Confronting the Allies west of Austerlitz, he feigned a desire for peace and surrendered the dominating plateau of the Pratzen Heights to lure his opponents into attacking him. He also sent part of his army off the intended battlefield to appear even weaker. The Allies took the bait; full of confidence, they attacked on 2 December 1805. The French Army that confronted them was at the height of military proficiency; they defeated the Austro-Russians, inflicting over 36,000 casualties. The Russians fell back to the east; the Austrians sued for another humiliating peace. This was Napoleon's greatest victory. It resulted in the death of the Holy Roman Empire of the German Nation, the birth of the pro-French Confederation of the Rhine in Germany and the death of William Pitt, the British prime minister.

1806 Despite the demonstration of French military might and the absence of viable allies, King Frederick William III of Prussia chose the summer of

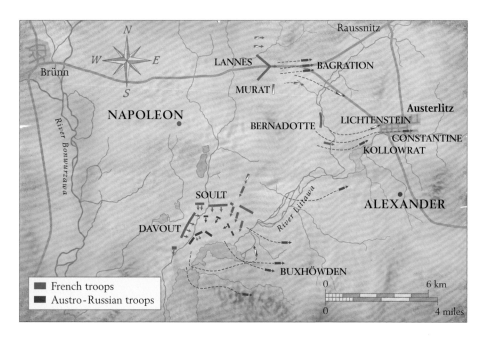

French troops
Austro-Russian troops

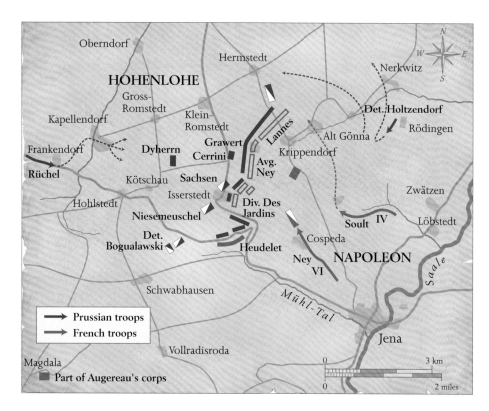

▲ The Battle of Jena, 14 October 1806, in which Napoleon defeated the smaller half of the Prussian field army.

1806 to challenge Napoleon. The emperor's response was crushing. With his usual speed and secrecy, he threw the Grand Army through central Germany onto the unsuspecting and divided Prussians. On 14 October he destroyed the minor half of their army at the Battle of Jena. That same day, 12 miles (20 km) north of Jena, a single French corps, commanded by Nicholas Davout, wrecked the main body of the Prussian Army at Auerstädt. The once-mighty Prussian Army burst apart; the state collapsed with it and was overrun, as mighty fortresses surrendered meekly to squadrons of French cavalry. The Prussian king, however, refused to accept defeat and withdrew into East Prussia. Czar Alexander, forgetting the lesson of Austerlitz, came to his aid, with a new Russian army in Poland.

On 21 November 1806 Napoleon published his Berlin Decree, opening total economic warfare on Britain, a power that he was unable to crush by military means. One of the wilder British schemes involved the invasion of Argentina from February to July of 1806; the hare-brained plan failed.

1807 The resulting winter campaign in the mud and desolation of Poland should have taught Napoleon that his invasion of Russia five years later was a fool's errand; the lesson was wasted. On 7–8 February a bloody stalemate battle took place at Preussisch-Eylau; both sides lost about 18,000 men. Further clashes took place and more Prussian cities and fortresses were starved into submission. Spring eventually came and the clashes continued with neither side willing to cede victory. On 10 June the Battle of

Heilsberg took place; the Allies claimed a victory and paraded three of Napoleon's precious Eagles in triumph. The French lost some 14,000 men, the Allies over 6,000. Four days later the end came at Friedland, where the Russian commander, General Bennigsen, was ill-advised enough to accept battle with a much stronger enemy and with a river positioned at his back. He was justly trounced, losing over 10,000 men. French losses were slightly higher, but the Russian Army was now a broken reed.

Alexander offered peace, abandoning Frederick William of Prussia. The Treaty of Tilsit resulted in the dismemberment of most of Prussia, the creation of the Grand Duchy of Warsaw and Russia's accession to Napoleon's Continental System, the economic weapon created by his Berlin Decree. Britain's European markets were to be sealed off; she was to be driven into bankruptcy, defeated by market forces.

Fearing the resurgence of hostile naval power, Britain again attacked Copenhagen, subjecting the city to bombardment from land and sea from 15 August to 5 September, laying much of the city to waste and causing over 2,600 civilian casualties.

▼ The hard-fought, indecisive battle of Eylau, February 1807, in which Marshal Augereau's VII Corps suffered heavy casualties.

▲ *Madrid, 1808, a struggle between the French forces and the people of Spain, who rose up against Napoleon's conquest.*

1808 Napoleon, having humbled all of northern mainland Europe, turned his attention to Spain. He kidnapped the Spanish royal family and set his brother, Joseph, upon the vacant throne. He also invaded Portugal, eager to close yet more ports to the British colonial and other goods, which poured into Europe despite all his efforts. Portugal asked Britain for aid; it was promptly and willingly given, and Junot's French Army was quickly beaten into submission and repatriated to France in British ships under the terms of the infamous Convention of Cintra. More French troops poured into Spain and the Spanish people rose in spontaneous revolt against the invaders and their new, unwelcome, king. Despite being repeatedly beaten in the field, the various Spanish armies always regrouped and came back for more. In this struggle they were eagerly supported by their civilian comrades. On 22 July a French corps under General Dupont was forced into a shameful capitulation with the Spanish General Castaños. This event reverberated around Europe.

Saragossa and other Spanish cities were besieged by the French and their allies, but offered bitter resistance. In November Napoleon decided to go to Madrid himself, to restore Joseph to the throne. On 30 November he forced the pass of Somosierra and entered Madrid on 4 December. The Spanish *Junta* asked Britain for help. The small British army in Portugal, under General Sir John Moore, was ordered to advance into Spain, ignorant of the topography and the road system and without any knowledge of the enemy they would have to face, or of the support that they would receive.

The Campaigns of 1809–12

This period of the conflict began with a European-wide explosion of uprisings against the French. Austria, subsidized by Britain, was again tempted to attack Napoleon in the Danube valley, the Grand Duchy of Warsaw, Bohemia, the Tyrol, northern Italy and Dalmatia. Dispossessed German princes invaded their old homelands to whip up revolt against the new French rulers. Prussia remained severely cowed; Russia waited on the sidelines.

1809 In this year, Austria's plans leaked through to Napoleon; in January he set off back to France from Madrid. Learning there was a small British force to the north-west of Marshal Soult's corps, he ordered him to destroy it. There followed the desperate chase through the Galician mountains to the port of La Coruña. There the British won the battle of that name; Sir John Moore was killed and the British Army successfully evacuated. In the emperor's absence, the set battles in

▼ *The Battle of Talavera, 27–28 July 1809, at which the Anglo-Spanish had the upper hand, but then had to withdraw when the superior forces of Marshal Soult arrived.*

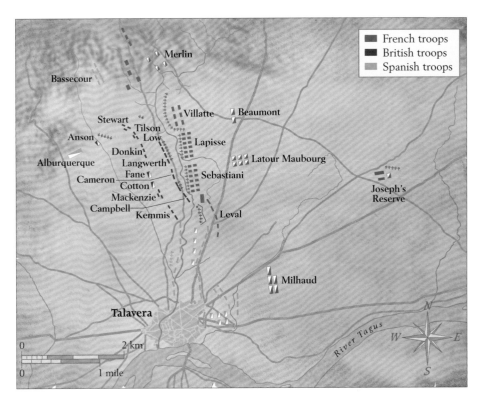

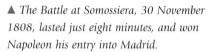
▲ *The Battle at Somossiera, 30 November 1808, lasted just eight minutes, and won Napoleon his entry into Madrid.*

▲ *At the Battle of Busaco, 27 September 1810. Wellington prepared a trap for Marshal Masséna's army, and won a brilliant victory.*

Spain usually went in favour of the French, but they were unable to stamp out the fires of rebellion. On 29 March the French won another decisive victory at Medellin; it brought no peace. Marshal Soult invaded northern Portugal again, took Oporto, and pushed on south. Napoleon and the Grand Army raced into the Danube valley to crush the Austrians and caught them off guard. The first clash came at Hirschau on 11 April; the Austrians were overthrown in a series of actions from Amberg, through Landshut, Regensburg, Abensburg, Eggmühl, Ebelsberg and Linz (on 17 May) before the opponent squared up for the Battle of Aspern-Essling, east of the Danube, near Vienna. Here, on 21 and 22 May, Napoleon failed to force the crossing of the river and fell back.

The raids into Germany by the princes fizzled out; Marshal Marmont defeated the uprising in Dalmatia and moved into northern Italy to aid Prince Eugène against Archduke John. John withdrew into Hungary to concentrate with the main Austrian army. The revolt in the Tyrol was successful; the Bavarian Army was thrown out of the province and could not reassert itself until the end of the year. On 5 July

Napoleon crossed the Danube; the next day he defeated Archduke Charles in the Battle of Wagram and Austria admitted defeat, again. General Arthur Wellesley took command of Anglo-Portuguese forces in Spain; on 12 May he threw Marshal Soult out of Oporto and chased him out of Portugal. On 27–28 July, aided by the Spanish, he won the Battle of Talavera against King Joseph Bonaparte, but had to withdraw into Portugal again, as superior enemy forces gathered at the rear.

At sea, British Admiral Gambier blockaded the squadron of Rear Admiral Williamez in Basque Roads and attacked it with a bold combination of fireships and rocket artillery on 11–12 April. Two French ships of the line were taken, and two more ships and a frigate were burned to prevent their capture.

With inexplicably bad timing, Britain decided to land a small army on the island of Walcheren, in the estuary of the River Scheldt on 30 July. After some initial successes for the British, the Franco-Dutch defenders flooded the island. The British troops wallowed about in the malarial mud for weeks before being withdrawn; some 4,000 of them died of fever, while just 106 were killed by enemy action. The usual harvest of enemy colonies began again, as Martinique was taken in February.

1810 The war in Spain and Portugal blazed on; men and cash flowed steadily from France into the Peninsula without any results. On 9 July the French captured Ciudad Rodrigo, one of the two key fortresses on the Spanish-Portuguese border. In September a French army invaded Portugal and was defeated by Wellington at Bussaco. Wellington withdrew into the Lines of Torres Vedras, a series of fortifications built to protect the port of Lisbon. Masséna sat down in front of this obstacle and let his army starve. In the West Indies, Guadaloupe was captured in February. In the Far East, Amboyna, Bourbon and Mauritius were taken from France.

1811 Again, the struggles between the French and the people of Spain raged on. The French captured Badajoz, the other key border fortress on the Spanish-Portuguese border, on 11 March. That same day, Masséna's starving army fought a rearguard action at Pombal, as they began to withdraw into Spain. Wellington followed, and on 3–5 May he and Masséna fought the Battle of Fuentes de Oñoro – an Anglo-Portuguese victory. Wellington then laid unsuccessful siege to Badajoz.

▲ Napoleon's invasion of Russia, showing the advance of the Grand Army as far as Moscow and Riga. The retreat followed a similar route.

1812 In south-eastern Spain Marshal Suchet took Valencia on 9 January, but the insurrection across the country held almost 300,000 French and allied soldiers fast in a bitter guerrilla war. On 20 January Wellington took the fortress of Ciudad Rodrigo, then moved south to attack Badajoz. On 6 April, at the third attempt, he took it. He could now move to invade Spain through either route. He chose the northern road and on 27 June he took Salamanca, north-west of Madrid.

Czar Alexander had abandoned Napoleon's Continental System by 1809; contraband British goods flowed through Russia into Germany and France. In 1810, Napoleon annexed Holland in order to stop the smuggling of colonial goods from Britain through that state. He then felt forced to do the same with the Hanseatic towns and Oldenburg. Unable to tolerate Alexander's flouting of his own wishes, Napoleon had been carefully planning the invasion of that country since 1810.

At the end of June 1812, with over half a million men, he crossed the River Niemen and rushed into Russia, intent on destroying its two separated and inferior armies within the first few days. But the Russians did not oblige

him and fell back rapidly to the east. What minor clashes did take place were Russian ambushes of his advanced guards. While the emperor raced for Moscow with the Grand Army, Marshal Macdonald, with the X Corps (including a large Prussian division) operated against the Latvian port of Riga, and the VII Saxon Corps and an Austrian corps guarded the exits of the Pripet Marshes in the south. Marshal Oudinot, with the II and VI Corps, stood as northern flank guard at Polotzk, opposed by General Wittgenstein's I Corps. The two Russian armies united at Smolensk and stopped Napoleon's advance on 17–18 August. The French logistical system had collapsed completely at the start of the campaign: 10,000 horses had died in an unexpected cold spell and by the time of this battle almost all regiments of Napoleon's main body were below half strength.

In Spain, Wellington had soundly defeated Marshal Marmont on 22 July at Salamanca; things were going in the Allies' favour. In Russia, Napoleon stumbled on eastwards. The Russians (now under the ageing Kutusov) stood again at Borodino, 62 miles (100 km) west of Moscow. On 7 September one

of the bloodiest battles of the era was fought; it was indecisive, but the Russians withdrew and abandoned Moscow to their enemies and to the fires they started themselves. Napoleon was baffled. He had not expected Alexander to be so stubborn. After wasting over a month in the ruined city, hoping for subservient peace feelers from Alexander, he was awoken to the true state of affairs by a Russian attack on Murat on 18 October.

Napoleon at last left Moscow, hoping to return to western Europe by a southerly route. This hope was dashed by the Battle of Malojaroslavetz on 24 October, and he was condemned to retrace his steps through the desert that his advancing army had helped to create. Various clashes marked the retreat, mainly those at Krasnoi on 14–18 November and the Battle of the Berezina Crossing on 26–28 November. Starvation and the cold weather helped to destroy those still with the Grand Army. Napoleon abandoned his survivors and returned to Paris. Prussian General von Yorck took his Prussian corps into neutrality in late December 1812. This act forced his king to break with France and join with Russia for the Wars of Liberation.

The Campaigns of 1813–15

The Russian adventure cost Napoleon 90 per cent of the men in his army and almost his entire artillery and cavalry. Napoleon could easily get men, in the form of young conscripts, and arms and equipment could quickly be manufactured, but horses were a problem: the French Army remained chronically short of cavalry for the remainder of the period.

1813 The Russians and Prussians advanced slowly westward; on 2 May the first major action, the Battle of Lützen (Gross-Görschen), was won by Napoleon but remained unexploited due to his lack of cavalry. On 20–21 May this story was repeated at Bautzen and Wurschen. The opponents agreed to an armistice. In Spain, King Joseph abandoned his kingdom and fled to France. Wellington intercepted him at Vittoria on 18 June and scattered his

army. There followed weeks of fighting in the Pyrenees between Wellington and Soult. The Battle of Sorauren (28–30 July) tipped the scales against Soult. In Germany, Austria had joined the Allies during the armistice and fighting broke out again on 22 August.

The Allies had developed the "Trachenberg Plan". They now fielded three armies: the army that was confronted by Napoleon would withdraw, while the other two operated against his flanks. This plan worked well. A string of battles, such as Gross-Beeren, the Katzbach, Dresden, Kulm, Dennewitz (Jüterbog), Teplitz and Wartenburg, led to the climactic Battle of Leipzig on 16–19 October.

Napoleon had taken a position with an impassable river and swamp to the rear; he was to pay dearly for this. Leipzig was the bloodiest battle of the Napoleonic Wars. The French lost 29 Eagles and colours, 325 guns and 60,000 men. The Allies lost 80,000 men. Napoleon's power was broken and he fled back to France, fighting his way through an Austro–Bavarian blocking force at Hanau (Bavaria had

▲ *Napoleon's army retreats from Moscow into the bitter cold of the Russian winter.*

also defected) on 30–31 October. In Spain, Wellington closed up to the French border; on 31 August he won the Battle of the Bidassoa. He then forced the French out of the strong position of the Rhune on 7–9 October. The fortress of Pamplona surrendered to the Spanish on 31 October after a long siege. Wellington pushed on into France, winning the Battle of the Nivelle on 10 November; on 9–13 December he fought and won the Battle of Bayonne.

Prince Eugène had been sent by Napoleon to co-ordinate the defence of Italy against the Austrians, but it was not until late August that the Austrians began their invasion through the town of Villach. They were held up at Feistritz on 6 September, but pushed on through the mountains of Slovenia and into the South Tyrol. On 7 October they took Tarvis on the River Fella. The port city of Trieste fell to an Anglo-Austrian force on 28 October. A rearguard action by Eugène at Bassano, on the River Brenta, on 30–31 October allowed him to cross intact. The Austrians captured Caldiero on 15 November and Ferrara three days later.

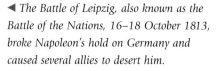

◄ *The Battle of Leipzig, also known as the Battle of the Nations, 16–18 October 1813, broke Napoleon's hold on Germany and caused several allies to desert him.*

1814 On New Year's Day, Prussian Field Marshal von Blücher invaded France, across the Rhine at Kaub, below Mainz. There followed the famous spring campaign, in which Napoleon's old genius flashed again and again. The Allies made his task much easier than it should have been by throwing the Trachenberg Plan out of the window and failing to co-ordinate their actions. On 29 January, Napoleon won the Battle of Brienne against the Russo-Prussians, although he suffered a defeat at La Rothière on 1 February. He trounced the Allies at Montmirail on 11 February, again at Vauchamps three days later, at Nangis four days after that and at Montereau on 18 February. The Allies finally managed to stop his run of successes at the Battle of Bar-sur-Aube on 26–27 February. They then defeated Marshal Macdonald at La Guillotière on 3–4 March and again defeated Napoleon at

▼ *Napoleon's defeat by the Allied army at the La Rothière, 1 February 1814, dispelled the myth of the emperor's invincibility.*

Craonne three days later. Another French defeat came at Laon on 9–10 March. On 21 March Napoleon was once more defeated at Arcis-sur-Aube; Allied inertia allowed him to escape destruction. Marshals Marmont and Mortier were beaten at Fère-Champenoise on 25 March and things looked bleak for the emperor.

Finally, Napoleon took a desperate gamble to try to lead his enemies away from Paris; they ignored this odd ploy and closed in on his capital city. On 30 March, Paris fell to the Allies.

▲ *At the Battle of Quatre Bras, June 1815, a square of the 28th Regiment of Foot stands against a French cavalry attack.*

Napoleon was forced by his battle-weary marshals to abdicate on 6 April.

In northern Italy, Prince Eugène held the Austrians in the Battle of the Mincio at Roverbella on 8 February; the struggle then halted along the line of the Mincio river, as the Austrians closed up to Mantua. Marshal Joachim Murat, King of Naples, had defected to the Allies by then and took command of an Austro-Neapolitan force, which forced the River Taro, west of Parma, on 13 April. This was the last action of any note in Italy that year. Wellington's thrust across southern France began on 15 February when he won the clash at Garris. This was followed by his victory at the Battle of Orthez on 27 February, and that of Vic-en-Bigorre on 19 March. His victorious campaign culminated in his winning the Battle of Toulouse on 10 April.

1815 Napoleon returned to France from his exile in Elba in February 1815. The reinstated King Louis XVIII fled to Belgium, leaving the throne for him to reoccupy. Months of frantic work reshaping the government and the army to his will followed as Napoleon sought to placate the fears of his old enemies. These old enemies, still sitting in the Congress of Vienna, would have none of his protestations of peaceful intent; they declared him an outlaw and mobilized to crush him. Their armies gathered on his northern and eastern borders; the Anglo-Dutch-

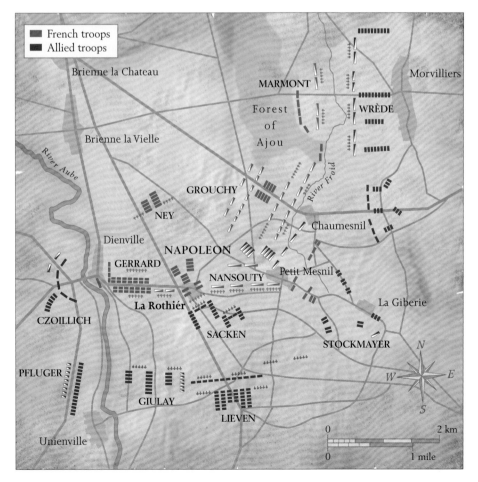

French troops
Allied troops

Brienne la Chateau

MARMONT

Morvilliers

Forest of Ajou

WRÈDE

River Aube

Brienne la Vielle

River Froid

GROUCHY

NEY

Dienville

NAPOLEON

GERRARD

NANSOUTY

Chaumesnil

Petit Mesnil

La Rothiér

La Giberie

CZOILLICH

SACKEN

STOCKMAYER

PFLUGER

GIULAY

LIEVEN

Unienville

0   2 km

0   1 mile

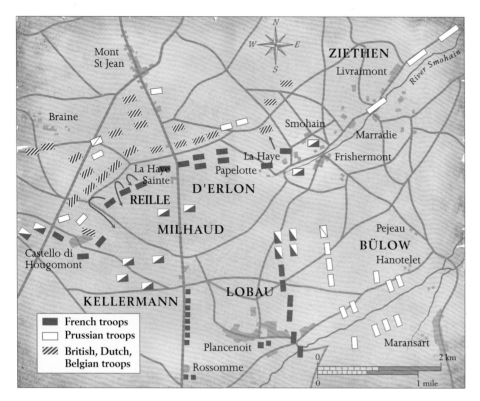

◄ The Battle of Waterloo, 18 July 1815, at the point of the defeat of the Old Guard, showing the position of the three armies.

Prussians in Belgium were the first to be ready. Napoleon recognized this imminent threat and moved against them with his characteristic speed and secrecy. Before this, Joachim Murat attacked the Austrians in Italy and was defeated at the Battle of Tolentino on 3 May. On 15 May, Napoleon attacked the Prussians at Fleurus, Gilly and Gosselies, throwing them back north. Wellington and Blücher had agreed to support each other, and this plan was to save them.

On 16 June, Napoleon assaulted the Prussian Army at Ligny and defeated it in a hard contest. That same day, Marshal Ney attacked the allied troops at Quatre Bras, west of Ligny, but was unable to break them. Wellington ordered a withdrawal northwards to his previously selected defensive position along a slight ridge at Waterloo, south of Brussels. Blücher had promised to come to his aid. Ney and Napoleon combined against Wellington, while Marshal Grouchy was sent to drive the beaten Prussians away to the east. He failed to catch them, with historically disastrous results for Napoleon. On 18 June, Napoleon's fate was decided at Waterloo. It is possible that he could have defeated Wellington, but for the fact that the Prussian Army had evaded Grouchy and drove deep into the French right flank, late in the afternoon of that fateful day.

The sodden state of the field on the morning of 18 June meant the French could not deploy their artillery until about 11 o'clock. The ill emperor was oddly inactive and mentally absent this day. He issued his orders and withdrew into himself as his subordinates mismanaged the battle. A supposed feint attack on the château of Hougoumont was allowed to become a struggle to the death, sucking in thousands of French troops. The great infantry assault on the Allied centre went in without cavalry support and was crushed. A subsequent cavalry charge (unsupported by infantry and artillery) also failed. The French Reserve Cavalry blundered into action without orders and were squandered, milling uselessly around the Allied infantry squares being shot to pieces. At about 4 o'clock the Prussians entered the field and thrust into Napoleon's right flank. Then came the humiliation that broke the will of the French army: the infantry of the Imperial Guard assaulted the right of Wellington's line, was defeated and fled. As darkness fell, the beaten French Army streamed away to the south. Napoleon's ambitions were finally wrecked; he abdicated on 22 June and was exiled to St Helena.

▼ The Battle of Waterloo, at the moment when the Scots Greys captured the Eagle of the French 45th Regiment.

FRANCE

The French Army had enjoyed a high reputation during the mid-eighteenth century, but the Revolution of 1789 all but destroyed it. In the years following the fall of the Bourbon monarchy, many aristocrats were either executed or obliged to flee abroad: as the nobles provided the army's entire officer corps, the effect on the French military may be imagined. The cavalry regiments – being the especial preserve of the nobility – suffered worst, the infantry fared a little better, and the practical, unglamorous artillery escaped almost unscathed. Thus it was the latter units, which largely maintained their discipline during the revolutionary mayhem that provided the cornerstone of Lazare Carnot's new Republican Army. After achieving a string of startling victories in defence of the Republic, this force would embark upon a series of dazzling campaigns of conquest under Napoleon. Starting in 1796 with his dramatic chase of the Austrians across northern Italy, Napoleon blazed his way into history. In 1798 he mounted his expedition to Egypt, then returned to France in late 1799 to seize power in the coup of *Brumaire*, in which he became First Consul.

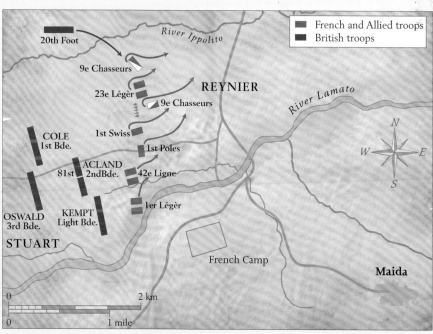

▲ *The Battle of Maida was fought in southern Italy in 1806. A small British force met and defeated the French in a battle that was a precursor to those fought in Spain and Portugal.*

◄ *Napoleon on the field at the Battle of Wagram, at which, on 6 July 1809, he defeated Archduke Charles of Austria.*

REVOLUTIONARY FRANCE
1789–96

on. Others were less able, but occupied positions in which they could cause much mischief.

The Government and the Army

This new government cast mistrustful eyes on the upper military hierarchy and rapidly instituted a system (as in Russia following their revolution of 1917) of sending trusted political agents – *Représentatives en Mission* – to oversee military planning and operations on the various fronts. These *Représentatives* had great powers over the military and could order officers to be arrested and sent back to Paris for trial if they thought fit. This made appointment to a position of command a less than joyful moment. The *Représentatives* involved themselves in strategic and tactical matters, questioning military decisions, slowing down the decision-making process and undermining the status of the commanding generals. Not all of them were malevolent, but even the most positive of them impeded military affairs. As long as the battle went in favour of the French, commanders

The social confusion caused by the French Revolution ripped the nation apart from top to bottom and produced – overnight – a nation almost wholly involved in political debate and activity, to the exclusion of most other matters. Politics in France – like all other European nations at that time – had been the reserve of that fortunate 4 or 5 per cent of the population with the money, time and interest to devote to matters other than the sheer fight for survival. In Paris, deprivation existed cheek by jowl with the opulence of the royal court, the upper clergy, the aristocracy and the successful merchants.

But traditional figures of authority in France were all to be questioned by the newly liberated political activists. The clergy and aristocracy now became

▲ *The decrepit Bastille symbolized the king's absolute power; when the Parisian mob stormed it on 14 July 1789, they smashed that power once and for all.*

hate-figures for the rest of the nation: it was open season on them all. Army officers, generals and admirals – most of whom came from the aristocracy – were also included. Many fled the country in the early stages of the Revolution, to join in the expatriate resistance flourishing in all of France's neighbouring states.

This decapitated the social, political, commercial and military structures of the nation. These vacuums were often filled by pushy, politically correct parvenus from the newly mobile lower orders. Some were men of talent, who brought order to chaos as time went

▲ *A French peasant woman carries the double burden of the Church and the aristocracy, in a picture entitled* The Great Abuse.

▲ *The young Napoleon Bonaparte at the beginning of his military career as a lieutenant of artillery.*

could rest relatively easy. But if the tactical situation turned against him – even for reasons totally outside his control – the unfortunate French general was liable to be clapped in irons and sent off to Paris to defend himself against charges of sabotage or treason. And the outcome of such trials was usually conviction and death: from April 1793 to July 1794, no less than 84 French generals and admirals were executed in this manner.

Several competent senior commanders found this operational climate intolerable and deserted to the Allies. They included General Dumouriez, commander of the Army of the North, which had been badly defeated by the Austrians at the Battle of Neerwinden on 18 March 1793. He was ordered to relinquish his command and return to Paris. Fearing the worst, he tried to convince his troops to march with him on the capital and overthrow the government: when they refused, Dumouriez deserted to the Austrians.

The turmoil of this time seeped down through the command structure of all the French armies. The brooding, threatening presence of the

▶ *French soldiers of the Revolutionary period: from left to right, a hussar, a heavy cavalryman and a grenadier of infantry.*

Représentatives made officers edgy, even if they were not of aristocratic origin. This undermined the cohesion and discipline of the armies to such a degree that morale was seriously affected. In the First Battle of Kaiserslautern (28–30 November 1793), when things began to go against the French, the cry went up in their ranks: "*Nous sommes trahis!*" (we are betrayed) and the army fled. Happily for France, the Prussians did not follow up their victory. Similar scenes were repeated on other battlefields. The men in the ranks had no faith in their officers: they were ready to run at the first setback.

It was not until after the end of the Terror, in mid-1794 – followed by a string of French victories and the withdrawal of Prussia from the war – that the morale of the French armies

was restored. They ended 1794 by driving the Allies out of Belgium and continued the sweep in 1795. By 1796, French soldiers were as confident of victory as any of their opponents.

In late 1793 a young officer of artillery, Napoleon Bonaparte, took command of the artillery besieging the Allied-held naval base at Toulon. By skilful use of his guns, he forced the invaders to evacuate the city on 18 December, and was consequently promoted. Being politically active as well as militarily competent, he rose quickly up the chain of command. On 5 October 1795, Napoleon saved the government from destruction by a royalist mob in Paris by his legendary "whiff of grapeshot". He was promoted again, and was soon to show the world just what he could do when given command of the Army of Italy.

NAPOLEON'S RISE TO POWER

The French government unleashed Napoleon into battle in northern Italy on 11 April 1796. He began with a victory over the Austro-Sardinian forces of Count Argenteau at Montenotte on 11 and 12 April, followed by rapid advances and more victories at Cosseria (13–14 April), Dego (14 April) and Mondovi (22 April), which caused Sardinia to sue for peace. More success followed at Lodi (10 May), Borghetto (30 May) and finally Milan (16 May–29 June), as he pushed the demoralized Austrians eastwards.

Napoleon and Mantua

Napleon's advance was stopped at Rivoli, east of Lake Garda, on 29 July. General Massena was defeated here by Field Marshal Wurmser. Napoleon now turned to the capture of the fortified city of Mantua. He used the Siege of Mantua to lure the Austrians into sending relief forces, confident that he could beat them in the open field and take Mantua as well.

▼ *Napoleon's victory at Rivoli in January 1797 sealed the fate of the city of Mantua and led to the defeat of the Austrians.*

The morale of the French Army under his command was now high, while that of the Austrians was rather rattled. They did as Napoleon wished and sent a first, hastily-assembled relief army down from Austria at the end of July. But the force was split into two parts, utterly divided by Lake Garda. Wurmser commanded the main body of 15,500 men, who advanced over the Brenner Pass and through Bolzano, down the eastern side of Lake Garda. Field Marshal Quosdanovich led another 15,000 men down the western side of the lake, through Brescia.

On 2 August Napoleon (with 20,000 men) defeated Quosdanovich at Lonato. Then, gathering a force of 35,000, he rushed eastwards to beat Wurmser at Castiglione on 5 August. Wurmser and Quosdanovich – having lost 6,000 men between them – fell back north. Napoleon laid siege to Mantua again.

The second attempt to raise the siege was made in early November: again, the Austrian force was split by Lake Garda. After initial successes, the Austrians were beaten by Napoleon at the Battle of Arcole from 15–17

November, largely because Field Marshal Davidovich, with 8,000 men in the Tyrol, refused to come to Field Marshal Alvintzy's aid, as his 18,500 men grappled with Napoleon's 20,000 in the flooded rice fields.

Alvintzy fell back north, up the eastern side of Lake Garda, while Davidovich – at last coming around the southern end of the fateful Lake Garda – soundly defeated General Vaubois' division at Rivoli on 17 November. By this point, the French had captured the detailed plans of Alvintzy's position and intentions. Napoleon at once decided to strike at Davidovich, while keeping Alvintzy at a distance. This led to the defeat of Davidovich at Rivoli on 22 November. The Austrians withdrew north again.

Urged on from Vienna, Alvintzy tried again to relieve Mantua with 24,000 men. This led to the Battle of Rivoli on 14–15 January 1797, in which he was again defeated by Napoleon, losing 12,000 men in the process. Meanwhile, Wurmser had raced for Mantua, where an action was fought on 16 January, Napoleon having left Rivoli to fight the next fire. Again, Wurmser lost and was forced to take refuge in the fortress, which was almost out of food. On 2 February Mantua surrendered. Napoleon's victory was complete: he occupied Lombardy and neutralized Venice.

Archduke Charles tried to advance from Udine, but was stopped at Valvassone on 16 March, ending Austrian efforts to retake northern Italy. On 18 April the Treaty of Leoben ended Franco-Austrian hostilities. Venice, which had broken the terms of its neutrality, was quickly overrun and converted into yet another pro-French republic at the end of May 1797.

Napoleon was now omnipotent. His army adored him and he showered the Directory in Paris with (some of) the vast collection of trophies he had amassed during this campaign.

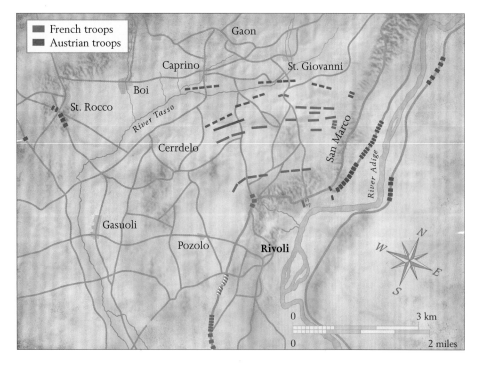

French troops
Austrian troops

Gaon

Caprino

St. Giovanni

Boi

St. Rocco

River Tasso

Cerrdelo

San Marco

River Adige

Gasuoli

Pozolo

Rivoli

N
W   E
S

0   3 km

0   2 miles

▲ *In Egypt Napoleon was so impressed with the Mamelukes in the Turkish ranks that he formed a squadron of them for his Guard.*

Napoleon in Northern Egypt

Following his victories in northern Italy, Napoleon was the darling of Paris, particularly as Archduke Charles had defeated General Moreau's Army of the Rhine and the Moselle in southern Germany in 1796. The Directory were aware of Napoleon's popularity and began to fear he might gather enough support to oust them from power.

Consequently, when he proposed an expedition to Egypt, in order to strike at Britain's eastern empire, the Directory quickly approved, and sent him on his way with the troops who had fought with him in Italy. Thus, at one stroke, a potentially dangerous rival – and most of his army – had been placed out of the realm of domestic French politics. Napoleon left France on 19 May with over 40,000 men, evaded Nelson's fleet (more by good luck than skill), forced Malta to capitulate on 11 June and took Alexandria on 2 July. But Nelson's crushing victory at the Battle of the Nile, on 1 August 1798, effectively marooned the French Army in Egypt,

as Britain assembled an army to destroy it. Napoleon rampaged through Egypt and Syria, easily defeating the impressive but largely ineffective hordes of Mameluke cavalry that were sent against him, until stopped by Anglo-Turkish forces at Acre on 21 May 1799. Made aware of the deteriorating political situation in France, Napoleon secretly abandoned his army in Egypt on 22 August and headed back to France, determined to squeeze political gain and glory from the national mess into which France had sunk. He landed in France on 9 October and at once hurried to Paris to begin plotting a seizure of power.

Suvorov in Italy

A major cause of France's misery had been the Allied reconquest of northern Italy in 1799. This had been achieved by Suvorov, the famous Russian commander. Although inter-Allied rivalry played into French hands, the collapse of the French in the region, coupled with increasing domestic financial crises, had made the Directory terminally unpopular.

The upshot was the coup of *Brumaire* (9 November 1799), in which the unwitting Abbé Sièyes helped Lucien Bonaparte push his brother,

Napoleon, into the post of one of the three new consuls. Within no time, Napoleon was First Consul and the other two – Sièyes and Roger Ducos – were nowhere.

Napoleon had arrived at the helm of France: it would take over 15 years for the combined powers of Europe to wrest it from his grasp again.

▼ *A portrait of Napoleon showing him in his role as First Consul of France.*

FRENCH ARMY UNIFORMS

The first mention of uniform clothing for the French Army was in 1670, when the dress of the foreign regiments was regulated. This was followed in 1690 by a ruling on the clothing of the French regiments. Coats were in mellow colours, the facings and small clothes were differentiating features. Pikemen wore the cuirass. From about 1715 white coats became the predominant colour for French units, the foreigners in French service wore red (Swiss and Irish) or blue (German). From about 1743 the English- or German-pattern fur cap began to be adopted for grenadiers.

At the outbreak of the Seven Years' War (1756–63), the French army coat adopted the same lapels and turnbacks of other armies.

In 1759 epaulettes were introduced as rank badges for officers. A colonel wore two, with heavy, bullion fringes; a lieutenant colonel one such on the left shoulder; a major wore two epaulettes with fine fringes, a captain had one on the right shoulder, lieutenants and second lieutenants one, with a diamond-shaped pattern on the strap and the fringes mixed with silk. All officers wore the gorget and the sash. Coat turnbacks were decorated with the fleur-de-lis for fusiliers, and with a grenade for grenadiers.

In 1786 the Colonel-General regiment adopted a steel helmet with a leopard skin turban, brass front plate and comb and a flowing, black horsehair crest. It was remarkably like the dragoon helmet that was later in service. Several variations of this helmet appeared in the Revolutionary period, with and without peaks.

Although Revolutionary fervour swept away royal crests and titles extremely rapidly, replacing the uniforms of an entire – and very numerous – army was a luxury that the nation in turmoil could not embark upon lightly. It is thus extremely likely that the regiments of the French Army fought for the first few years in their old, royalist costumes. The change to dark blue coats would have come gradually and patchily, from 1795, as old uniforms became unavailable.

◀ REGIMENT COLONEL-GÉNÉRAL NO. 1, 1791 *In 1793 this old regiment was formed into the 1st and 2nd Demi-Brigades, which later converted to the 31st Line and 9th Line respectively. This individual wears the traditional white coat of the royal French infantry and the soon to be replaced helmet with a black horsehair crest and leopardskin turban. This cumbersome headgear would be revived for dragoons under the empire.*

▼ OFFICER, SWISS REGIMENT SALIS-SAMADE NO. 64, 1791 *Like all other Swiss regiments that were in the French army in 1789, this regiment, raised for French service in 1672, fell under the suspicion of the Revolutionary government and was disbanded in 1792. All 14 Swiss regiments in French service at this time wore red coats. In March 1805, Napoleon raised four regiments of Swiss infantry for French service. They fought with their customary valour throughout the imperial period and into the Hundred Days. This officer wears a bicorn, and his long-skirted coat is faced with yellow. He wears his hair in a pigtail, a custom abolished in the French Army in 1805.*

THE REPUBLICAN INFANTRY

The years following the Revolution saw great changes for the French Army: the old royalist infantry regiments were to serve as the stiffening for the tens of thousands of new volunteers who answered the patriotic call to arms. Most of the old regiments consisted of two battalions, though some had four. In the First Amalgamation of 1794, each old royalist battalion was put together with two new volunteer battalions, to become a *demi-brigade de bataille*, of which there were 198 in the line and 15 of light infantry. Only the old battalions were capable of manoeuvring efficiently in the extended, three-deep line, eight fusilier companies wide. They were placed between the two volunteer battalions, which marched in battalion columns. Each battalion also had a grenadier company and these three would be concentrated together on either flank, or to the rear of the *demi-brigade* as needed. This was the origin of the famous *ordre mixte*, which was in use up to 1815.

▼ **SERGEANT, WITH COLOUR, OF THE 8TH LIGHT INFANTRY REGIMENT, 1800** *The 8th served at Austerlitz, Jena, Friedland, Essling and Wagram. They then went to Spain and fought at Talavera and Barossa, where, on 5 March 1811, they lost their eagle to Sergeant Masterson of the 87th British Foot. They stayed in Spain to the end of the war there, but also had battalions in Saxony in 1813 and later fought at Waterloo. Although the shako was introduced in 1804, it took some years for the bicorn, as worn here, to entirely disappear. The regimental colour, however, was replaced when the regiment was issued with an Eagle and imperial colours in 1804.*

▼ **REPUBLICAN INFANTRY KIT** *1 The bearskin cap worn by line infantry grenadiers. 2 The calfskin pack and rolled blanket or greatcoat used by all French infantry. Into this the soldier had to cram all his personal possessions when in the field. 3 This black felt cocked hat was in near-universal use for civilian and military use across Europe at this time. The colouring of the round cockade showed the national colours, the pompon was in the colour of the wearer's company. 4 A remnant of the armour once worn by knights, the gorget was the badge of an officer when on duty. It would usually carry the crest of the ruling monarch; this is a Republican model. 5 The canvas cover worn over a cartridge pouch.*

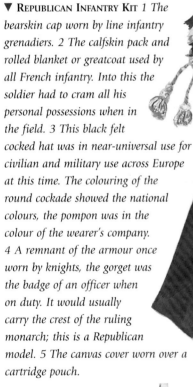

1
3

2

4

5

55 ème
de Ligne
Premier Bataillon
Comp. des Grenadiers

The Line Infantry

The First Amalgamation was followed in 1795 by a second, reducing the *demi-brigades* of the line (as they were now termed) to 100 and the light to 30. In 1796 the line was increased to 110, but some of these numbers were vacant. In 1803 a *voltigeur*, or light company, was added to each light infantry battalion, and in 1804 the same happened in the line battalions. By 1805 the title *demi-brigade* had been replaced by the old royalist term *régiment*. It was not until February 1808 that the well-known French infantry battalion organization of one

▼ OFFICER, 13TH LINE INFANTRY, 1796 *This officer wears the new, dark blue Revolutionary tunic, originally worn by the National Guard, but extended to the regular army early in the period. His epaulettes, gorget and sword strap are all badges of his officer status.*

Regimental Distinctions: Line Infantry 1789

No./Title/Date raised	Facings	Buttons	Pockets*	Cuffs**	Collar/cuff flaps***
*vertical or horizontal, ** in the facing colour *** in the facing colour					
1 Colonel-Général 1780	black	yellow	H		
2 Picardie 1557	black	yellow	H		YES
3 Piémont 1558	black	yellow	H	YES	
4 Provence 1776	black	white	H		
5 Navarre 1558	black	white	H		YES
6 Armagnac 1776	black	white	H	YES	
7 Champagne 1558	black	yellow	V		
8 Austrasie 1776	black	yellow	V		YES
9 Normandie 1616	black	yellow	V	YES	
10 Neustrie 1776	black	white	V		
11 La Marine 1635	black	white	V		YES
12 Auxerrois 1776	black	white	V	YES	
13 Bourbonnais 1672	violet	yellow	H		
14 Forez 1776	violet	yellow	H		YES
15 Béarn 1684	violet	yellow	H	YES	
16 Agénois 1776	violet	white	H		
17 Auvergne 1606	violet	white	H		YES
18 Royale-Auvergne 1776	violet	white	H	YES	
19 Flandre 1597	violet	yellow	V		
20 Cambrésis 1776	violet	yellow	V		YES
21 Guyenne 1610	violet	yellow	V	YES	
22 Viennois 1776	violet	white	V		
23 Royal 1656	violet	white	V		YES
24 Brie 1775	violet	white	V	YES	
25 Poitou 1616	pink	yellow	H		
26 Bresse 1775	pink	yellow	H		YES
27 Lyonnais 1616	pink	yellow	H	YES	
28 Du Maine 1775	pink	white	H		
29 Dauphin 1667	pink	white	H		YES
30 Perche 1775	pink	white	H	YES	
31 Aunis 1621	pink	yellow	V		
32 Bassigny 1775	pink	yellow	V		YES
33 Touraine 1625	pink	yellow	V	YES	
34 Angoulême 1775	pink	white	V		
35 Aquitaine 1604	pink	white	V		YES ▶

grenadier, one *voltigeur* and four fusilier companies was adopted. The uniforms of the line regiments were defined by the regulations of October 1786. A revised regulation was published in November 1789, but it is very unlikely that it was implemented. The infantry wore long-tailed coats, most of them white. Nine regiments wore dark blue coats, 14 wore red. Regimental identity was shown by the seven different facing colours and the white or yellow buttons. With so many regiments in the army, further

differentiations had to be incorporated in the uniforms to give each its own, unique dress.

A batch of 12 regiments all wore the same facing colour: six wore brass buttons, six wore pewter. All regiments wore coloured lapels and turnbacks. Six regiments had horizontal pocket flaps in the tails, the others had vertical flaps. Four regiments of each group, or series wore facing colours on the collar, lapels, cuffs, cuff flaps, turnbacks and piping to white shoulder straps and pocket flaps. Of the eight other

No./Title/Date raised	Facings	Buttons	Pockets*	Cuffs**	Collar/cuff flaps***
36 Anjou 1775	pink	white	V	YES	
37 Maréchal de Turenne 1625	sky blue	yellow	H		
38 Dauphiné 1629	sky blue	yellow	H		YES
39 Ile-de-France 1629	sky blue	yellow	H	YES	
40 Soissonnais 1598	sky blue	white	H		
41 La Reine 1661	sky blue	white	H		YES
42 Limosin 1635	sky blue	white	H	YES	
43 Royal-des-Vaisseaux 1638	sky blue	yellow	V		
44 Orléans 1642	sky blue	yellow	V		YES
45 La Couronne 1643	sky blue	yellow	V	YES	
46 Bretagne 1644	sky blue	white	V		
47 Lorraine 1644	sky blue	white	V		YES
48 Artois 1615	sky blue	white	V	YES	
49 Vintimille 1647	crimson	yellow	H		
50 Hainault 1651	crimson	yellow	H		YES
51 La Sarre 1651	crimson	yellow	H	YES	
52 La Fère 1654	crimson	white	H		
53 Alsace 1655	red	yellow	H		
54 Royal-Roussillon 1655	crimson	white	H		YES
55 Condé 1635	crimson	white	H	YES	
56 Bourbon 1644	crimson	yellow	V		
57 Beauvoisis 1667	crimson	yellow	V	YES	
58 Rouergue 1667	crimson	yellow	V		YES
59 Bourgogne 1668	crimson	white	V		
60 Royal-Marine 1669	crimson	white	V		YES
61 Vermandois 1670	crimson	white	V	YES	
62 Salm-Salm 1670	red	white	H		YES
63 Ernest-Suisse 1672*	black	white	H		YES
64 Salis-Samade-Suisse 1672*	yellow	yellow	H		YES
65 Sonnenberg-Suisse 1672*	sky blue	white	V		
66 Castella-Suisse 1672*	dark blue	white	H		
67 Languedoc 1672	scarlet	yellow	H		
68 Beauce 1763	scarlet	yellow	H		YES
69 Vigier-Suisse 1674*	buff	yellow			YES
70 Médoc 1674	scarlet	yellow	H	YES	
71 Vivarais 1674	scarlet	white	H		
72 Vexin 1674	scarlet	white	H		YES
73 Royal-Comtois 1674	scarlet	white	H	YES	
74 Beaujolais 1674	scarlet	yellow	V		
75 Monsieur 1674	scarlet	yellow	V		YES
76 Lullin de Chateuavieux -Suisse 1677*	yellow	white	H		
77 Lamark 1680	red	white	H		
78 Penthièvre 1684	scarlet	yellow	V	YES	
79 Boulonnais 1684	scarlet	white	V		
80 Angoumois 1684	scarlet	white	V		YES
81 Conti 1684	scarlet	white	V	YES	
82 Saintonge 1684	blue	yellow	H		
83 Foix 1684	blue	yellow	H		YES
84 Rohan 1681	blue	yellow	H	YES	
85 Diesbach-Suisse 1689*	grey	white	H		cuff flaps in the coat colour ▶

regiments in the series, four had white collars and cuff flaps piped in the facing. The last group of four regiments had white cuffs piped in the facing colour. Small clothes and belts were white. Fusilier companies wore the peaked casque. Resembling the Tarleton helmet in style, it had a stiff black, horsehair crest and mock leopardskin turban. On the left hand side were the white cockade, loop and button and company badge. It was very

▼ FUSILIER, 96TH LINE INFANTRY REGIMENT, 1800 *The French Army's line infantry had emerged from the chaos of the Revolutionary period with a uniform that was practical and reasonably easy to manufacture. The only distinguishing regimental feature was the regiment's number on the buttons.*

cheaply made and production ceased in 1795, when it was replaced by the bicorn. The casque continued in use until 1799, when it was banned. From 1788 grenadier companies wore red epaulettes. Buttons bore the regimental number within a French ring.

Drummers wore dark blue coats with extensive decoration in the royal livery of red and white. This was replaced by tricolour lace. Many of the regiments of the line were foreign and were distinguished from native French regiments by coat colours: the 53rd, 62nd, 77th, 89th, 94th, 96th, 98th, 99th, 101st wore sky blue coats; the 63rd, 64th, 65th, 66th, 69th, 76th, 85th, 86th, 87th, 88th, 92nd, 95th, 97th, 100th wore red coats. In 1795

▼ **GRENADIER DRUMMER, 93RD DEMI-BRIGADE, 1796** *This young drummer wears a bearskin decorated with a tricolour plume and copper front plate bearing a grenade.*

No./Title/Date raised	Facings	Buttons	Pockets*	Cuffs**	Collar/cuff flaps***
86 Courtin-Suisse 1689*	sky blue	white	H		YES
87 Dillon 1690	black	yellow	V		
88 Berwick 1690	black	yellow	V		YES
89 Royal-Suédois 1690	red	white	V		
90 Chartres 1691	blue	white	H		
91 Barrois 1692	blue	white	H		YES
92 Walsh 1689	black	yellow	V	YES	
93 Enghien 1706	blue	white	H	YES	
94 Hesse-Darmstadt 1709	red	white	V		YES
95 Salis-Grisons 1734*	dark blue	white	H		YES
96 Nassau 1745	red	yellow	V	YES	
97 Steiner-Suisse 1752*	dark blue	white	H		cuff flaps in the coat colour
98 Bouillon 1757	black	white	H		
99 Royal-Deux-Ponts 1757	black	white	H		YES
100 Reinach-Suisse 1758*	white	white	H	YES	
101 Royal-Liégeois 1787**	black	white	H	YES	
102 1791	blue	yellow	H		
103 1791	dark green	yellow	H		YES
104 1791	dark green	yellow	H	YES	
105 1791	dark green	white	V		

The 106th to 110th regiments were raised in the colonies in 1792 and the 111th in France also in 1792

*regiments were disbanded in 1792 **emigrated en masse in 1792

most of these were replaced by the royal blue of the National Guard.

In the line infantry, regiments had lapels in the facing colour: variations in the colouring of collars, cuffs and cuff flaps then differentiated between other regiments in each group, which shared the same facings. Later all line infantry regiments went into dark blue, with white lapels and turnbacks.

The Light Infantry

France began to experiment with light infantry in 1740 and several legions were raised by 1749. At the same time, a battalion of *chasseurs à pied* (literally hunters on foot) was attached to each of the six newly-raised regiments of *chasseurs à cheval* (mounted hunters). In 1788 these battalions were separated from the cavalry, and six more were raised to give the following light infantry in 1791. They were designed to perform scouting duties and to act as advance and rear guards. According to the regulations of 1784, their uniforms were of the same cut as those of the line, but in dark green, with pewter buttons bearing a hunting horn enclosing the battalion number. On the right shoulder was a dark green *contre-epaulette*, on the left shoulder was an epaulette with a white strap and fringes and a lozenge pattern on the facing colour.

New uniform regulations were issued in 1789: buttons were now to be of brass and the coat was piped in white. The turnbacks were to be in the facing colour, with green hunting horns. Small clothes and belts were white, gaiters black. Musicians wore reversed colours. The elite company was entitled *carabiniers* and these troops wore red epaulettes and bearskins with red plumes, white cords, a red top patch with a white cross and no front plate. The other companies wore the peaked casque, with stiff black horsehair crest and mock leopard skin turban. On the left-hand side were a brass hunting horn badge, a company pompon and the

The headgear was a green leather casque, replaced by the shako in 1801. By 1800 these regiments were armed with the same smooth-bore musket as their comrades in the line.

The National Guard

The first National Guard units were formed in 1789. Standardization on royal blue was achieved in 1792. Red cuffs and collar were piped white, white lapels and turnbacks were piped red. Fusilier companies wore a bicorn with tricolour cockade; grenadiers wore black bearskins, tricolour plume and cockade, white cords, and brass plate.

▼ OFFICER, LIGHT INFANTRY, 1796 *The light infantry were among the first to adopt the shako, in 1799, although officers usually retained the bicorn. This officer wears silver epaulettes and hussar-style boots.*

▲ LIEUTENANT OF CHASSEURS, 4TH LIGHT INFANTRY, 1804 *This light infantry officer wears a shako, silver buttons and a blue waistcoat edged in white. He has silver Hungarian knots on his trousers and has hussar-style boots. The red collar and cuff-flaps are not regulation; they should have been blue.*

tricolour cockade. For parades a white plume, tipped in the facing colour would be worn. Two more battalions were raised in 1791: the 13th, with white collar, cuffs and flaps; and the 14th, with white cuffs only. In March 1793 the free corps and legions raised since then were reorganized into the 15th–21st Battalions. In September 1793 the light infantry changed their green coats for the same dark blue as was now worn in the line, with pointed lapels, white piping, yellow buttons, red collar and cuff flaps. Small clothes were dark blue, belts white.

Regimental Distinctions:
Chasseurs à Pied Battalions

1st Chasseurs Royaux de Provence: red collar, cuffs and cuff flaps.

2nd Chasseurs Royaux du Dauphine: red cuffs only.

3rd Chasseurs Royaux corses: red collar and cuff flaps only

4th Chasseurs corses: bright yellow collar, cuffs and cuff flaps.

5th Chasseurs cantabres: bright yellow cuffs only

6th Chasseurs bretons: bright yellow collar and cuff flaps.

7th Chasseurs d'Auvergne: pink collar, cuffs and cuff flaps.

8th Chasseurs des Vosges: pink cuffs only.

9th Chasseurs des Cévennes: pink collar and cuff flaps.

10th Chasseurs du Gévaudan: crimson collar, cuffs and cuff flaps.

11th Chasseurs des Ardennes: crimson cuffs only.

12th Chasseurs du Roussillon: crimson collar and cuff flaps.

THE REPUBLICAN CAVALRY

The cavalry regiments suffered a drain of officers following the revolution of 1789. By 1796, however, the cavalry was on the road to recovery and began to improve. The backbone of the cavalry was the dragoons and *chasseurs à cheval*: the cuirassiers and lancers would achieve fame under the Empire.

The Carabiniers

There were two regiments of carabiniers, which were always brigaded together. Their title derived from the short musket, or carbine, with which they were armed. The uniform was originally dark blue with

Regimental Distinctions: Dragoons 1789

No./Title	Coat	Waistcoat	Facings
1 Colonel-Général	red	blue with white edging	blue
2 Mestre-de-Camp Général	red	red	white
3 Royal	blue	red	red
4 du Roi	blue	red	white
5 La Reine	red	blue	blue
6 Dauphin	blue	blue	blue
7 Orléans	red	blue	blue
8 Beauffremont	red	red	yellow
9 Choiseul	red	red	dark green
10 d'Autichamps	red	red	light green
11 La Ferronnaye	red	red	red
12 Flammarens	red	red	black
13 Nicolai	red	red	light blue
14 Chapt	red	red	yellow
15 Marboeuf	red	red	red
16 Langedoc	blue	blue	red

◀ TROOPER OF CARABINIERS, 1791 *This trooper wears a uniform, the style of which was almost universal for heavy cavalry in Europe at this time. The two carabinier regiments were descendants of the first cavalry to be equipped with carbines. They were ranked as the senior regiments in the line cavalry and were always brigaded together in the field.*

▶ OFFICER, 1ST DRAGOONS, 1792 *Dragoons were trained to fight on foot as well as on horseback, and were equipped and armed accordingly. The ubiquitous cocked hat was replaced by the elegant Grecian-style helmet as early as 1762. Each regiment of dragoons procured their own uniforms, so variations from the prescribed norm were inevitable and common.*

red lapels, collar, cuffs, long turnbacks, with dark blue grenade badges, and small clothes, but the latter were buff by 1789. The 1st Carabiniers had red cuff flaps with dark blue piping, the 2nd had dark blue cuff flaps with red piping. The dark blue shoulder straps were edged red. The bicorn had a wide white edging and red, drooping feather plume, decorated by the tricolour cockade and a white loop and button. Small clothes were deep yellow, buttons and belts were white. The straight-bladed sword was carried in a black sheath. Saddlery was dark blue with white edging and grenade badges. harness was black with steel fittings.

The Cuirassier and Horse Regiments

There were 11 regiments of Royal Horse in 1789: the 1st–7th and the 9th–12th. Only the Cuirassiers du Roi, later the 8th Regiment, wore body-armour (the cuirass). No more such regiments were raised before 1802.

The Dragoon Regiments

There were 18 regiments of dragoons in 1792. The 19th–21st were raised in 1793: the 21st disbanded again in 1798. They wore a medium green coat and brass helmet with comb, drooping black horsehair crest, red plume and turban, without a peak.

The *Chasseurs à Cheval*

There was no practical difference in the tactical employment of *chasseurs à cheval* or hussars and very little sartorial difference either. Both carried the same weapons and adopted the costume of the Hungarian hussars, although the *chasseurs* wore no pelisses or sabretasches. Even allowing for the large size of the French Army, the emphasis on a powerful light cavalry arm is impressive.

In 1779 the first six regiments of *chasseurs* appeared in the Army List. During the Revolutionary period they wore green coats and breeches with white trim; a hussar dolman was worn,

together with the infantry-style crested helmet. This helmet was then replaced with the winged cap or replaced with the *mirliton* in the facing colour, edged in the button colour. The hussar costume in dark green and white was retained (belts were white) but without a pelisse. Weapons were the curved, hussar-pattern sabre with brass hilt, a carbine and a brace of pistols.

▲ OFFICER, 8TH CAVALRY REGIMENT, 1794
From 1792 to 1802, this was the only cavalry regiment to wear armour. The bicorn was worn until 1804 and then replaced by a steel helmet. That same year the number of cavalry regiments wearing armour was raised to 12, although sources are contradictory as to the level of protection afforded by the steel cuirass.

Regimental Distinctions: *Chasseurs à Cheval* 1800

No./Raised	Collar	Collar Piping	Cuffs & Edging
1 1651	scarlet	green	scarlet
2 1673	green	scarlet	scarlet
3 1675	scarlet	green	green
4 1675	yellow	green	yellow
5 1676	green	yellow	yellow
6 1676	yellow	green	green
7 1747	pink	green	pink
8 1749	green	pink	pink
9 1757	pink	green	green
10 1758	crimson	green	crimson
11 1762	green	crimson	green
12 1769	crimson	green	green
13 1793	orange	green	orange
14 1793	green	orange	orange
15 1793	orange	green	green
16 1793	sky blue	green	sky blue
17 1793 disbanded 1795; the number remained thence vacant.			
18 1793	sky blue	green	green
19 1793	orange	green	orange
20 1793	green	orange	orange
21 1793	orange	green	green
22 1793	dark orange	green	dark orange
23 1793	green	dark orange	dark orange
24 1793	dark orange	green	green
25 1795	madder red	green	madder red

Regimental Distinctions: Hussars 1792						
No./Title/Raised	Dolman	Pelisse	Lace	Breeches	Sash	Mirliton
1 Bercheny 1720	sky blue	sky blue	white	sky blue	crimson & yellow	red & black
2 Chamborant 1735	brown	brown	white	sky blue	crimson & sky blue	sky blue&black
3 Esterhazy 1764	light grey	light grey	red	light grey	crimson & white	white & black
4 Saxe* 1743	green	green	yellow	red	crimson & green	green
5 Colonel-General 1779	dark blue	red	yellow	blue	crimson & yellow	black
6 Lauzun 1783	sky blue	white	yellow	sky blue	crimson & sky blue	red & black

*this regiment emigrated en masse in 1793; the old 5th and 6th became the new 4th and 5th at that point.

The Hussars

Although light cavalry was well represented by the numerous regiments of *chasseurs à cheval*, the French also raised six regiments of

hussars prior to 1792. In that year the old royalist regimental titles were officially abolished, but continued in barrack usage for years afterwards.

French hussar regiments modelled their uniforms very faithfully on those pioneered by the Hungarian horsemen, including the winged cap, or *mirliton*, plus the braided dolman and pelisse, each with 18 rows of buttons and lace on the chest. Some regiments wore five buttons in each row on the chest, others, including the 2nd, 4th, 5th, 9th and 10th regiments wore only three. The pelisse was $7^3/4$ in (20 cm) longer than the dolman and could be worn as a jacket in winter, but it was usually fastened by a cord and slung over the left shoulder, to act as protection against sabre cuts. French hussars also wore the decorated breeches, woollen barrel sash (crimson and white or yellow according to the button colour), short boots, dangling sabretasche and curved sabre of their

◀ OFFICER, 5TH HUSSARS, 1794 *This was the old Lauzun Hussars, raised in 1783 and numbered "6th" until 1793, when the 4th Hussars emigrated* en masse *and the other two, junior, regiments moved up in seniority. Hussars were popular regiments in most European armies, a combination of dashing reputation and colourful uniform.*

▶ TROOPER, 1ST HUSSARS, 1806 *This regiment had been raised in 1720 by Comte Ladislas-Ingace de Barcheny. The uniform was typically Hungarian, and in 1792 was topped off with a red and black Mirliton. The sash was crimson and yellow. During the Revolutionary and Naopleonic wars, the 1st Hussars fought in northern Italy, but did not accompany Napoleon to Egypt. They were in Spain in 1812 and did not fight at Waterloo.*

worn slung over the left shoulder. The dolman was usually in the colours of the pelisse, but there were exceptions.

The Hungarian breeches had decorative knots on the thigh vents and similar braid up the outside of each leg and across the backside, where there would be a loop. These were protected in the field by buttoned overalls, having 18 buttons to each side, usually in the same colour as the pantaloons and reinforced with black leather inside the legs and around the bottoms. The boots had steel, screw-in spurs and the tops were cut out in the front centre, edged with white or yellow cord and had a tassel in the front cut-out.

Instead of the royalist lilies or crowned cipher, the sabretasches were decorated with the Cap of Liberty atop the *liktor*, flanked by

two discs bearing "R" and "F". Officers' bandoliers were decorated in gold and silver edging plus picker equipment. They were often protected by red Morocco leather cases, closed with regimental buttons.

Horse furniture was of traditional hussar cut, in the dolman colour, edged and decorated with the lace colour. The cylindrical portmanteau bore the regimental number on each end. White sheepskin saddle covers, edged in the facing colour, were often worn. The traditional wooden Mongolian Bock saddle was used, keeping the rider well off the horses' withers. Hussars were armed with a curved sabre with brass hilt, two pistols and the M 1786 carbine. Hussar regiments bore standards and later Eagles, but not in the field.

▲ *This picture of an officer of the hussars dates from the early Revolutionary period and just oozes all the panache and swank that went with the uniform.*

Hungarian counterparts. Badges of rank were chevrons in the button colour placed above both cuffs: these were worn on dolman and pelisse.

The farrier (*maréchal ferrant*) wore a horseshoe (points down) on the upper sleeve in white or yellow. Belts were white, the was harness black with steel fittings. Hussars had their own hair styles: the usual pigtail, plus one plait of hair in front of each ear (known as *cadenettes*). Moustaches were worn. The traditional *mirliton*, or peakless, winged cap, was originally in the form of a truncated cone, with a long flap of cloth (the *flamme*), in the facing colour and edged in the button colour, wrapped around it or allowed to fly free.

In barracks the shako would be replaced by a soft cap, the *bonnet de police*, in the dolman colour, decorated in the lace colour or the facing colour. The pelisse bore 18 rows each of five ball buttons and was lined with white sheepskin, edged with black lamb's wool. It was usually

◄ **FIELD OFFICER, 6TH CHASSEURS À CHEVAL, 1796** *This individual shows how influential hussar-style uniforms were on the* chasseur *regiments. Tactical use of this light cavalry arm was as for the hussars, and their uniforms were very similar. The officer wears a* mirliton, *the wing of which was either wound around the cap (as here) or worn flying free.*

THE REPUBLICAN ARTILLERY, ENGINEERS AND MINERS

The artillery was relatively unaffected by the upheaval of the Revolution, largely because it had never been the preserve of aristocratic officers, like the cavalry. Thus it maintained its efficiency while other units were thrown into chaos by the mass desertion (or murder) of the nobility. Napoleon was a gunner himself, and following his seizure of power in 1799, began transforming the artillery into the most powerful branch of the French Army. The engineers had originally been part of the artillery but, in 1793, a corps of engineers, composed of 12 battalions of sappers and six companies of miners, was established. French engineers were certainly among the best in Europe and enjoyed an excellent reputation.

The Artillery

French foot artillery wore dark blue, with similar collar and lapels piped red, red cuffs and turnbacks, blue cuff flaps piped red, with yellow buttons. From 1792 the horse artillery wore a dark blue hussar uniform with red lacing and yellow buttons, together with the Tarleton helmet.

The 1st–5th foot artillery regiments were raised in 1720, the 6th in 1757, the 7th in 1762, the 8th in 1784 and the 9th followed later in 1810 from the ex-Dutch artillery. Horse artillery did not make an appearance in the French Army until 1792, relatively late on. By 1795 there were eight such regiments. Companies of these regiments fought separately, as the tactical situation dictated, often scattered over several fronts. Guns and limbers followed the Gribeauval design, introduced in an attempt to impose a level of standardization, which had been a major step forward and was to be reintroduced in 1818. A new artillery design was imposed from 1803 but it proved problematic and many French batteries would make use of captured weapons, mainly Austrian pieces.

The Artillery Train

This was the organization that drove the guns and ammunition vehicles. Initially the task of transporting guns and ammunition had been given to hired civilians but this proved highly unsatisfactory. In 1800 the train was militarized with drivers incorporated into the army. They wore a shako with white metal, rhombic plate and chin scales, red cords and plume, grey, single-breasted coat with light blue facings piped red, grey shoulder straps piped red, grey waistcoat laced with red, white buttons, grey breeches with red thigh knots, and riding boots.

Engineers and Miners

From 1776 there was a battalion of engineers and in 1793 this was expanded into a corps of 12 battalions of sappers and six companies of miners. The uniform was dark blue with black collar, lapels, cuffs and cuff flaps all piped red, red turnbacks, yellow buttons, dark blue small clothes, white belts, shako with red cords and plume.

Engineer officers were primarily employed in siege works or in building and improving existing defences such as the series of forts guarding France's eastern frontier. These played an

◀ **ARTILLERY OFFICER, 1796** *This officer is from the foot artillery. As Napoleon was himself a trained artillery officer, he kept a special eye on the performance of this arm of the service and was a master of its effective use on the battlefield. The colouring of the artilleryman's uniform was relatively practical, with dark blue predominating, which was essential given the masses of black smoke and powder given off by cannon.*

▲ *Napoleon's artillery train, with its heavily loaded wagons, crossing the Sierra Guadarrama in Spain in December 1808.*

important role in the campaigns of the French Revolution, particulary in 1793 when Mainz and Maubeuge played important roles. Later, when the Revolutionary forces went on the offensive, the engineers were again crucial, particularly in the Low Countries and in the numerous attempts to cross the Rhine. Napoleon had relatively few good engineers with him in 1796 in Italy. Aside from building or destroying fortifications, engineers could be used to oversee

◀ GUNNER, HORSE ARTILLERY, 1800

Horse artillery was not designed to operate exclusively with cavalry formations, although this was often the case. The light cavalry flavour of the horse artillery was followed in many European armies and is readily apparent in this individual's uniform. The fur colpack, the hair worn in a pigtail, the dolman and lace, the breeches with Hungarian thigh knots and the boots all suggest the influence of the hussars.

▶ OFFICER OF ENGINEERS, 1796

The engineers were essentially a branch of the artillery service and these officers were highly schooled in mathematics and science. Engineer officers took years to train and were, therefore, highly prized individuals. The dark blue uniform with black collar, cuffs and cuff flaps was a distinguishing feature of the engineer's uniform. This unusual cut of coat was later replaced by a single-breasted variation with black lapels.

earthworks or fieldworks. Sappers did the spadework or were tasked with destroying enemy defences or, occasionally, leading attacks against besieged emplacements.

Miners were used to dig trenches or, more specifically, to mine beneath city walls, place explosives and, ideally, bring whole sections of wall tumbling down. They were to earn lasting fame under the empire during the siege of Saragossa. Miners were often issued with rudimentary trench armour as they were frequently the most exposed in the initial stages of a siege. Another specialist arm was that of the *pontonniers* (bridge-builders), first seen in the French Army in Strasburg in 1792. They became famous for their building of the Beresina bridges in November 1812 during the ill-fated retreat from Moscow.

THE ARMY IN EGYPT 1798–1801

A French army landed in Egypt in July 1798 and was soon in conflict with the wild, but relatively ineffective, Islamic Mameluke forces. However, following the destruction of the French navy on 1 August of that year, regular communication between Egypt and France – and consequently any new supplies of equipment, weapons and ammunition – was ended. Even when Napoleon entered Cairo, less than a month after

Regimental Distinctions: Infantry of the Army of Egypt 1798–1801

Unit	Coat turnbacks	Collar	Cuffs	Piping	Cap tuft
2nd Light	light green	dark blue	dark blue	white	green
4th Light	light green	dark brown (crimson)*	dark brown (crimson)	white	white & green
21st Light	sky blue	yellow	yellow (red turnbacks)	white	yellow & green
22nd Light	sky blue	maroon	maroon	white	red over green
9th Line	red	green (blue)	green (white)	green	red
13th Line	brown (crimson)	blue	dark brown (puce)	white	dark blue
18th Line	red (brown)	dark brown (scarlet)	yellow (blue)	yellow	black
25th Line	pink	pale blue	pale blue	white	white & red
32nd Line	pink (brown)	dark blue (red)	dark blue (orange)	white	white & blue
61st Line	dark brown (crimson)	orange (blue)	orange (blue)	yellow	black & white
69th Line	brown	red	red	white	white over yellow
75th Line	red	sky blue	sky blue	white	red over dark blue
85th Line	dark brown	red	buff	white	red & yellow
88th Line	crimson (violet)	dark blue (white loop)	green (dark blue)	white	blue over yellow

* Colours that changed from October 1799 are shown in brackets.

landing, many of the men were in rags. Local sources provided plenty of cotton, so new uniforms were made up of this material. Locals were even recruited into the army, although the Naval Legion and the Maltese Legion were quickly broken up and distributed among the *demi-brigades*.

◀ **TRUMPETER OF DROMEDARIES, 1799**
Realizing the limitations of horses in soft sand, Napoleon ordered two squadrons of dromedary-mounted troops be raised to operate with the infantry in the desert. Although this trumpeter wears a bicorn, the officers and men wore a shako with a yellow rhombic plate, white cords and plume on the left side. Although very hot by day, North Africa can be cold at night, thus the pelisse and burnous. The regiment, possibly the most unusual to serve under Napoleon, was disbanded at the end of the campaign.

The uniforms that the men had worn in Italy were the usual dark blue, with only the unit numbers on the buttons giving any clue to unit identity.

Uniform Regulations

In October 1799 General Kléber issued new uniform regulations, but until then the army presented a very motley appearance, with each *demi-brigade* designing its own costume. Lack of standardization of materials and processes meant that varieties of shades and colours were legion.

The infantry seem to have abandoned the bicorn and adopted a black leather peaked cap in September 1798, with flaps which could be let down to cover the ears and neck. Each unit was distinguished by a coloured tuft on the crown of the cap. The infantry were supposed to have

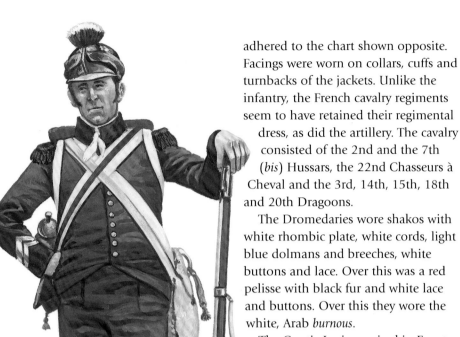

adhered to the chart shown opposite. Facings were worn on collars, cuffs and turnbacks of the jackets. Unlike the infantry, the French cavalry regiments seem to have retained their regimental dress, as did the artillery. The cavalry consisted of the 2nd and the 7th (*bis*) Hussars, the 22nd Chasseurs à Cheval and the 3rd, 14th, 15th, 18th and 20th Dragoons.

The Dromedaries wore shakos with white rhombic plate, white cords, light blue dolmans and breeches, white buttons and lace. Over this was a red pelisse with black fur and white lace and buttons. Over this they wore the white, Arab *burnous*.

The Coptic Legion, raised in Egypt in 1799, wore the bicorn with light green tunics, with similar facings, but with a yellow collar and piping, white buttons and small clothes and black belts. When the French army was ejected from Egypt by the British in October 1801, these legions went back to France with them. The Dromedaries were transferred into the Gendarmerie, the Naval Legion was transferred to the navy, the Guides later went into the Imperial Guard and the remainder became the *Chasseurs d'Orient*.

▼ CORPORAL, 18TH DRAGOONS, 1800
This was the old Du Roi Dragoons, which had been with Napoleon in Italy in 1796. Once cut off in Egypt, difficulties with supplies of cloth and dyes forced the French to use what could be had locally: uniformity was a luxury that could not be afforded. Even so, this individual's turnout largely conforms to regulations and makes few concessions to the heat of Egypt. The regiment fought at the Pyramids on 21 July 1798 and took part in the failed invasion of Syria in 1799. It was General Kleber who raised the Mamelukes for service in the French Army on 25 September 1799, just after Napoleon had left Egypt to return to France. The men were selected from Syrian Janissaries who had taken part in the unsuccessful siege of Acre.

▲ SERGEANT, 4TH LIGHT INFANTRY, 1800
This regiment had fought under Napoleon in Italy. Shipped to Egypt, the 4th fought at El Arish (14–20 February 1799), Mount Tabor (16 April), and participated in the failed invasion of Syria. In 1800 the 4th Light was in action at Heliopolis and in 1801 at Lake Mareotis and the French defeat at Alexandria on 21 March. Blue cloth was hard to come by in Egypt and many regiments took to wearing variations of green, brown and red and also white. Note also the unusual leather cap.

▼ 18TH DRAGOONS KIT *1 The standard French cavalry pistol; like most pistols of that time, it was of very limited practical use.*
2 The M 1777 infantry musket, easily recognizable by the three brass rings used to fix the barrel into the stock.
3 The dragoon-pattern sword, a heavy weapon used more for stabbing than slashing.

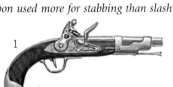

THE IMPERIAL GUARD

The Imperial Guard was created in 1804 and was among the youngest formations of Napoleon's army, taking its heritage from the *Garde de l'Assemblée Nationale*, which was raised on 20 June 1789. In September 1792 this body became the *grenadiers de la gendarmerie*, in July 1795 the *grenadiers de la convention* and in November 1795 the *Garde du Directoire*. It was later restyled the *Garde Consulaire*. Between 1804 and 1815, regiments of the Guard were classed in accordance with their dates, hence the Old Guard, Middle Guard and Young Guard designations.

The Old Guard

The grenadier regiment wore a semi-circular brass bearskin plate bearing a grenade over "GARDE DES CONSULS", within laurel branches. Following Napoleon's coronation as Emperor of the French in December 1804, this regiment became part of the Imperial Guard, a formation of towering – slightly unearned – combat stature. On 15 April 1806 a second such regiment of two battalions was raised and on 13 September 1810 the grenadiers of the Royal Dutch Guard became the 3rd Regiment. This unit wore white uniforms with crimson

▼ SERGEANT, GRENADIERS OF THE IMPERIAL GUARD, 1812 *The grenadier regiments of the Imperial Guard were composed of veterans and were the elite of Napoleon's Guard. The bearskin was more substantial than those worn by grenadiers of the line. This non-commissioned officer wears golden chevrons on the lower arm. In 1812 the grenadiers formed part of the expedition to Russia and suffered heavily.*

facings and brass buttons. On 9 May 1815 a 4th Regiment was raised, but disbanded again in September: it is doubtful if it was ever completed. All units of the Guard wore the brass button bearing the imperial eagle.

The uniform was a dark blue coat and collar, white lapels and cuff flaps, red cuffs and turnbacks, red, fringed epaulettes, white small clothes and belts, gold grenades on the turnbacks. The bearskin had a copper plate bearing the crowned imperial eagle and flanking grenades, white cords, red plume, red top patch with yellow grenade. The special blue-within-red-within-white cockade had a gold crowned eagle in the centre.

The uniform for the *chasseurs à pied* was as for the *grenadiers à pied* but

▼ GRENADIERS OF THE IMPERIAL GUARD KIT
1 *The sabre of a grenadier.* 2 *The backpack of the infantry of the Guard, far superior in quality to those issued to the line.* 3 *Cartridge pouch belonging to the* grenadiers à pied. 4 *The embroidered cockade of the Guard.* 5 *An epaulette of a lieutenant of the Guard.* 6 *A detail of the cuff and buttons of the 1st Grenadiers à Pied.*

◄ **PRIVATE, CHASSEUR À PIED, 1805** *The Chasseurs were supposed to be light infantry, a role this uniform scarcely reflects. Note the green base of the plume, swordknot and epaulettes fringed in red.*

tailed, dark blue naval uniform, with gold anchors in the turnbacks.

GRENADIERS À CHEVAL. These mounted grenadiers were raised on 2 December 1799. Uniform as for the *grenadiers à pied,* but no plate to the bearskin and an orange cross to the red top patch; gold and red aiguillette to the right shoulder, white breeches, buff gauntlets with white cuffs; heavy cavalry boots.

CHASSEURS À CHEVAL. Also raised on 2 December 1799, the *chasseurs à cheval* uniform was a dark green dolman with crimson cuffs, gold buttons and lace; red waistcoat with gold buttons and lace; dark green breeches laced in gold; bearskin with red bag, gold tassel, cords and chin scales; dark green and gold sash. The sabretasche was dark green with a coloured imperial eagle on a crowned ermine coat and six crossed lances. These men often escorted the emperor.

MAMELUKES. A single-squadron light cavalry unit, the Mamelukes were raised from Syrian Janissaries on 25 September 1799. Their uniform was a fanciful Turkish costume, which altered frequently, but seems to have included a green or red fez, orange turban and waistcoat, and red breeches.

LÉGION DE GENDARMERIE D'ÉLITE. The Elite Gendarmes were raised on 19 March 1802 and disbanded on 23 April 1814. Their uniform was as for the *grenadiers à cheval* but with white buttons, white grenade on the red bearskin top patch, and on the red turnbacks; white chin scales and plume, white trefoil and aiguillette on the left shoulder; yellow small clothes and gauntlets, and yellow belts edged with white.

► **TROOPER, GRENADIERS À CHEVAL, 1812** *Raised in 1799 as light cavalry, the* grenadiers à cheval *were converted to heavy cavalry in 1800. This trooper is wearing field service dress. A gold aiguilette was worn on the right shoulder.*

COMPAGNIE DE GENDARMES D'ORDONNANCE. Raised in 1806 but disbanded in 1807, the uniform was a shako with white rhombic plate and chin scales, white plume and cords; dark green tunic, white buttons and aiguillette on the right shoulder; dark green breeches laced white; red waistcoat with white lace and buttons; black belts.

DRAGONS DE LA GARDE. Raised on 15 April 1806, the Guard Dragoons' uniform consisted of a brass dragoon helmet with red plume, black horsehair crest, leopardskin turban, and chin scales; dark green tunic, white lapels, dark green collar, red turnbacks, brass buttons, gold *contre-epaulette* and aiguillette on the right shoulder; white belts and small clothes.

without a plate to the bearskin, red over green plume, green epaulettes edged and fringed in red.

MARINS. On 29 July 1804 a battalion of Sailors of the Guard (*Marins*) was raised. The uniform was a shako with orange top and bottom bands, orange cords, red pompon and plume, copper badge of a crowned eagle on a thunderbolt, in waves, on an upright anchor, a badge also worn on pouch and belt plate. Dark blue dolman and trousers, orange piping and lace, orange braid edging to dark blue collar and pointed red cuffs, brass buttons and shoulder scales, the latter on red backing. Black belts, black and brass sheath to sabre. Officers wore long-

CHEVAU-LÉGER LANCIERS. The 1st Chevau-Légers (Light Horse), later referred to as the Chevau-Légers lanciers, was a Polish regiment, raised on 2 March 1807, and consisting of four squadrons. The troops wore Polish costume: square-topped cap (*czapka*) and traditional Polish tunic (*kurtka*) in slate blue with crimson facings and silver buttons and lace; silver aiguillette on the right shoulder; slate blue breeches with twin crimson side stripes. The *czapka* had a crimson top, white plume, gold sun-ray plate with a silver centre bearing the crowned golden "N".

The 2nd Chevau-Léger lanciers was raised on 13 September 1810 from the cuirassiers and hussars of the

▶ GRENADIER OF THE 1ST GRENADIERS, MIDDLE GUARD, 1812 *The Guard were very conservative and retained queued and powdered hair long after the line abandoned it. This figure is in full parade dress, with bearskin, cords and plume. All items of equipment for the Guards were of a higher quality than for those of the line.*

Royal Dutch Guard. Again the costume was entirely Polish, but in red with dark blue facings and yellow buttons and lace. The 3rd Chevau-Léger lanciers was raised on 5 July 1812 as two squadrons, which were destroyed at the clash at Slonim on 19 October 1812. Their costume was the same as the 1st Lancers but with yellow lace and buttons.

TATARS LITHUANIENS. A single squadron of Tartars was raised at Vilna in 1812. The hat was of black astrakhan with green bag and gold tassel, yellow turban and black peak. On the front of the hat was a crescent moon (points up) under three stars. They wore a red jacket, black bolero-style waistcoat, wide blue pantaloons, black belts.

GARDES D'HONNEUR. Consisting of four regiments, each of ten squadrons, raised on 3 April 1813 and incorporated into the Imperial Guard on 29 July. They wore red shakos with white top band, eagle and chin scales, green dolman and pelisse, white lace and buttons, red collar, cuffs and breeches, the latter decorated in white braid, crimson and white sash; black sabretasche with white crowned eagle. The regiments were distinguished by the tips to their green plumes: 1st, red; 2nd, blue; 3rd, yellow; and 4th, white.

ARTILLERIE LÉGER. Raised on 2 December 1799, in April 1806 with six companies. The unit was re-raised for the Hundred Days. The hussar-style uniform consisted of fur cap or

◀ SAPPER, GRENADIERS OF THE GUARD, 1810 *The sappers were supposed to be able to move ahead of the marching column to clear obstacles, build bridges, etc, often under enemy fire, and wearing this equipment. Obviously no expense was spared on the uniforms of the Guard: whether it was well spent is another matter.*

colpack, a dolman in dark blue, with red facings and lace, brass buttons, white belts. The brass plate on the headgear bore the crowned eagle on crossed gun barrels.

ARTILLERIE À PIED. The foot artillery was raised on 7 April 1808. Costume was as for the Grenadiers of the Guard, but the bearskin had a black peak and no plate, red cords and plume. The coat and small clothes were dark blue; turnbacks, cuffs, epaulettes and piping red; collar, lapels and cuff flaps dark blue; buttons brass; gaiters black, and belts white.

TRAIN D'EQUIPAGE. Raised on 24 August 1811. The shako plate bore the crowned eagle on crossed cannon barrels on a label pierced with "N" within laurel branches. The uniform was as for the artillery train.

BATAILLON PRINCIPAL DU TRAIN. Raised on 8 September 1800, the uniform was grey with dark blue facings, red piping, white buttons.

ENGINEERS. The uniform featured a polished steel helmet with brass trim, chin scales, comb and eagle badge, black crest, red plume. The coat was dark blue with black collar, lapels, cuffs and cuff flaps all piped red; red turnbacks with yellow grenades; yellow buttons; dark blue small clothes, and white belts. The Corps of Engineers was raised in 1808. The uniform was dark blue, faced black, yellow buttons.

OUVRIERS D'ADMINISTRATION. Raised on 15 April 1806. Uniform was as for the artillery but with bicorns.

The Middle Guard

FUSILIERS-GRENADIERS. Raised on 19 September 1806. Uniform was as for the 1st Grenadiers but the shako had white side struts and cords, with red plume and brass eagle plate. The coat had red epaulette straps with two white stripes along them, and white fringes. In the long turnbacks, the corners were white with crowned eagles.

FUSILIERS-CHASSEURS. Raised on 15 December 1806. The uniform was as for the *chasseurs à pied* but the shako had white side struts, a brass eagle plate and cords, and green plume tipped with red. The coat had green epaulette straps with red crescent and fringes, and white, crowned eagles in the long, red turnbacks.

BATTALION OF VÉLITES OF FLORENCE. Raised March 1809 with the Battalion of Vélites of Turin, they wore the uniform of the Fusiliers-Grenadiers.

The Young Guard

TIRAILLEURS-CHASSEURS Raised in January 1809, becoming the 1st and 2nd Voltigeurs on 30 December 1810. Their uniform was as for the Tirailleurs-Grenadiers, except for the following: white cords, green pompon to the shako, green shoulder straps piped red, green eagles, and hunting horns on the turnbacks.

CONSCRITS-GRENADIERS. The Conscript Grenadiers became the 3rd and 4th Tirailleurs-Grenadiers on 10 February 1811. Their uniform was: shako as for the Fusilier-Grenadiers but with red cords; short dark blue tunic with dark blue collar, lapels (piped white) and shoulder straps (piped red); red cuffs, white flaps, white turnbacks with red piping and eagles; yellow buttons, white belts and small clothes.

TIRAILLEURS. Meaning literally "skirmishers", they comprised 19 regiments and a depot, raised from December 1810 to 1814. Uniform: see the Tirailleurs-Grenadiers above.

VOLTIGEURS. Meaning literally "leapers" or "vaulters", comprised 19 regiments raised from December 1810 to 1814. Uniform: see the Tirailleurs-Chasseurs above.

FLANQUERS-GRENADIERS. Raised on 4 September 1811. Uniform details: shako with white side struts, red cords and yellow, pear-shaped pompon with a red tip; green Spencer tunic with green collar, lapels and shoulder straps; pointed red cuffs all edged yellow; red turnbacks, piped yellow and with white eagles; white belts and small clothes.

FLANQUERS-CHASSEURS. Raised on 4 September 1811. Their uniform was as for the Flanquers-Grenadiers but with white shako cords, yellow over green pompon, green cuffs and green hunting horns

▶ BATTALION COMMANDER (CHEF DE BATAILLON) OF THE FUSILIER-GRENADIERS, IMPERIAL GUARD, 1812 *The Guard marched into Russia in 1812. This officer's rank is shown by his epaulettes and the gold embroidery on the shako.*

on the turnbacks.

ARTILLERIE À PIED. Raised in June 1809. The uniform was as for the artillery of the Old Guard but with shakos.

ARTILLERIE À CHEVAL. Raised in late 1813. The uniform was as for the artillery of the Old Guard but with shakos.

TRAIN D'ARTILLERIE. Raised in 1808. The uniform was as for that of the artillery of the Old Guard but with shakos instead of bearskins.

▼ SERGEANT, TIRAILLEURS-CHASSEURS, 1809 *The Young Guard uniforms were much more like those of the line than those of the Old Guard, but they still wore the coveted button and enjoyed better pay than the line. The chevrons on the cuffs replaced the simple bars for regiments with pointed cuffs.*

THE IMPERIAL LINE AND LIGHT INFANTRY

The nucleus of Napoleon's Grand Army was formed in 1803. That same year, the old royalist term *régiment* was reinstated, replacing the republican *demi-brigade*, which subsequently referred to provisional units only. At the time, only some 90 infantry regiments existed, the majority of them consisting of three battalions. By 1804,

▼ VOLTIGEUR, 22ND LINE, 1807 *The 22nd Line was one of the regiments selected to pilot the reintroduction of white tunics for the French Army in 1806. The* voltigeur *company was distinguished by the buff collar and green and yellow plume, epaulettes and sabre strap.*

each battalion had been obliged to convert one of its fusilier companies into *voltigeurs*, thus augmenting the French light infantry establishment.

The Line Infantry

By a decree of 25 April 1806 Napoleon reintroduced white coats for the line infantry, but in the event, only 11 regiments actually received the new clothing. They were the 3rd, 4th and 8th (dark green facings), 14th, 15th (black facings), 17th, 18th, 19th, 21st, 22nd and 33rd (red facings). Dark blue tunics were issued again in May 1807. Line grenadiers often wore bearskin bonnets in the early days of the empire, grenadiers of the line had brass plates with a grenade badge, the grenade and the number, or just a grenade itself, either plain or pierced with the regimental number.

The shako plate of this period was supposed to be a rhombus bearing the crowned imperial eagle over the regimental number stamped through the brass. There were many variations to be seen. In 1812 the more ornate crowned eagle over a semi-circular Greek shield with the number stamped through was introduced. Some of these plates were plain for all companies: others were differentiated by the company of the wearer for example; some grenadier companies had shields decorated with grenades, while *voltigeurs* had hunting horns and centre companies lions' heads.

Other variations of shako plates included a sunburst with the crowned eagle in the bottom centre, or a crowned "N"; a crowned eagle on a rectangular label with lightning flashes; or a crowned eagle on a label with the regimental number or abbreviated designation. Octagonal and pentagonal plates were also worn. The tricolour cockade was worn above the plate, extending to the top of the shako. Above this was the company pompon. Grenadiers gradually abandoned the

▲ PIONEER, 94TH LINE, 1807 *It seems that regimental commanders exercised considerable control over the uniforms of pioneers, as well as their musicians. Pioneers in certain regiments wore sets of crossed axes on each sleeve and various brass badges were worn on their bandoliers.*

expensive bearskin caps and wore the shako, with red top and bottom bands and red side struts. Above their cockade was the red pompon and plume. The *voltigeurs* had yellow top, bottom and side trim to the shako and yellow or green pompon and yellow plume with green tip. The fusilier pompons were green for the 1st company, sky blue for the 2nd, orange for the 3rd and violet for the 4th. Those of the 1st battalion would be in solid colours, the pompons of the 2nd and subsequent battalions had white centres or rims.

In 1812 the Spencer tunic was introduced. The red collar was closed and piped white to top and front; the white lapels and turnbacks were piped red; the red cuffs were piped white and the blue cuff flaps were piped white. Grenadiers had red, fringed epaulettes; *voltigeurs* had yellow collars and green epaulettes with yellow crescents. Fusiliers had dark blue, trident-ended shoulder straps piped red. In the four corners of the turnbacks were company emblems: grenadiers, red grenades; *voltigeurs*, green horns; fusiliers, a crowned "N" in blue or a blue, five-pointed star.

The brass buttons bore the regimental number within a ring. The vertical skirt pocket flaps were piped in red. Small clothes and belts were white.

The Light Infantry

The same multiplicity of shako plates existed in the light infantry as in the line, they were usually of tin. Variants of the rhombic plate included the eagle over a hunting horn enclosing the regimental number, the eagle holding the horn over the number, a horn over the number, embossed or pierced, a plain horn enclosing the pierced number or without a number at all. The regiments' equivalent to the line's grenadiers were the carabiniers, who often wore grenades. The 1812-style eagle and Greek shield plates also came in various versions. Tin chin scales, with hunting horns on the bosses, were worn. The 1812 dark blue coat had dark blue lapels, pointed cuffs and turnbacks all piped white. It seems that some regiments retained their old square cuffs with red flaps piped white.

Carabiniers wore the same red badges as the grenadiers of the line; *voltigeurs* had yellow collars, green

and yellow epaulettes and shako decorations as those of the line, with yellow horns on the turnbacks. *Chasseur* company pompons were as for the line. Buttons were of pewter with the regimental number within a hunting horn, itself within a ring. Small clothes were also dark blue. Belts were white, short black gaiters with red, yellow or white trim and tassel according to company.

▼ Officers' Epaulettes *Epaulettes (in the regimental button colour) were the badges of status for officers. The French were among the first to design a system that codified and exhibited the exact rank of the wearer.*

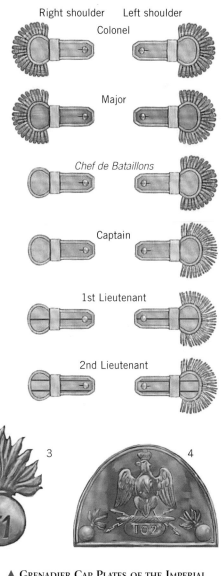

Right shoulder   Left shoulder
Colonel

Major

Chef de Bataillons

Captain

1st Lieutenant

2nd Lieutenant

1

2   3   4

◄ Tambour Major, 16th Light Infantry Regiment, 1807 *Some Tambour Majors (Drum Majors) were decked out in even greater splendour than this figure from the 16th. Huge tricolour plumes and wide, embroidered sashes were often seen.*

▲ Grenadier Cap Plates of the Imperial Period *These French cap plates show that many regimental commanders ignored instructions and procured their own patterns. 1 Unknown regiment; copper. 2 42nd Line; brass. 3 71st Line; brass. 4 102nd Line; brass.*

THE IMPERIAL CARABINIERS AND CUIRASSIERS

The two regiments of carabiniers survived the upheavals of the Revolutionary period to become the elite units of Napoleon's heavy cavalry. Meanwhile, armoured cuirassiers were formed from the old regiments of cavalry, being equipped with iron helmets and the cuirass like the 8th Regiment of Cavalry-Cuirassiers, which served as the general model. Napoleon reserved these iron-clads for heavy battlefield blows, rather than scouting or outpost duties, which were the preserve of the light cavalry, who had

Regimental Distinctions: the Cuirassiers 1812

Number	Date Raised	Collar & turnbacks	Cuffs	Cuff flaps	Pockets horizontal or vertical
1	1657	red	red	red	H
2	1635	red	red	blue	H
3	1654	red	blue	red	H
4	1643	orange	orange	orange	V
5	1653	orange	orange	blue	V
6	1635	orange	blue	orange	V
7	1657	yellow	yellow	yellow	H
8	1638	yellow	yellow	blue	H
9	1665	yellow	blue	yellow	H
10	1643	pink	pink	pink	V
11	1652	pink	pink	blue	V
12	1668	pink	blue	pink	V

performed their role famously well at Eylau, during the charge of the Reserve Cavalry against the Russian centre; at Borodino; at Quatre Bras in 1815; and at Waterloo, where they were mishandled by Marshal Ney and led, fruitlessly, against Allied squares.

The Carabiniers

The old uniform was worn into the Empire period: the dark blue grenade badges on the turnbacks were replaced by white in 1808. Red epaulettes were worn. Belts were yellow with white edging. The bicorn was replaced by the bearskin in 1801: it was supposed to be 12$\frac{1}{2}$ in (32 cm) tall, but this height was unofficially extended to 13$\frac{1}{2}$ in (35 cm). The red top patch was decorated with a white cross and a red plume was worn on the left-hand side.

◀ CAPTAIN, 1ST CARABINIERS, 1809
The carabiniers were in action throughout Napoleon's campaigns and were present at Austerlitz, Jena, Eylau, Friedland, Eggmühl, Wagram and Borodino. In the Hundred Days, both regiments were heavily engaged at Waterloo. This uniform is the better-known version of their uniform, which was worn from after the Battle of Wagram in 1809. It shows the yellow copper helmet but the brass-plated steel cuirass is not being worn.

When hair was cut short in 1808, the old method of securing the unstable bearskins by means of ribbons under the pigtail no longer worked. In some early actions of the 1809 campaign, several carabiniers were wounded in the head as their bearskins trailed behind them in the mud. In December 1809 Napoleon ordered that the carabiniers be armoured as for the cuirassiers. This led to the introduction of the yellow copper helmet, with red crest, copper comb, front and rear peaks, and steel chin scales and front plate. They were also issued cuirasses with a thin layer of brass covering the steel.

It was at this point that the old uniform was replaced with white, single-breasted tunics, having sky blue collars and turnbacks. The 1st Regiment had red cuffs, with white cuff flaps edged sky blue; the 2nd Regiment had sky blue cuffs and flaps edged white. There were white grenade badges in the four turnback corners, on the square brass belt buckle and on the cartridge pouch. White breeches or buttoned overalls were worn.

Through 1812 trumpeters wore reversed colours and sky blue helmet crests, but no body armour. From 1813 they wore red crests, dark green tunics

Regimental Distinctions: the Cuirassiers 1812

No.	Date Raised	Collar & turnbacks	Cuffs	Cuff flaps	Pockets horizontal or vertical
1	1657	red	red	red	H
2	1635	red	red	blue	H
3	1654	red	blue	red	H
4	1643	orange	orange	orange	V
5	1653	orange	orange	blue	V
6	1635	orange	blue	orange	V
7	1657	yellow	yellow	yellow	H
8	1638	yellow	yellow	blue	H
9	1665	yellow	blue	yellow	H
10	1643	pink	pink	pink	V
11	1652	pink	pink	blue	V
12	1668	pink	blue	pink	V
13	1808	lilac	lilac	lilac	?
14	1810	lilac	lilac	blue	?

with sky blue collars and turnbacks, regimental cuffs and the imperial livery braid to sleeves, chest and facings.

The carabiniers were clearly elite regiments and were treated as such. General Kellerman vainly kept them back as a reserve at Waterloo even while Ney was sending the cuirassiers to their destruction against the Allied squares. They did not escape the same fate but were the very last regiments to be sent forward into battle in the futile cavalry charges.

▼ *French cuirassiers charge a square of the 42nd Royal Highlanders at the Battle of Quatre Bras, 16 June 1815.*

The Cuirassiers

By 1802 the heavy cavalry regiments began to be issued with the steel cuirass. By 1804 there were 12 such regiments and in this year the elegant steel helmet replaced the old bicorn. The helmet had a black fur turban extending down over the brass-edged peak, a copper comb and flowing, black horsehair crest. Brass chin scales secured the helmet and a red plume was worn on the left. Each regiment procured their own items, so there were numerous slight deviations to be seen. The facings were as shown in the table above left (all buttons were white). All regiments wore red, fringed epaulettes and

▶ **Officer, 10th Cuirassiers, 1809** *Cuirassiers rode the largest horses of all cavalry regiments, usually blacks or bays. These were in short supply after 1812. This officer has blue saddle furniture trimmed in pink. The 10th Cuirassiers won the following battle honours in the later campaigns: Ulm, Austerlitz, Jena, Eylau, Eggmühl and Wagram.*

had dark blue grenade badges on their turnbacks, although this was not officially sanctioned. All coats were dark blue, buttons white, as were the grenade badges in the turnbacks. Breeches and belts were white.

By 1809 a dark blue, single-breasted jacket (*habit-surtout*) was introduced. It was closed with ten buttons, facings were worn on collar, cuffs, turnbacks and pocket piping. This was replaced by a version with shorter skirts in 1812. The leather breeches were covered with buttoned overalls in the field; mostly these were grey. Trumpeters had white horsehair crests, and often had multi-coloured

plumes. They wore reversed colours until 1812, the dark green, decorated with the imperial livery. Some regimental commanders attempted to ensure their trumpeters rode grey horses, a luxury that was abandoned in the shortage of horses after the 1812 campaign. Saddle furniture was dark blue, trimmed in the facing colour and with a grenade badge in the rear corner. The regimental number was shown on the ends of the rectangular portmanteaux. Two more regiments were raised during the empire period. The 13th Regiment was formed from provisional units serving in Spain, and it seems that some of the regiment's personnel wore

▲ HEAVY CAVALRY SADDLERY, 1812 *This is an example of the typical heavy cavalry saddlery, with the English saddle, the brief, square shabraque and the sheepskin saddle cloth. The crupper helped to maintain the saddle in the desired position.*

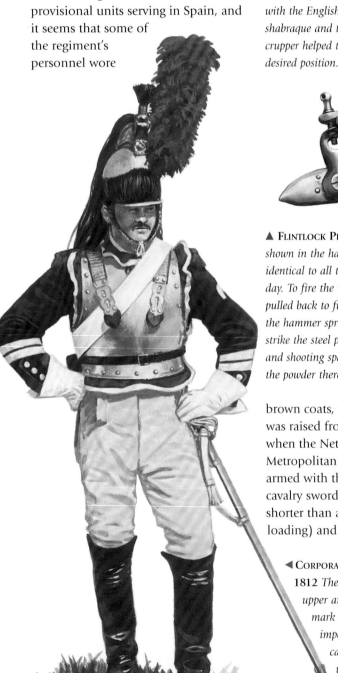

▲ FLINTLOCK PLATE *This flintlock plate, shown in the half-cocked position, is almost identical to all those of other armies of the day. To fire the weapon, the hammer would be pulled back to full cock; pulling the trigger let the hammer spring forward, the flint would strike the steel pan cover, throwing it open and shooting sparks into the pan and igniting the powder there.*

brown coats, whilst the 14th Regiment was raised from a Dutch cuirassier unit when the Netherlands was absorbed by Metropolitan France. Cuirassiers were armed with the long, straight heavy cavalry sword, a carbine (slightly shorter than a musket for ease of loading) and a brace of pistols.

◀ CORPORAL FARRIER, 1ST CUIRASSIERS, 1812 *The white horseshoe badge on the upper arm was the distinguishing mark of all the farriers, an important individual in any cavalry regiment. He displays white leather gauntlets and the long, straight sword typical of heavy, armoured cavalry across Europe.*

▲ TRUMPETER, 14TH CUIRASSIERS, 1812 *By this time, the imperial livery was being introduced for musicians, replacing the tradition of musicians wearing coats of the facing colours. Trumpeters were distinguished by their white crests and epaulettes and did not wear armour. This unit was Dutch.*

The effectiveness of the cuirass in protecting the cuirassier is a subject of continuing debate. Certainly, body armour was little protection against well-directed musket fire (and the horses were always vulnerable in any case) but it could be of some use in hand-to-hand fighting.

THE IMPERIAL DRAGOONS AND LANCERS

Historically dragoons were mounted infantry, which rode to the battlefield before dismounting and fighting on foot. Several of Napoleon's dragoon regiments served as infantry in 1803, 1805 and 1806. As for the lancers, it is likely that the dramatically destructive charge of the lancers of the Vistula Legion at the Battle of Albuera, which took place on 16 May 1811, was the catalyst for the creation of more of these regiments.

The Dragoons

The distinctive dragoon helmet was introduced in 1804. It was all of brass, with chin scales, a high comb, flowing black horsehair crest and fur turban usually extending down the brass-edged peak. As each regiment procured its own items, variations from the official norm were frequent. A plume was worn on the left side for parades. In 1807 the following plume colours were recorded:

Red: 1st, 2nd, 9th, 17th, 22nd, 30th
Red–white–red: 3rd
White: 4th, 5th, 8th, 11th, 16th, 17th, 19th, 21st, 23rd, 24th, 28th, 29th
Red and green: 7th, 8th, 12th, 13th
Crimson: 10th
Red and white: 12th, 18th
Green topped in the facing colour: 1st, 2nd, 6th, 19th, 20th, 25th

As some regiments appear more than once, with different coloured plumes, it is clear that many colonels ignored the regulations. Facing colours remained as they had been in the Revolutionary period. From 1804 to 1812 the tunic became sharper and more close-fitting; the skirts shorter. By 1810 the turnbacks extended to the bottom edge of the skirt and were

decorated with white, or medium green grenade badges. Trumpeters wore reversed colours: from 1812 dark green with the imperial livery braid decoration. The regimental pioneers wore elite company bearskins and distinctions. Saddlery was in the coat colour, heavy cavalry style, edged in the facing colour, with the regimental number in the rear corner and on the rectangular portmanteaux. Later the numeral on the saddle cloth was replaced by a grenade.

◀ CORPORAL, 16TH DRAGOONS, 1800–09
This man is dressed for dismounted duty, hence the musket fitted with a bayonet; the sword would be hooked up on the bandolier. His cavalry boots, however, must have made acting as a foot soldier difficult. The practice of using dismounted dragoons as foot soldiers became rarer but dragoons always carried the musket so that they could serve as infantry. His rank would be shown by two stripes on the lower arm.

▶ FARRIER, 2ND DRAGOONS, 1804 *The farrier is also dressed for dismounted duty, with his musket. Note his fatigue cap rolled up under his cartridge pouch. The pewter button bears "2" in a French ring and the regimental number was also borne on the dragoons' white buttons.*

▶ CHEVAU-LÉGERS LANCIERS KIT
*1 A lancer officer's sabre belt. Hussars'
belts would have additional straps
for the sabretasche.
2, 3, 4 Various views of an
officer's helmet.*

▼ TROOPER, 1ST CHEVAU-
LÉGERS LANCIERS, PRE-1812
*This regiment was originally
the 1st Dragoons and was
converted to 1st Lancers
in June 1811. They
were intended
to act as light
cavalry for heavy
cavalry formations and were
usually brigaded with
cuirassiers. The formation of
lancer regiments in the French
Army can be attributed to the success of
Polish lancers in Spain and their
devastating use of the lance against both
formed and broken infantry. Lance pennons,
traditionally deemed to frighten or deter
enemy horses, were universally red and
white. This trooper wears the field service
dress, with overalls, and has a hay net
and oat sack for his horse, hanging
from the saddle. He also carries a
carbine and pistols.*

The Cheveau-Légers Lanciers

The 1st–6th regiments were converted
to lancers from the 1st, 3rd, 8th, 9th,
10th and 29th Dragoons in June 1811.
They also had the brass helmet, but
with peaks fore and aft. The brass
comb bore the Medusa's head over
crossed lances on the front and the
black crest was in caterpillar form.
Troopers had brown fur turbans,
which do not seem to have
covered the black, brass-
edged peak. Officers
had leopardskin
turbans,
extending over
the peaks. Their
uniform was also
medium green, but the cuffs
were pointed and had no flaps.
Facings were worn on the
collar, lapels, cuffs, turnbacks
and pocket piping. There was no
effort made to emulate the Polish
czapka and *kurtka*-style uniforms
for these six regiments. Facings
were as follows (all buttons were
yellow): 1st, scarlet; 2nd, orange;
3rd, pink; 4th, crimson; 5th, sky
blue; 6th, madder red.
In 1811 three more regiments were
raised: they wore dark blue uniforms,
probably retaining their Polish
costumes. Facings were as follows: 7th,
yellow; 8th, yellow; 9th, yellow. The
9th Regiment had a red *czapka* top, a
green plume with a yellow tip, a red
tunic with yellow facings, and white
buttons. The 7th and 8th
Regiments were raised
from the 1st and 2nd
Lancers of the Vistula

Regimental Distinctions: the Dragoons 1805

Regiment	Raised	Lapels & turnbacks	Collar	Cuffs	Cuff flaps	Pockets horizontal or vertical
1*	1656	scarlet	scarlet	scarlet	scarlet	H
2	1635	scarlet	green	scarlet	green	H
3*	1649	scarlet	scarlet	green	scarlet	H
4	1667	scarlet	scarlet	scarlet	scarlet	?
5	1668	scarlet	green	scarlet	green	V
6	1673	scarlet	scarlet	green	scarlet	?
7	1673	crimson	crimson	crimson	crimson	H
8*	1674	crimson	green	crimson	green	H
9*	1673	crimson	crimson	green	crimson	?
10*	1674	crimson	crimson	crimson	crimson	V
11	1674	crimson	green	crimson	green	V
12	1675	crimson	crimson	green	crimson	V
13	1676	pink	pink	pink	pink	H
14	1672	pink	green	pink	green	H
15	1688	pink	pink	green	pink	H
16	1718	pink	pink	pink	pink	V
17	1743	pink	green	pink	green	V
18	1744	pink	pink	green	pink	V
19	1793	yellow	yellow	yellow	yellow	H
20	1793	yellow	green	yellow	green	H
21	1793 disbanded in 1798.					
21	1801	yellow	yellow	green	yellow	H
22	1635	yellow	yellow	yellow	yellow	V
23	1671	yellow	green	yellow	green	V
24	1671	yellow	yellow	green	yellow	V
25	1665	orange	orange	orange	orange	H
26	1671	orange	green	orange	green	H
27	1674	orange	orange	green	orange	H
28+	1802	orange	orange	orange	orange	V
29+*	1802	orange	green	orange	green	V
30+	1802	orange	orange	green	orange	V

*converted to Chevau-Légers lanciers in June 1811.

+raised in 1802 from the 7th bis, 11th and 12th Hussars respectively.

Legion respectively on 18 June 1811; the 9th Regiment was raised from the 31st Chasseurs à Cheval and the cavalry of the Hanoverian Legion on 18 June 1811.

The terrible effects of the 1st Lancers of the Vistula Legion against a brigade of British infantry in the Battle of Albuera on 16 May 1811 prompted Napoleon to introduce lancer regiments into the French Army proper. General Colborne's brigade of the 2nd British Division was almost destroyed in a matter of minutes. Only the front rank carried lances; the second rank were armed with carbines and sabres.

▲ JUNIOR OFFICER, 8TH CHEVAU-LÉGERS LANCIERS, 1812 *The two Polish lancer regiments continued to wear their slate blue Polish costume, with the characteristic cut of the tunic tails, but with the French cockade. Officer's rank was shown by epaulettes and silver lacing on the thighs and over the cuffs.*

◀ LANCER'S KIT 1 *An officer's bandolier and cartouche. The stripes were in the facing colour, the braid in the button colour.*
2 *A trooper's bandolier (with carbine hook) and cartouche.*

THE IMPERIAL *CHASSEURS À CHEVAL*

It was at this point that the long romance with hussar-style costume began to wane, but the nature and tactical role of both light cavalry arms remained the same: patrolling, scouting, screening, pursuit and rearguard actions. In 1805 the shako began to be introduced. It bore the tricolour cockade, regimental loop and button and a variety of plates adorned the fronts, including the 1812 eagle on a Greek shield, with the number stamped through it, and – in earlier years – the simple rhombus, with the eagle or hunting horn over the regimental number. White chin scales were worn with white cords

added for parades or ceremonial duties. Dark green plumes usually had tips in the regimental facing colour.

The fatigue cap (*bonnet de police*) was dark green, trimmed in the facing colour and bearing a white tassel and white hunting horn or regimental number on the front. These caps were usually made up by the regimental tailor from old dolmans or pelisses. The dolman gave way to the dark green, double-breasted tunic (*surtout*) from 1805, although some dolmans were still to be seen in 1808. The tunic lapels were in the coat colour, piped in the facing colour. Facings were also worn on the collar, pointed cuffs and turnbacks; white hunting horns were worn on the latter and on the cartouche. In 1812 the *surtout* was replaced by the single-breasted Spencer

tunic in the same colours. The elite company wore fur colpacks with bags in the facing colour, red plumes and fringed epaulettes.

Officers protected their expensive cartouche bandoliers when in the field with red Moroccan leather cases, closed along their lengths with regimental buttons. In 1812 the facing colours were as shown in the table opposite; all lapels and tunics were dark green, buttons and lace were white. Regiments wore white-braided waistcoats in the facing colour. The dark green overalls had side stripes in the facing colour and up to 14 pewter buttons. The *chasseurs* retained the wooden Bock saddle and the hussar-style black harness with steel fittings, as well as the long-tailed shabraques and cylindrical portmanteaux in dark

◄ **OFFICER, 13TH CHASSEURS À CHEVAL, 1809** *This officer is attired in* tenue de fantasie *or walking-out dress, in which much latitude was allowed. He wears an off-duty* bonnet de police, *more comfortable than a shako, although bicorns were also popular. Chasseur officers did not, as a rule, wear epaulettes but their ranks were indicated by chevrons above their cuffs.*

▼ **CHASSEURS À CHEVAL KIT** *1 An example of the standard French cavalry pistol. 2 A sabre of the light cavalry and its steel sheath. 3 A shako of a centre company of a chasseur regiment, with its green and red plume and additional cords for parades. 4 Detail of the brass hilt of the sabre. 5 The exposed Bock saddle, used by hussars and other light cavalry regiments, made from birch wood.*

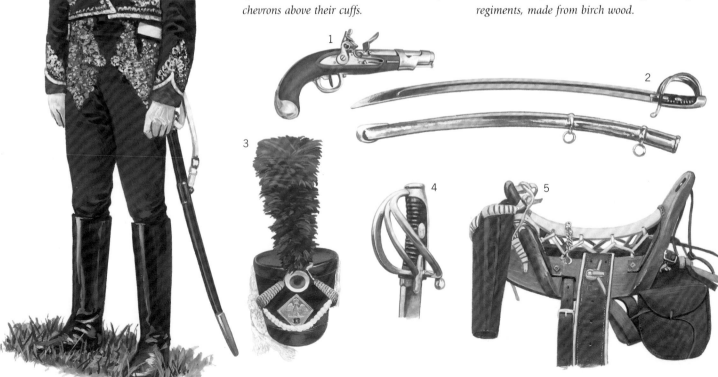

Regimental Distinctions: *Chasseurs à Cheval* 1811

No./Raised	Collar	Collar piping	Cuffs/Edging	No./Raised	Collar	Collar piping	Cuffs/Edging
1 1651	scarlet	green	scarlet	17 1793 disbanded 1795; remained thence vacant.			
2 1673	green	scarlet	scarlet	18 1793	sky blue	green	green
3 1675	scarlet	green	green	19 1793	orange	green	orange
4 1675	yellow	green	yellow	20 1793	green	orange	orange
5 1676	green	yellow	yellow	21 1793	orange	green	green
6 1676	yellow	green	green	22 1793	dark orange	green	dark orange
7 1747	pink	green	pink	23 1793	green	dark orange	dark orange
8 1749	green	pink	pink	24 1793	dark orange	green	green
9 1757	pink	green	green	25 1795	madder red	green	madder red
10 1758	crimson	green	crimson	26 1802	green	madder red	madder red
11 1762	green	crimson	green	27 1808	green	madder red	green
12 1769	crimson	green	green	28 1808	maroon	green	maroon
13 1793	orange	green	orange	29 1808	green	maroon	maroon
14 1793	green	orange	orange	30 remained vacant through Empire period.			
15 1793	orange	green	green	31* 1811	buff	green	buff
16 1793	sky blue	green	sky blue	*converted to the 9th Chevau-Légers lanciers in June 1811.			

green, trimmed in the facing colour and decorated with the regimental number. The original 25 regiments were increased by a further six from 1802, but the 31st, raised in 1811, was converted almost at once to the 9th Chevau-Légers lanciers.

◄ TROOPER, 5TH CHASSEURS À CHEVAL, ELITE COMPANY, FIELD SERVICE DRESS, 1812
Although many elite companies wore the colpack, the tradition was not universal. The sabre, hilt and steel sheath are shown in detail, as are the wooden Bock saddle, the pistol and the shako with rhombic plate with eagle and regimental number.

◄ TRUMPETER, 24TH CHASSEURS À CHEVAL, 1811 *The tradition of allowing musicians to wear coats of the facing colour is shown here. This trumpeter wears orange. He also wears an elaborate colpack, the 'bag' of which drops down among cords and loops.*

THE IMPERIAL HUSSARS

The hussars enjoyed great popularity in most armies, in none more so than the French. The thing that set these light cavalrymen apart from the rest of the line regiments was their history. Originally, hussars (meaning corsairs, pirates or raiders) were irregulars, often fighting for booty alone. Their origins lay in the Mongolian raiders who plundered their way through eastern Europe in the thirteenth century. These excellent horsemen, on their tough little ponies, scoured ahead of their main army, striking terror into the enemy population. Part of their stock in trade was to wear a wolf's skin across their left shoulder, and this acted as a light shield against sabre cuts, as well as lending a rakish air to the rider. They wore long moustaches and their hair was worn in *cadenettes* (three plaits: one at the rear and one in front of each ear). The Mongols settled in some areas of Hungary, becoming less warlike, and influenced the Hungarians' national costume, which featured the dolman with the typical multiple rows of buttons and lace. The wolf's skin was replaced by the pelisse

◀ TROOPER, 2ND HUSSARS, 1807
This figure is in winter dress, wearing his pelisse over his dolman and buttoned overalls over his breeches. The chinstrap bosses are unusually shown as stars, instead of being circular. The man wears his pelisse, which probably places the uniform in Poland in early 1807.

▲ TROOPER, 1ST HUSSARS, 1812 *The shako worn here bears the 1812 model plate; no plume or cords are worn, as this man is on campaign. The small pistol was a signalling device, its accuracy was poor. Rank is shown by the gold decoration to shako, sleeves and thighs. Note that he wears just a red ribbon (and a white one) on the pelisse, instead of the actual medal of the Legion of Honour.*

(a corruption of the word *pelz* or animal skin) and elaborately decorated breeches were worn.

In the wars of the eighteenth century, the hussars of the Austrian Army scored some notable victories over the Prussians, and with their

▲ *The romantic, dashing reputation of the French hussars was fostered by flamboyant figures such as the Comte de Lassalle.*

colourful and flamboyant costumes, the popularity of the hussars spread across Europe, firing the blood of many a youth. In the Napoleonic era, one man in France came to personify their racy, irreverent, spirit more than any other: Antoine-Charles-Louis, Comte de Lasalle.

The Ultimate Hussar

Born in Metz on 10 May 1775, Antoine de Lasalle was of noble birth. On 19 June 1786 he was appointed *sous-lieutenant* in the Alsace Infantry Regiment; on 25 May 1791 he transferred to the 24th Cavalry Regiment, but lost his commission on 4 May of the next year, as did many other aristos. On 10 March 1795 he was commissioned; family connections then came into play and on 6 May he was appointed ADC to General Kellermann, in the Army of the Alps. Lasalle was captured by the Austrians at Brescia on 29 July of that year,

released on the following 7 November and promoted to captain the same day. He distinguished himself in action at Vicenza on 17 December and Napoleon appointed him to command a squadron of the 7th (*bis*) Hussars on 6 January 1797. Seven days later, at Rivoli, he charged and took prisoner a complete battalion of Austrians.

One episode in this campaign involved a liasion with an Italian noblewoman in Vicenza. One night he led a group to the lady's chateau, behind Austrian lines. During his stay there, the Austrians discovered his presence and he and his companions had to fight their way to safety. He then fell in love with, and later married, Marshal Berthier's sister-in-law, Josephine.

Lasalle went to Egypt with Bonaparte's expedition; where he performed prodigies of valour, but it was during the 1806 campaign in Prussia that Lasalle really shone. His brigade was in action at Schleiz on 9 October, Jena on 14 October, then had a successful clash with General von Schimmelpfennig's brigade at Zehdenick on 26 October. As the beaten Prussian Army scattered away to the north-east, Lasalle bluffed General Prince von Hohenlohe into capitulation at Prenzelau with almost 10,000 troops, 64 guns and a score of colours and standards. Four days later, backed only by his own brigade, he again bluffed the commandant of Stettin, 81-year-old General von Romberg, to surrender the fortress, together with 5,300 men and 281 guns.

Lasalle could not resist cultivating his legend as a swashbuckler at every opportunity. He could ever be seen "drinking, swearing, singing, smashing everything up" as his contemporary,

▶ **COLONEL, 9TH HUSSARS, 1812** *Resplendant in his uniform, dripping with gold lace, this officer of the 9th is shown without the customary bandolier, which would have been in the button colour, with a central stripe in the facing colour. Hussar officers did not wear epaulettes. This man's rank is shown by the gold braid chevrons above the cuffs, on the thighs and on the shako.*

Marbot wrote. Such pantomimes often inspired his juniors with ambition to outdo him on the battlefield, sometimes with fatal results for his doting admirers.

In 1809 Lasalle served at Aspern-Essling on 21–22 May, then went to the Siege of Raab from 15 to 24 June. His final action was the Battle of Wagram, where he was killed by a musket ball on 6 July. Lasalle once remarked that any hussar who was not dead by the age of 30 was a blackguard; by dying aged 34 he missed his own target by only a small margin.

The Hussar's Uniform

The ubiquitous shako appeared in the hussars from 1803. It was decorated with a regimental button, loop and tricolour cockade, later with the rhombic plate with the eagle over the regimental number stamped through. From 1812 the eagle on the Greek shield bearing the number was introduced. The peak was edged in the button colour and chin scales were worn with cords and a plume added for parades. At the top, above the

▼ CHEF D'ESCADRON, 8TH HUSSARS, GRANDE TENUE, (FULL-DRESS UNIFORM) 1809 *This figure shows hussar costume at its most dashing. He has a black fur-trimmed green pelisse thrown over his shoulder and traditional Hungarian breeches. All hussar regiments had black fur on their pelisse with the exception of the 11th, which had white. This officer's rank is shown by the silver chevrons on cuffs and thighs.*

▲ *This portrait is reputed to be of Eugene de Beauharnais; it was painted in 1814 and illustrates just how exotic hussars were seen to be. His arab steed is seemingly invincible!*

cockade, was the pompon in the squadron colour: 1st, red; 2nd, sky blue; 3rd, dark yellow; 4th, violet. The cords were held at the sides of the top by hooks set into five-pointed stars. The elite company of the 1st squadron wore bearskin colpacks with bag in red, red pompon, plume and cords. In 1813 the tall, cylindrical shako came into service.

Badges of rank were in the form of chevrons above both cuffs. The breeches, with coloured thigh knots and side seams were mostly covered on campaign with similar coloured overalls, reinforced in black leather, closing with eighteen metal buttons on the coloured side stripe. The sabretasche

◀ CAPTAIN, 7TH HUSSARS, 1809 *This officer is shown (unusually) without his pelisse. He wears the buttoned overalls that were worn in the field to protect the expensive, embroidered breeches. The shako is without the green plume and gold cords, which were added for parades.*

Regimental Distinctions: the Hussars 1812

No./Date raised	Dolman	Collar	Cuffs	Pelisse	Lace & buttons	Breeches	Shako/Plume
1 1720	sky blue	sky blue	red	sky blue	white	sky blue	black/black
2 1735	brown	brown	sky blue	brown	white	sky blue	black/?
3 1764	grey	grey	red	grey	red & white	grey	black/black & red
4 1779	royal blue	royal blue	red	red	yellow	royal blue	red/black & green
5 1783	sky blue	sky blue	white	white	yellow	sky blue	red/white & blue
6 1792	red	red	red	royal blue	yellow	royal blue	red/?
7 (*bis*)* 1793	dark green	red	red	dark green	yellow	red	green/white & red
8 1793	dark green	red	red	dark green	white	red	red/black
9 1793	red	light blue	light blue	light blue	yellow	light blue	red/black & red
10 1793	sky blue	red	red	sky blue	white	sky blue	black/red
11 1793 converted to the 29th Dragoons in 1802							
11 1810	royal blue	red	red	royal blue	yellow	royal blue	black/yellow
12 1794 converted to the 30th Dragoons in 1802							
12 Feb 1813							
13 1792 converted to the 13th Chasseurs in 1793							
13 Jan 1813 disbanded Dec 1813							
13 Jan 1814 from Westphalian Hussars, who wore red uniforms							
14 Mar 1813 disbanded in Nov 1813							
14 Feb 1814							

*converted to the 28th Dragoons in 1802

was in the facing colour, decorated and edged in the button colour. There were several variants of decoration of this item: for troopers it was usually the regimental number within laurel branches and under a laurel wreath. Later in the period the crown replaced the wreath over the regimental number. Officers often had the crowned imperial eagle over the number. Later in the period many regiments adopted plain black leather sabretasches with just the number in the button colour as decoration.

From 1807 new-style, steel-hilted sabres in steel sheaths began to be introduced. Saddle furniture was in the dolman colour, edged and decorated in the button colour, usually with the regimental number. In 1812 the colour-scheme of the hussar regiments was as shown in the table.

The Westphalian hussars of King Jerome`s Guard were mostly Frenchmen and in January 1814 most of them fled back to France with him. They were designated the 13th and wore red shakos and dolmans, dark blue pelisses and breeches with yellow lace and buttons. Their nickname in Westphalia was "The Lobsters".

▶ SERGEANT, 5TH HUSSARS, 1812 *This figure's rank is shown by the gold chevron over his cuffs; he wears a long-service chevron on his upper left arm. The sabretasche is red, instead of being in the cuff colour. The barrel sash, which was crimson and white or yellow, depending on the lace and button colour, is shown off to good effect here.*

THE IMPERIAL ARTILLERY, ENGINEERS AND MINERS

The famous Gribeauval artillery system, which was a development of the Austrian Liechtenstein system, was used widely in the French Army at this time. Among its advantages was a reduction in the different sizes of wheels used on the guns and vehicles and a reduction of the guns' calibres. It also introduced elevation screws, which enabled range to be altered with fine accuracy, and shorter gun barrels, making the French artillery more mobile. For Napoleon's taste, however, Gribeauval's 8-pounder field guns were still too heavy, and he replaced them with 6-pounders. Originally part of the artillery, the engineers developed into a distinct branch of service in the Revolutionary wars. Primarily used to improve fortifications, or conduct sieges of enemy fortifications, engineer officers were highly-prized specialists. Miners were used in siege works to dig under walls, lay charges and open breaches for the attacking troops. They could also be used to dig trenches.

The Artillery
The foot artillery uniform retained the traditional dark blue coat, faced red with brass buttons. In 1810 the shako with grenade and crossed cannon barrels badge replaced the bicorn. The brass rhombic badge bore the crowned eagle on crossed cannon barrels over the regimental number, but there were numerous variations.

The horse artillery had the same colour scheme but with the dark blue *surtout* and red-laced waistcoat, hussar-style, and dark blue breeches with red lace and piping. Initially they wore the crested helmet of the *chasseurs à cheval*, then took the shako with red pompon, plume and cords. The brass badge included the following designs: a grenade, a grenade on crossed gun barrels, the grenade and regimental number. The sabretasche bore the regimental number. The train wore iron grey uniforms and buff small clothes with blue collar, lapels, cuffs and turnbacks piped red. Buttons and belts were white. The shako had a brass eagle plate and chin scales, red pompon and cords, red epaulettes.

The Engineers and Miners
The engineer uniform was dark blue with black collar, lapels, cuffs and cuff flaps all piped red, red turnbacks, yellow buttons, dark blue small clothes, white belts, shako with red cords and plume. The miners wore brass, crowned eagles over a label bearing the company designation ("3e COMPe MINEURS"). When working in trenches in range of enemy fire, the men wore black-painted steel helmets and cuirasses.

◀ GUNNER, HORSE ARTILLERY, 1806–14
The influence of the hussars is unmistakable in this uniform. Many horse artillery officers sported a colpack to reflect their elite status.

▶ SERGEANT, MINERS, FIELD SERVICE ORDER, 1809 *If working under enemy fire, the miners wore this heavy helmet and body armour, which must have made digging all that more difficult, but undoubtedly saved lives. It was blackened to minimize reflection and thus render the wearer less conspicuous.*

FOREIGN AND AUXILIARY TROOPS

Despite the massacre of the Swiss Guard in Paris on 10 August 1792, the French felt unable to abandon the services of foreign troops. Polish and Swiss contingents formed the core of these mercenaries.

The Polish Legions

Among the most enthusiastic of Napoleon's foreign supporters were the Poles, of whom thousands of expatriates roamed Europe after the partition of that country in 1795. Napoleon raised the three Polish legions in northern Italy: the 1st in January 1797, the 2nd in the June of that year – only to be swept away in the capitulation of Mantua – and the 3rd in 1800.

FIRST AUXILIARY POLISH LEGION IN LOMBARDY. Raised under General Jan Henryk Dabrowski (or Dombrowski) on 2 January 1797 with three battalions and reorganized on 2 June 1797. Renamed the Polish Auxiliary Legion of the Cisalpine Republic in November 1797.

SECOND AUXILIARY POLISH LEGION IN LOMBARDY. Also known as the Polish Auxiliary Legion of the Cisalpine Republic, this unit was also raised by General Dabrowski on 2 June 1797 from the First Legion. It existed until 27 April 1800.

1ST POLISH LEGION. The 1st, 2nd and 3rd Battalions were raised on 2 June 1797 in Milan, Ferrara and Bologna respectively. The grenadier battalion was raised in March 1799 and disbanded in early 1800 and the *chasseur* battalion was also raised in March 1799 and disbanded in 1800.

2ND POLISH LEGION. The 1st, 2nd and 3rd Battalions were raised on 2 June 1797 in Mantua, Tortona and Milan respectively. The cavalry regiment of the legion was raised in 1799. This unit later became the 1st Polish Hussars and on 20 March 1808, the Vistula Lancers (see overleaf). There was also an artillery battalion. These troops wore the traditional Polish *czapka* and *kurtka* in slate blue, with facings shown on collar, lapels, cuffs, turnback edging and on the side stripe to the breeches. One battalion had yellow facings, the second scarlet, the third green. Buttons and belts were white. The plumes to the *czapkas* were in the tricolour: red, blue and white.

3RD POLISH LEGION. Raised by General Dabrowski in 27 April 1800, this legion, also known as the Polish-Italian Legion, became the 1st Demi-Brigade Polonaise on 21 December 1801. In March 1802 the unit passed into the service of

▲ INFANTRY COLOUR, POLISH LEGION 1800
A representation of a rare relic: the colour of the Polish Legion of 1800 in French service.

the Italian Republic and on 5 August 1806 into Neapolitan service. The Legion consisted of the 1st–7th Infantry Battalions in addition to an artillery battalion.

1ST POLISH DEMI-BRIGADE. Commander General Jozef Grabinski. Raised on 21 December 1801 from the Polish-Italian Legion of General Dabrowski (see above); transferred to Italian service on 5 February 1802, to Neapolitan service in 1804 and back to French service in 1808.

2ND POLISH DEMI-BRIGADE. Commander General Wincenty Aksamitowski. Raised December 1801 from the Polish-Italian Legion; transferred to French service as the 114th Demi-Brigade, December 1802.

3RD POLISH DEMI-BRIGADE. Commander General Wladyslaw Jablonowski. Raised in March 1802 from the Danube Legion (see overleaf); transferred to French service as the 113th Demi-Brigade on 2 September 1802. On 24 January 1803 sent out to St Domingue and destroyed there by

◀ OFFICER, 3RD POLISH LEGION, 1800
He wears a costume that is unmistakably Polish. The czapka, *with slate-blue top, has silver braid whilst the blue* kurtka *is almost obscured by a lavish silver and crimson sash. This unit served in Italy and would later be transformed into the famous Vistula Legion.*

disease. The uniform consisted of a dark blue *czapka*, dark blue *kurtka* tunic and breeches, crimson collar, lapels, cuffs and turnbacks, with white buttons and belts.

THE DANUBE LEGION. Initially called the Legion of the Rhine, this unit was raised on 8 September 1799 and disbanded in March 1802. It had three battalions of infantry, each of 10 companies; a regiment of lancers, of four squadrons; and a battery of horse artillery. The cavalry and artillery were incorporated into the army of the Cisalpine Republic on 31 December 1801. The infantry became the 3rd Polish Demi-Brigade and later the 113th Demi-Brigade (see above). The cavalry was transferred to Neapolitan service on 4 August 1806 and back to French service on 2 February 1807. On 27 October 1807 it took in the men of the 1st Polish Hussars, which had been disbanded, and on 11 November 1807 went into Westphalian service, returning

to French service on 20 March 1808 as the lancers of the Vistula Legion (see below). The lancers wore slate blue dolmans faced in crimson and piped white. The artist Knötel shows them in French-style uniforms with bicorns, red collars, cuffs, cuff flaps and piping, white lapels, turnbacks, small clothes and belts, yellow buttons. The artillery wore the same dark blue dolmans and breeches as the lancers, red cords and piping, yellow buttons, black *czapkas*.

THE 1ST AND 2ND LEGIONS OF THE NORTH. The 1st Legion was raised on 20 September 1806 in Hagenau; the 2nd was raised on 23 September 1806 in Nuremberg. During 1807 the two legions were reduced to one and in March 1808 this became the 5th Infantry Regiment of the Grand Duchy of Warsaw.

THE VISTULA LEGION. Raised on 31 March 1808 from the Polish-Italian Legion and new Polish recruits. It reached a strength of three infantry regiments and a regiment of lancers (the ex-lancers of the Polish-Italian Legion; later the 1st Polish Hussars). On 18 April 1811 this regiment

became the 7th Chevau-Légers lanciers of the French line. A 2nd Vistula Legion was begun in July 1808 but in February 1809 this unit became the 4th Regiment of the old Vistula Legion. This legion also had two regiments of lancers. The uniform was a traditional *kurtka* in dark blue, with yellow

◄ LANCER, LEGION OF THE DANUBE, 1799
This regiment of cavalry was the first unit of Polish lancers employed by the French, although it also briefly served the Neapolitans and Westphalians. They wore the czapka and, initially, blue dolmans faced with crimson.

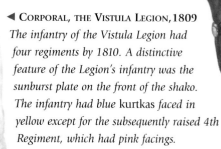

◄ CORPORAL, THE VISTULA LEGION, 1809
The infantry of the Vistula Legion had four regiments by 1810. A distinctive feature of the Legion's infantry was the sunburst plate on the front of the shako. The infantry had blue kurtkas *faced in yellow except for the subsequently raised 4th Regiment, which had pink facings.*

facings, lining and buttons, shako with brass sunburst plate, white belts and small clothes, French badges of rank and distinction. These lancers became the 7th and 8th of the French line on 18 June 1811. In June 1813 the infantry was concentrated into the Vistula Regiment of two battalions, which fought at Leipzig in October 1813 and in the defence of Soissons and the Battle of Arcis-sur-Aube in 1814. All these troops were disbanded on 12 May 1814. In April 1815 the Poles formed the 3rd Foreign Regiment and the 7th Chevau-Légers.

The Swiss Regiments

Napoleon recruited several regiments of Swiss infantry. These were raised by a military capitulation between France and the Helvetian Republic on 19 August 1798. Originally there were to be six demi-brigades, but only three were actually raised: the 1st Demi-Brigade, which became the 3rd battalion, 1st Swiss Infantry Regiment in 1805; the 2nd Demi-Brigade, which became the 4th battalion, 1st Swiss Infantry Regiment in 1805; and the 3rd Demi-Brigade, which went to St Domingo in 1803 and was destroyed by disease. Recruitment for the 4th, 5th and 6th demi-brigades began but they melted away with desertion.

THE SWISS DEMI-BRIGADES. The demi-brigades wore red coats, the 1st with white facings and blue piping, the 2nd with blue facings and white piping and the 3rd with yellow facings and sky blue piping.

OTHER SWISS UNITS. The Swiss contributed yet more men to Napoleon's cause: the 1st to 4th Swiss Regiments, raised between 1805 and 1807. These regiments wore French uniforms and badges. Their coats were red, buttons yellow, small clothes and belts white. The 1st Regiment had yellow facings; the 2nd, dark blue; the 3rd, black; and the 4th, sky blue. These regiments were destroyed in Russia. On 20 March 1815 a 2nd Foreign Regiment (Swiss) was raised from the remnants of the four Swiss regiments.

THE VALAISAN BATTALION. This unit was raised in October 1805. In September 1811 it was merged into the 11th Light in Wesel, together with the Tirailleurs du Po. They wore a dark red coat with white collar, cuffs, lapels, turnbacks, small clothes and belts. Brass buttons bore the peripheral inscription "Empire Francais"; and within this: "Bataillon Valaison".

▲ SAPPER, NEUFCHATEL BATTALION, 1812
Marshal Alexander Berthier, created Prince of Neufchatel in 1806, raised this battalion in 1807. Due to the somewhat flamboyant yellow colour of their coats, they were known as the "Canaries". This sapper carries a heavy axe and might have worn a leather apron when on campaign.

▲ OFFICER, 1ST SWISS INFANTRY REGIMENT, 1812 *Unlike the Canaries, the four Swiss regiments raised in 1805 maintained the tradition of wearing red. This individual wears a wide bicorn, suggesting he is off duty. A shako with brass eagle plate, chin scales and a white plume and cords was more commonly worn on active service.*

THE NEUFCHATEL BATTALION. Raised in May 1807 and then disbanded in June 1814. It wore an unusual uniform, which consisted of a deep yellow coat with scarlet collar, lapels and cuffs, white lining, small clothes and belts. Tin buttons had the peripheral inscription: "Empire Francais"; and within this: "Bataillon de Neufchatel".

Balkan Troops

When France took control of Austria's provinces in the Balkans, a number of units passed into French service.
ILLYRIAN REGIMENT. Sometimes known as the Dalmatian Regiment, it was raised by imperial decree of 16 November 1810, of local levies by Marmont at a strength of five light infantry battalions. The uniform was of French light infantry cut, all dark blue, with red collar and cuffs piped white, white buttons and belts.
PROVINCIAL CROATIAN REGIMENTS. Apart from Marmont's local levies, six regiments of Austrian Border Infantry passed into French service from 1809 to 1813: 1st Regiment (Licca), 2nd Regiment (Ottochatz), 3rd Regiment (Ogulin), 4th Regiment (Szluin), 5th Regiment (1st Banat), 6th Regiment (2nd Banat). These regiments wore green uniforms of light infantry cut,

◀ OFFICER, 1ST CROATIAN INFANTRY REGIMENT, 1812 *When Austria's Adriatic borderlands fell to France after the 1809 campaign, the six old Border Regiments were formed into three Croatian regiments. They wore a uniform in the style of the French light infantry, although the shako is evidently Austro-Hungarian in origin.*

green lapels, yellow collar, pointed cuffs, turnbacks and pocket piping, green breeches, yellow waistcoats, white buttons, shako with white eagle plate and chin scales, tricolour cockade, white loop and button.
1ST REGIMENT OF CROATIAN HUSSARS. Raised on 23 February 1813, and later used to form the Croatian Pioneer Battalion. They wore a sky blue dolman and pelisse, buff collar and cuffs, white buttons and lace, shako with white rhombic plate, white belts.

Other Balkan troops included the Albanian Regiment, Septinsulaire infantry, chasseurs and artillery.

Iberian Troops

The French invasion of Spain and Portugal led to the raising of local troops, often from prisoners of war.
THE SPANISH REGIMENT (JOSEPH NAPOLEON). Raised by decree of 13 February 1809 from Spanish prisoners of war at a strength of four field battalions and a depot. They wore French uniform in white with light green collars, cuffs and lapels, brass buttons, white belts and small clothes.
THE PORTUGUESE LEGION. Raised May 1808 at paper strength of five infantry and two cavalry regiments; by May 1811 these had been reduced to three and one respectively. They wore Portuguese shakos with brass front band, brown tunics and breeches, red facings, white piping, white buttons and belts. French badges.

German Troops

France retained some units of German mercenaries throughout the period.
THE WESTPHALIAN REGIMENT. Raised on 11 December 1806 in Posen from Prussians and recruits from Brunswick, Erfurt, Fulda, Minden and Münster. There were four battalions of light

infantry each of six companies. On 30 September 1808 it was merged into the Hanoverian Legion.
THE HANOVERIAN LEGION. Raised on 13 April 1804 with three infantry battalions and a regiment of *chasseurs à cheval* of three squadrons. On 30 September 1809 it absorbed the 1st Battalion of the Westphalian Regiment. The infantry of this legion seemed to have worn their old Hanoverian uniforms: red coats, dark blue facings, white turnbacks, buttons, belts and small clothes. The cavalry wore dark

▼ OFFICER, PORTUGUESE LEGION, 1812 *This unusual French unit retained a Portuguese influence in their uniform. The infantry wore a shako similar to the belgic shako adopted by the British but the cavalry wore this elegant crested helmet. The uniform colour was brown for both infantry and cavalry.*

green, single-breasted coats, yellow facings, lining and buttons, yellow waistcoats and breeches. On 9 August 1811 the legion was disbanded: the infantry became the 127th, 128th and 129th Line, the cavalry the 1st Hussars and 9th Chevau-Légers lanciers.

Other Foreign Regiments

Napoleon raised a number of units from various soldiers from Germany, Ireland, Albania, Greece and Egypt,

▼ FUSILIER PRIVATE, HANOVERIAN LEGION, **1810** *Raised from the old army of the Electorate of Hanover in April 1804, they wore their old Hanoverian uniforms but carried and used French equipment. Legend has it that their red uniforms led to them being mistaken for British infantry in the Peninsular War.*

among others. Chief among these units were four foreign regiments.

1ST FOREIGN REGIMENT. Raised on 30 September 1805 at Weissenburg from Germans and others as the Régiment de La Tour d'Auvergne with three battalions. In August 1811 it became the 1st Foreign Regiment (Régiment Étranger). They wore dark green tunics, cuffs, turnbacks and breeches; red collar and cuff flaps; white waistcoats, belts and piping.

2ND FOREIGN REGIMENT. Raised on 1 November 1805 in Mainz from Germans at three battalions as the Regiment of Issembourg. On 3 August 1811 it became the 2nd Foreign Regiment. They wore a sky blue coat, cuffs, turnbacks and breeches; yellow collar and cuff flaps. White belts and buttons with the peripheral inscription: "RÉGIMENT ÉTRANGER", and in the centre the number "2".

3RD FOREIGN REGIMENT. Raised on 13 August 1803 as the Irish Legion (really only one battalion), in 1809 it was increased to two battalions and then to three. On 3 August 1811 it became the 3rd Foreign Regiment. The uniform included white buttons with the peripheral inscription: "RÉGIMENT ÉTRANGER", and in the centre the number "3".

4TH FOREIGN REGIMENT. Raised on 13 November 1806 in Leipzig from Prussian prisoners by the Prince of Isenburg-Birstein as the Regiment of Prussia. On 3 August 1811 it became the 4th Foreign Regiment. The uniform included: dark green coat and breeches; red facings and turnbacks; brass buttons. White buttons with the peripheral inscription: "RÉGIMENT ÉTRANGER", and in the centre the number "4".

THE MIDI LEGION. Raised on 18 May 1803 in the newly annexed departments at a strength of three line infantry battalions, two light battalions (all with five companies) and a company of artillery. It was disbanded in 1811 and the men went to the 11th and 33rd Light. The legion wore brown coats with royal blue collar, lapels and cuffs, white cuff flaps, buttons, small clothes, belts and turnbacks. The

▲ OFFICER, 1ST FOREIGN REGIMENT, 1808
The regiment wore a light infantry uniform with green tunic and green breeches. The buttons were inscribed with "RÉGIMENT ÉTRANGER", in the centre the number "1".

fusiliers wore the old French fusilier helmet, the grenadiers wore bearskins with tin plate bearing a grenade. The light company wore the shako. All wore the usual French badges.

INDIAN TROOPS. Dating back to 1737, France raised native troops on the Indian subcontinent, and up to 1792 they had the Regiment of Pondicheri in that town. The native *Cipahis* wore white turbans and short, dark green coats with red collar, lapels, pointed cuffs and yellow buttons. Native legwear of white shorts or *dhoti* and white belts were worn.

GREAT BRITAIN

Safe behind the wooden walls of her Royal Navy, Britain remained an implacable enemy to Revolutionary and Napoleonic France for almost 23 years. Fearful of a French invasion, and determined to enforce a balance of power in Europe in order to establish a lasting peace, Britain (or "Perfidious Albion" as Napoleon preferred to call her) committed a small but highly skilled army, a huge navy, and a truly colossal amount of cash (over £1 billion in total, which should be multiplied by a factor of at least 50 for a modern equivalent) to the pursuit of victory. The British army was to be virtually excluded from continental Europe after 1795 and until the Battle of Maida in 1806. Lessons from the early fighting were learned and when the British returned to the fight, first to southern Italy, then to Spain and Portugal and finally to Waterloo itself, the reforms bore fruit and contributed significantly towards final victory.

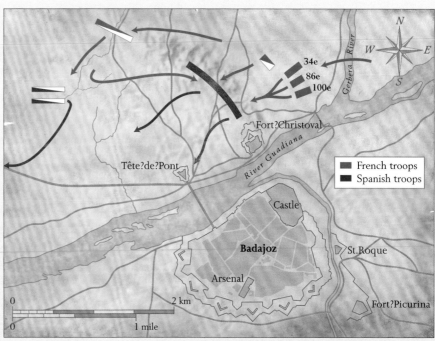

▲ *The Battle of Rio Gebora in early 1811. The loss of this battle by the Spanish led directly to the fall of the strategically vital frontier fortress of Badajoz on 11 March 1811, setting back Wellington's plans for the invasion of Spain for months.*

◄ *The Battle of Trafalgar: the French ship* Redoubtable *is about to surrender to the* Victory. *This justifiably celebrated victory of Admiral Horatio Nelson and the Royal Navy, in 1805, ensured Britain's global supremacy for the next 100 years.*

BRITAIN'S GOVERNMENT AND THE BIRTH OF HER EMPIRE

In 1792 Britain was ruled by the House of Hanover. The reigning monarch, George III, was bound by the terms of the unwritten constitution and could do very little without the agreement of the bicameral Houses of Parliament. These consisted of the House of Lords and the House of Commons; membership of the former was by right of aristocratic birth but the financial power was firmly in the hands of the Commons, which was an elected chamber. Fair and democratic elections were totally alien to the system of national government of that day. All parliamentary elections were accompanied, as a matter of course, by bribery, intimidation, corruption, perjury and riot. It goes without saying, that standing for election to such a political body was open only to rich men who knew how to pull the strings of power. Indeed, the privilege of being able to cast a vote in parliamentary elections was reserved for those who owned land worth at least 40 shillings freehold. Even in 1831, from a population of 24 million in the United Kingdom, the electorate numbered only 516,000, or 5 per cent.

The populace was being comprehensively taxed without being properly represented, and thousands were dying from want. Care of the

▲ *Geroge III, painted in 1771. Although viewed by the American colonists as a tyrant, George III was an enlightened ruler, far from being as despotic as is sometimes suggested.*

poor, the aged and the infirm was non-existent. The conditions endured by the workers and their families in the many new mills, mines and factories were incredibly hard. None of this, it seems, impinged upon the consciences of the Members of Parliament, who

indulged themselves in their privileges and concentrated upon increasing their already-considerable wealth.

The fact that only in France had the populace risen and overthrown the established monarch indicates that contemporary life in Britain was relatively bearable. At least there was an electorate in Britain, to which the government had some responsibility: nothing like it existed within the European monarchies of the day.

There were fears, however, among the governing classes in Britain – as elsewhere – that the lower orders might revolt. Thus, the regular army and the militia were viewed as police forces for internal security duties as much as weapons of national defence against external enemies. Further, Britain had been working hard for centuries to collect enemies, creating a global climate of competition and conflict in the scramble for overseas riches and colonies.

Britain and France had been involved in fierce rivalry on the North American continent since 1607: France had lost Canada to Britain in 1763 and Britain had been thrown out of the United States (with much aid from the French) 20 years later.

Gibraltar had been taken from the Spanish by the British in 1702, thus ensuring British control of the western end of the Mediterranean Sea and easing British mercantile traffic. Unable to gain much of a foothold in South America, Britain had raided the Spanish treasure convoys returning to Europe since the sixteenth century, approaching such operations with schoolboyish glee. In 1807 a British expedition even managed to seize Montevideo for a short time.

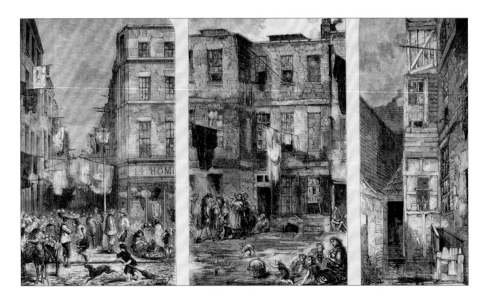

◀ *Living conditions for the new proletariat in London during the 18th and 19th centuries were dire. Poverty inevitably drove many into the armed forces to escape the deprivation that this illustration depicts.*

▲ *This typical trading port in West Bengal shows how commerce (in this case conducted by the Honourable East India Company) opened the door for the establishment of permanent empire.*

▼ *Perhaps the one man who did more than any other to carve out and establish the British Empire was Captain James Cook, who dedicated his life to claiming as much of the globe as possible for his country.*

Colonial Influence

Britain had been extremely active over the world's oceans, grabbing territories left and right, particularly during the exploratory career of Captain James Cook (1768–80), which added islands, archipelagos and the continent of Australia to the Crown's possessions. By 1792, British commercial interests had set up warehouses, depots and factories in many foreign locations where commodities were to be found for which European markets existed and vice versa.

Chief among these areas were the East and West Indies. British merchants fought tooth and nail against similar entrepreneurs from France, Holland, Spain, Portugal and Denmark for the lion's share of these markets, with the British government firmly in the back seat, but with its members' interests in these commercial ventures influencing national policy on several occasions. The Dutch colony on the strategically vital Cape of Good Hope was snatched by the British in 1795, and although it was returned to Holland at the Peace of Amiens, it was later reoccupied.

In the East Indies, it was the Honourable East India Company (John Company) that had clawed a toe hold on the Indian subcontinent in the reign of Charles II, negotiated treaties with local rulers and recruited their own troops (both native and European) for the protection of their investments. Ships of the Honourable East India Company were among the best British craft of this time. They were heavily armed and well constructed, being virtually cargo-carrying ships of the line.

The French presence was considerable in India. It was formally ended by the fall of Pondicherry in 1793. John Company now ruled the roost, together with its allied native principalities. It was not until after the Indian Mutiny of 1857 that the British government took over direct rule of that vast subcontinent. In the West Indies, commerce led the way but the British Army and the Royal Navy were thrust forward to try to eliminate other European interference.

THE STRUCTURE OF THE BRITISH ARMY

The British Army of 1792 had no designated Commander-in-Chief in peacetime: the Secretary at War (a civilian appointee, answering to the sovereign and to Parliament) exercised that office. There were no organizations larger than a regiment in the British Army, no brigades or divisions, and only one training camp – set up in July and August of that year to introduce the new Prussian drill.

Command was similarly illogical and fragmented: the Commander-in-Chief, in Horse Guards, Whitehall, actually commanded only the infantry and cavalry of the line. The Board of Ordnance, a separate organization, and until part-way into the Napoleonic period, largely civilian in character, commanded the artillery, engineers and such other technical troops as existed. The sovereign commanded the Household Troops and the Home Office commanded the militia.

There were military units scattered all over the globe, each small detachment fighting in isolation,

▼ The famous charge of the Scots Greys at Waterloo. Such stirring depictions lent a cloak of glamour to the hard years of fighting, terrible deprivation and continuous marching through Europe and across the globe.

mostly in terribly hostile climatic conditions, at the ends of command chains often thousands of miles long. It often took months for orders to reach remote commanders from London. But military administration was in a similar state: it had often fallen into the wrong hands, corruption was rife, and when an English army was sent to Ireland in 1689 the unfortunate troops went unclothed and unpaid and many died of starvation. This scandalous state of affairs was destined to become a recurrent theme throughout the history of the British armed services.

Purchasing Commissions

Up until the Crimean War, it was common practice for officers' commissions to be offered for sale in Britain. In 1795 the system went as follows: to purchase a commission, an officer placed his name with the financial agent of his desired regiment. The officer would be placed in the regimental seniority list and these lists were correlated throughout the army. The prices one paid for commissions had been set in 1756 and remained unaltered until well into our period. They varied according to how fashionable a regiment was.

The Duke of York's Reforms

Following Britain's reverses in the campaigns of 1793–95 the process of officer selection was regulated by the reforms of the Commander-in-Chief of the army, Frederick Augustus, Duke of York: "No person is considered eligible for a commission until he has attained the age of sixteen. All recommendations shall certify the eligibility of the person recommended in respect of character, education and bodily health, and that he is prepared immediately to join any regiment to which he may be appointed. His Christian names and place of address must be particularly stated." The letter of recommendation had to be signed by a major or higher rank.

The Duke of York also ruled that officers would have to spend much more time with their regiments and certain minimum periods in a rank before being able to purchase or be promoted to the next rank: "No officer may acquire a captaincy until he has served two years as a subaltern, and he must have six years commissioned service before becoming a major." The duke also instituted annual reports on each officer by their commanding officer. No officer could be promoted without a satisfactory report.

The Duke of York had no control over the artillery, engineers, or the supply services, and the militia, yeomanry, volunteers and fencibles came under Home Office control. Yet he was able to accomplish a great deal despite these limitations. In 1801 he established the Duke of York's Royal Military School for soldiers' children, which still exists today. The duke also had greatcoats issued to soldiers free of charge. Next year the Royal Military College opened in Woolwich, a "New Land Pattern" musket was introduced and Colonel Shrapnel's explosive shells were bought for the artillery. In 1803 he formed the Royal Wagon Train.

Military hospitals with wards for soldiers' wives were built, which required that the names of soldiers who became casualties were to be reported instead of just their numbers. The duke insisted on better treatment of soldiers and issued the "Rules & Regulations for the Formations, Field-Exercises and Movements of His Majesty's Forces" in 1803, making all regiments practise a uniform system of evolutions for the first time.

Light infantry regiments were introduced to the regular army in 1803 by converting the 43rd and 52nd Regiments to that role. In 1805 the Duke introduced volunteering from the militia into the line. The Corps of Captains, Commissaries and Drivers was formed in 1794, disbanded in 1801 and then replaced by the Corps

of Military Drivers. In 1806 this became the Royal Artillery Drivers.

General Sir John Moore commanded the model brigade at Shorncliffe that served as a showpiece of these reforms.

▲ *Frederick Augustus, the Duke of York, in the uniform of a Colonel of the Coldstream Guards. The duke is unfortunately now remembered better as a mention in a nursery rhyme rather than for his intelligent and far reaching military reforms.*

Officers' Commissions and Purchase Prices 1756				
Rank	**Foot Guards & Dragoons**	**Horse Guards**	**Dragoon Guards**	**Foot Regiments**
Lieutenant Colonel	£6,700	£5,200	£5,350	£3,500
Major	£6,300	£4,250	£4,250	£2,600
Captain with rank of Lieutenant Colonel	£3,500			
Captain Lieutenant with Rank of Lieutenant Colonel	£2,600			
Captain	£3,100	£3,150	£1,500	
Captain Lieutenant with Rank of Captain	£2,100	£950		
Lieutenant with Rank of Captain	£1,500			
Lieutenant		£1,750	£1,365	£500
1st Lieutenant in Fusilier Regiment				£550
Cornet		£1,600	£1,102	
2nd Lieutenant in Fusileer Regiment				£450
Ensign	£900			£400

THE BRITISH ARMY IN THE NAPOLEONIC WARS

The years 1793–1815 represented a steep learning curve for the British Army. Regiments were frequently sent on campaign with little or no experience of battle, their knowledge of military arts being limited to parade-ground manoeuvres and drill. Experience had to be "bought" on the battlefield and the cost was high.

The War in Flanders

The performance of the few regiments that the British government could scrape together for the 1793–95 campaigns in Flanders – with the exception of the Guards and a few others (mainly cavalry regiments) – was of very mixed quality. This was largely due to the fact that most of the men were new, untrained recruits when they landed on the Continent. Matters were made worse by the fact that many of their officers were rich, ignorant teenagers, with little professional knowledge, who owed their positions purely to their wealth, and who could not be bothered to learn how to drill

▼ *The Battle of Aboukir, 1 August 1798, saw Nelson destroy the French fleet and place Napoleon's expedition to Egypt in peril.*

their men or to even care for them. Despite these drawbacks, the army managed to hold together under the shock of combat and even scored some victories. Indeed, quite a few battle honours were awarded to the regiments involved in the fighting in this phase of the wars.

After initial success, defeat at Tourcoing in 1794 meant that the Austrian government lost the will to continue the war in the Netherlands and began to withdraw their army.

In June of that year French pressure began to tell, as Generals Macdonald and Souham, with 24,000 men of the Army of the North, defeated the Allies at Hooglede. On 14 and 15 September, General Pichegru attacked and overran the exposed Allied outpost at Boxtel.

As winter closed in, the British and Hanoverians fell back to the north-east on Bremen, suffering great privations on the way. The British Army's involvement on mainland Europe fizzled out like a damp squib.

The Effects of the Colonial Wars

The war on mainland Europe was patently not going to yield much cash for Britain: her small field army was no

match for those of Austria or Prussia, thus, even if they all agreed to a fair share of any booty, Britain's share would be very small. This situation was reversed if one regarded the global situation. Due to the size and combat efficiency of the fleet, and quality of its commanders, the Royal Navy very soon ruled the waves and Britain could be master of pretty much any coastal location that she put her mind to. This brought in its wake the British control of many rich sources of income from those goods on which Europe had developed a dependence: coffee, cocoa, tea, tobacco, fruits, spices of all types, silks, cottons, dyes.

Far-away ports from which these commodities originated were identified, targeted, taken and garrisoned. The problem with these conquests was that many of these commodities grew in places like the West Indies, where diseases such as malaria and the almost certainly fatal yellow fever were rampant. Yellow fever had been brought to the Caribbean by the African slaves imported to work on the plantations. No complete figures exist for British losses to disease in the West Indies, but the total is believed to lie in the region of 100,000 men.

Nevertheless, the Revolutionary Wars saw Britain grab numerous colonies and engineer a French defeat in Egypt (aided by Nelson's destruction of the French fleet at Aboukir).

Reform

The decade after 1795 marked a period of learning lessons for the British military led by the Duke of York and other officers such as Sir John Moore. Among those regiments that underwent Moore's training system there were the 43rd, 52nd and 95th: the forerunners of the famous Light Division of the Peninsular War. Moore was an enlightened officer, who urged relaxation of the rigid code of discipline. The professional quality of

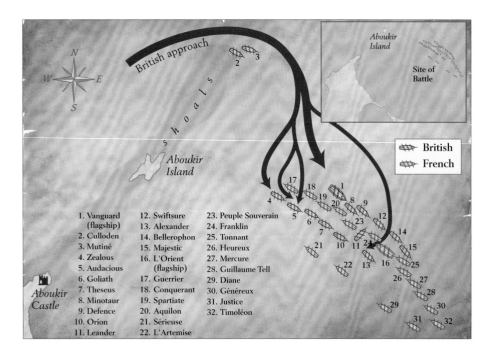

1. Vanguard (flagship)
2. Culloden
3. Mutiné
4. Zealous
5. Audacious
6. Goliath
7. Theseus
8. Minotaur
9. Defence
10. Orion
11. Leander
12. Swiftsure
13. Alexander
14. Bellerophon
15. Majestic
16. L'Orient (flagship)
17. Guerrier
18. Conquerant
19. Spartiate
20. Aquilon
21. Sérieuse
22. L'Artemise
23. Peuple Souverain
24. Franklin
25. Tonnant
26. Heureux
27. Mercure
28. Guillaume Tell
29. Diane
30. Généreux
31. Justice
32. Timoléon

the officers, men, organization and procedures of the British Army were to improve markedly after the dark days of 1795 and were honed by experience of battle. Following the Battle of Trafalgar on 21 October 1805, the Royal Navy commanded the seas of the world. Napoleon's success at Austerlitz did nothing to shake this, but it did make him almost omnipotent on the European mainland.

The Victory at Maida

In 1806 Napoleon resolved to eliminate the Bourbon Kingdom of the Two Sicilies, whose King Ferdinand and Queen Caroline had – rather rashly – opted to support Austria in the last conflict. On 9 March 1806 the French scattered the Sicilians at the Battle of Campo Tenese and took possession of southern Italy. The local Calabrian peasants rose in revolt whilst the Bourbon royal family withdrew to Sicily, where 7,000 British soldiers were stationed. General Sir John Stuart decided to mount a spoiling attack on the mainland in support of the rebels. He embarked 5,200 men at Messina on 29 June in transports and on 1 July the British landed unopposed.

The French general, Reynier, acted with speed and energy, concentrating as many troops as he could. The two forces clashed on 4 July, Reynier assaulting Stuart's force with 6,440

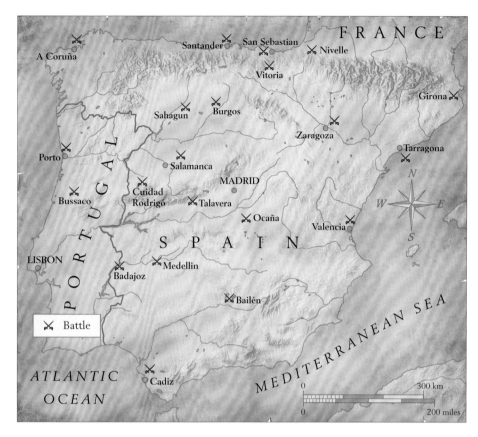

men. Stuart's troops deployed into line as Reynier's infantry advanced, still in columns of companies, with regimental frontages of about 60 men, being 14 men deep. The outnumbered British held their fire until the enemy was within half a musket shot, then opened up at less than 150 yd (140 m). The French 1st Light took a second volley at 80 yd (73 m) and a third at 20 yd (18 m).

▲ Map of the Peninsular campaigns. Britain's involvement in the wars in Spain and Portugal ran from 1808 to 1814. It was a severe testing ground for a reformed army and saw the making of Wellington's reputation.

By this time the losses of the 1st Light were so heavy (427 killed or wounded out of 1,810) that they turned and fled. This triumph of British tactics was repeated along the rest of the battlefield. Total French losses: 490 killed, 870 wounded, 722 men and four guns captured. British losses: 45 killed, 282 wounded.

Peninsular Performance

Sir Charles Oman documented many British victories in Spain and Portugal and credited them all to the "column versus line" syndrome, claiming that the French insisted on attacking in columns, with their limited firepower and vulnerable depth, against the two-deep British line, which shot the hapless columns to pieces, achieving victory. He later retracted this assertion.

◀ The Battle of Maida. Sir John Stuart's victory here on 4 July 1806 proved how the British Army had improved since 1793.

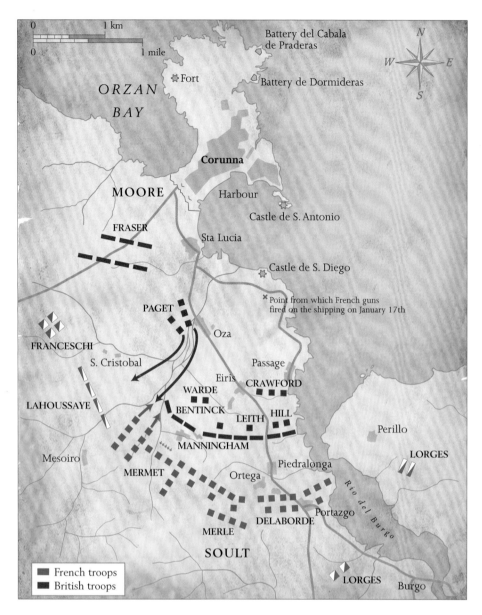

■ French troops
■ British troops

◄ *During the Battle of Corunna, Moore's British turned on their French pursuers and gained sufficient respite to embark and slip away. The battle was notable for the defeat of repeated French attacks and for hard fighting in the villages on the approaches to Corunna.*

On 17 August the British won the first clash at Roleia. Four days later, at Vimiero, the British line convincingly destroyed the composite grenadier column of Colonel Maransin and won the battle. French losses were 1,500 killed and wounded, 300 captured and 12 guns. Anglo-Portuguese losses were 134 killed, 534 wounded, 51 missing. Junot sued for peace and his army was evacuated under the terms of the notorious Convention of Cintra. This victory was followed by defeat when Moore was chased out of Spain but, even then, some pride was salvaged when the British beat off their pursuers at the Battle of Corunna. Moore, sadly, was one of the casualties.

The next – very convincing – instance of the superiority of British infantry tactics came at Bussaco on 27 September 1810. Here, Wellington, with 32,000 men, deployed along a ridge in his classical manner and soundly defeated Marshal Masséna's 58,000 men, causing them 4,479 casualties for a loss of 1,252. The pattern was repeated again at Barossa on 5 March 1811, where Marshal Victor's 10,700 men were defeated by Sir Thomas Graham with 8,270. The French lost over 2,000 casualties (and an Eagle) to the Allies' 1,600.

Towards the end of the French occupation of Spain, steady British infantry were the key to many victories, in both an offensive as well as defensive role. Wellington's victories at the battles of Salamanca, Vittoria, the Nivelle, Nive, Orthez and Toulouse were just the major examples of the high quality of both the commander and his army.

The Battle of Waterloo

Napoleon returned to France from his first exile on the island of Elba on 1 March 1815. All of Europe mobilized against him and it fell to the British,

It seems, in fact, that Wellington played a major role in these victories. He always took time to seek out an optimal defensive position, usually along a ridge with good lateral communications along the side away from the enemy. He then deployed his infantry in line on the reverse slope, well out of sight of the advancing French and covered them with a heavy line of skirmishers. The skirmishers, fighting in open order from behind cover, usually outnumbered the French and gained the upper hand.

The French main line advanced in battalion columns in order to cover the open ground as quickly as possible, to get to grips with the British. As they toiled up the slopes of the ridge, the British skirmishers fell back over the crest, the British line stood up, advanced over the crest and poured volley after volley into the surprised French columns before they had time to deploy. Whatever actually happened on the ground so many times in the Peninsular War, the British victories cannot be ignored. Waterloo was their ultimate confirmation.

The Spanish Campaign

France invaded Spain in June 1808. The British government jumped at the invitation from the Spanish to come to their aid, and in August a British expeditionary force landed in Portugal. It was commanded by Sir Arthur Wellesley (the future First Duke of Wellington). The country had been invaded by a French army under General Junot and this army came up to stamp on the British.

▲ *One of the Army's most promising commanders and leading reformers, Sir John Moore, had his career cut short on 16 January 1809 during victory at the Battle of Corunna.*

Netherlanders, Prussians, Hanoverians and Nassauers in Belgium to be the first to cross swords with him.

On 16 June Napoleon defeated Blücher's Prussians at Ligny, while Ney failed to break the Netherlanders and some Allied troops at Quatre Bras. Two days later, Wellington had concentrated much of his polyglot army along the ridge just south of the village of Mont

St Jean. He had 106,000 men to stop Napoleon's 72,000. But not only was his army far from homogeneous, much of it was also composed of raw troops, many of his Peninsular veterans having been sent to America and Canada. The duke deployed most of his troops, so as to make the most of the terrain features. Wellington knew the Prussians had been badly beaten at Ligny, but they had promised to come to his aid at Waterloo. The French assaulted in "the same old way", as the duke later said. On the west flank they became embroiled in a desperate

struggle for possession of the chateau of Hougoumont, which distracted their infantry from attacking the main Allied line lying in the dead ground behind the crest of the ridge.

D'Erlon's I Corps infantry attack the Allied centre but was wrecked by British cavalry, which in true British fashion, went out of control. The massive French cavalry charges that followed – launched too soon and without infantry or artillery support – mostly broke on the Allied infantry squares and were thus squandered. By evening, the Prussians arrived and drove deep into the French right flank at Plancenoit. The Allied crisis was over. Nevertheless, the Imperial Guard charged, but were repelled, with heavy losses. They ran, and the rest of the French Army ran with them.

British losses were 7,000 men; the Netherlands' army lost 4,000, the Hanoverians 2,000, the King's German Legion lost 1,600, the Brunswickers and the Nassauers 700 each. The French losses were estimated at 42,000.

▼ *"Hard pounding" was how Wellington described the Battle of Waterloo. This painting shows one of the French cavalry charges on the afternoon of that costly day.*

THE GENERALS, GENERAL STAFF, ROYAL WAGON TRAIN AND GUARDS

Traditionally, British soldiers wore the highly visible red coat, the exception being the artillery and certain cavalry regiments. The complex system of rank badges was simplified during the course of the wars.

Generals

Infantry generals wore red coats faced dark blue with gold buttons and lace and a gold aiguillette on the left shoulder. Ranks were shown by

▶ OFFICER OF THE GENERAL STAFF, 1805 *The requirements for members of this elite corps were a good family tree and the right schooling. Compared to staff organizations in other armies, Britain's was very small. This officer wears epaulettes, a badge of rank introduced after 1791, a crimson sash and the appropriate lacing to sleeve and cuffs. High boots and spurs complete his aristocratic, expensive costume.*

buttons and gold lace chevrons on the forearm, the lowest of which was on the indented cuff. A field marshal wore six chevrons, regularly spaced, a general four, a lieutenant general six in two groups of three, a major general two groups of two and a brigadier general one on the cuff and two higher up the sleeve. The waist sash was crimson and gold silk, the bicorn edged with white feathers.

General Staff

The quartermaster general's staff, the adjutant general's staff and brigade majors wore red coats, silver buttons and lace (with tassels), dark blue collars and cuffs. They all wore aiguillettes on the left shoulder in the button colour, except aides-de-camp, who wore the same but with gold lace and buttons. Rank was denoted by gold/silver lace chevrons on the cuff and lower sleeve.

The commissary general's department, the paymaster general's staff and the storekeeper general's staff all wore plain dark blue coats with yellow buttons.

The Royal Wagon Train and Royal Staff Corps

The men of the Royal Wagon Train wore red coats, dark blue facings and white buttons and lace. The Royal Staff Corps was founded by the Horse Guards in 1798 to alleviate the shortage of qualified engineering officers. By 1809 it had grown to battalion size, equipped as infantry. They wore red, faced dark blue, without any lace decoration.

Life Guards

The 1st and 2nd Life Guards had red tunics, dark blue facings and gold buttons and lace in pairs and white breeches. The Royal Horse Guards (The Blues) had dark blue tunics, red

▲ *British wagons, such as the one shown here, proved to be too cumbersome for the rough tracks of Portugal and Spain. The lighter native ox carts were used to move everything from wine to the unfortunate wounded.*

▲ **BRITISH GENERAL, 1798** *The rather odd system of generals' rank badges shown on this figure, of chevrons, points down, on the cuffs, could well have been mistaken for similar decorations worn by some of the British heavy cavalry regiments. The much clearer system of epaulettes came in later.*

▲ **SERGEANT TRUMPETER, 1ST LIFE GUARDS, 1815** *Lace for all ranks in the Life Guards was gold, instead of the usual worsted worn by the men of line regiments. The helmet design seems to have borrowed heavily from that of the Austrian cuirassiers. The 1st Life Guards were brigaded together at Waterloo with their sister regiment (the 2nd), the Royal Horse Guards and the 1st Royal Dragoons in the 1st Brigade.*

▲ **DRUMMER, 1ST FOOT GUARDS, 1815** *The white-over-red plume indicates a centre company. The 1st was an elite unit and this individual's turnout is inevitably finer than that of his line counterpart. He wears a considerable amount of lace, including the drummers' swallows' nests on the shoulder. He wears the "Belgic Cap" shako introduced in 1812 with the high, rounded front plate. The plume and cockade (black for British and Hanoverian units until 1803) is worn on the left side of the shako. Drums were brass with hoops in the facing colour.*

facings, yellow buttons and buff breeches. At the beginning of the period, the cavalry wore the usual huge bicorns and their tunics had long tails. On campaign it was common for brass chin scales to be added to the bicorns. By 1811 the tunic skirts had been shortened and the Austrian-style helmet had replaced the bicorn. There were two versions of this: the first had a "stuffed sausage" crest or "roach". But this was unpopular and replaced with a flowing black horsehair crest.

Foot Guards

In 1815 there were three regiments of Foot Guards, all in red tunics, faced dark blue, with yellow buttons and lace grouped as per their seniority numbers. The 1st Foot Guards had bastion-ended lace, the other two had pointed lace. All the lace was plain white. The grenadiers wore bearskins with brass front plates, white cords and

white plume on the left-hand side on parade, otherwise they wore the shako like the other companies. The 1st Foot Guards had square belt plates, that of the 2nd Foot Guards (Coldstreams) were oval. Each regiment wore the cap badge on the pouch lid.

THE LINE INFANTRY

Britain's line infantry were generally organized into regiments of one or two battalions, each consisting of 10 companies. One of these companies was designated as grenadiers and another was deemed a light company. These elite companies, often called flank companies from the position

▼ PIONEER, 23RD FOOT, 1792 *This pioneer is bearded and wears a bearskin and buff leather apron, a common practice among European armies at the time. He also wears below-the-knee black gaiters and white breeches; these were replaced by trousers in 1810. The 23rd was a fusilier regiment, so called because originally they had carried short muskets known as "fusils".*

they adopted "in the line of battle", were sometimes grouped on campaign to form composite battalions.

Regiments of Foot

Bicorns would give way to shakos at the very start of the nineteenth century and a short-tailed, single-breasted jacket replaced the old-fashioned long-tailed coat. Officers, however, retained the long-tailed coat. Further reforms in 1812 led to the adoption of the Belgic shako with a tall front plate. The reforms also led to grey overalls replacing white breeches and gaiters.

Traditionally, hair was worn in a pigtail but these were abolished in 1808 much to the relief of the rank and file. However the 23rd Foot, the Royal Welch Fusiliers, retained the traditional style.

All regiments of the line wore red tunics with white turnbacks. Facings were worn on collars, cuffs and shoulder straps; collars and shoulder straps were edged in white lace. The centre companies wore a white, worsted tuft at the outer end on the shoulder strap, and a white-over-red tuft on the shako. The two flank companies wore wings in the facing colour, edged and barred in white tape and often having worsted tufts all along their outer edges. The light company wore a green tuft and a small hunting horn badge. There is evidence that these elite company badges were worn on the shoulder wings and the tunic turnbacks as well.

At the beginning of the period, grenadiers wore a small, black bearskin cap, with a brass front plate bearing the royal cipher, a scroll reading: "NEC ASPERA TERRENT" ("By Difficulties Undaunted") and decorative scroll work. On the back of the headband was a white grenade with the regimental number in black. The top patch of the cap was plain red, except for the six senior regiments and the royal regiments, who had their badges

worked on them in white thread. The black cockade was worn on the left-hand side, with the white plume issuing from it. White worsted cords hung across the front. When this cap gave way to the stovepipe shako in 1802, the fur cap was reserved for ceremonial use by the Guards regiments only. The grenadier

▼ OFFICER OF GRENADIERS, 28TH FOOT, 1802 *The rather short bearskin cap was regarded as a status symbol and was worn by all line infantry grenadiers until 1802, when it was replaced by the shako. White plumes were worn. Grenadiers wore red shoulder wings decorated in white lace.*

Line Infantry Regimental Distinctions: 1792–1815 (Badges are "GR" and number unless otherwise shown)

No./Title/Date raised	Facings	Officers' Lace	Pairs or single	Lace square or bastion
1 Royal Regiment of Foot/1633 Badge: thistle and crown	dark blue	gold	pairs	square
2 Queen's Royal Foot/1661 Badge: the Lamb	sea green	silver	single	square
3 (East Kent) Foot/1665 Badge: a rose and crown	buff	silver	pairs	square
4 (King's Own) Foot/1680 Badge: the lion of England	dark blue	silver	single	bastion
5 Foot (Northumberland Fusiliers)/1674 Badge: a rose and crown; St George and the Dragon	gosling green	silver	single	bastion
6 (1st Warwickshire) Foot/1673 Badge: an antelope within the garter	yellow	silver	pairs	square
7 (Royal Fusiliers) Foot/1685 Badge: the red and white roses within the garter under the crown	dark blue	silver	single	square

▶

company now wore the shako with a plain white plume and a small grenade badge on the shako plate underneath the regimental badge or royal cipher. Non-commissioned ranks all wore pewter buttons; officers wore silver or gold buttons and lace.

Badges of rank for the non-commissioned officers (NCOs) were not defined in clothing regulations until 1822. Until that time, they were the responsibility of the colonels of the regiments, who made their own arrangements with the contractors who supplied the clothing. There was a guideline that these ranks were to be shown by a series of chevrons – point down – on the upper right arm. These chevrons were to be backed on cloth in the regimental facing colour and to be set 1/2 in (12.7mm) apart. Lance corporals wore a single chevron in the

◀ LIGHT COMPANY OFFICER, 88TH FOOT, **1802** *This light company officer wears "wings" on his shoulders and has a green plume in his top hat to distinguish him from centre company officers. The 88th Foot was an Irish regiment with a distinguished service record, the famous Connaught Rangers.*

▶ PIPER, LIGHT COMPANY 42ND FOOT, 1812 *By this time it was often the case that pipes would be decorated with small banners, usually in the regimental facing colour and bearing the unit designation.*

regimental lace; corporals two such chevrons. Sergeants and quartermaster sergeants wore three stripes in white lace, the latter with a crown above the chevrons. Company sergeant majors wore four chevrons and a crown. Sergeants and above also wore crimson waist sashes with a central stripe in the facing colour, and sergeant majors' chevrons were of gold or silver lace; they also wore gold or silver epaulettes and carried canes. Colour sergeants wore a variety of badges, some with, some without chevrons. These generally took the form of crossed swords, a union flag and laurel wreaths, all in gold, in a gold frame

Regiments with buff facings wore buff small clothes (except the 36th Foot, whose troops wore white), otherwise small clothes were white. Highland Scottish regiments wore the kilt, in various tartans. Lowland Scottish regiments wore trews (close-fitting tartan trousers).

▲ **SERGEANT, 24TH FOOT, 1798** *The 24th were known as Howard's Greens on account of their facings. This sergeant wears a double-breasted, short-tailed coat. Sergeant majors would wear officer-style coats. He has a crimson waist sash with a central stripe in the regimental colour (green) and would have carried a spontoon. Chevrons would have been added to his sleeves in 1801, generally with points down. Unusually he wears an unadorned and rather simple shako instead of the regulation bicorn.*

◀ **DRUMMER, 27TH FOOT, 1800** *This drummer wears reversed colours, in this case a buff coat with red facings. He wears the newly introduced stovepipe shako – headgear that would remain in service for the next 12 years. The regimental badge (Enniskilling castle) appeared on the front of the shako and the black cockade was held in place by a regimental button beneath the plume. This drummer boy is heavily laden with pack, blanket and brass drum.*

Those regiments that had no special badge wore the royal cipher "GR" and their number on the shako plate.

Fusiliers

In 1792 there were three regiments of fusiliers in the British Army: 7th (Royal), 21st (Royal North British) and

▼ **OFFICER, 9TH FOOT, 1800** *Reflecting some of the diversity in headgear in the British Army of the period, this officer wears the impressive Tarleton helmet with its brass chin scales and peak edging, bearskin crest and plume on the left side. The turban could have been fashioned from extremely expensive leopard skin (or cheaper cloth painted to imitate leopard skin) or, more usually, the regimental colour (yellow). The Tarleton was named after the celebrated British general of the American War of Independence. It was a favourite of light troops, being worn by both the light dragoons (although discontinued for them after 1812) and the horse artillery.*

No./Title/Date Raised	Facings	Officer's Lace	Pairs or Single	Lace square or bastion
8 Foot/The King's Regiment/1685	dark blue	silver	single	square
badge: the white horse of Hanover within the garter				
9 (East Norfolk) Foot/1685	yellow	silver	pairs	square
badge: britannia				
10 (North Lincoln) Foot/1685	yellow	silver	single	square
badge: from 1802 the sphinx				
11 (North Devon) Foot/1685	dark green	gold	pairs	bastion
12 (East Suffolk) Foot/1685	pale yellow	gold	pairs	bastion
13 (1st Somersetshire) Foot/1685	yellow	silver	pairs	bastion
badge: from 1802 the sphinx				
14 (West Yorkshire) Foot/1685	buff	silver	pairs	bastion
15 (York, East Riding) Foot/1685	yellow	silver	pairs	bastion
16 Foot/1688	yellow	silver	single	square
From 1782 Buckinghamshire Foot; from 1809 Bedfordshire				
17 (Leicester) Foot/1688	pearl grey	silver	pairs	square
18 (The Royal Irish) Foot/1688	dark blue	silver	pairs	square
badge: the rose and crown; from 1802 the sphinx				
19 (1st York North Riding) Foot/1688	dark green	silver	pairs	square
20 (East Devonshire) Foot/1688	pale yellow	silver	pairs	square
badge: from 1802 the sphinx				
21 (Royal North British Fusiliers) Foot/1678	dark blue	silver	pairs	square
badge: the thistle within the ring of St Andrew under a crown				
22 (Cheshire) Foot 1689	buff	silver	pairs	bastion
23 (Royal Welsh) Foot/1689	dark blue	silver	single	bastion
badge: the Prince of Wales' crest				
24 (2nd Warwickshire) Foot/1685	willow green	silver	pairs	square
badge: from 1802 the sphinx				
25 (Sussex)/1689	dark blue	gold	single	bastion
From 1782 to 1805 The King's Own Borderers Foot				
badge: from 1802 the sphinx				
26 (Cameronians) Foot/1689	pale yellow	silver	pairs	square

▶

23rd (Royal Welsh); this remained the position in 1815. The designation "fusiliers" related to the fact that these regiments were originally raised and equipped with "fusils" – muskets that were shorter than the usual infantry

▶ 9TH FOOT INFANTRY KIT: *1 This officer's gorget carries the royal cypher "GR" and was tied behind the collar with ribbons. Gold gorgets were worn by dismounted officers. 2 The 9th's badge was of Britannia, during the Peninsular War it was mistaken for the madonna by the local inhabitants. This led to the regiment being nicknamed the "Holy Boys". 3 An example of the regiment's lace. This was worn in pairs and had two black stripes. Officers' lace was silver. 4 Two variations of the regimental button.*

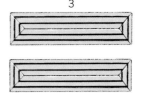

weapons. They were distinguished from other Foot regiments, in that they wore black bearskin caps, similar to those worn by grenadiers, but slightly shorter. The other distinction was that all their companies wore wings on their shoulders. Fusiliers wore the same badges of rank as did the light infantry regiments. Officers wore a grenade at the lower ends of their epaulettes, and all officers wore two epaulettes.

▼ PRIVATE, 61ST FOOT, 1795 *This soldier wears a wide-brimmed hat much favoured by all European troops serving in the West Indies, East Indies or in India. He also wears long and loose trousers rather than breeches and gaiters. The regiment's territorial designation was South Gloucestershire. Regimental titles relating to a particular region of Britain do not necessarily mean that the regiment was filled with personnel from that area, largely due to the habit of recruiting heavily from militia regiments throughout Great Britain or drafting in Irish recruits.*

From the time of the American War of Independence, the expensive bearskin cap became reserved for parade and ceremonial duties, the usual shako being worn for everyday duty and in the field. Apart from these small differences, fusiliers and light infantry wore line infantry uniforms and carried standard muskets.

Light Infantry

Light infantry regiments were formed in 1803 by converting line regiments. They could also fight as line but were

▼ PRIVATE, LIGHT COMPANY, 91ST FOOT, 1801 *In 1796 the old 98th Foot was renumbered '91', but retained their old facings and buttons. Their trews were in the "Government sett", as worn by the 42nd Foot. There is some evidence to suggest that the tartan later had a red stripe added to it.*

trained to excel in skirmishing. The 13th, 43rd, 51st, 52nd, 68th, 71st, 85th and 90th were officially designated as being light infantry, although the latter regiment only received that designation in 1815.

▼ OFFICER, 95TH FOOT, 1809 *Perhaps the most famous of all the British units of the Napoleonic period, the 95th Foot, or Rifles, were something of an elite force. Equipped with Baker rifles and dressed in green, they fought throughout the campaigns in Spain and Portugal and were then at Waterloo. The unit began as Manningham's Sharpshooters but were brought into the line to satisfy the need for light infantry. The 95th's officers dressed in something akin to a hussar's uniform, with pelisse and light cavalry sabre. The folding peak on the shako was a distinctive feature. The shako has the bugle horn badge above the regimental number. The green uniform was of such dark colour it was almost black.*

No./Title/Date raised	Facings	Officers' lace	Pairs or single	Lace square or bastion
27 (Enniskillen) Foot/1689	pale buff	silver	single	square
Badge: Enniskilling castle				
28 (North Gloucestershire) Foot/1694	bright yellow	silver	pairs	square
Badge: since 1780 the royal crest; from 1802 the sphinx, also on the back of the hat on account of the regiment having faced back to back in Egypt to repel French cavalry				
29 (Worcestershire) Foot/1694	bright yellow	silver	pairs	square
Badge: the royal crest, the lion				
30 (Cambridgeshire) Foot/1702	pale yellow	silver	single	bastion
Badge: from 1802 the sphinx				
31 (Huntingdonshire) Foot/1702	buff	silver	single	square
32 (Cornwall) Foot/1702	white	gold	pairs	square
33 (1st Yorkshire West Riding) Foot/1702	red	silver	pairs	bastion
34 (East Lancashire) Foot/1702	white	gold	pairs	square
35 (Royal Sussex) Foot/1701	orange	silver	pairs	square
Dorsetshire 1782–1805, Sussex from 1805				
36 (Herefordshire) Foot/1702	willow green	silver	pairs	square
37 (North Hampshire) Foot/1702	bright yellow	silver	pairs	square
38 (Staffordshire Volunteers) Foot/1702	yellow	silver	single	square
Badge: from 1802 the sphinx				
39 Foot/1702	willow green	silver	pairs	square
East Middlesex 1782–1807, Dorsetshire				
Badge: castle, key and motto: "MONTIS INSIGNIA CALPE" for Gibraltar 1779–83; and the sphinx				
40 (2nd Somersetshire) Foot/1717	buff	silver	pairs	square
Badge: the Prince of Wales' crest				
41 (The Welch Regiment) Foot/1719	red	gold	single	bastion
Badge: rose and thistle within the garter				
42 (Royal Highland) Foot/1739	dark blue	gold	single	bastion
Badge: thistle and crown; from 1802 the sphinx				
43 Foot/1741	white	silver	pairs	square
Monmouthshire from 1782, Monmouthshire Light Infantry from 1803				
44 (East Essex) Foot/1741	bright yellow	silver	single	square
45 (Nottinghamshire) Foot/1741	lincoln green	silver	pairs	bastion
46 (South Devonshire) Foot/1741	light yellow	silver	pairs	square
47 (Lancashire) Foot/1741	white	silver	pairs	square
48 (Northamptonshire) Foot/1741	buff	silver	pairs	square
Badge: from 1802 the sphinx				
49 (Hertfordshire) Foot/1743	dark green	silver	single	bastion
50 (West Kent) Foot/1755	black	silver	pairs	square
Badge: from 1802 the sphinx				
51 (2nd Yorkshire, West Riding) Foot/1755	olive green	silver	pairs	square
Converted to light infantry in 1809				
52 Foot/1755	buff	silver	pairs	square
Oxfordshire 1782–1803				
53 (Shropshire) Foot/1755	red	gold	pairs	square
54 (West Norfolk) Foot	popinjay green	silver	pairs	square
55 (Westmoreland) Foot	dark green	gold	pairs	square
56 (West Essex) Foot	purple	silver	pairs	square
57 (West Middlesex) Foot/1755	bright yellow	gold	pairs	square
58 (Rutlandshire) Foot	black	gold	single	square
59 (2nd Nottinghamshire) Foot	white	gold	single	bastion
60 (Royal American) Foot/1755				
Dark green dolmans, dark blue breeches, red facings, silver officer's lace, hussar-style lace; later King's Royal Rifle Corps ▶				

The light regiments never adopted the Belgic shako and all of them wore light company distinctions, namely wings and hunting horn badges. Officers of light infantry regiments wore a stringed bugle horn on their epaulettes.

Rifle Corps

In the early Revolutionary period Britain again attempted to purchase the services of German mercenaries but, as the conflict dragged on, it became more difficult. Some German riflemen were added to the 60th (Royal American) Foot and formed a fifth battalion dressed in green. This battalion was often deployed as separate companies. They wore green jackets and had

blue breeches. They wore the stovepipe shako and wore black leather equipment.

The 95th Rifles was formed from an Experimental Corps of Riflemen trained by colonels Coote Manningham and Stewart. There were three battalions in all and they were dressed in the famous rifle green jackets, green overalls, black facings, white piping and black equipment. The 95th and the 5/60th were armed with the Baker rifle.

Highland Regiments

In 1809 the Highland corps consisted of the 42nd, 78th, 79th, 92nd and 93rd regiments. In addition to the kilt these Scottish troops also wore feathered bonnets and their officers had crimson silk sashes from the left shoulder to the right hip. Tartans of the era were all derived from the

◀ OFFICER, 60TH FOOT, 1812 *The 60th were formed from loyalist Americans during the American War of Independence They later became the receptacle for the remnants of many of the old French émigré regiments in British service and for many disbanded units of German mercenaries. Like the 95th, they were uniformed in green. This officer wears his pelisse in the hussar style and has a stylish leather trim to his overalls. As the 60th carried no colours, being light infantry, they wore their battle honours (some 22 by 1815) on their cap badges.*

▶ PRIVATE, 71ST FOOT, 1812 *This regiment, later to be called the Highland Light Infantry, served in India from 1780 to 1806 (and suffered heavy casualties at the Battle of Assaye), then fought in Portugal in 1808 and took part in Sir John Moore's raid into Spain and the subsequent ordeal of the retreat to Corunna. They suffered heavy casualties at Waterloo. Note the grey overalls worn while on campaign. The stovepipe shako with tartan turban was unique to the regiment and was retained throughout the Napoleonic period. The bugle horn badge on the shako was the recognized badge of light regiments throughout Europe, here it is worn around the regimental number. The shako was still being worn at Waterloo because the light regiments did not adopt the Belgic shako in 1812.*

official Black Watch with various white, yellow or red lines added to provide a regimental distinction.

Infantry Equipment

Rifleman Costello of the 95th regiment informs us that men of his unit habitually carried 80 llbs (175 kg) of equipment. This was by no means unusual. In addition to a musket or rifle, British infantrymen would probably be required to carry a haversack, canteen, ammunition pouch (with contents), ball bag and belts. In or on his haversack he would have two spare shirts, stockings, a spare pair of shoes with extra heels and soles, a pair of trousers or breeches and a greatcoat. Then there were various brushes, a razor, a bar of soap, a box of whitener or blacking, a

No./Title/Date raised	Facings	Officers' lace	Pairs or single	Lace square or bastion
61 (South Gloucestershire) Foot	buff	silver	single	square
62 (Wiltshire) Foot/1758	buff	silver	pairs	square
63 (West Suffolk) Foot/1758	dark green	silver	pairs	square
64 (North Staffordshire) Foot/1758	black	gold	pairs	square
65 (2nd Yorkshire, North Riding) Foot/1758	white	gold	pairs	square
66 (Berkshire) Foot	dark green	silver	single	square
67 (South Hampshire) Foot	pale yellow	silver	pairs	square
68 (Durham) Foot/1782	dark green	silver	pairs	square
69 (South Lincolnshire) Foot	willow green	gold	pairs	square
70 (Surrey) Foot 1782–1812	dark blue	gold	single	square
Glasgow Lowland 1812–1825				
71 (Highland) Foot/1771	buff	silver	single	square
A regiment of light infantry they wore the stovepipe shako even after 1812				
72 (Highland) Foot/1777	light yellow	silver	single	bastion
73 Foot/1786	dark blue	silver	single	bastion
The Highland Regiment to 1809:				
74 Highland Foot	yellow	gold	single	square
75 Highland Foot	yellow	silver	pairs	square
Badge: from 1807 the Indian tiger				
76 Foot	red	silver	single	bastion
Hindoostan 1807–1812; then '79'; then The Queens Own Cameron Highlanders.				
77 (East Middlesex) Foot	yellow	silver	single	square
Badge: from 1810 the Prince of Wales' crest				
78 (Highland or Rosshire Buffs) Foot/1793	buff	silver	single	bastion
79 Foot (Cameronian Volunteers) 1793	dark blue	gold	pairs	square
The Cameron Highlanders from 1804, Badge: from 1802 the sphinx				
80 Foot	yellow	gold	pairs	square
81 Foot	buff	silver	pairs	square
82 (Prince of Wales' Volunteers) Foot	yellow	silver	pairs	bastion
83 Foot/1793	bright yellow	gold	pairs	square
84 Foot/1794	yellow	silver	pairs	square
The York and Lancaster Foot from 1809				
85 (Buckinghamshire Volunteers) Foot	yellow	silver	pairs	square
86 Foot/1793	bright yellow	silver	pairs	square
The Leinster Regiment in 1809; The Royal County Down Regiment from 1812, Badge: from 1802 the sphinx				
87 (Prince of Wales' Irish Foot)/1793	dark green	gold	pairs	square
The Prince of Wales' Own Irish Regiment from 1811,				
Badge: Prince of Wales' crest; sphinx from 1802, an Eagle of the French 8th Line from 1811 in recognition of them having				
taken an Eagle in Spain				
88 Foot/1779	bright yellow	silver	pairs	square
Disbanded 1783; re-raised 1793 as Connaught Rangers, Badge: from 1802 the sphinx				
89 Foot/1793	black	gold	pairs	square
90 (Perthshire Volunteers) Foot	dark buff	silver	pairs	square
badge: from 1802 the sphinx				
91 Foot/1779	white	silver	pairs	square
Disbanded 1783; re-raised in 1793, disbanded 1795				
From 1798 the 98th was renumbered 91st, The Argyllshire Regiment				
92 (Gordon Highlanders) Foot	yellow	silver	pairs	square
Renumbered from 100th in 1798				
93 Foot/1793	yellow	silver	pairs	bastion
Disbanded 1796; re-raised 1800, mainly from the Sutherland Fencibles				

▶

mess tin and rations. Up to three days' rations could be carried and this usually consisted of a pound of bread and a pound of meat per day. The standard musket carried by British infantry would normally have been the M1794 "India pattern" (most famously known as the "Brown Bess") or the "Land Pattern".

▼ SERGEANT, 93RD FOOT, 1815 *This regiment was another casualty of the army reductions of 1881. As befits a Highland regiment, this NCO wears trews and a sash in scarlet and the regimental colour (yellow). His fatigue cap would have been replaced by the feathered Highland bonnet on duty. Also shown is the regimental badge and a detail of the regimental lace.*

The Fencibles

Britain's sophisticated system of Militia and Fencible regiments provided Britain with a Home Guard and a source of recruits for the regulars. Militia were raised in particular counties and embodied in wartime. Most were volunteers but ballots were often drawn among the able-bodied to make up the numbers. Volunteer regiments were raised by the dozen in the great invasion scare of 1803 to 1805. They were uniformed, equipped and paid by the government. Some regiments were mounted, and termed yeomanry, and there were also some volunteer artillery for service in coastal batteries. Fencibles were regular regiments intended for home service.

▼ OFFICER, 54TH FOOT, 1815 *This is the uniform that would have been worn at the Battle of Waterloo in June 1815. The distinctive Belgic shako replaced the stovepipe in 1812 and, although it took a few years to reach all units, it was certainly in general service by 1815. Plumes remained unchanged from the traditional white over red. His shako has gold cords. The green shade of their facings led to this unit being nicknamed the "popinjays".*

◀ CORPORAL, 48TH FOOT, 1812 *Officers of the 48th wore buff breeches, but this corporal is dressed in functional grey trousers. He wears chevrons in white tape on his sleeve to indicate his rank. He has the stovepipe shako and this would soon be replaced by the Belgic shako with its raised front. The regimental cap badge was a sphinx, due to distinguished service in Egypt in 1800 and 1801 against the remanants of Napoleon's army. The regimental badge would also probably have been painted on to the front of the white haversack and on the round canteen and the canvas pack. His lace is of narrow red and black stripes.*

No./Title/Date raised	Facings	Officers' lace	Pairs or single	Lace square or bastion
94 Foot/1794	dark green	gold	pairs	square
Disbanded 1795; re-raised 1802; Badge: from 1807 the elephant				
95 Foot/1802				
This regiment wore dark green dolmans	black	silver		hussar-style
96 Foot/1793	buff	silver	pairs	square
Disbanded 1795; raised 1802: The Queen's Royal Irish Regiment				
97 Queen's German Foot	black	gold	pairs	square
Badge: from 1802 the sphinx, from 1794–1795 there was a 97th (Inverness-shire Highland) regiment, in 1798 the Minorca Regiment was raised; in 1801 this became the Queen's Germans, see the section on foreign regiments in British service for more details.				
98 Foot/1794	buff	single	single	square
Renumbered 91st in 1798; re-raised 1804; disbanded 1818				
99 Foot/1794	yellow	silver	pairs	square
Disbanded 1796; raised 1804: The Prince of Wales' Tipperary Regiment				
100 Foot/1780	yellow	silver		none
Badge: the Prince of Wales' crest; disbanded 1784; re-raised 1794 as the Gordon Highlanders; renumbered 92nd in 1798; a new regiment was raised in 1804: HRH The Prince Regent's County of Dublin Regiment				
101 (Irish) Foot/1794	white	silver	pairs	square
Disbanded in 1795; re-raised in 1806: The Duke of York's Irish Regiment				
102 Foot/1808	yellow	silver	pairs	square
103 Foot/1794 Loyal Bristol Volunteers	buff	silver	single	square
Disbanded 1796; re-raised in 1808 from the 9th Garrison Battalion				
104 Foot/1794 Royal Manchester Volunteers				
Disbanded 1795;	buff	silver	pairs	square
re-raised 1810 from the New Brunswick Fencibles				
105 Foot/1794 Leeds Volunteers, disbanded 1796				
106 (Norfolk Rangers) Foot/1794, disbanded 1795				
107 Foot/1794 then disbanded				
108 Foot/1794 then disbanded				
109 Foot /1794 then disbanded in 1795				

According to the Army List of 1815, there were also six Garrison battalions raised with dark blue facings and 13 Veteran battalions, again with dark blue facings

▼ **93RD FOOT KIT** *1 This officer's silver belt plate was worn around 1800. By 1810 the corners were clipped off and the shamrock removed. 2 The bastion-ended regimental lace; buttons were placed opposite the bastion.*

1

2

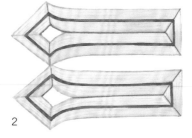

▶ **DRUMMER, 17TH FOOT, 1812** *The swallows' nests are clearly shown on this image as are the chevrons down each sleeve. Reversed colours were quite normal for musicians in all armies but the British were never quite as lavish in the uniforming of their drummers as the French were in the heyday of empire. There is comparatively little lace and the shako is very simple with almost no adornment.*

THE HEAVY LINE CAVALRY

In 1792 the cut of the uniforms of the heavy cavalry was completely conventional. Headgear was a large bicorn with black cockade, white plume with red base, hat cords and edging in the button colour. It was not until 1811–12 that the old bicorns of the heavy dragoons were replaced by black leather helmets with combs and flowing black horsehair crests, rather like those of the French cuirassiers. These helmets had brass-edged black peaks, a brass front plate bearing the

Regimental Distinctions: Line Cavalry 1768				
No./Title	Facings	Buttons	Small clothes	Hat & lace
HORSE REGIMENTS				
1 Horse	dark blue	white, pairs	white	silver
2	dark green	yellow pairs	white	gold
3	white	white pairs	white	silver
4	black	yellow pairs	buff	gold
Lapels in the facing colour. Badge: IH				
DRAGOON GUARDS				
1	dark blue	yellow, pairs	buff	gold
2 *	buff	yellow 3 & 3	buff	gold
3	white	yellow pairs	white	gold
4 Royal Irish				
Lapels in the facing colour. Badge crowned GR and garter				
*Also known as The Queen's Bays				
DRAGOONS				
1	dark blue	yellow, pairs	white	gold
2	dark blue	white, pairs	white	none
3	dark blue	yellow, threes	buff	gold
4	dark green	white pairs	white	silver
5	dark blue	white, threes	white	silver
6 Carabiniers	dark yellow	white, pairs	white	silver
7	white	white 3 & 3	white	silver
8	yellow	white, threes	white	silver
9	buff	white, pairs	buff	silver
10	dark yellow	white, 3, 4 & 5	white	silver
11	buff	white 3 & 3	buff	silver
12	black	white pairs	white	none
13	dark green	yellow 3 & 3	buff	gold
14	lemon	white, 3 & 3	white	silver
No lapels worn, except the 12th				

crowned royal cipher "GR" and a brass comb, the front of which was decorated with the head of the gorgon Medusa from Greek legend. At the bottom centre of the front plate was a small oval, bearing the regimental title. The headband was covered with brass scales, as was the chinstrap, which was held by brass rosettes.

◀ SERGEANT, 2ND DRAGOON GUARDS, 1798
The system of rank badges was complex. This sergeant's cane, a badge of office, can be seen tucked into his crimson and blue sash. Facings were now black. This regiment was known as the Bays because of the colour of their horses.

Rank Badges

In 1800 a system of rank badges for officers was introduced. Field officers wore two fringed epaulettes in the button colour; captains and lieutenants wore one. A colonel wore a crown over a star, the exact design of which varied from regiment to regiment. A lieutenant colonel wore a crown, and a major a star. Junior officers wore the epaulette on the right shoulder: a captain wore two stars, a lieutenant one, a second-lieutenant the epaulette.

Officers wore crimson silk waist sashes, senior NCOs wore crimson waist belts with two dark blue lines

▲ *Sergeant Ewart of the Scots Greys in the moment of taking the Eagle of the 45th French Line Regiment at Waterloo.*

and large chevrons in the facing colour on the upper left arm. Corporals wore one chevron, sergeants two and sergeant majors three. The senior NCOs also had silver or gold buttonhole lace and wore crimson waist sashes with a central stripe in the facing colour. They also carried canes. Trumpeters and kettle drummers generally wore reversed colours: trumpeters rode greys and drum horses were piebald.

As is usual in the British Army, tribal customs ensure that general rules on clothing were circumvented at every possible occasion. The 2nd Dragoon Guards had the following system of rank badges in 1799: sergeant major, three chevrons in the facing colour on the upper left arm, silver buttonhole laces and crimson silk waist sash with a central stripe in the facing colour, white gloves and cane; sergeants wore the gloves, sash, silver buttonhole lace, two chevrons and also carried a cane; corporals wore one chevron, no sash and plain white buttonholes.

Uniforms

According to the Royal Warrant of December 1768, the uniforms of the line cavalry regiments, which wore red coats, were as in the table opposite.

The great exception to wearing the bicorn was the 2nd (North British) Dragoons, better known to many as the Royal Scots Greys from the fact that the whole regiment rode greys, although some say it is because the regiment was dressed in grey when first raised. It was the custom in other regiments that only trumpeters rode greys. The 2nd Dragoons also wore a bearskin cap, with brass-edged peak, yellow cords and red top patch, bearing the white horse of the House of Hanover.

From 1811 onwards, the huge, and impractical, old bicorns and the stovepipe shakos of the cavalry began to be replaced with the "Roman" style, black leather helmet, with brass front plate and "turban" of brass scales. It had a comb covered in brass, surmounted by a flowing black horsehair mane. To the left-hand side was a white-over-red plume. There was a front peak edged in brass.

By 1814 the red tunics were single-breasted and hooked together. For dragoon regiments, broad braid, in the button colour and with a central dotted line in the facing colour, ran up both sides of the tunic edges and up the front of the collar. This lace also edged the cuffs and the very short turnbacks, which were in the facing colour. Dragoon regiments now had conventional pointed cuffs,

▼ Sergeant, North British Dragoons, 1815 *Later to become the Royal Scots Greys, this regiment is most famous for the Battle of Waterloo, where Sergeant Ewart took the Eagle of the 45th French Line Regiment: the Greys subsequently became known as "The Birdcatchers". This shows the man in marching order, with the foul-weather cover on his bearskin cap and with grey overalls. This tunic pattern was worn by dragoon guards and dragoons from 1812 to 1815. The brown strap was for the water bottle; the white canvas strap underneath it for the haversack. In 1794 the regiment was in Flanders and earned the battle honour "WILLEMS" for breaking a French square. The regiment did not serve in the Peninsular War, but had their day of glory on 18 June 1815, when, brigaded with the 1st and 6th Dragoons, they charged and lost 199 men, over half of them killed.*

Regimental Distinctions: Dragoon Guards 1792–1815

No./Title	Facings	Buttons & lace
1 King's	dark blue	gold
2 Queen's	black	silver
3 Prince of Wales'	white	gold
4 Royal Irish	dark blue	silver
5 Princess Caroline of Wales'	green	gold
6 Carabiniers	white	silver
7 Princess Royal's	black	gold

Regimental Distinctions: Dragoons 1792–1815

No./Title	Facings	Buttons & lace
1 Royal	dark blue	gold for officers, white for the men
2 North British	dark blue	gold
3 King's Own	dark blue	gold
4 Queen's Own	green (light blue by 1814)	silver
5 Royal Irish	blue	silver
6 Inniskilling	yellow	silver

the training of new recruits. Compared to the armies of the Continental powers, Britain could field precious few heavy cavalry. A typical regiment fielded an average of some 600 men.

The British cavalrymen had peformed very well in 1793 against the French in the Low Countries. But they had a major defect: lack of discipline. Once they had been loosed on the enemy, they could be written off: the chances of getting them under control again were negligible. They would charge at and through almost anything, then just gallop on until their mounts were blown, by which time they might be miles away from the original action and tactically useless. Their officers joined in this mad chase or failed to exert control.

while the Dragoon Guards had red front ends to their collars and the broad braid on the chest stopped at the collar. Regiments of dragoon guards were distinguished from the dragoons by having red patches to the fronts of their collars. Sashes were generally yellow with twin, narrow blue stripes, although officers wore gold and crimson. Heavy cavalry had black sabretasches. British cavalry were organized into regiments of five squadrons. Generally one of these was retained as a depot for

▶ TROOPER, 1ST DRAGOON GUARDS, 1812
This private carries the straight heavy cavalry sword as well as a carbine. This would have had a stirrup under the muzzle which held the ramrod so it would not fall out, rendering the firearm useless. The blanket has been rolled and placed before the rider to give extra protection to his legs. This image shows the classical helmet with flowing horse mane introduced in 1812. The daily rates of forage for dragoon regiments was 10 lb (4.5 kg) of oats, 12 lb (5.4 kg) of hay and 8 lb (3.6 kg) of straw: rations designed to extract speed and power.

THE LIGHT LINE CAVALRY AND HUSSARS

Austria raised a regiment of hussars in 1703, Prussia had a hussar regiment in 1721 and several others were raised in the 1740s. The Seven Years' War saw many such units in most of the Continental armies.

England was much more conservative, however, and retained only regiments of "horse", "dragoons" and "dragoon guards". There simply was no light cavalry.

In 1745, at the time of the Jacobite Rebellion, the Duke of Kingston raised – at his own expense – a regiment of "Light Dragoons", mounted on small horses and armed with light, curved sabres and carbines. It was disbanded the next year, but almost at once another such regiment was raised, incorporating many of the men of the original unit. This regiment was disbanded in 1748.

At last, in 1756, Horse Guards ordered that a troop of light horse be attached to each cavalry regiment. These new units proved so useful in the Seven Years' War that in 1763 the 15th Dragoons were converted into light dragoons, as were the 17th–20th.

By 1798 this arm had increased to some 23 regiments: the 7th–14th Dragoons had been converted, and 15 new regiments had been raised and retained in service. The 30th–33rd

Regimental Distinctions: Light Dragoons 1768			
No.	Facings	Buttons	Small Clothes
15	dark blue	white, pairs	white
16	dark blue	white, pairs	white
17	white	white, pairs	white
18	white	white, pairs	white

Light Dragoons had been raised in 1794, but with Britain's eviction from Europe in 1795, they were disbanded again early in 1796. No details of their uniforms are known, and it is very doubtful they ever reached full strength.

In 1784 these light cavalry regiments changed their red coats for dark blue and the helmet assumed the form known as the "Tarleton", with black fur crest, turban in the facing colour and the regimental badge on the left-hand side.

In 1806 the 7th, 10th and 15th Dragoons were also "converted" – or rather "re-costumed" – to light dragoons. All wore dark blue dolmans or tunics. In 1803 the 10th Light Dragoons "converted to hussars".

▶ TROOPER, 10TH LIGHT DRAGOONS, 1795

In 1784 the light dragoons adopted blue coats that were very similar to the dolmans of the hussars, together with the elegant Tarleton helmet. Light dragoons carried curved sabres and carbines with brass fittings. The horse's tail has been docked to give it uniform length, a practice some observers thought cruel and unnecessary. This regiment was the Prince of Wales's Own Royal, hence his badge on the saddle cloth and over the pistol holster.

This conversion consisted mainly of sartorial changes: they abandoned the Tarleton helmet for the winged cap (*mirliton*), adopted the fur-lined pelisse, the barrel sash and the Mongolian Bock saddle. Forty of Ezekiel Baker's new rifled carbines were also issued to them, making them the first British cavalry regiment to use rifled weapons. In general, however, the old bicorns of the light dragoons and the Tarletons of the hussars were replaced by the shako at this time.

Each regiment wore a facing colour on collar, cuffs and turnbacks. Pink seems to have been an unpopular facing colour: the 21st was given permission to change to black in 1814 and the 22nd to white in the following year.

So finally, the British Army had its colourful, flamboyant hussars – even if they still referred to them as "light dragoons". How were they to be

▼ OFFICER, 15TH LIGHT DRAGOONS, 1809
Hussar costume was officially approved for the 7th, 10th and 15th Light Dragoons in 1805, and they revelled in it. This is the uniform worn during the Peninsular War and at Sahagun on 21 December 1808. The regiment was known as the "Tabs" on account of the large number of journeymen tailors in the ranks. A tab was the small piece of cloth a tailor incorporated into clothing to identify his work. The distinctive red shako would have been worn in a black oilskin cover on campaign and, as here, the pelisse worn as a jacket rather than slung over the left shoulder. Sabretasches were generally black although evidence exists for them being in the regimental colour.

▲ LANCE-CORPORAL, OR CHOSEN MAN, 12TH DRAGOONS, 1812 *This uniform is the "home service" dress of the cavalry: on campaign, grey overalls would have covered the white breeches. The tunic is a copy of the traditional Polish* kurtka, *worn by lancer regiments on the Continent, and this regiment indeed later converted to that arm.*

employed tactically? It was left to a Captain Hinde to publish his work entitled *Discipline of the Light Horse* in 1778. Even so, throughout the Napoleonic period, British light cavalry suffered from that want of discipline alluded to by the Duke of Wellington, who commented that "I considered our cavalry so inferior to the French from want of order, that although I considered one of our squadrons a match for two French, yet I did not care to see four British opposed to four French, and still more as their numbers increased." A striking example was the 23rd's charge at Talavera in 1809. Casualties were so heavy that the Baden infantry, serving with the French, equipped their entire band of musicians with Tarleton helmets either discarded by desperate horsemen or taken from the dead.

The 1812 Uniform Changes

In 1812 the French-style shako was introduced for the light dragoons. It had a black-within-white frontal cockade, regimental loop and button, traditional white over red plume and top band and chin scales in the button colour. The tunics were also changed from a dolman to a short-skirted double-breasted tunic in dark blue with facings shown on the collar, lapels, cuffs, turnbacks and piping around the pocket.

Regimental Distinctions: Light Dragoons/Hussars 1806

No./title	Facings	Lace & buttons	Sash or belt
7 Queen's own (Hussars)	white	silver	blue and white sash
8 King's Royal Irish*	red	silver	blue and red belt
9	red	gold	blue and yellow belt
10 Prince of Wales' Own Royal	red	silver	red and yellow sash
11	buff	silver	blue and buff belt
12 Prince of Wales'	yellow	silver	blue and yellow belt
13	buff	gold	blue and buff belt
14 Duchess of York's Own	orange	silver	blue and orange belt
15 King's (Hussars)	red	silver	red and yellow sash
16 Queen's	red	silver	blue and red belt
17	white	silver	blue and white belt
18 (Hussars)*	white	silver	blue and white sash
19	yellow	gold	blue and yellow belt
20	orange	gold	blue and orange belt
21	pink	gold	blue and pink belt
22*	pink	silver	blue and pink belt
23	red**	silver	blue and red belt
24	grey	gold	blue and grey belt
25*	grey	silver	blue and grey belt
26*	purple	silver	blue and purple belt
27	white	silver	blue and white belt
28*	yellow	silver	blue and yellow belt
29	pale buff	silver	pale buff and blue belt

*These regiments wore grey dolmans
**In 1803 Charles Philip de Bosset (later to serve as a lieutenant in the King's German Legion) produced a chart of the light dragoons, showing this regiment with yellow facings

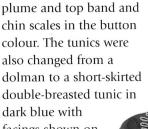

The tunic was in a completely lancer-style fashion with the coloured lapels folded back in imitation of Napoleon's Polish lancers. The men even wore a waist belt or sash with two dark blue stripes on a backing colour, and in the small of the back they had the "waterfall" of the lancers. White breeches or grey overalls were worn on campaign with twin stripes in the facing colour. Hussars wore a brown fur busby with red bag (except the 18th which had blue). Dolman, lace, facings and buttons were as before, a dark blue pelisse with a red and yellow barrel sash was worn by the men, crimson and gold for the officers.

◀ OFFICER, 12TH DRAGOONS, 1809 *The light dragoons fought most of the Peninsular War dressed in uniforms such as these. The regiment was the Prince of Wales', hence the prince's feathers on the saddlecloth.*

THE ARTILLERY AND ENGINEERS

The Royal Artillery of the period was commanded by the Board of Ordnance, as distinct from the Horse Guards, which commanded the infantry and cavalry. This rather odd arrangement reflected the specialist status of the artillery, which was then regarded rather as a tradesmen's guild.

▼ OFFICER, ROYAL HORSE ARTILLERY, 1800
The unmistakable Tarleton helmet and the hussar costume allude to the high mobility of this relatively young branch of the Royal Artillery. This officer wears his fur-lined pelisse as a hussar would: slung over the left shoulder as some protection against enemy sabre blows.

Foot Artillery
The uniform of the foot artillery consisted of a dark blue coat, faced red, with yellow buttons and lace, white breeches, black gaiters. In 1793 there were four battalions of foot artillery, increased by 1801 to seven.

Horse Artillery
This first appeared in the British Army relatively late, in January 1793, when two companies of 100 men each were formed. They had their own trained drivers and all members of the crew were mounted. The horse artillery adopted foot artillery colours but wore Tarleton helmets and dark blue dolmans with yellow buttons and lace, white breeches and short boots. By July 1794 the two companies had grown to four troops, with over 800 men and 1,000 horses. In October 1801 there were 10 such troops.

In 1801 the foot and horse artillery had over 9,000 men, excluding the drivers of the foot artillery, who belonged to the Corps of Captains-Commissary and Drivers, founded in 1794. It was not until the expedition to Holland in 1799, under General Abercromby, that an army-level "Commander of the Artillery" was then introduced.

Up until 1801 it was the custom for each regiment of light dragoons to provide an officer and 18 men to be trained to operate the "galloper guns" attached to it: an infantry regiment had to provide an officer and 34 men for their guns. The galloper guns were of 3-pound calibre; the infantry used 3-pounders and light 6-pounders.

British field artillery of the Revolutionary period was heavy, 24-pounders being used. The foot artillery was equipped with 9-pounders, which also superseded the 6-pounders. Siege artillery – of which Wellington was always short – was still of the 12- and 24-pounder class, and naval pieces were sometimes used for this work. It was clear even then that there was a trend to take the battalion and galloper guns from the regiments to form into batteries for better tactical effect. Many commanders thought the battalion guns were more trouble than they were worth, as they severely limited the mobility of the infantry and cavalry. The disadvantages of such heavy old weapons were so clearly demonstrated that they were rapidly replaced by 6- and 9-pounder cannon and 5 in (14cm) howitzers. Meanwhile, the British introduced a gun trail for cannon made of a single wooden block, thus saving much weight and allowing a tighter turning circle than the Gribeauval-type design. The British howitzer still used the double trail.

Engineers
The Corps of Royal Engineers was formed in April 1787. It was an all-officer corps and in 1792 had only 73 members. Even in 1813 there were only 262 of them. Lack of such

◄ ROYAL ARTILLERY KIT
1 Artilleryman's belts complete with powder flask, bayonet and spikes. 2 Shako badge of the Royal Artillery with royal cipher.

Sappers and Miners was founded. In 1813 it became simply The Royal Sappers and Miners. These support troops were organized into companies and commanded by officers of the Royal Engineers. The Royal Engineers wore dark blue, with black facings, gold buttons and white skirt lining. In 1811 this was changed to a red coat with "Garter blue" facings and gold buttons. The Sappers and Miners wore red, faced dark blue, yellow lace, white buttons.

▲ ROYAL ARTILLERY KIT
1 An officer's Belgic shako with gold chin scales. 2 A private's shako with yellow lace and a less elaborate plume.

▼ GUNNER, ROCKET TROOP, 1813 *In this costume, one could be forgiven for mistaking this man for a lancer: the "lance" was, in fact, a rocket-launching stick. A battery of rocket troops with 32 launchers and 151 men served with the Allies and came into action on 18 October 1813 at Paunsdorf, north-east Leipzig, where it served with credit.*

▲ SERGEANT MAJOR, FOOT ARTILLERY, 1806
This uniform was worn from 1806 to 1814, although there is some controversy as to whether the red lapels were generally adopted or whether the men just wore six yellow, bastion-ended loops to single-breasted tunics. His white gloves would not have been practical but, like the sash and whistle, were a badge of office.

experts severely hampered Wellington's sieges in Spain.

In October 1787 a corps of Military Artificers was founded. It was to be commanded by the Board, and the uniform consisted of a dark blue coat, black facings, white buttons, yellow lace, white turnbacks. In April 1812 the corps of Royal Military Artificers or

THE KING'S GERMAN LEGION AND THE BLACK BRUNSWICKERS

The most important of Britain's foreign units was the superb King's German Legion and perhaps the most infamous was the black-clad Brunswick corps.

The King's German Legion

France overran the Electorate of Hanover in 1803 and disbanded its standing army, raising the Hanoverian Legion from those willing to serve. In October 1803 many hundreds of ex-Hanoverian soldiers made their way to England, wanting to fight against France. The King's German Regiment was formed and soon expanded into a legion of eight battalions of line infantry and two of light, two heavy dragoon regiments, three light dragoon regiments, four batteries of foot artillery, two of horse artillery and a corps of engineers. The heavy dragoons converted to light in 1813 and the light dragoons into hussars at this time.

The infantry of the Legion dressed exactly as their British counterparts, with unit designations on shako and shoulder belt plates, packs, water

▼ BUGLER, KING'S GERMAN LEGION, 1812 *The uniform is completely British: regimental identity being shown on buttons, water bottles, packs, cap and belt plates. Several of the Legion's units won British battle honours, and the Hanoverian regiments, which sprang from these units in 1815, continued to wear them until 1918.*

▼ JÄGER, BRUNSWICK AVANT-GARDE, 1815 *This was the uniform worn at Waterloo. The Corsican hat was a favourite with German light troops. Note the ducal badge, a white horse, and the green band around the hat. The Brunswickers were quite young and inexperienced but fought well at Quatre Bras, where their duke was killed, and Waterloo.*

▼ SERGEANT MAJOR, KING'S GERMAN LEGION, 1812 *The legion was formed in 1803 and expanded during the wars by enlisting German exiles and prisoners of war. There were eight line battalions and particular unit distinctions were only shown on the shako plates, buttons and on badges on the officers' turnbacks.*

bottles and buttons. The line battalions of the Legion wore red coats, dark blue facings, yellow buttons, white, square-ended lace loops with a central dark blue line, in pairs. The two light battalions wore rifle green dolmans, faced black, white buttons, black lace.

By 1812 there were two regiments of light dragoons in dark blue tunics, faced red: the 1st had yellow buttons; the 2nd white. The hussar regiments would wear dark blue dolmans: the 1st faced red; the 2nd white; the 3rd yellow. The 1st and 2nd had yellow buttons and lace, the 3rd white. Sashes were red plus the button colour.

The Black Brunswickers

This corps was raised in Bohemia in 1809 by Frederick William, ex-Duke of Brunswick, dispossessed by Napoleon in 1807. It consisted of an infantry

regiment and a hussar regiment and was equipped with Austrian items. There was a regiment of three battalions of infantry and a company of riflemen (*Jägers*), plus a regiment of hussars with a squadron of lancers (*Ulans*) and a battery of horse artillery.

Infantry and artillery uniform was all black, including buttons and lace; facings were light blue. The *Jägers* wore dark green, faced red and with yellow buttons; they wore Corsican hats with the left-hand brim turned up. The hussars also wore black with light blue facings, while their sashes were yellow and light blue. The shakos of infantry, hussars and artillery bore a silver skull and bones badge. The lancers were dressed exactly as for the 1st Austrian Ulans: green uniform, faced red, brass buttons and yellow *czapka* (square-topped Polish cap) top.

The Brunswickers invaded Saxony then came to England and were taken into British service. In 1815 the reconstituted Duchy of Brunswick sent its army to join the Allies at Waterloo. It consisted of two companies of riflemen, two of light infantry, three battalions of light infantry, three of line infantry, a regiment of hussars with a squadron of lancers, a battery each of foot and horse artillery.

▼ **OFFICER, BRUNSWICK HUSSARS, 1809** *Black was the predominant colour of the Brunswickers between 1809 and 1815, often with light blue facings. The drooping plume was a distinctive badge of the Brunswickers. The hussars fought for the British in Spain.*

▼ **BRUNSWICK EQUIPMENT:** *1 A czapka of the lancer squadron from 1809. 2 The Jingling Johnnie, carried in a Brunswick regimental band. So-called Turkish music was very popular at this time. 3 A shako plate of the line battalions from 1815. 4 An artillery shako dating from 1815. 5 An infantryman's shako from the time of the formation of the corps in 1809.*

THE EAST AND WEST INDIAN REGIMENTS AND THE AFRICAN CORPS

Britain's growing empire increasingly relied upon native troops for defence and policing duties. These local units were officered by Europeans. At this time India was administered by the Honourable East India Company. The British army of India sprang from the troops organized in the three presidencies of Bengal, Bombay and Madras, which had been formed from the myriad native principalities, largely by the Honourable East India

▼ SERGEANT OF LIGHT INFANTRY, MADRAS ARMY, 1810 *This uniform is very British in tone, although some allowance for local conditions and for the Indian climate was made in terms of headgear and trousers. Badges of rank were as for the British Army. Turbans were worn by the troops of all three presidencies. The pencil moustache seems to have been universal.*

Company. They were the backbone of British rule in India. Native regiments wore short-tailed tunics, turbans and shorts (*dhoti*).

The Bengal Army

The Bengal infantry (the European Regiment and the 1st–27th Native Infantry regiments) wore red coats, yellow facings, plain, square-ended lace worn singly, white belts and small clothes. The 1st–8th Native Cavalry regiments wore dark blue dolmans, orange facings, white buttons and lace, white small clothes and belts.

The Bengal foot artillery wore dark blue coats, red facings, yellow buttons and square-ended lace, worn in pairs. They had white small clothes and belts. The Bengal horse artillery wore

Madras Cavalry Regimental Distinctions: 1792–1815

No.	Facings	Buttons and lace
1	black	yellow
2	black	yellow
3	brown	white
4	yellow	white
5	black	white
6	blue	white
7	yellow	white
8	yellow	white

Bombay Infantry Regimental Distinctions: 1792–181

No./Title	Facings	Buttons and lace
1 European	black	yellow
2 Native	black	yellow
3 Native	brown	white
4 Native	yellow	white
5 Native	black	white
6 Native	blue	white
7 Native	yellow	white
8 Native	yellow	white
Marines	dark blue	white

dark blue dolmans with red facings, yellow buttons and lace, white breeches. The engineers wore all dark blue coats with yellow buttons and lace, square-ended, worn in pairs.

The Bombay and Madras Armies

Bombay infantry had red coats, white belts and small clothes and single, square-ended buttonhole lace. Artillery wore dark blue coats faced red; the engineers had red coats faced dark blue, with yellow buttons.

The Madras Native cavalry wore red dolmans with white breeches and belts. The Madras infantry all wore red coats with white, square-ended laces, worn singly, white breeches and belts;

▼ GRENADIER SERGEANT, BENGAL ARMY, 1805 *Note the grenadiers' shoulder wings in addition to his shoulder straps. Aside from the headgear, this is a close imitation of British Army uniform. This native NCO even wears full-length trousers rather than shorts.*

Madras Infantry Regimental Distinctions: 1792–1815

No./Title	Facings	Buttons and lace
1 European	blue	yellow
2 Native	black	yellow
3 Native	red	white
4 Native	yellow	white
5 Native	black	yellow
6 Native	chestnut	white
7 Native	blue	white
8 Native	yellow	white
9 Native	black	white
10 Native	red	yellow
11 Native	chestnut	yellow
12 Native	green	white
13 Native	buff	white
14 Native	black	white
15 Native	white	white
16 Native	buff	white
17 Native	yellow	yellow
18 Native	black	white
19 Native	chestnut	white
20 Native	green	yellow
21 Native	yellow	yellow
22 Native	buff	yellow
23 Native *		
24 Native	white	yellow
25 Native	white	yellow
* Mutinied in 1806 and disbanded		

▲ NAIK, BOMBAY GRENADIER BATTALION, 1801 *The flavour of the native costume was retained by the British, as in this elaborate headgear, while they imposed their own trademarks of facings and badges of rank and company. In this year, Indian troops were employed as part of the expedition to oust the French from Egypt.*

▲ PRIVATE, WEST INDIAN REGIMENT, 1812 *Note the rounded lapels and the blue trousers. This man wears the Belgic shako only just introduced in that year. The unit's personnel was often recruited from freed or escaped slaves. Relatively immune to the devastating yellow fever, these men served well and made good soldiers.*

the facings and buttons were as shown above. The foot artillery wore dark blue coats, faced red, with yellow buttons and lace; the horse artillery wore the same colour scheme in hussar style. The engineers had dark blue coats and facings and yellow, square-ended lace and yellow buttons in pairs. Pioneers had dark blue coats faced dark blue, white buttons and no lace buttonholes.

The West Indian Regiments

These wore shakos, red coats, all with red collars, facings shown on the plain round cuffs; all lace was square-ended and worn singly, breeches were dark blue, belts were white.

The African Corps

This unit had red coats, black facings, white buttons, white lace with a red and a black line, white belts and white small clothes.

West Indian Regiments' Regimental Distinctions: 1792–1815

Regiment	Cuffs	Buttons	Lace
1st	white	white	white with outer black stripe
2nd	yellow	yellow	white with black and a yellow stripe
3rd	yellow	white	white with inner black stripe
4th	yellow	white	white with central yellow and two outer black stripes
5th	dark blue	yellow	plain white
6th	yellow	white	white with outer black stripe
7th	yellow	white	white with outer yellow and inner black stripe
8th	dark blue	white	plain white

OTHER FOREIGN REGIMENTS

The outbreak of war with Revolutionary France in February 1793 found Britain totally unprepared for the conflict. The army was run down and in a parlous condition. The usual panic measures were resorted to, which included buying the services of German mercenaries, paying subsidies to the King of Prussia and other monarchs, using the army of the Electorate of Hanover and throwing money at dubious recruiters who offered to raise bodies of men for service at great speed. Among these soldiers were many French *émigrés* who had fled to England, Spain or to south-western Germany to escape the Terror. Some of these regiments wore the old French white cockade, others the black of Britain. Some commissions were signed by the king, others by the Duke of York. The white cockade units (raised by Frenchmen) formed in 1794 mostly failed to reach their agreed establishments and were disbanded in 1795. Many regiments recruited from among French prisoners of war were confined on the prison hulks; they ended up with their ranks filled with republicans who deserted at the first opportunity or – as at Quiberon – betrayed their regiments and joined in their destruction.

◄ **PRIVATE, HUSSARS DAMAS LEGION, 1794** *Damas raised a legion of infantry, cavalry and artillery in 1793, in British pay. The hussars wore this elaborate costume. There were many republicans in the legion's ranks, as they recruited from French prisoners of war, who were willing to sign anything to get out of captivity. On 16 July 1795, 17,000 émigré troops were landed on the Quiberon peninsula under Royal Navy protection. They were opposed by General Lazare Hoche, with 13,000 men. Droves of deserters from the émigré units went over to them, betraying plans and passwords. Within four days, the royalists had suffered around 1,700 killed and wounded and some 6,300 captured.*

The following émigré regiments were destroyed at Quiberon in July 1795 or disbanded by 1797 and are not dealt with in the uniform section; Beon's Infantry, Beon's Hussars, Ulans Britanniques (Bouille's), De Castries' Regiment, Choiseul's Hussars, Damas' Legion, Henry Dillon's, Du Dresnay's, Royal Foreign Artillery (Rotalier's), Hector's Royal Marine Regiment, Hervilly's Royal Louis, Hompesch Chasseurs a Pied, Hompesch Hussars, Jerningham's, La Chatre's Loyal Emigrants, Maclean's (or French) Chasseurs, aka 'the Corsicans', Montalembert's Chasseurs Britanniques de St Domingo, Perigord's, Rohan's Hussars, Light Infantry and Horse Artillery, Royal Louis (Boisgelin's), Salm's Hussars, Salm's Light Infantry, Waldstein's, York Rangers (Ramsay's).

The ruins of the Quiberon regiments were drafted into other *émigré* regiments, most of whom were promptly shipped off to the West Indies to die of yellow fever. The few survivors were all drafted into various battalions of the 60th Regiment or the York Rangers in 1798.

Six of these regiments survived the Peace of Amiens and continued in British service until 1815: Chasseurs Britanniques, Dillon's, Stuart's Minorquins, de Meuron's Swiss, de Roll's Swiss and de Watteville's Swiss.

Uniforms

The *émigré* regiments chose costumes for themselves, which covered the entire palette of military fashion, many based on the uniforms of Austria and the Swabian German contingents. We can give only brief details here, since few of these exotic units survived the Napoleonic Wars and details on their organization and uniform are sparse and patchy. Personnel was recruited wherever and whenever possible and officers were frequently either very young, very poor or very incompetent.

▲ PRIVATE, HOMPESCH FUSILIERS, 1796 *This was one of the more permanent foreign regiments, fighting in Egypt in 1801; they were disbanded in 1802. The uniform is Germanic in style, especially the shako, which reflects the uniforms of Wurttemberg.*

The following list contains only those regiments which were actually accepted into British service.

CHASSEURS BRITANNIQUES. Raised in May 1801, this regiment was in action in 1807 at Alexandria and was involved in the fighting at Naples in 1809. In the Peninsula War it fought at Fuentes d'Oñoro, La Hermandad, Vitoria and Sorauren. Disbanded in August 1814. Personnel included Frenchmen, Italians, Swiss, Poles and a few Russians. The regiment initially seems to have worn green coats but then adopted British light infantry uniform.

CORSICAN RANGERS. Raised in 1799 on Minorca, they fought in the Egyptian campaign of 1801, suffered heavy casualties and were disbanded in Malta in July 1802. In September 1803 a new regiment was raised and took part in the fighting on Capri. The uniform consisted of a green coat with red facings and breeches.

EDWARD DILLON'S. This regiment was raised in 1795 in northern Italy. It went to Egypt in 1801 and fought at Alexandria on 21 March. In 1812 the regiment took part in the raids on the eastern coast of Spain. The regiment was disbanded in December 1814. The uniform consisted of a red coat with buff facings, white buttons, white, bastion-ended lace with a royal blue line, worn singly. The small clothes were white.

HOMPESCH FUSILIERS (or Light Infantry). Raised in March 1796, this unit was sent to the West Indies in December 1796. On 1 May 1798 the survivors were absorbed into the 2nd and 5th Battalions of the 60th Foot.

HOMPESCH CHASSEURS À CHEVAL. Raised in July 1796, this unit fought at Lake Mareotis on 13 March 1801 with Finch's cavalry brigade. It was disbanded in Ireland on 28 September 1802. The uniform consisted of a black shako with red turban, dark green coat faced red and red (or light blue) breeches.

LÖWENSTEIN'S CHASSEURS. Raised in April 1795, the regiment was sent to the West Indies in 1796 and disbanded in December 1797. The men were then transferred into the 5th Battalion, 60th Regiment. The uniform consisted of a Corsican hat with the left-hand brim turned up, a blue coat and breeches with green facings and half lapels.

LÖWENSTEIN'S FUSILIERS. The regiment was raised in August 1795, and the following year joined Abercromby's expedition to Martinique, Puerto Rico and Barbados. The unit was disbanded in December 1797, the men transferring into the 5th Battalion, 60th Foot. The uniform consisted of a Corsican hat, left brim turned up, white cockade, loop and plume, yellow button. They wore a short, light blue

(some sources say red) coat and breeches, green half lapels, collar, shoulder straps, round cuffs and turnbacks, yellow buttons, black gaiters and belts.

LÖWENSTEIN'S JÄGERS or Light Infantry. Raised in January 1800, the *Jägers* fought at Alexandria in General Moore's Reserve. They were disbanded in April 1802; the men went into the 5th Battalion, 60th Foot. The uniform consisted of a Corsican hat and a blue coat with green facings.

▼ PRIVATE, CORSICAN RANGERS, 1799 *This unit, sometimes called the Royal Corsican Rangers, was raised in 1799. Detail on the uniform conflicts. The coat is sometimes shown as a dolman and the breeches are variously given as red, white or blue. Such confusion surrounds the foreign corps raised at a time when Britain's military budget was stretched. Hudson Lowe, Napoleon's jailer on St Helena, was colonel of the unit for a while.*

DE MEURON'S. This Swiss regiment was in Dutch service on the Cape of Good Hope in October 1795, when that colony was captured by the British. The unit was taken into British service and sent to the Madras Presidency, where it was disbanded in July 1816. The uniform consisted of a brimmed round hat with black crest, white-over-red plume; red coat, royal blue facings, white buttons, white bastion-ended lace with a red line, spaced singly. They wore white small clothes and belts, black gaiters.

MINORCA REGIMENT (Stuart's or 'the Queen's Germans'). Raised in

▼ PRIVATE, WURTTEMBERG CAPE REGIMENT, 1795 *This regiment was raised and recruited in Swabia, south-western Germany, and served in South Africa. It was uniformed and equipped in a German manner and evidently no adjustment was made for the local climate or conditions. These troops also fought for the British in the East Indies.*

▲ OFFICER, LEGION DE MIRABEAU, 1795 *Another unit with a brief lifespan, this regiment was lavishly equipped in black coats and elaborate headgear. Although officers were often royalist many of the men were drafted prisoners or foreigners and this, generally, led to very poor performance or a natural reluctance to place the unit in the front lines.*

November 1798 on the island, following its capture by the British. In 1801 the title changed to Queen's Germans and in 1805 the unit became the 97th Foot (see the British infantry section for uniform details).
MORTEMARTE'S. Raised in 1794 and disbanded on 24 August 1802. The uniform was a bicorn with yellow edging, loop and button, white plume and cockade. They wore a red coat with

▼ PRIVATE, DE MEURON'S, 1800
De Meuron's regiment was in the service of the Dutch East India Company on the Cape of Good Hope when the British landed there in 1795. The regiment took British service and were sent to the Madras Presidency, where they were disbanded in 1816. This illustration shows a private in the original Dutch uniform. In the military museum in Geneva is a set of 15 watercolours of the "Regiment de Meuron Hollandais 1781" and another of the same regiment in British service from 1795 to 1805. The latter shows this uniform. Officers wore gorgets bearing the cipher "VOC" for United East Indian Company and a silver silk sash over the left shoulder. The helmet plate bore "VOC" over a shield with three chevrons on the central, vertical strip. An officer is shown in "gala" uniform. It was a single-breasted royal blue coat, faced red, with silver buttons and lace decoration down the front. The waistcoat and breeches were red, the former with silver lace trim. He wore white silk stockings and silver shoe buckles.

black facings, yellow buttons, white small clothes and belts, black gaiters.
DE ROLL'S. Raised in December 1794 in Swabia, south-west Germany. In 1801 the regiment was shipped briefly to Egypt. In 1807 the unit went back to Egypt and fought at Alexandria and Rosetta in a brief and unsuccessful campaign against the Turks. The regiment was disbanded in 1816. The uniform consisted of a red coat with royal blue facings, white buttons, white buttonhole lace with a royal blue line, in pairs, with white tassels. They wore white small clothes and belts. Fortescue states that De Roll's was amalgamated with Dillon's, but this is untrue.

DE WATTEVILLE'S. Raised in spring 1801, this unit fought at the Battle of Maida on 4 July 1806 in Oswald's brigade. Like many foreign regiments, the unit was disbanded in 1816. The uniform was a conical British shako, red coat, black facings, white buttons, white, bastion-ended lace with a black line, in pairs on the chest. Small clothes and belts were white.

ROYAL YORK FUSILIERS (Hardy's). The uniform was a small black cap with transverse crest and crescent badge as for the Perigord regiment, but with dark green plume to right-hand side. The green coat and breeches had yellow buttons, red collar, cuffs, shoulder straps, waistcoat and turnbacks. Their distinction was a red and yellow striped lace edging to facings. Over each cuff were three yellow and red tape chevrons, points down. The short black gaiters had yellow and red lace top trim. Black belts were worn.

YORK HUSSARS (Irwine's). Raised in May 1794, the regiment left for the West Indies on 28 February 1796. The unit was disbanded at Weymouth on 24 July 1802. The uniform consisted of a peakless dark green shako with white cords and plume and a white and green cockade. The red dolman and breeches had white buttons and lace and dark green facings. The dark green pelisse was edged in grey fur. White belts were worn.

YORK RANGERS (Ramsay's) This regiment

was raised in Germany in July 1793. In January 1796 it sailed from the Elbe for the West Indies. The unit was disbanded in August 1797, the men transferring into the 3rd Battalion, 60th Foot. The uniform consisted of a hat with an eight-pointed white star over a white scroll. Light royal blue coat and breeches with white facings, white buttons and waistcoat. At the shoulders were swallows' nests in the coat colour, edged and trimmed in yellow. They wore short black gaiters and black belts.

Other foreign regiments in British service during the period included the Dutch Artillery, the Curacao Detachment, the Dutch Emigrant Brigade, the Royal Dutch Battalion (Coehorn's) and the Loyal Orange Battalion (van Well's).

▼ **TROOPER, YORK HUSSARS, 1795** *This trooper wears the fashionable mirliton but the unit could have worn a shako. The regiment was raised in May 1794 and contained many ex-French cavalrymen, though the regimental staff and all captains were British. The York Hussars embarked for the West Indies on 28 February 1796. During their stay in this inhospitable theatre of war they took part in the capture of St Lucia in 1796 and in the savage wars of extermination against the Maroons and the Caribs among the islands. They absorbed the remnants of Rohan's Hussars and the Hompesch Hussars. After hard service, the York hussars were disbanded at Weymouth on 24 July 1802. A regiment of York Rangers was also in British pay. They mostly fought in the West Indies.*

THE AUSTRIAN EMPIRE

By 1792 Austria was the centre of a sprawling empire consisting of the dynastic possessions of the Habsburg family, which had ruled in Vienna since 1278. Furthermore, the Habsburgs were the traditional sovereigns of the Holy Roman Empire, thus giving them hegemony over the tangle of tiny states that made up much of Germany and Italy at that time. Little surprise, then, that Austria should oppose French attempts at Continental domination, and the two powers went to war on no less than six occasions between 1792 and 1815. Despite being repeatedly defeated by France in 1794–98, Austria, together with Russia, swept the French out of northern Italy in 1799, leading to the downfall of the Directory and to Napoleon's seizure of power in the November of that year. The year 1800 saw another Austrian defeat, as did 1805 and 1809. In 1812 Austria provided Napoleon with a corps that acted as his southern flank guard in Russia. In 1813 they were finally rewarded for their tenacity, when they took part in his defeat at Leipzig.

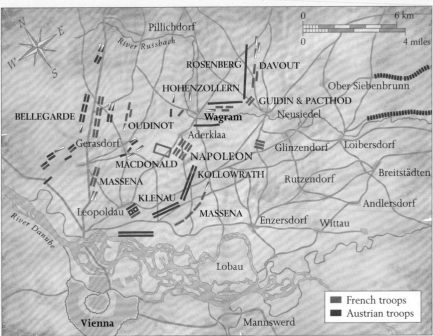

▲ *The Battle of Wagram saw the Austrians perform with much credit. Archduke Charles demonstrated many of the talents that made him Austria's foremost general.*

◄ *At the Battle of Hanau, 30–31 October 1813, Napoleon exploited an Austro-Bavarian force's poor tactics, burst through their blockade and continued his retreat to France.*

AUSTRIA'S EMPIRE

Like all other European states of this era, Austria was an absolutist monarchy with a feudal, largely agrarian, society. The emperor governed with the aid of several substantial institutions: the civil service, the Roman Catholic Church, police forces and the army. But this did not mean all of life within the imperial borders was ruled with a rod of iron from Vienna. With its multicultural, multilingual character, the Austrian Empire was – like the widespread British Empire that followed – almost a club. In the kingdom of Hungary, in particular, the emperors of Austria had learned to wear kid gloves if they wished to obtain co-operation from their independent-minded subjects. Government of this rather ramshackle political edifice was exercised from Vienna by an oligarchy: a system not usually guaranteed to produce dramatic decisions. Indeed, during the period 1792–1815 the Austrian court was frequently split into pro-French and anti-French factions. This latter faction gained a temporary ascendancy in 1810, when, for dynastic reasons, Kaiser Franz consented to Napoleon's request for his daughter's hand in marriage. The Archduchess Marie

Louise duly married Napoleon by proxy in Vienna before travelling to Paris, where she presented Napoleon with a son on 20 March 1811.

Austrian Rule

In 1792 the Austrian Empire sprawled across Europe, encompassing many nations and tongues. To the north of Vienna lay the Austrian provinces of Bohemia and Moravia (now the Czech and Slovak republics), and beyond them, Prussia, Poland and Russia. The Kingdom of Prussia was an old enemy who had ripped the rich Polish province of Silesia from Vienna in the War of the Austrian Succession and the Seven Years' War. Russia, too, was a competitor for the ownership of Polish territory, and by 1799 had – along with Austria and Prussia – carved up this ancient kingdom. Austria's share was the southern province of Galicia, in which was the old Polish capital city of Krakow.

To the east of Vienna lay one of the oldest components of the empire, the Kingdom of Hungary, which came voluntarily into Austrian possession in 1527 through the decision of the parliament (*Reichstag*) of Pressburg (present-day Bratislava).

▲ *Emperor Franz II. When the Holy Roman Empire was abolished, Franz was forced to change his title to Franz I of Austria.*

To the south, Austrian influence extended into the Balkans as far as Dalmatia, where it abutted the decaying Ottoman Empire, with which wars flared up now and again. In fact, the areas along the border with the Ottoman Empire formed a special territory, in which border (*Grenze*) regiments were recruited and stationed. These territorial defence regiments were kept in a state of high alert, constantly repelling Turkish border raids. In 1683, 140,000 Turks, under Kara Mustapha Pasha, had laid siege to Vienna. A force drawn from various European nations, led by the Polish King Jan Sobieski, defeated the

◄ *This is a rare Austrian view of the early part of the action at the bridge of Lodi, northern Italy, 10 May 1796, which ended in a French victory.*

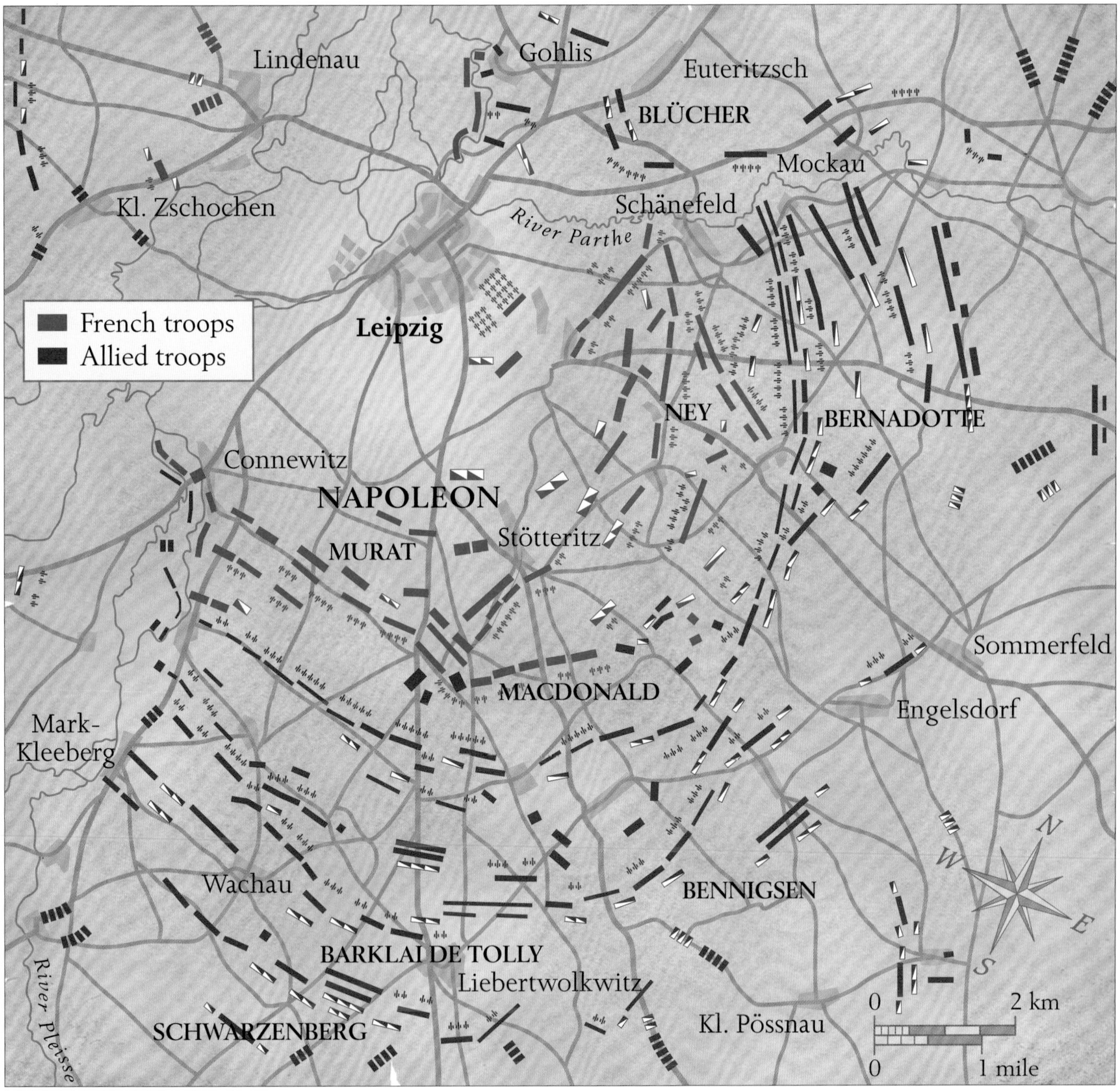

Lindenau

Gohlis

Euteritzsch

BLÜCHER

Mockau

Kl. Zschochen

Schänefeld

River Parthe

■ French troops
■ Allied troops

Leipzig

NEY

BERNADOTTE

Connewitz

NAPOLEON

MURAT

Stötteritz

Sommerfeld

Engelsdorf

MACDONALD

Mark-
Kleeberg

Wachau

BENNIGSEN

River Pleisse

BARKLAI DE TOLLY

Liebertwolkwitz

Kl. Pössnau

0   2 km

SCHWARZENBERG

0   1 mile

▲ *The Battle of Leipzig saw Napoleon badly defeated by the Allies over three days. He lost 75,000 men, 325 guns, 900 wagons and 28 eagles, colours and standards. Austria played a key role in the fighting to the south of the city.*

Ottomans at the Battle of Kahlenberg and Turkish influence in the region began to ebb away. But the frontier with the Ottomans was still dangerous and needed guarding. To the west, large tracts of northern Italy, including Venice from 1797, were under rule from Vienna until Napoleon's victory at Marengo in 1800 established French hegemony in the region.

Meanwhile, to the north-west of Vienna (where the present-day Federal German Republic lies) lay an amorphous mass of princely and ducal states, imperial free cities and bishoprics, squeezed between Austria and Prussia, Saxony and Hanover, which formed the Holy Roman Empire of the German Nation. Traditionally, Austria had provided almost all the emperors of this political anachronism. Thus, in 1792 Franz, of the Austrian House of Habsburg, was Emperor Franz II of the Holy Roman Empire. But following Napoleon's crushing victory over the Austrians and their

Russian allies at Austerlitz in 1805, the balance of power in Germany shifted in favour of France, and the Holy Roman Empire was replaced by the pro-French Confederation of the Rhine. Franz, therefore, was obliged to renounce his former title, becoming simply Franz I of Austria.

Even further away to the north-west, on the North Sea coast, separate from the rest of the empire, lay the Austrian Netherlands, present-day Belgium. The effort required to defend this province in the early Revolutionary Wars would prove to be too much for Austria, and in 1795 it fell to France.

THE AUSTRIAN ARMY

The Aulic Council (*Hofkriegsrat*) was the Austrian War Cabinet, responsible for managing the armed forces and the planning and conduct of campaigns. The council contained both military and civilian members, and like the rest of the Austrian government of this period, was a strictly conservative, hidebound beaurocracy. Indeed, the council was in no way fitted for the job of combating the military might and genius of Napoleon Bonaparte. Local field commanders were strictly subject to decisions made by the council and had very limited leeway for initiative. Once Napoleon emerged on to the European stage, having combined the roles of army commander- in-chief and head of state, any local commander opposing him – given the painfully slow communications of the day – was at a serious disadvantage. Meanwhile, fudged political compromises in the Aulic Council often condemned their unfortunate distant field commanders to humiliating catastrophy.

Senior Army Commanders

While most Austrian officers were traditionally drawn from the aristocracy, it was possible for commoners to flourish in the system. Anton Freiherr Zach entered the engineers in 1765 and worked his way up to being Melas' chief of staff in 1800 at the Battle of Marengo. In 1801, Zach was ennobled for his gallantry. He died in 1826 as a *Feldzeugmeister*, a technical field marshal.

Command of an army in a theatre of war was often given to an archduke, a sibling of the emperor. Where it was felt such an imperial appointee lacked the experience and training to wield this command in reality, a tried and successful general would be appointed to oversee operations as his loyal assistant (*adlatus*).

The most successful Austrian field commander of the Revolutionary and Napoleonic Wars was Archduke Charles. Born in 1771, he was the emperor's younger brother and had been adopted by the Duke of Saxe-Teschen, under whom he was trained to be a commander from an early age. He commanded a brigade at the Battle of Jemappes on 6 November 1792 and was distinguished at the Battle of Neerwinden on 18 March 1793. In 1796 he commanded the Army of the Rhine in southern Germany, winning a series of victories over General Moreau, one of France's ablest commanders of the period and a serious rival to Napoleon. In 1799, Charles was employed in Italy, but difficulties with the Russians led to his retirement. In 1805 he commanded in Italy again, but events at the capitulation of Ulm, in October, overshadowed him. In 1809 he commanded in Germany, inflicting a stinging defeat on Napoleon at Aspern-Essling on 20–21 May. His subsequent defeat at Wagram (5–6 July) was due, in large part, to the late arrival of his younger brother, Archduke John. Following this defeat, Charles retired from military life.

Archdukes John and Ferdinand also exercised military command but were mediocre. John – apart from arriving late at Wagram in 1809 – was also defeated by Eugène de Beauharnais at the Battle of Raab on 14 June in the same campaign. But perhaps more famously, John had been beaten by Moreau at the critical Battle of Hohenlinden, nine years earlier, in December 1800. His brother Ferdinand's performance in Bohemia, during the campaign of 1809, was lacklustre and ineffective.

Other, more successful Austrian commanders of the era, however, included generals Alvintzy (who defeated Napoleon at Bassano on 6 November 1796), Bellegarde, Colloredo-Mansfeld, Crenneville, Frimont, Albert Gyulai, Hardegg-Glatz, Friedrich Hessen-Homburg, Ludwig Hohenlohe, Hohenzollern-Hechingen,

▲ *Archduke Charles, Austrian commander, army reformer and military tactician.*

Kienmayer, Klenau, Kray, Alois Liechtenstein, Meerveldt, Melas, Nostitz, Radetzky, Saxe-Coburg, Schwarzenberg and Wurmser.

The Austrian General Staff

Any senior commander (or manager) needs a team of trusted helpers to enable him to be successful. The military term for these helpers is the French aide-de-camp, or ADC. By 1792 these ADCs formed the nucleus of the general staff of any army, corps or division. Commanders usually hand-picked their ADCs – young, competent, trusted officers, often members of their own families – and took them with them when they changed commands. This custom had been first formalized in the Austrian Army in 1757. From 1805 the staff was commanded by the chief of staff (usually a major general or colonel), a close confidante of the commander, responsible for all aspects of staff-work, as well as intelligence and cartographic matters.

On 4 April 1809 Archduke John formalized the structure and duties of his headquarters staff in an Army Order. John's system envisaged three sections working together: first, his own chancery and the Detail Chancery managed by Adjutant-General Count Morzin; second, the Operations Chancery under the Quartermaster General Colonel Count Nugent; third, the Army Headquarters under *Feldmarschalleutnant* Baron Gorup.

John's chancery handled all reports and communications with the Aulic Council, Archduke Charles (the Generalissimo) and provincial governments. It also formulated and distributed proclamations, accounted for the use of secret funds, censored outgoing correspondence and distributed all incoming mail. The Technical Engineering Corps also reported directly to Archduke John. Meanwhile, the Detail Chancery drafted duty rosters, muster rolls, army orders and correspondence, and was responsible for the the war diary. All incoming situation reports were sent from here to Archduke John.

Quartermaster General Colonel Count Nugent's Operations Chancery handled all things relating to the tactical operations of an army: marching orders, orders of battle, orders for assaults and defence. It also questioned prisoners and deserters and prepared all reports relating to

operations, as well as maintaining their own war diary. It was responsible for the upkeep of operational maps and military files, and for the management of the engineers, *pontonniers* and *Tschaikisten* (boatmen on the Danube and other waterways). Finally, it took care of the domestic management of the whole headquarters.

Feldmarschalleutnant Baron Gorup's Army Headquarters was responsible for transport (such as horse teams and pack animals), the commissary (rations, clothing and exchange, deliveries and payments), field hospitals, the cashier, and legal affairs.

This new organization was formulated at Graz on 4 April 1809 and it is of interest that John (commander of the Austrian Army in Italy) chose this date to redefine the duties of the most important organ of his army. One week after this instruction was given, the Austrians had pushed into French-held territory and clashed with Prince Eugène's Army of Italy at Venzone. That same day, at Hirschau in the Danube valley, the main Austrian army, commanded by John's brother, Archduke Charles, clashed with Napoleon's Grand Army. The war was on, and at a fast and furious pace: scarcely the environment

in which to try out experiments. It seems that this system was a success despite such testing conditions, and survived the unfortunate Danube campaign of 1809: the organization of the Austrian general staff of the Army of Bohemia at Leipzig in 1813 looks remarkably similar to John's model.

Tactics

In the eighteenth and nineteenth centuries, armies used the smoothbore musket as the main infantry weapon and had adopted the linear formation for infantry in battle, in order to achieve maximum fire-power from the available muskets. Columns were used for rapid movement and squares were infantry's defensive measure against cavalry attack, but were very vulnerable to artillery fire.

Austria's light cavalry (hussars, lancers, mounted rifles) were used to scout, screen and patrol, although increasingly, they took part in charges in set-piece battles. Heavy cavalry were used for shock action on the battlefield: ideally, they would catch the exposed ends of a line of infantry and roll it up with devastating effect.

▼ *A wide variety of Austrian infantry and artillery officers can be seen here.*

THE AUSTRIAN ARMY'S RECORD

In all the wars against France, there was an international coalition, usually supported financially by Britain. In all such cases, the Allies were mutually suspicious of one another and operated on external lines of communication, and their individual actions were often counter-productive.

The Revolutionary Wars broke out in April 1792, when the French attacked the Austrians and their allies in the Austrian Netherlands – and were promptly repulsed. Tactical victories alone were, however, not enough to withstand the energy and weight of these massive French armies. The extremely long Austrian and Prussian lines of supply and communication also worked against them. Despite Allied victories at Orchies, on 15 July and Longwy, on 23 August, no decision was achieved, and the stand-off at Verdun in September resulted in the Allied withdrawal and the fall of Mainz and Frankfurt.

In 1792–95 the land war was fought out in the Netherlands and along the Rhine. The Austrian armies fought well, despite some extreme supply and

reinforcement problems, which aggravated the sickness figures. It was in 1794 that Prussia left the coalition to concentrate on securing its part of Poland. Austrian will to retain a hold on the Netherlands was broken, and France overran Belgium, Holland and Luxembourg.

Campaigns in Italy

In 1796, with no threat from the north, France's aggressive government

▲ Austria's Field Marshal Count Wurmser yielded the fortress of Mantua to General d'Allemagne on 2 February 1797.

transferred its attentions to the south, against Austria. While General Moreau struggled haplessly in Germany against Archduke Charles, northern Italy became the major theatre of the war, heralding Napoleon's debut as a stunningly successful army commander there. The local Austrian commander, the 71-year-old General Baron Johann Beaulieu, was no match for the young whirlwind of twenty-seven. By June the battered Austrian field army was shut up in the fortress of Mantua. After four hasty, careless attempts to relieve the place, it was forced to capitulate on 2 February 1797. Austria sued for peace at Leoben. Another anti-French coalition had collapsed. The fault for the disaster in northern Italy lay with the Aulic Council, which decided to concentrate its efforts on relieving Mantua, rather than on destroying Napolen's army, which would automatically have achieved their

◀ At the Battle of Hohenlinden, 3 December 1800, General Moreau's French Army of the Rhine comprehensively defeated a combined Austro-Bavarian force commanded by Archduke John of Austria.

desired aim. Thus, Austria's successes in Germany were negated by the disaster in Italy.

Austria's next campaign took place in 1799, in Germany and northern Italy. Archduke Charles fought successfully in Germany against General Jourdan, while General von Kray led the offensive against the French General Scherer. The Austrians in Italy were joined by a Russian army under Field Marshal Count Alexander Suvorov, and together they swept the French westwards, back to their border.

The victorious Allies then quarrelled: Suvorov was sent north into Switzerland, where, after losing much of his train and baggage in the mountains, he had to flee to the north-east to save his men. On 25 September Masséna defeated a second Russian force at the Battle of Zürich and cleared the Allies out of Switzerland. Once again, high-level Austrian political blunders had ruined the achievements of their army in the field.

Bonaparte returned from his failed Egyptian adventure in late 1799, came to power as First Consul by the coup of *Brumaire* and launched himself into the famous Marengo campaign in 1800. Suffice it to say that generals Desaix and Kellerman saved the day for him after he had thrown that battle away. Italy was lost: the Holy Roman Empire would follow later.

Wars against Imperial France

Despite these setbacks, Austria mounted the invasion of Bavaria in 1805 – against the advice of Archduke Charles – with an army under General Karl Freiherr Mack. This commander's stunning incompetence led to the capitulation of Ulm, on 15 October, and the loss of that army. There followed the disaster of Austerlitz on 2 December, where Russia and Austria were soundly beaten by Napoleon, Emperor of the French. By the Treaty of Pressburg, Austria lost the Tyrol, Salzburg, Venice and other provinces.

At last, in 1808, Archduke Charles was able to abolish the life-long service liability for the army, increase the number of young recruits, pension off the old soldiers and older officers and thus reduce the average age of the army dramatically. The old soldiers now formed the cadres for the new militias.

This became law on 12 February 1808, and on 9 June 1808 the *Landwehr-Patent* was also passed, whereby all fit adult males between the ages of 18 and 45 were required to take up arms in defence of their homelands. But the parlous condition of Austria's finances hampered these efforts and progress was agonisingly slow. When, in 1809, Austria opened the war with France again (Archduke Charles had warned against it but was overruled) the *Landwehr* proved to be poorly trained and equipped, and had minimal combat value.

Archduke Charles's victory over Napoleon at Aspern-Essling on 20–21 May was cancelled out by his defeat at Wagram. Austria had gambled in vain on a general uprising against Napoleon in Germany. Meanwhile, the Treaty of Vienna, of 14 October, saw Austria lose Trieste, Istria, Croatia and Galicia. In 1812 Austria was forced to provide a corps to support Napoleon's invasion of Russia. It was commanded by Prince Schwarzenberg and fought with success and distinction in the Pripet Marshes in the Ukraine, together with the Saxon VII Corps. It suffered relatively light losses in the 1812 disaster and was able to play a major role in the fateful campaign in the following year.

▲ *The capitulation of Ulm, 15 October 1805, was a blow to Austria and a demonstration of General Mack's incompetence.*

In 1813 Vienna was initially neutral, but joined the Allies during the armistice of the summer months and made a major contribution to the resounding Allied success at Leipzig on 19 October, which broke Napoleon's hold on Germany. The Allies fielded three armies; co-ordinating these forces was Prince Schwarzenberg's great achievement. Napoleon was forced to flee back into France.

In 1814 Napoleon worked miracles to rebuild his army and fend off the invaders. The Allies forged relentlessly on and the dynamic struggle in Champagne swung back and forth. The Austrian armies performed well in difficult conditions, being severely tested by Napoleon's strategic mastery. Despite this, they pushed on and the Allies captured Paris on 30 March. This event led directly to Napoleon's first abdication. On 8 February 1814 an Austrian army had crossed the River Mincio and pushed into Italy; by 13 April they had forced their Franco-Italian foes to lay down their arms.

At Napoleon's return to France from exile in Elba, in the spring of 1815, Austria again fielded two armies to fight against him. The years of combat experience had honed the Austrian army and forged it into a fine weapon.

THE *LANDWEHR* IN 1809

The name *Landwehr* means territorial defence force, and initially these militia were intended for service within the borders of the Austrian Empire only. The most militantly patriotic Austrian province was the Tyrol, where a large percentage of the adult males were authorized to carry rifles. Each group of villages would form a shooting club (*Schützenverein*). The shooting clubs of the Tyrol were tailor-made to be used in defence of their homelands: they knew every cave and mountain path and were already in a hierarchical, quasi-military structure.

In 1796, 1797, 1800, 1802 and 1804 the governor of the Tyrol mobilized these shooting clubs for defence of the province against French invasion. In 1805 these companies were available but it was only in 1808 that they were rationalized by Archduke Charles's army reforms.

▼ *The Battle of Aspern Essling in May 1809 was an Austrian victory, buying time to complete preparations for war.*

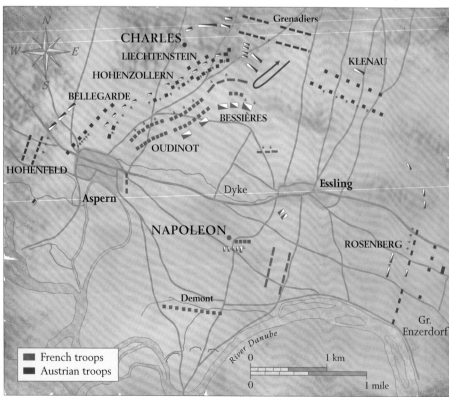

▲ *Andreas Hofer, the Tirolese patriot, centre, with some of his compatriots. Hofer led a revolt against the French and Bavarians. His men wore local, traditional costume.*

These saw a mobilization that occurred in three phases:
• The *Landesschützen* companies: formed from the shooting clubs.
• The volunteer *Scharfschützen* companies: made up of all other adult males, not in the *Landesschützen*, who were trained in marksmanship.
• The *Landsturm* or Home Guard: men, from 18 to 50, excluded or exempted from the other categories.

Theoretically, dress and equipment for the *Landesschützen* were to be as for the *Jägers* of the line: although, most just wore national costume (*Landestracht*), but when on campaign, each man wore a green and white armband. However, local councils could buy uniforms, weapons, and ammunition for the volunteers if they so decided. A structure as mature as that of the Tyrol did not exist in other Austrian provinces, where the ownership of firearms by the general public was frowned upon by the government.

In 1796 the city council of Vienna had proposed arming the general populace, but only a few companies were raised that year, and again in 1797 and 1800. Also in 1796, a militia (*Landesmiliz*) had been raised in Bohemia. In December 1800 this example was followed by the provinces of Goriza, Krain,

Lower Austria, Upper Austria, Salzburg, Steyermark and the city of Vienna. Apart from registering lists of volunteers, nothing came to fruition.

The 1809 Campaign

In 1808, Archduke Ferdinand and Count von Wallis raised 16 battalions of *Landwehr* in Bohemia and ten more in Moravia and Silesia. Archduke John was in charge of Carinthia, Krain and Steyermark; ten battalions were raised there. Count Wurmser raised 26 more in Galicia, Count Bissingen raised eight battalions in Lower and Upper Austria. In Hungary 28 battalions of infantry and ten regiments of hussars were raised by Archduke Joseph in the *Insurrektion*, as the *Landwehr* was known there. On paper the Austrians were richer by 98 battalions of infantry and ten regiments of cavalry.

The *Landwehr* consisted only of infantry and cavalry units: there was no artillery. The thought was that *Landwehr* units would be integrated into regular formations. But money was short, and time even shorter. Napoleon unleashed his imperial thunderbolts against Austria before these militia regiments were fully trained, clothed and armed. The first clash of the campaign in the Danube valley took place at Hirschau on 11 April 1809; the Battle of Aspern-Essling was fought on 20–21 May and although this battle was a definite defeat for Napoleon, all of Austria west of the Danube, including Vienna, was in enemy hands. Efforts to raise the *Landwehr* were just too little, too late.

The raw *Landwehr* regiments came into action most significantly on 14 June at Raab, where Archduke John's force, including many Hungarian *Insurrektion* units, was defeated by Eugène de Beauharnais' Army of Italy. The other major occasion was at Graz on 24, 25 and 26 June. Here Ignaz

◄ PRIVATE, AUSTRIAN LANDWEHR, 1809 *This man wears a Corsican hat, with upturned brim, and the traditional Austrian sprig of oak leaves. His uniform is simple and cheap, as befits a man from a unit raised quickly and at minimum expense.*

Gyulai's *Insurrektion* troops just dropped their weapons and fled. In the Tyrol the situation was very different. The *Landesschützen*, *Scharfschützen*, and *Landsturm* put up a terrific resistance against the Bavarian, German and French invaders, even after Wagram had sealed Austria's fate. The fight, under the leadership of Andreas Hofer, went on until 1 November.

▼ OFFICER, TRIESTE CITY LANDWEHR BATTALION, 1809 *Trieste was the home of Austria's navy at this period but it was lost to France in 1809. This rather composite uniform combines Austrian, Italian and Hungarian elements.*

GENERALS, FIELD MARSHALS AND STAFF

From early times the hallmark of Austrian generals had been their plain red breeches. Even today, Austrian generals wear wide, double, red side stripes to their trousers. The plume was of dark green cock's feathers and the hat (bicorn) had a 2¼ in (6 cm) wide gold braid edging. In the corners of the hat were black-within-gold rosettes, bearing the gold cipher "FII" for "Franz II" ("FI" from 1806). Each general would carry the sword of the regiment from which he came. It would be carried on red leather slings, fitted and embroidered in gold. The waistcoat was red and the buttons in gold. All German generals wore the gold lace decoration to collar and front of tunic; the exact rank could be seen by the thickness of the gold edging to the cuffs. A field marshal's cuffs were edged in broad gold braid with an oak-leaf pattern and had three gold buttons along the top.

Epaulettes were not worn. The sash and sword strap and knot were of gold and black silk. Generals carried a Malacca cane with ivory knob, gold cord and tassels and gold shoe. Horse furniture was red, of dragoon cut, and edged with three wide bands of gold braid. In the front and rear corners were ciphers or trophies of arms. By 1813 a field uniform had

◄ **GERMAN MAJOR GENERAL, 1809**
Officers of this rank commanded brigades in the Austrian Army. Note the cipher which now bears "FI" for Franz I of Austria and the 1.7 in (4 cm) of gold edging to the cuffs, denoting the status of the wearer.

been introduced for generals. It consisted of a single-breasted, pike grey coat, with red collar. The edges of the cuffs, lapels, pocket flaps and collar were edged in gold braid. With this were worn pike grey overalls with small gold buttons down the sides of the legs.

Rank badges were in the form of gold braid edging to the cuffs. The general of cavalry, general of infantry, and *Feldzeugmeister* (technical field marshal) wore two rows of braid, each 2¼ in (6 cm) wide. The *Feldmarschalleutnant* (commander of a division) wore one such band. Major generals had one row of braid ¾ in (4.5 cm) wide.

The Hungarian Generals

These wore red hussar dolman and breeches with gold buttons and lace, and a white pelisse trimmed with sable fur. The colpack was brown with red bag and white plume. The barrel sash was black, yellow and gold. Rank was shown by increasing amounts of gold lace embroidery on the cuffs and the thighs. The Hungarian harness of their horses was most elaborately decorated with gold studs. The undress uniform was as for the dress uniform, but with a pike grey pelisse, and the colpack was replaced with a shako with triple gold edging to peak, top band and neck shield and a 9¾ in (25 cm) high, dark green cock's feather plume. They could wear yellow leather breeches or pike grey overalls.

Staff Officers

The general staff wore its own uniform, and officers chosen for this specialized branch tended to see out the rest of their service there. Nowadays, armies demand that officers qualifying for staff duties rotate back to regimental duty between each stint on the staff. This is to ensure they remain

▼ **AIDE-DE-CAMP (FLÜGELADJUTANT), 1795**
*An aide-de-camp was selected by a general to help
him with his duties. To emphasize his role and
position, this field officer
wears his waist sash en
bandolier; his gold
and black sword
belt, with silver
buckle plate
and gold
double-headed
eagle badge is
clearly
visible.
German
saddle and
harness are
used.*

► **OFFICER, GENERAL STAFF, 1795** *This man's
rank of field officer, is displayed by the gold
lace edging to his cuffs. Once again,
German saddle and harness are used. The
Austrian general staff struggled in the
1790s and was to be thoroughly reformed
following defeat in 1805. Note the
distinctive black collar and gold-piped cuffs
and the overall plain and functional
appearance of the uniform.*

in close touch with experiences at the
sharp end and do not remain remote,
issuing plans that have little to do with
the reality of soldiering.

General Adjutants and ADCs

Plain bicorn with dark green plume,
bottle green tunic, red facings, gold
buttons and cord along the left
shoulder, under which the sash ran.
Waistcoat and breeches were buff.
Bottle green greatcoat. All other details
as for officers of German fusiliers. The
ADC to the generals' uniform was as
for general adjutants but with silver
buttons. This was a reasonably

well-regulated uniform, the Austrians
turning their backs on some of the
more individualistic uniforms favoured
by aides-de-camp of some French
marshals, for example.

Officers of the General Quartermaster's Staff

All details were as for officers of
German fusiliers, except that the tunic
was bottle green with black collar and
cuffs, red lining, gold buttons. The
bicorn had a green plume, the
waistcoat was buff. They carried curved
sabres instead of swords. The greatcoat
was bottle green with black facings.
  Other staff officers wore plain
bicorns, dark blue coats and
waistcoats, yellow buttons and
white breeches. They wore no
sash, but had the usual gold
portépée to their swords. The
facings to the coats varied with
different branches of service:
Field Commissariat, red;
Ration Supply, buff;
Records, sky blue.

GERMAN FUSILIERS AND GRENADIERS

The Austrian infantry was divided into German and "Hungarian" regiments. German units actually included Dutch, Italian and Polish troops.

Fusilier Privates

The term fusilier originally denoted a soldier who carried a fusil, or flintlock. Likewise, grenadiers were originally soldiers armed with grenades. Eventually, the latter constituted the infantry's elite whilst fusiliers were line infantry. The fusilier's uniform was also worn by the other nationalities in the Imperial Army,

apart from the Hungarian infantry. In 1798 a Roman helmet had replaced the *Kasket* for the infantry. The solid leather comb was topped by a black-over-yellow woollen crest. The brass front plate bore the imperial cipher and two flat, iron wires ran up the sides of the crown to add protection from sabre cuts. The chinstrap was of plain black leather. When on field service, a sprig of oak or fir leaves was worn in the left-hand chinstrap boss. Hair was queued and the men were clean-shaven.

The single-breasted tunic was pearl grey in colour, closed with 8–10 regimental buttons according to the height of the wearer. Facings were worn on the collar, cuffs, turnbacks and piping to shoulder straps and skirt tails. Waistcoats and breeches were also "white", gaiters black. The greatcoat was in grey. Belts were white, the pack was of calfskin. Fusilier privates did not carry a sabre.

◀ Fifer, German Infantry Regiment
Neugebauer No. 46, 1798 *Fifers wore scalloped white lace edging to collar and cuffs and swallows' nests in the facing colour at the shoulders. The front peak of the headgear, known as the Kasket was extended and worn turned up at the front. The brass fife case, which hung from a white shoulder strap, was decorated with the crowned double-headed eagle. This regiment was recruited in Galicia from largely Polish personnel.*

▶ Private, Infantry Regiment
Württemberg No. 38, 1798 *The rather impractical leather hat bore the double-headed eagle badge on the brass front plate by 1798. Previously it bore the crowned cipher "MTJ" (Marie-Theresia and Joseph). The calfskin pack was carried on a single bandolier over the right shoulder and the wooden water canteen was sealed with beeswax. Although this man is from a so-called German regiment, this unit was actually recruited in Galicia. The uniform had pink facings and brass buttons.*

Fusilier NCOs and Officers

Corporals wore uniforms as for privates, but carried a hazelnut stick and had a black and yellow woollen fist strap and tassel to their sabres. Sergeants carried a Spanish cane. Pioneers wore moustaches as for grenadiers. They carried an axe and a hatchet and wore a protective brown leather apron.

From lieutenant to captain, officers wore the same helmet as the men did, but of better quality and finer workmanship, all brass parts being gilt,

as were the front and sides of the comb and the reinforcement struts. The crest was of silk threads and the chinstrap was covered with a double gilt chain. The tunic was of better cloth than that of the ranks, having no shoulder straps, and the skirts reached to the back of the knee. Facings were worn only on collar and cuffs. White breeches were worn and straight-topped black boots.

The white leather sword belt, with rectangular silver buckle plate, bearing the double-headed eagle, was worn under the yellow and black worsted waist sash, which was worn only when on duty. A straight sword in a brown sheath was carried, the sword had a gold *portépée*. In the field, officers wore a grey,

double-breasted jacket (*Überrock*), with regimental buttons and facings on collar and cuffs. Field officers (majors, lieutenant colonels, colonels) had helmet crests of black and gold bullion fringes, and the cuffs were edged in gold or silver lace, 3/4 in (2 cm) wide. The waist sash was in yellow and black silk. The tassel of the *portépée* bore the double-headed eagle on one side, the cipher "FII" on the other. Officers wore silver, buckle-on spurs.

In 1806 the shako began to be introduced for all ranks. It had eye and neck peaks and a small leather flap over each ear. The chinstrap was plain black leather. At the top front was a black-within-yellow pompon. The regimental sergeant major had the cipher "FI" in yellow silk in the central, black field. Officers wore the "FI" in gold. Extending down from the pompon was a brass "loop" held at the bottom by a regimental button, all within a crimped brass ring. The oak leaf sprig was worn behind the pompon. Corporals' shakos had a 1/2 in (1.25 cm) wide yellow top band, sergeants had two such stripes. Second lieutenants had two gold stripes separated by a black stripe; lieutenants and captains had one wide gold stripe.

Grenadiers

All uniform details were as for the German fusiliers except the lid of the cartridge pouch bore a flaming grenade in brass and a brass match case was

worn on the bandolier. All men carried a sabre and their muskets were of brown walnut with brass fittings. Instead of the helmet or shako, grenadiers wore the black bearskin with decorated brass front plate and, initially, no peak. The back of the front plate was decorated with a bag in the facing colour, with white braid, ending in the black-within-yellow pompon on the right hand side of the plate. Sergeants had silver or gold braid to their bags. Officers' cap plates had finer workmanship, and they all carried sabres; field officers wore bicorns. In 1803 peaks were added to the bearskins; officers' peaks had a gilt rim. In 1811 the bearskin cap backing to officers' bearskins was made yellow for all regiments. In 1809 the match cases on the bandoliers were abandoned.

◀ **GERMAN GRENADIER, INFANTRY REGIMENT DE LIGNE NO. 30, 1769–98** *The grenadier still wears a brass match case on his bandolier, a survival from the days when they lit and threw grenades in battle; this was replaced by a flaming grenade badge in 1809. The bearskin front plate bears the crowned double-headed eagle amid trophies of arms. This regiment was recruited in the French-speaking Walloon provinces until 1802, thence in Galicia.*

▶ **GERMAN FUSILIER DRUMMER, INFANTRY REGIMENT DE LIGNE NO. 30, 1769–98** *Drummers were distinguished by white lace edging to collar and cuffs and the swallows nests at the tops of the sleeves.*

HUNGARIAN FUSILIERS AND GRENADIERS

Reflecting the multinational character of the Austrian Empire, Hungarian units included troops from Transylvania and Croatia. These were recruited via a mixture of voluntary enlistment and conscription.

Infantry Organization

The established strength of an infantry regiment in 1792 was 4,580 men in four battalions, each of six companies. Each regiment had 22 companies of fusiliers and two of grenadiers. In times of war, the grenadier companies would be taken from their parent regiments and combined into battalions of grenadiers, six companies strong. When on campaign, each regiment was allocated one 6-pounder and four 3-pounder guns. In June 1805

▲ *Various Austrian grenadier regiments, probably in the 1815 period of the Congress of Vienna, just before Napoleon escaped from the island of Elba to burst onto the European stage for his final fling.*

this was altered to four companies per battalion, and there were now the 1st–4th Field Battalions and one Grenadier Battalion (each four companies strong) in each regiment. Following the end of the 1805 campaign, the old infantry organization was reverted to, and a regiment consisted of three battalions of fusiliers (the 3rd having only four companies) and two companies of grenadiers. In 1809 each infantry regiment had two grenadier and 18 fusilier companies in three battalions, plus a depot of two companies. A German regiment thus had 5,170 men. Hungarian regiments had 5,065 men,

◀ SENIOR OFFICER, HUNGARIAN INFANTRY, INFANTRY REGIMENT NO. 32, 1798–1805
This shows a field officer. His status is given by the gold lace edging to his cuff, gold bullion sword knot and the gold bullion fringes to the helmet crest. Although he is from a Hungarian regiment, German saddle and harness are used. Officers of Hungarian regiments wore sabres as opposed to swords. The cipher in the saddle cloth corner is "FII".

Line Infantry Regimental Distinctions: 1792–1815

No.	Title/date raised	Facings	Buttons	Nationality
1	Kaiser/1715.	pompadour	yellow	Moravian
2	Archduke Ferdinand/1741	emperor yellow	yellow	Hungarian
	Hiller/1806, 1 Alexander, Czar/814			
3	Archduke Charles/1715	sky blue	white	Austrian
4	Hoch-und Deutschmeister/1696	sky blue	yellow	Austrian
5	or 1st Garrison Regt/1762	dark blue	white	
6	or 2nd Garrison Regt/1764	black	white	
7	Schroeder/1691	dark blue	white	Moravian
	Ferdinand/1809			
8	Huff/1642	poppy red	yellow	Moravian
	1810	grass green		
	also Galician from 1807, Archduke Ludwig/1801			
9	Clerfayt/1725	apple green	yellow	Wallonian
	Galician from 1804			
10	Kheul/1715	parrot green	white	Bohemian
	Moravian from 1807, Anspach/1802			
	Mittrowsky/ 1806, Reisky/1809			
11	Wallis/1629	pink	white	Bohemian
	1810	dark blue	yellow	
	Archduke Rainer/1801			
12	Manfredini/1702	dark brown	yellow	Moravian
	Liechtenstein			
13	Reisky/1642.	grass green	yellow	Austrian
	re-raised/1814	pink	yellow	Italian
	Wimpffen/1815			
14	Klebeck/1733	black	yellow	Austrian
	Archduke Rudolf/1811			
15	D`Alton/1701	madder red	yellow	Bohemian
	Oranien/1797, Moravian/1807, Riese/1801, Bohemian/1809,			
	Zach/1806, Moravian/1812			
16	Terzy/1703	violet	yellow	Steyermark
	1810	yellow		
	Archduke Rudolf/1802, Lusignan/1806			
17	Hohenlohe-Kirchberg/1674	light blue	white	Bohemian
	Reuss-Plauen/1801			
18	Stuart/1682	pompadour	white	Bohemian
	D`Aspre/1809, Reuss-Greitz/1809			
19	Alvincy de Berbereck/1734	light blue	white	Hungarian
20	Kaunitz-Rietberg/1681	lobster red	white	Silesian
21	Gemmingen-Hornberg/1733	sea green	yellow	Bohemian
	Rohan/1808			
	Gyulai (Albert)/1810			
22	Lacy/1709	emperor yellow	white	Moravian
	Sachsen-Coburg-Saalfeld/1802, Nassau-Usingen/1815			
23	Archduke Ferdinand/1672	poppy red	white	Galician
	Mauroy de Merville/1814	crimson	white	Lombardian
24	Preiss/1771	dark blue	white	Austrian
	Auersberg/1801, Galician/1807, Strauch/1808			
25	Brechainville/1672	sea green	white	Bohemian
	Spork/1801, Zedwitz/1808, De Vaux/1810			
26	Schroeder/1717	parrot green	yellow	Carinthian
	Hohenlohe-Bartenstein/1803, Wilhelm of Oranien/1814			

▶

▼ PIONEER, HUNGARIAN GRENADIERS, INFANTRY REGIMENT ALVINTZY NO. 19, 1812
The fur on the front of these caps pointed upwards, to give greater emphasis to the height of the wearer. The pioneers were an elite force who wore a thick leather apron and were equipped with heavy axes. These troops acted as sappers and were tasked with various duties such as destroying obstacles, battering down doors, or building earthworks. In 1796 this regiment was one of those in Wurmser's corps, which was forced to take refuge in Mantua fortress when the second attempt to relieve that place failed on 15 September 1796. They fought in northern Italy in 1805 and 1809, where they were in the battles of Sacile, the River Piave and Raab. In 1812 they were in Schwarzenberg's corps in Russia and fought at Podubnie and Wolkowisk.

▲ HUNGARIAN INFANTRY REGIMENT SWORD
The sword carried by all officers of the German and Hungarian infantry regiments had a superb hilt, decorated with a lion's head motif, and a gold and black tassel.

20 men more in each fusilier company, but only 465 men in the depot. During the wars of 1813–15 each line regiment had a *Landwehr* battalion attached to it as its 4th Battalion.

In the British Army, the numbering of regiments is strictly according to age, the 1st Foot (The Royal Scots) having been raised in 1633. In the Austrian Army this was ignored, the oldest regiment being number 11.

Fusiliers

Uniforms for Hungarian fusiliers were as for their German counterparts, except that the cuffs were pointed and decorated with regimental lace and button – "the bear's claws". Instead of white breeches and gaiters, Hungarian regiments wore long, sky blue trousers decorated at the thighs and down the sides with black and yellow cords; no gaiters were worn. For officers the lace was silver or gold and they wore the same boots as the German officers.

Grenadiers

Hungarian grenadiers wore the same fur bonnets as their German grenadier comrades; their jackets were of the same design as the Hungarians', with pointed cuffs and bear's claws. Grenadiers also wore the light blue breeches of the Hungarian infantry.

No.	Title/date raised	Facings	Buttons	Nationality
27	Strassoldo/1682 Chasteler/1809	emperor yellow	yellow	Steyermark
28	Wartensleben/1698	grass green	white	Bohemian
29	Wallis/1709 Lindenau/1803	light blue	white	Moravian
30	De Ligne/1725 Nugent/1815	pike grey	yellow	Wallonian 1802 Galician
31	Benjovszky/1741	emperor yellow	white	Hungarian/ Siebenburgen
32	Gyulai, Samuel/1741 Esterhazy/1802	light blue	yellow	Hungarian
33	Sztaray/1741 Colloredo-Mansfeld/1809	dark blue	white	Hungarian
34	Kray/1733 Davidovich/1804, Wied-Runkel/1815	madder red	white	Hungarian
35	Brentano-Cimaroli/1683 Wenkheim/1793, Modena/1802, Archduke Maximilian/1803 Nepomuk/1807, Argenteau/1809	madder red	yellow	Bohemian
36	Kinsky/1683 Fuerstenberg/1797, Kolowrat-Krakowsky/1801	pink	white	Bohemian
37	De Vins/1741 Auffenberg/1803, Auersperg/1808, Wiedenfeld/1808, Mariassy/1813	poppy red	yellow	Hungarian
38	Wuerttemberg/1725 1815 re-raised/1815 Prohaska	pink pink	yellow white	Galician Lombardian
39	Nadasdy/1756 Duka/1803	poppy red	white	Hungarian
40	Mittrowsky/1733 Wuerttemberg, Ferdinand/1813	crimson 1810 light blue	white	Moravian
41	Bender/1701 Wuerttemberg, Wilhelm/1803, Saxony-Hildburghausen/1805 Kottulinsky/1808, Hohenlohe-Bartenstein/1815	sulphur yellow	white	Austrian
42	Mathesen/1674 Erbach-Schoenberg/1793	orange	white	Bohemian
43	Thurn-Valle-Sassina/1715 Simbschen/1806 re-raised/1814	sulphur yellow crimson	yellow yellow	Austrian Lombardian
44	Belgiojoso/1744 Bellegarde/1801,	madder red	yellow	Italian 1807 Galician
45	Lettermann/1682 De Vaux/1806	crimsom	yellow	Salzburg
46	Neugebauer/1769 Chasteler/1808	French blue	yellow	Galician
47	Kinsky/1682 Vogelsang/1805	steel green	white	Bohemian
48	Schmitfeld/1721 re-raised 1798 Vukassovich/1799, Simbschen/1809, Radivojevich/1815	light blue steel green	yellow yellow	Italian Hungarian
49	Pellegrini/1715 Kerpen/1797	light pike grey	white	Austrian
50	Stain/1762	violet	white	Galician
51	Splenyi/1702	French blue	yellow	Hungarian/ Siebenburgen ▶

▼ GRENADIER SERGEANT MAJOR, HUNGARIAN INFANTRY REGIMENT ERZHERZOG FRANZ NO. 52, 1805 *This regiment recruited in Hungary, and this NCO thus wears the appropriate uniform complete with pompadour facings. To untutored eyes, the badges of rank may almost be overlooked, but they consist of the officer-style pompon with gold embroidered imperial cipher "FII", the impressive Spanish cane with white leather fist strap, the boots and the special sabre hilt with lion's head pommel, and the gold and black silk fist strap and tassel. The white lace and tassels on the cuffs were known as bear's claws. The cane could be used to punish private soldiers. The regiment's title can be translated as Archduke Franz.*

No.	Title/date raised	Facings	Buttons	Nationality
52	Archduke Anton/1741 Archduke Franz	pompadour	yellow	Hungarian
53	Jelachich/1741 Hiller/1814	pompadour	white	Hungarian/ Croatian
54	Callenberg/1661 Morzin/1802, Froon/1805	apple green	white	Bohemian
55	Murray de Melgum/1742 Reuss-Greitz/1803	light blue	yellow	Galician
56	Colloredo-Waldsee, Wenzel/1684	steel green	yellow	Silesian/ Moravian
57	Colloredo-Waldsee, Joseph/1688	pink	yellow	Bohemian
58	Beaulieu/1763 from 1798	black	white	Wallonian Bohemian
59	Jordis/1682	orange	yellow	Austrian
60	1798 Gylai, Ignaz/1801	steel green	white	Hungarian
61	1798 St Julien/1802	grass green	yellow	Hungarian
62	1798 Jelachich/1802, Wacquant-Geozelles/1810	grass green	white	Hungarian/ Siebenburgen
63	Archduke Joseph/1799 Baillet-Mermet/1807, Bianchi/1811	light blue	yellow	Wallonian/ Italian/Galician
64	1801 Chasteler/1802	green	yellow	Tyrolian

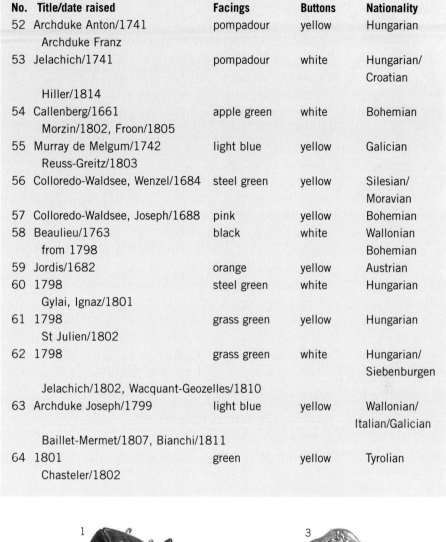

▲ HUNGARIAN INFANTRY REGIMENT KIT
1 The black oilskin cover to the grenadier bearskin, with neck and cheek flaps extended.
2 The same headgear with cheek-pieces tied above the brass front plate (bearing the "FII" cipher of Franz II).
3 A grenadier cap plate, in brass, in use up until 1806.
4 Front and side view of an officer's pompon.

THE LIGHT INFANTRY

Traditionally, the skirmishing function in the Austrian Army had been carried out by volunteer Free Corps (*Freikorps*) and by the Border Infantry Regiments. By 1798 the scarcity of light troops for skirmishing duties in dispersed order

▼ PRIVATES OF LIGHT INFANTRY, 1800 *On the left is a figure from the 1st Battalion (Strozzi) with madder red facings and the German-style breeches and boots; on the right is a figure from the 13th Battalion (Zechmeister) with sulphur yellow facings and the Hungarian-style breeches and cuffs as worn by the non-Italian units. Both have yellow buttons. The battalions were disbanded in 1801, the men going mainly to the newly formed* Jäger *battalions.*

was being keenly felt. The single regiment of *Jägers* was just overwhelmed by the task. A solution was sought in taking the various Free Corps, which were serving in the field, and reorganizing them into battalion-sized units. Thus regular light infantry units entered the Austrian Army lists for the first time.

Light Infantry Units

The uniform was as for the German fusiliers, but without the brass front plate, this being replaced with the brass cipher "FII". The centre companies had black-over-yellow crests, white belts and were armed with muskets; the sharpshooter (*Scharfschützen*) company had green crests and black belts and were armed with rifles. The five battalions that were raised in Italy wore

German-style breeches, while the others wore long, Hungarian-style, light blue trousers, together with the pointed cuffs and bear's claws. The tunic was pike grey.

Instead of drummers, the light infantry used hornists (*Waldhornists*) to relay signals. They wore the decorated swallows' nests, collars and cuffs. Line

▼ OFFICERS OF LIGHT INFANTRY, 1800 *Again it is odd that officers in these battalions did not carry curved sabres. The waist sashes cover the black and gold sword belts. On the left is an officer from the 10th Battalion (Greth); on the right one from the 4th Battalion (Otto). Both units have Hungarian-style cuffs and breeches.*

Light Infantry Regimental Distinctions 1798

No./Title	Facings	Buttons	Raised from Freikorps wearing uniforms as below
1 Strozzi	madder red	yellow	O'Donell's Freikorps. Kasket green coat, poppy red facings and breeches, yellow buttons
2*Rohan	madder red	white	Rohan's émigrés. Kasket sky blue coat, poppy red facings, yellow buttons, green breeches.
3*Watlet	brick red	yellow	Grün Laudon's Freikorps. Kasket green coat and breeches, madder red facings, yellow buttons.
4*Otto	brick red	white	Grün Laudon's Freikorps. See 3rd Regiment above.
5 Radivojevich	orange	yellow	1st Battalion Serbian Freikorps. Kasket with black plume, short brown coat with red facings, light blue Hungarian breeches, black belts.
6 Trauttenberg	orange	white	Gyulai's Freikorps. Low brimmed hat, brown coat red facings, edged with black and yellow cord, light blue Hungarian breeches with black and yellow lace decoration, yellow Hungarian boots.
7 Schmelzern	steel green	white	Gyulai's Freikorps. See 6th Regiment above
8 Not raised			
9 Siegenfeld	crimson	yellow	Gyulai's Freikorps. See 6th Regiment above
10 Greth	dark blue	white	Gyulai's Freikorps. See 6th Regiment above
11*Carneville	dark blue	yellow	Carneville's: bicorn, green coat, black facings, yellow buttons. Liege: bicorn, sky blue coat and breeches, lobster red facings, white buttons. Anhalt-Zerbst: grenadier caps, white coat, red facings.
12 Steigentesch	steel green	white	O'Donell's Freikorps. See 1st Regiment above.
13 Zechmeister	sulphur yellow	yellow	Gyulai's Freikorps. See 6th Regiment above.
14* Reichenstein	black	white	Rohan's émigrés. See 2nd Regiment above.
15 Mihanovic	black	yellow	2nd Battalion Serbian Freikorps. See 5th above.
16 Ertel (aka the Dalmatian Light Battalion)			They wore the helmet with Turkish costume.
17 Buonacorsi (aka the Italian Light Battalion)			Dark blue coat, red facings.

NB In 1814 four Italian light infantry battalions were raised; they wore dark green coats, emperor yellow facings and yellow buttons. *Raised in Italy.

infantry badges of rank were used. These battalions were short-lived. In 1801, with the advent of peace at the end of the War of the Second Coalition, they were all disbanded. This left only three "rifle" units: the Tyroler Scharfschützen, the German Feld-Jäger-Corps Kurz and the Belgian Feld-Jäger-Corps Le Loup.

After consulting with the Tyrolean leaders, the emperor decided to raise a new regiment of *Jägers* in that province. Apart from the Tyroler and Kurz units, all Tyroleans in the Le Loup Feld-Jäger and the Infantry Regiment Neugebauer No. 46 were to form the basis for this new regiment. It received the number "64" and was named after its colonel-in-chief, the *Feldmarschalleutnant* (lieutenant general) Marquis Chasteler. The uniform was pike grey, with green facings, brass buttons and black belts. The regiment was organized in three battalions each of six companies. After

the 1809 campaign, it was reorganized into nine *Feld-Jäger* battalions. In 1813 the battalions were increased to 12. When Tyrol reverted to Austrian rule by the Treaty of Ried (8 October 1813) the Fenner Jäger-Corps was raised in the province.

The new colonel-in-chief, Franz Fenner von Fennerberg (born in 1762), had fought against the Turks in 1778–79, and in the early Revolutionary campaigns. By 1809 he was a major general and commander of the defence of the Tyrol. In 1813 Fenner von Fennerberg commanded the right wing of the Army of Inner Austria and was distinguished in the raids on the Mühlbacher Klause on 11 September and 7 October, which cleared the enemy out of the southern Tyrol. In 1814 he liberated the Pusta valley. He died in 1824. On 1 January 1816 this regiment became the Kaiser-Jäger Regiment.

▶ *JÄGER*, FIELD SERVICE DRESS, 1798–1805
With the subdued uniform colours of pike grey and green and the black belts, it is clear that the Austrian riflemen were following the examples of their civilian hunter colleagues. In 1805 the Roman helmet was replaced by the Corsican hat with the left brim turned up. Those Jägers *armed with rifles had a wooden mallet with which to drive the tightly fitting ball into the rifle's barrel.*

THE BORDER INFANTRY

These regiments were recruited in the Balkan provinces, up against the border with the Ottoman Empire. In this region, all able-bodied adult males were liable for military service. Called *Grenzers*, the Border Infantry units carried out the duties of light infantry and were mostly deployed with the advanced guards. They were named after the regions in which their men were recruited.

All uniform details were as for Hungarian fusiliers, except that belts were black. In 1792 most coats were white but some units had tobacco brown tunics. In 1808 all coats were ordered to be in tobacco brown, but the change took years to complete.

Campaign of 1809

In 1809 there was a minor – but hard-fought – campaign in Dalmatia and Croatia, which had been under French occupation since 1805. It demonstrates just how tough these Border troops were. The major French garrisons were in Ragusa (Dubrovnik) – two battalions – Castelnuovo, Cattaro and Zadar (one

battalion each). As the storm clouds gathered, Marshal Macdonald (French commander in the region) also quickly repaired the forts at Klissa, Knin and Sibenik and put garrisons into them.

Marmont gained Turkish support against the Austrians by having them raid into the areas of old Turkish Croatia ceded to Austria by the Peace of Sistova in 1791. It was Marmont's plan to invade Lika as soon as Viceroy Eugène had achieved a victory in northern Italy. By the end of March he had concentrated his mobile troops around Kistanje, Knin, Obrovac, Ostrovica and Zadar. His corps headquarters was at Ostrovica, which was fortified.

He was opposed by Lieutenant General Graf Ignaz Gyulai, Banus of Croatia and Slavonia and commander, IX Austrian Corps. Gyulai's primary task in 1809 was in covering Archduke John's rear and southern flank. His secondary duty was to pin down Marmont's corps.

The Austrian force initially available here was just a brigade commanded by Major General Andreas von Stojcevic. It consisted of the local Border Infantry. Stojcevic knew that he was heavily outnumbered and requested reinforcements; he was sent one 6-pounder battery of field artillery and was told to activate the newly organized *Landwehr* (militia).

In great haste three local, composite *Grenzer Landwehr* battalions were scratched together from the home areas of the six regiments of the Karlstadt and Warasdin commands. They consisted of untrained boys and old men, short of clothes, arms, food and equipment. Most arrived without shoes; two-thirds of the available muskets were unusable.

▶ **PRIVATE, KREUTZER BORDER INFANTRY REGIMENT NO. 5, 1812** *The Border Infantry regiments were some of the first to wear the felt shako. By 1812 the 6th, 12th and 15th Regiments were wearing brown coats; the rest were still in white. The 5th Regiment was in Russia in 1812 and fought in the Pripet Marshes, where they had heavy losses due to the exhaustion of the men towards the end of the year.*

◀ **DRUMMER, 2ND SZECKLER WALLACHISCHES BORDER INFANTRY REGIMENT NO. 15, 1812** *The drummer wears the yellow top band to the shako and the yellow and black sabre fist strap of a junior NCO or corporal; he thus also carries the hazel stick as his badge of office.*

Stojcevic also raised a Dalmatian Free Corps of one battalion on 8 April 1809; the commander was Major Ugarkovic, the garrison was in Udbina and its strength rose to 1,400 men. It was armed with carbines. The local population in Dalmatia was pro-Austrian and several spontaneous uprisings took place against the dispersed French garrisons. Marmont fought his way, against fierce resistance, up out of Croatia to join up with Prince Eugène's Army of Italy and take part in the campaign in Hungary. Dalmatia was occupied by the

Border Infantry Regimental Distinctions 1798

No.*/Title/Raised	Facings	Buttons
1 (60) Liccaner/1746	violet	yellow
2 (61) Ottocaner/1746	violet	white
3 (62) Oguliner/1746	orange	yellow
4 (63) Szluiner/1746	orange	white
5 (64) Warasdiner Kreutzer/1749	lobster red	yellow
6 (65) Warasdiner St Georger/1749	lobster red	white
7 (66) Brooder/1747	pink	yellow
8 (67) Gradiscaner/1747	pink	white
9 (68) Peterwardeiner/1747	grey	yellow
10 (69) 1st Banal/1750	crimson	yellow
11 (70) 2nd Banal/1750	crimson	white
12 (71) Deutsch-Banater/1765	sky blue	white
13 (72) Wallachisch-Illyrisch/1766	light grey	white
14 (73) 1st Szeckler (aka /1762 Siebenburger-Szeckler)	pink	yellow
15 (74) 2nd Szeckler/1764	pink	white
16 (75) 1st Wallachisches/1798	poplar green	yellow
17 (76) 2nd Wallachisches/1798	poplar green	white

*In 1792 there were 17 regiments, numbered 60 to 76 (shown above in brackets). In 1798 they were given their own series running from 1 to 17.

Austrians, using the available troops under command of the retired Major General Peter Freiherr von Knezevic. The French garrisons left in the province were attacked and isolated, and news arrived from Vienna on 29 July of the ceasefire signed by Austria and France. The Austrians ceased hostilities and began negotiations.

On 4 November, news of the Peace of Schönbrunn reached Zadar and with it the news that Dalmatia was to be among those areas transferred back to French control. In total, the French took over the following six regiments from among the Border Troops: 1st Banal (Glina), 2nd Banal (Petrina), Lika, Ogulin, Otocac, Sluin. In all, this made up 12 field and six reserve battalions. These became the 1st–4th Croatian Regiments in French service, two of which served in Russia in 1812. Two Croatian officers, Captain Colic and Lieutenant Mudrovcic, of that contingent were awarded the *Légion d'Honneur* for their bravery in battle.

The French occupation of Croatia and Dalmatia lasted until October 1813, when their state officials quietly withdrew. The jubilant population returned with enthusiasm to the rule of the House of Habsburg and remained part of the Austrian Empire for more than a century.

◀ JUNIOR OFFICER (LEFT), SZLUINER BORDER INFANTRY REGIMENT NO. 4, 1798 *The Regiment No. 4 served in Italy against the French but when Austria lost her Balkan provinces it served with the French from 1809 to 1813 as the 2nd Croatian Regiment. The coat is white but in 1808 would become brown.*

◀ SERGEANT (RIGHT), DEUTSCH-BANATER BORDER INFANTRY REGIMENT NO. 12, 1809 *Changes in uniform regulations led to the adoption of brown coats, as for this sergeant of the 12th. This unit fought in the Tyrol in 1805 and in Germany and Bohemia in the 1809 campaign.*

THE CARABINIERS AND CUIRASSIERS

Austria's heavy cavalry consisted of two carabinier regiments, considered to be elite units, and the formidable armoured cuirassiers (*Kürassiers*).

From 1798 the Roman helmet replaced the bicorn. It was of infantry pattern, with peaks to front and back, the front peak edged in brass, and the brass front plate bearing the uncrowned imperial cipher "FII" until 1806, thence "FI". There was a brass covering to the comb for officers, and a black-over-yellow caterpillar crest (red for trumpeters). Two brass struts to each side of the helmet, running down from the centre of the crown to the sides of the round, brass chinstrap bosses, and plain black chinstrap. An improved version was introduced in

1811, with enhanced comb. The tunics were as for the German infantry but with shorter, white skirts, edged in the facing colour. Facings were worn on the round cuffs, the turnbacks and on two small, lozenge-shaped patches on the front of the white *paroli* (collar). Each patch had a regimental button in the rear top corner. Only the front plate of the cuirass was worn. It was black, edged in red, with white leather straps. Junior officers had a gilt "peak" to the chest of the cuirass, reaching about one-third of the way down; for

▶ CUIRASSIER REGIMENT NO. 3 (ALBERT), 1798 KIT *1 A trooper's German-style saddle. 2 The officer's version of the same saddle, used throughout the heavy cavalry regiments.*

Cuirassier Regimental Distinctions

Until 1798 all cavalry regiments shared a common series of numbers. These are shown in brackets behind the new numbers, which were allocated in that year.

No./Title/Date raised	Facings	Buttons
1 (15) 2nd Carabiniers/1768	pompadour (1768–98)	white
Kaiser Kürassiers in 1793		yellow (1798)
		white (1810)
2 (29) EH Franz/1672	black (1792–1815)	white
3 (5) Albert (1st) Carabiniers/1768	pompadour (1792–1868)	yellow
Albert Kürassiers No. 3 in 1798		
4 (27) Czartoryski/1682; disbanded in 1802	crimson (1792)	yellow
	dark blue (1798–1815)	yellow
5 (10) Zeschwitz/1682; disbanded in 1802	dark green (1792)	yellow
	grass green (1798)	yellow
6 1798: converted to the 6th Dragoons in 1802		
7 (21) Wallisch/1663; Lothringen; No. 7 in 1798	dark blue	white
8 (4)/1691		
Hohenzollern in 1792	poppy red (1792)	white
8th Kürassiers in 1798; Grand Duke Constantine in 1813	scarlet (1798)	yellow
9 (14)/1721; Nassau in 1792;	light blue (1792–1868)	white
renumbered 5th Kürassiers in 1802; Sommariva in 1806		
10 (20)/1701; Mack in 1792:		
renumbered 10th Kürassiers in 1798;	black	yellow
renumbered 6th Kürassiers in 1802;		
vacant 1807; Liechtenstein in 1809		
11 (33) Brandenburg (Anspach)/1702; disbanded in 1802	parrot green (1792)	white
	poppy red (1798)	white
12 (12) Kavanagh/1672; EH Ferdinand in 1801;	dark green (1792)	white
renumbered to 4th Kürassiers in 1802	grass green (1798)	white

◀ TROOPER, CURASSIER REGIMENT NO. 3 (ALBERT), 1798 *This regiment had been the 5th Cavalry Regiment (1st Carabiniers) until this year. The facings were pompadour, the buttons brass. Only the front plate of the cuirass was worn. As time went on, the helmet became more classical in style, with a higher comb, arching over to the front. The regiment was with Mack's army at Ulm in 1805, but escaped capture with Archduke Ferdinand, making their way to Bohemia.*

▼ CURASSIER REGIMENT NO. 3 (ALBERT), 1798 KIT.
1 *A junior officer's cuirass showing the gilt peak which denoted the rank of the wearer. Austrian cuirassiers did not wear a back plate.*
2 *The harness of an officer's cuirass.*
3 *Sword belt and steel scabbard (an officer's scabbard would be black).*
4 *The heavy, straight-bladed sword was a fearsome weapon.*
5 *Detail of the cuirass strap.*

majors and colonels the peak reached down to the bottom. White breeches were normally worn with high boots, but grey overall trousers were worn in the field in winter. Officers' overalls had a side stripe in the facing colour. In 1798 the knee cuffs on the boots were removed.

The cuirassiers were armed until 1798 with the straight-bladed heavy sword, a carbine and a pair of pistols. Following the reorganization of this year, only the eight sharpshooters per squadron carried rifled carbines, eight others per squadron had hussar-pattern, smoothbore weapons; the

others had no carbines. Officers' *portépées* had a black leather strap with two stripes of gold stitching along it and the normal gold tassel. The lid of the black leather cartridge pouch bore a round brass plate with the double eagle. The saddle cover was of white sheepskin with red edging; the red shabraque had a slight rear peak in which was the crowned imperial cipher in yellow. It was edged in black and yellow cord; inside this was a wide yellow lace with a black central stripe. A red, round portmanteau was carried. The harness was of German pattern, black with brass fittings.

The changes that affected the German cavalry through this period border on the bewildering and are difficult to follow. From 1769 the carabinier regiments were made up of three "line" divisions, each of two squadrons, and a fourth *chevauxlégers* (light horse) division. A carabinier squadron was to have 174 men (including 151 troopers) and a *chevauxlégers* squadron had 193 men, including 170 troopers. In time of war each cavalry regiment had to form a reserve squadron, made up of six men from each field squadron. Each squadron was commanded by a captain (*Rittmeister*), and had two first and two second lieutenants, two sergeants, eight corporals and two vice corporals. Every cavalry regiment that fought in the war in Lower Hungary against the Turks in 1788–90 had an increase of six mounted riflemen, armed with rifled carbines.

In 1798, 15 regiments of dragoons and *chevauxlégers* were converted into light dragoons, and the carabiniers and cuirassiers were reshuffled into cuirassiers, with no regard for their old numbering. In 1801 they were again reshuffled and divided into the original categories, with no regard for their historic origins. From 1802 the heavy cavalry consisted of the cuirassiers and dragoons; the term light

▶ STANDARD BEARER, KÜRASSIER REGIMENT KRONPRINZ FERDINAND NO. 4, 1809 (*the old Kavanagh No. 12 until 1802) The standard bandolier was in the facing colour (grass green), trimmed in the button colour, which was silver. The silver fringing to the edges of the standard was unofficial. The red and white triangles in the edging are the colours of the state of Austria; the black and yellow triangles reflect the Austrian Empire.*

cavalry now covered the *chevauxlégers*, hussars and lancers (*Ulans*). It was ordered that all cavalry regiments were to have eight squadrons and several regiments were disbanded; the new squadrons were to be made stronger than heretofore.

Following the 1805 disaster, all heavy cavalry regiments were reduced to six squadrons. The number of standards carried was reduced to one per division. They were now square, the sovereign's standard being white, the others being yellow. The sovereign's standard bore the blessed virgin on one side, the small imperial crest on the other; the regimental standards had the small crest on both sides. The standard bandoliers were in the facing colour, embroidered in the button colour. Kettle drums were abolished and trumpeters introduced.

The blade of the sword of heavy cavalry units was 35 in (89 cm) long and sharpened only on one side. It was carried in an iron sheath. The hilt was of brass, the pommel in the form of a

◀ JUNIOR OFFICER, KÜRASSIER REGIMENT ARCHDUKE FERDINAND NO. 4, 1815 *In 1802 this regiment became Kürassier Regiment No. 4. The facings had changed in 1798 from dark green to grass green; the buttons remained white. Being a squadron-level officer, the gilt peak at the top of his cuirass extends only a short way down from the neckline. The sides of the gilt comb – far more pronounced than in earlier models of the helmet – are decorated with crouching lions. Trumpeters wore red crests.*

lion's head. At about this point the decoration of the saddlery was standardized: instead of bearing the colonel-in-chief's crest, all now bore the imperial cipher.

Austrian generals failed to adopt Napoleon's fashion of forming a large reserve of artillery and heavy cavalry, to be used in decisive, mass actions. Even at the critical Battle of Leipzig (16–19 October 1813), the Austrian Reserve Corps consisted of two infantry divisions and a single cavalry division of 28 squadrons. Compare this with Napoleon's total of 217 squadrons that he was able to bring to the battle.

THE DRAGOONS, *CHEVAUXLÉGERS* AND MOUNTED RIFLES

Originally horse-mounted infantry, which rode to battle before dismounting and deploying, dragoons had become regular cavalry by the end of the eighteenth century. In 1792 Austria had six regiments of dragoons, and until 1798 they were dressed as cuirassiers, but without the cuirass.

The Dragoons

All details as for the cuirassiers unless noted here as being otherwise; they wore no cuirass. Officers and dragoons wore the bicorn, then, as from 1798, the Roman helmet. Dragoon regiments had white tunics and turnbacks, edged in the facing colour. Coat as for the infantry with facings shown on the collar, cuffs and on the braid that edged the white turnbacks. In 1798 the coats were changed to dark green. White breeches and belts, below-knee boots. They carried straight, heavy swords in steel sheaths on white slings. It had a plain, white leather fist strap for privates. Long carbines – some 52 in (132cm) in length – were carried by the dragoons; those of the *chevauxlégers* were only 33 in (84cm) long. NCOs and the eight sharpshooters per squadron carried rifled carbines. These were 27 in (69 cm) long and had eight grooves in the

► Trooper, Dragoon
Regiment No. 8
(Württemberg), 1798
In 1802 the uniform of this regiment changed to white coat, crimson facings with white buttons. All regiments used the same red saddle furniture. This figure is in field service dress and carries a picket stake strapped to his carbine. He wears grey, buttoned overalls over his white breeches. German saddle and harness were used.

barrel. The Model 1798 cavalry pistol was some 18¹/₂ in (47cm) long. The lid of the black leather cartridge pouch bore a round brass plate with the double eagle.

The *Chevauxlégers*

These light horse regiments had first appeared in the Austrian Army from 1758, during the Seven Years' War. They were equipped with small horses as they were to be the German light cavalry equivalent of the Hungarian hussars. They used the Hungarian Bock saddle. In 1786 each *chevauxlégers* regiment was increased by a division (two squadrons) of lancers. One squadron came from the Galician Ulan Corps, which had been raised in 1785 the other squadron was to be newly raised. The lancer squadrons had the same organization as the *chevauxlégers* squadrons. Most of the lancers wore white *kurtkas*, regimental facings and blue, Hungarian breeches. Those in the regiments Kaiser and Richecourt, who wore green *kurtkas* and white breeches. All troopers wore low-crowned, square-topped *czapkas*, officers wore white. Officers wore the bicorn, the men of the *chevauxlégers* initially wore the *Kasket*; from 1798 the Roman helmet was introduced.

The *chevauxlégers* wore grass green coats with red turnbacks; all other details as for the dragoons. With all the chopping and

changing that took place between 1798 and 1802, it is very doubtful if these regulations were exactly followed, as old coats would have worn out over a two-year period. In 1802 white coats were ordered for the *chevauxlégers*. Facing colours were allocated in pairs: the dragoon regiment of the pair wore white buttons, the *chevauxlégers* wore yellow. In 1806 the regiments 1, 2 and 4 were permitted to wear green tunics again. These regiments were armed with short carbines.

The Mounted Rifles

The Bussy Mounted Rifle Regiment was raised in 1798 at eight squadrons and disbanded in 1802. They wore the Roman helmet with dark green crest and the crowned imperial cipher "FII" on the front. Pike grey coat, and breeches, black belts, green facings, yellow buttons. This

▶ TRUMPETER. CHEVAUXLÉGERS REGIMENT VINCENT NO. 4, 1809 *This was the old Cavalry Regiment (Latour Dragoons) No. 31 until 1798, then Dragoon Regiment No. 11 until 1802, when it was renumbered 4. It was one of the three* chevauxléger *regiments to wear green coats. Note the red comb to the robust Roman helmet, distinguishing the wearer as a trumpeter, and the way in which the chinstrap has been placed out of the way.*

regiment was armed with short carbines, pistols and sabres. In time of war each regiment had to form a reserve squadron, made up of ten men from each field squadron.

Kettle drums were abolished and trumpeters introduced in 1790. The organizational changes inflicted on Austria's cavalry were extremely

◀ OFFICER, CHEVAUXLÉGERS REGIMENT KLENAU NO. 5, 1809 (LEFT), AND TROOPER, DRAGOON REGIMENT NO. 1 (KAISER), 1812 (RIGHT) *The development of the Roman helmet of the German cavalry is clearly shown here, in that the crest and comb increased in height and jutted more forward as the years moved on. In 1812 the gilt-plated comb of officers' helmets was decorated on both sides with a crouching lion. The Regiment Klenau fought in southern Germany in 1800, at the battle of Hohenlinden in December, among other actions. In 1805 the main body of the regiment escaped from encirclement at Ulm and made their way to Bohemia. The Dragoon Regiment No. 1 had two squadrons at Austerlitz in 1805; in 1809 they were in the II Corps and fought at Aspern, Wagram, Korneuburg and Znaim. The dragoons and chevauxlégers used the same heavy sword as the cuirassiers.*

Chevauxlégers Regimental Distinctions: 1798

No./Title/Date raised*	Coat	Facings	Buttons
1 (1)/Kaiser Chevauxlégers/1688	white	pompadour	yellow
converted 1st Dragoons 1798			
re-converted 1st Chevauxlégers 1802	dark green 1815		
2 (3)/Kaiser Dragoons/1685, disbanded 1802	dark green	emperor yellow	white
3 (26)/Archduke Johann Kürassiers/1682	white	crimson	white
converted 1st Dragoons 1802		black	white
1798	dark green	orange	yellow
1802		black	white
4 (18)/Karakzay Chevauxlégers/1733	white	dark green	white
converted to 4th Dragoons 1798			
converted to 2nd Chevauxlégers 1802			
Hohenzollern 1803	dark green 1815		
5 (13)/Modena Dragoons/1706	dark green	orange	white
disbanded in 1802			
6 (37)/Coburg Dragoons/1683, disbanded 1802	dark green	poppy red	white
7 (39)/Waldeck Dragoons/1701	dark green	dark blue	white
converted to 2nd Dragoons Hohenlohe 1802	white	crimson	white
converted to Knesevich 1809			
8 (38)/Württemberg Dragoons/1688			
1792	white	black	white
1798	dark green	pink	yellow
converted to 3rd Dragoons 1802	white	crimson	white
9 Staff Dragoons/1798, disbanded 1802	grass green	black	yellow
	dark green 1798		white 1798
10 (28)/Lobkowitz Chevauxlégers/1718	white	poppy red	yellow
converted to 3rd Chevauxlégers 1802			
11 (31)/Latour Chevauxlégers/1725	white	dark blue	yellow
converted to 4th Chevauxlégers 1802			
La Tour 1803			
Vincent 1806	dark green by 1815		
12 (7)/Kinsky Chevauxlégers/1631	white coat	light blue	yellow
converted to 12th Dragoons 1798			
converted to 5th Chevauxlégers 1802, Klenau 1803			
13/Rosenberg/1798, renumbered 6th Chevauxlégers 1802	white	black	yellow
14 (19)/Levenehr Dragoons 1733			
renumbered 4th Dragoons 1802	dark green	emperor yellow	yellow
15 (9)/Savoy Dragoons/1682	[??]	dark green	white
converted to 5th Dragoons 1802			
7th Chevauxlégers raised in Italy in 1814	dark green	crimson	white

*Regiment numbers are those of the 1798 series; numbers following in brackets denote the 1792 series

complex. In 1798 it was decided that only the 12 cuirassier regiments would be classed as heavy cavalry; the light German cavalry would consist of 15 regiments of light dragoons, each of six squadrons. To achieve this, the six old dragoon regiments and seven *chevauxlégers* regiments changed their titles, the existing Italian Staff Dragoon Regiment was converted to a line unit and a new regiment was raised from the 4th Divisions of two *chevauxlégers* regiments and some *émigré* French troops.

These light cavalry regiments were equipped with small Polish horses, and the colour of their coats changed from white to dark green. As light cavalry, they were issued the Hungarian Bock saddle, as used by the hussars and lancers. This all changed in 1802, when they were reclassified as heavy cavalry. They received larger, German horses and used the German saddle again. It was ordered that all cavalry regiments were to have eight squadrons and that several regiments were to be disbanded; the new squadrons were to be stronger than heretofore. The eight sharpshooters per squadron had rifled carbines and the rest of the men were equipped with a smoothbore version.

THE HUSSARS

Hussars Regimental Distinctions: 1792–1802

No.*/Title	Dolman & pelisse	Facings	Buttons	Lace	Fur	Breeches	Cap	Sabretasche
2 (1)/Kaiser	dark blue	yellow	yellow	yellow	white	dark blue	dark blue*	dark blue
11/(9)/Nadasdy	dolman red, pelisse dark blue	red	yellow	crimson	brown	dark blue	black	crimson
16 (6)/Hadik	dark blue	red	white/red	white	brown	red	red	orange
17 (2)/Kalnoky	light blue	light blue	yellow	yellow	?	red	red	crimson
30 (8)/Nauendorf	light green	red	yellow	light red	white	light green	black	light red
32 (3)/Esterhazy	light blue	yellow	yellow	yellow	brown	red	red **	dark green
34 (4)/Desöffy	light green	red	yellow	white	?	red	red	light red
35 (10)/Bethlen	light blue	?	yellow	light red	?	red	green	light red
44 (11)/Szeckler	dark blue	yellow	white	?	white	dark blue	black	?

* Number in 1769 shown first, 1798 number shown in brackets

The following regiments were also present during the Seven Years' War, but were disbanded shortly afterwards:

Regiment	Dolman & Pellise	Facings	Buttons	Lace	Breeches	Cap
Baranyay	green	green	yellow	red	light blue	red
Sczeczeny	dark blue	red	yellow	red	dark blue	dark blue
Palffy	light blue	pink	yellow	pink	light blue	pink
Carlstädter	dark blue	red	yellow	yellow	dark blue	red
Kukez	red	red	white	white	red	red
Esclavonier	green	green	yellow	yellow/white	red	red

*black in 1772 **light grey in 1772 +light blue in 1772

Hussars originated in Hungary; their title originally meaning corsair or raider. Their flamboyant costume and their reputation for daredevil acts acquired during the Seven Years' War with Prussia made them immensely popular in all armies in Europe. Naturally, the Austrian armed forces could call upon the services of considerable numbers of such individuals and hussar units were the mainstay of the empire's light cavalry.

During the Napoleonic period hussars, as in all armies, were employed as scouts, given raiding missions or despatched to harry and pursue a defeated enemy on the run. Mounted on light, nimble horses, they performed so well in the Austrian forces of the Seven Years' War that the vast majority of continental European armies raised similar units for their own armies.

The Hussars 1792–1802

In 1767 new uniform regulations were introduced. Prior to this, the hussars wore their own interpretation of Hungarian national costume. This had largely consisted of a fur colpack with coloured bag, a dolman (with coloured cuffs and collars) or waist-length jacket and a fur-lined pelisse, both having five rows of buttons on the chest, all linked with coloured lace, decorated breeches and short boots. The laces on

▶ TROOPER, HUSSAR REGIMENT NO. 3 (ARCHDUKE FERDINAND), 1798–1806 *This was the only hussar regiment to have an ash grey shako. Unusually, this man is shown wearing his pelisse over the dolman. The breeches were dark blue, but have been covered here by grey, buttoned overalls for field service. He wears the red leather fist strap of his sabre around his wrist, as was required when going into action.*

▲ SERGEANT, HUSSAR REGIMENT NO. 10
(STIPSICZ), **1809** *The twin gold braids around
the top of the shako, the gold embroidered
imperial cipher "FI" in the pompon and the
yellow and black sabre fist strap were all
badges of rank, as was the polished cane. In
1799 the regiment fought in Switzerland and
in 1805 they were in northern Italy. In 1809
they were distinguished at Aspern and
Wagram. They were not mobilized in 1812
and fought in Italy in 1813 and 1814.*

the chest were in the button colour for
officers and for the sergeant major; for
other ranks they were as shown in the
chart on the left. A curved sabre and a
coloured sabretasche hung from the
waist belt.

It must be mentioned that the
documentation of these uniforms for
this period is somewhat fragmentary
due to the lack of adequate sources. It
seems that many of the details
(including the design of the crests on
the sabretasches) were actually decided
by the colonel-in-chief himself. By
1792 all sabretasches were red and
bore the imperial cipher "FII".

In 1767 the fur colpack was retained
only by officers, sergeants and the
standard-bearer. All others now wore a
felt cap or *mirliton*; NCOs had a yellow
band around the tops of their caps.

The *Grenz* hussar regiments
Banalisten and Warasdiner had been
disbanded in 1780. In 1798 it was
decided that the Hungarian cavalry was
to consist of twelve regiments, each
containing eight, instead of the
previous ten, squadrons. Each branch
of the cavalry arm now adopted its
own numbering system.

In 1798 the hussars were
renumbered: Kaiser No. 2 became No.
1; Nadasdy No. 11 became No. 9;
Haddik No. 16 became No. 6; Kalnoky
No. 17 became No. 2; Nauendorf No.
30 became No. 8; Esterhazy No. 32

▲ HUSSAR KIT *1 A dolman showing the
intricate lace arrangement across the chest
and down the back.*
*2 A pelisse as worn by the Erdoedy Regiment.
Note the cords to fasten the pelisse so it can
be worn over the left shoulder, thereby not
interfering with the sword arm and offering
some protection from sword cuts.*
*3 Detail of the black leather bandolier straps
and the cartouche, which bears the double-
headed eagle.*
*4 The standard hussars' black and yellow
barrelled sash.*
*5 A crimson sabretasche showing in detail the
Hungarian royal crown of Saint Stephen.*

became No. 3; Desöffy No. 34 became
No. 4; and Bethlen No. 35 became No.
10; and Szeckler No. 44 became No.
11. Regiments No. 5 and No. 7 were
raised in the same year, formed from
amalgamating the 5th Divisions of the
existing eight regiments. The Szeckler
Hussars and the newly raised Croatian-
Slovenian Grenz Hussar Regiment
joined the line as regiments No. 11 and
No. 12. This latter regiment was
disbanded again in 1802, and the
Hungarian Palatinal Hussars became
the new Regiment No. 12.

The Hussars 1803–15

In 1802 the staff of the regiment was increased from 30 to 32 men and each division of two squadrons was given a senior and a junior surgeon. Each squadron now had 12 corporals, six vice-corporals, two trumpeters, 156 mounted and 35 unmounted troopers. The peace establishment of a hussar regiment was 1,816 men and 1,488 horses. In time of war there was also a reserve squadron with 186 men and 177 horses. In 1805 each squadron was increased by one trumpeter.

During the wars of 1813–15 each hussar regiment (except the Szeckler Grenz Hussars No. 11) was increased by two "Vélite Divisions"; these were made up of patriotic volunteers and noblemen.

All details as for the German fusiliers except as noted below. The shakos introduced in 1798 had black and yellow cords and flounders and these regiments wore the traditional Hungarian costume. The fur trim to the pelisses was black. Officers had black bandoliers with gilt picker equipment. Their shakos were decorated with elaborate gold lace. The barrel sash was black and yellow; the red sabretasche was edged in black and yellow and decorated with the crowned imperial cipher. Belts were white. Weapons were a curved sabre with a steel hilt in a steel sheath on red leather slings, pistols and short carbines. The saddle cover was black sheepskin edged red. The red shabraque had long rear corners; it was edged and decorated as for the dragoons. The portmanteau was round and red and all sabretasches were now red with black and yellow decoration and crowned cipher. In 1802 all regiments were ordered to adopt light blue dolmans, breeches and pelisses with black and yellow lace and yellow buttons.

▲ JUNIOR OFFICER, HUSSAR REGIMENT NO. 9 (ERDOEDY), 1812 *Here, the black shako has officer's gold lace decoration and lions' heads to the sides, the officer wears a dark green dolman and pelisse, gold buttons and lace, crimson breeches. All hussar regiments wore the same red saddle furniture with black and yellow edging and the same red sabretasches. Senior officers had a second row of gold lace to the shako with thicker gold lace to the peak. The rear peak was also edged in gold and the embroidery on the sabretasche was augmented with trophies of arms.*

◄ TROOPER, HUSSAR REGIMENT ARCHDUKE CHARLES No 2, 1805 *Prior to 1798 this regiment bore the number 17 in the combined list of all the cavalry regiments. The shako colour is described as madder red. Examples of such items in the Army Museum in Vienna show the loop and cockade to have been made of brass. The flat leather fist strap was 1 in (2.5 cm) wide; the method shown here of attaching it to the sabre hilt is very unusual.*

Development of Regimental Titles 1803–15

Numbers in brackets show the number of that regiment in 1769–98

1 (2) Kaiser. Raised 1756.

2 (17) EH Leopold; 1795 EH Joseph. Raised 1742.

3 (32) 1792 vacant Esterhazy; 1794 EH Ferdinand. Raised 1702.

4 (34) Vecsey; 1803 Hessen-Homburg. Raised 1733.

5 Raised in 1798. 1801 Ott; 1809 Radetzky. Raised 1798.

6 (16) Blankenstein; 1814 Württemberg. Raised 1734.

7 Raised in 1798. 1801 Liechtenstein. Raised 1798.

8 (30) Wurmser; 1799 Nauendorf; 1802 Kienmayer; 1814 Kürfürst von Hessen. Raised 1696.

9 (11) Erdoedy; 1806 Frimont. Raised 1688.

10 (35) Barco; 1802 Stipsicz; 1814 King Friedrich Wilhelm III of Prussia. Raised 1741.

11 (44) Szeckler; Raised 1762.

12 (Croatisch-Slavonisches Grenz Hussar Regiment). Disbanded 1802; the Hungarian "Palatinal Hussars" (raised in 1800) became the new 12th Regiment.

► A43 TROOPER, HUSSAR REGIMENT NO. 4 (VECSEY), 1815 *An example of a hussar's uniform at the very end of the Napoleonic Wars. This trooper wears a blue shako, poplar green dolman and pelisse, poppy red breeches, white buttons and lace. The barrel sash is black and yellow.*

They were to be distinguished by the colour of their shakos. The scheme was never put into effect, however, and the regimental colour scheme remained pretty much as it was before.

◄ TRUMPETER, HUSSAR REGIMENT NO. 1 (KAISER), 1812 *The red plume and swallows' nests are the badges of the trumpeter. Trumpeters wore distinctive uniforms, so they could be quickly identified by the commanding officers. They could then be instructed to give certain signals, for example to rally and reform after a successful charge. Their role was therefore vital if a unit was to act in a co-ordinated, disciplined way. Light cavalry were notorious for getting out of hand and had a particular need for discipline.*

Hussar Regimental Distinctions: 1803–15

No./Title	Shako	Dolman & pelisse	Buttons	Breeches
1 (2)/Kaiser	black	dark blue	yellow	dark blue
2 (17)/EH Joseph	madder red	light blue	yellow	light blue
3 (32)/EH Ferdinand	pike grey	dark blue	yellow	dark blue
4 (34)/Vecsey	light blue	parrot green	white	poppy red
5 (**)/Ott	madder red	dark green	white	madder red
6 (16)/Blankenstein	black	light blue	yellow	light blue
7 (**)/Liechtenstein	grass green	light blue	white	light blue
8 (30)/Wurmser	black	parrot green	yellow	poppy red
9 (11)/Erdoedy	black	dark green	yellow	crimson
10 (35)/Meszaros	grass green	light blue	yellow	light blue
11 (44) Szeckler	black	dark blue	white	dark blue
12 (**) Palatinal	black	cornflower blue	white	cornflower blue

(*) 1792 numbers are shown in brackets behind the new, 1798 series. (**) Raised after 1798. The titles in this table are as for 1798.

THE LANCERS

The lancers (*Ulans*) were the junior regiments of the Austrian cavalry, the first being raised in 1784 under Joseph II from the ex-Polish provinces of Galicia and Lodomeritz, which had been Austrian since 1772. The regiment (*Pulk*) had 300 *Towarziki* and 300 *Pozdonen*. The former were members of the minor Polish aristocracy, the latter their servants. The costume was of traditional Polish cut. As of 1792 the uniform was grass green; the 1st wore white breeches but in 1798 these changed to grass green. The 3rd and 4th regiments wore dark green; all had yellow buttons. The facings of all regiments were poppy red and were worn on the collar, pointed cuffs, lapels, skirt turnbacks and piping to seams on the back of the tunic and the sleeves. They were differentiated by the colour of the upper part of the square-topped *czapka*. This traditional square Polish headgear was topped by the black-over-yellow plume and the black-within-yellow pompon.

Trumpeters wore red plumes. All ranks wore broad black and yellow waist belts.

The front rank carried lances with black-over-yellow, swallow-tailed pennants and light cavalry sabres. The rear rank were armed with the sabre and a carbine. The lance was made of beech wood and decorated with a black and yellow pennant. The butt end of the lance sat in a shoe on the right stirrup and was equipped with a strap, through which the rider put his right arm. The lance was well known in armies in eastern Europe, but it was not until 1811, after the success of the Lancers of the Vistula against the British at Albuera, that it took hold in the French army.

In 1798 all lancer regiments were ordered to wear grass green uniforms.

◄ COLONEL, MERVELDT REGIMENT, 1812 *The square top of the* czapka *was much taller than it had been originally; there were now four regiments of lancers in the Austrian Army, all clad in green uniforms faced red, and having brass buttons. They were differentiated by the colour of the top of the* czapka: *1st, yellow; 2nd, grass green; 3rd, red; 4th, white. As classic light cavalry, their role was mainly in the advanced patrolling, intelligence gathering and screening of operations from prying enemy eyes. The costume is entirely Polish in character.*

▼ TROOPER, ULAN REGIMENT No. 2 (MOTSCHLITZ), 1798 *The uniform of Austrian lancer regiments was copied – as in other armies – from the Polish national dress. The first Austrian lancer regiment was raised in 1784 and was an irregular unit. The square-topped* konfederatka *had a noticeably lower crown at this time than in later years. In 1805 Prince Schwarzenberg became colonel-in-chief of this regiment.*

Regimental Distinctions: Lancers

1 Meszaros; raised in 1784 as a Free Corps; title in 1797 Merveldt, emperor yellow *czapka*.

2 Ulanen-Freikorps Degelmann; raised 1790; title changes: 1793 Schwarzenberg; 1794 Keglevich; 1797 Motschlitz; 1805 Schwarzenberg, green *czapka*.

3 Raised 1801; title Archduke Charles, scarlet *czapka*.

4 Raised 1813; title Kaiser, white *czapka*.

Instead of the waist sash, officers were identified by cartouche bandoliers of black lacquered leather, decorated with gold ornaments.

Organization

These regiments were organized as hussars. In 1785 the regiment was increased to three divisions, each attached to the *chevauxlégers* regiments Lobkowitz, Levenehr and Modena. Next year it was decided that the other *chevauxlégers* regiments should also have a division of lancers attached.

After the end of the war with the Turks in 1790, it was decided to concentrate these lancers into one regiment of four divisions. Meanwhile, Colonel Count O'Donell had raised a corps of volunteers in Galicia, including two lancer divisions. By Order of 20 April 1791, these lancers were taken from O'Donell's corps, given a third division, and became the Ulan Volunteer Corps, bearing the name of its commander, Major Degelmann. In 1798 it became the 2nd Ulans. Each squadron had 168 troopers.

▶ LANCER SADDLE *The hussars and the lancers used the same saddle furniture and harness and both rode the Hungarian Bock saddle, which was made of wood and looked rather like a sawing horse. It had the advantage of keeping the load of the rider and his equipment well clear of the horse's spine.*

▲ THE POLISH CZAPKA *The czapka developed out of the traditional Polish square-topped* konfederatka. 1 *Originally this had a low crown, and was rather squat, but during the Napoleonic period the headgear grew markedly taller. By the 1790s it was as 2 and by 1809 it had developed into the tall* czapka *which lent its wearer the appearance of great height 3. The* czapka *was adopted by many nations for their lancer regiments and remained in use in the Prussian Army until 1918. The modern Polish army still wears a square-topped fatigue cap.*

▶ TRUMPETER, ULAN REGIMENT NO. 4 (KAISER), 1813 *Note the distinctive red plume of the trumpeter and the gold and black trumpet cords, typical of Austrian light cavalry. The black turnups of the grass green breeches are practical but boots are also worn underneath to protect the ankle.*

THE ARTILLERY AND PIONEERS

Until about 1734 the artillery were regarded more as a guild of craftsmen that soldiers. The first uniform was wolf grey, with red cuffs and yellow buttons, but in 1760 the coat and breeches became deer brown until 1798, when wolf grey was reintroduced. The Roman helmet for artillery officers had black-over-yellow crests and the cipher "FII" on the front plate;

those of the men had red crests. The helmet was not fully introduced; officers and men then wore the bicorn. All field artillerymen wore boots.

Artillery Organization

The artillery was divided into the field artillery and the garrison artillery in the fortresses. From 1765–72 artillery pieces were divided into line and reserve guns according to calibre. Line guns were 3-pounders and they were distributed with the infantry battalions. Reserve artillery guns were 6- and 12-pounders, with 7-pound howitzers. These guns were grouped in three or four concentrations, either on the wings of the line of battle, or in the centre. It was only in the Revolutionary Wars that batteries began to appear. To distinguish them from siege and fortress guns of similar calibres, these guns were referred to as "mobile" or "flying" batteries.

It is worthy of note that the continued supply of ammunition for muskets, carbines and guns on the battlefield was the responsibility of the commander of the Artillery Reserve.

In 1778, Colonel Rouvroy of the 2nd Artillery Regiment, proposed the introduction of horse artillery to the army. Prussia's Frederick the Great had first raised such units in 1759, at the start of the Seven Years' War.

◀ SENIOR OFFICER, ARTILLERY, 1798 *The artillery wore coats of infantry cut, and dragoon boots. They also wore the Roman helmet with front and rear peak. Although brown coats were experimented with, the artillery elected to use white, which was a thoroughly impractical choice.*

▶ SENIOR OFFICER, PIONEERS, 1798
Interestingly, this technical corps wore the Corsican hat with the rear brim turned up. The field officer has a broad silver cuff edging and hatband in addition to the hat brim edging. The cane is a badge of office as is the golden sash.

Despite the name, these highly mobile batteries were not intended for use with the cavalry; they were just assets that could be sent rapidly to the desired point. For this purpose, 6-pounders with lightened barrels were used, and the gun trails were extended to provide a box-seat on which five of the six-man gun crew could ride.

Ballistic Performance at the End of the Eighteenth Century

Calibre	Range in paces (ball – first strike)	Range in paces (ball – with riccochet)	Range in paces (canister)
Line 3-pounder	1,200	1,500	300–400
Line 6-pounder	1,400	2,100	300–600
Line 12-pounder	1,600	2,400	300–1,000*
Battery 12-pounder	1,125	–	–
Battery 24-pounder	1,250	–	–
		High trajectory	**Low trajectory**
7-pounder howitzer		1,100	1,900

(*increased range due to the use of heavier balls)

As the top of the box was padded with brown leather, it became known as a "sausage gun". The sixth member of the crew rode on the lead horse. Three of the crew were gunners and three were infantry fusiliers. A mounted corporal commanded two guns. Part of the ammunition for the gun was carried in the box-seat. Six-pounder howitzers were also added to the horse artillery. Ammunition for the horse batteries was carried on pack horses, four per gun. Usually two accompanied the piece and two were in the reserve. One driver managed two pack horses. In 1788, Prince Josias of Sachs-Coburg-Saalfeld took the crew off the trail box and mounted them on hussar horses, thus pointing the way towards real horse artillery. Twenty-four 6-pounder horse guns and eight horse howitzers were used in the 1778 campaign. It became usual to group four cannon and a howitzer into a battery.

In the Revolutionary Wars each infantry battalion in Italy and the Tyrol was given two 3-pounder guns whilst those in the Netherlands and Germany had two 6-pounders. The 12-pounders and the howitzers were held in the artillery reserve, along with three guns per infantry regiment.

In 1796, 460 guns were in the line, 371 in the reserve, and the latter grew in proportion to the line. In 1799–1800 the line had 492 pieces, the reserve 497. In 1805, each infantry regiment had six guns, and those troops in the Tyrol were issued with 1-pounder mountain guns. In 1808 batteries were introduced as permanent tactical groupings of men, guns, ammunition and horses. Guns were withdrawn from the infantry and concentrated into "Brigade Batteries of eight" pieces, all of the same calibre. The infantry were no longer required to provide assistants to the artillery and a new Artillery Assistants' Corps (*Handlanger-Corps*) was formed to help the gunners. This corps was not part of the field artillery, but was administered by the Artillery Directorate.

Apart from the Brigade Batteries, there were "Position Batteries" (of four 6- or 12-pounder cannon and two 7-pounder howitzers) and "Cavalry Batteries" of four 6-pounder horse guns and two 7-pounder horse howitzers. Brigade batteries were under command of the brigade commander, usually split into two equal halves. Position batteries remained in reserve, under corps command. Archduke Charles formed an Army Artillery Reserve in 1809. In 1813 it was initially dispersed, but soon reconstituted. Men of the artillery train wore white coats, emperor yellow facings, brass buttons.

Pioneers and *Pontonniers*

The artillery looked after the pioneers, engineers, sappers, miners, *pontonniers* and *Tschaikisten*, all of whom wore

▶ PONTONNIERS, **1800** *The pontonniers dealt with all bridging operations required by the army. Their uniform was dark blue with red facings and white buttons. The collar is unusual as are the tops to the man's boots. The pontonniers were technical troops and were counted as a branch of the artillery.*

pioneer uniform, but with the left-hand brim of the hat turned up; the sappers and miners had crimson facings, the engineers pompadour.

The *pontonniers* wore grey, faced red with silver buttons. Apart from the pioneers and *pontonniers,* there was also a small regular corps of *Tschaikisten,* managing the shipping traffic on the Danube. *Tschaikisten* wore Hungarian fusilier uniform, but with a peakless shako, cornflower blue coat, red facings, white buttons, black belts.

THE IMPERIAL CONTINGENTS

▲ GRENADIER, FUERSTENBERG INFANTRY REGIMENT, 1795 *This regiment was part of the Swabian contingent. This figure is shown with a brown bearskin with brass front plate bearing the arms of the principality, white coat, waistcoat, breeches and cartridge pouch bandolier. The waist belt, musket sling and sword belt were of brown leather. Facings and lining to the coat were red; buttons were brass. It is most unusual to see an infantry unit wearing knee boots and it probably made marching long distances very uncomfortable.*

All member states of the Holy Roman Empire were called upon to support the imperial war effort, either with a contingent of troops or, alternatively, with a sum of money. States could be called upon to provide the "simple" contribution, a double or triple amount of men or money. Major states of the empire, such as Saxony, Hessen-Cassel, Hessen-Darmstadt and Bavaria, provided relatively large armed contingents. The minor states were grouped into ten Imperial Regions (*Reichskreise*) and clubbed together to raise a single battalion or squadron for imperial service.

In 1792 there were 20 battalions of infantry from the various German states in Austrian service. Since the early eighteenth century the Austrians had followed the custom of clothing their infantry in pale grey or white and this custom was adopted by the other Catholic states of the empire.

Unless otherwise mentioned, all regiments wore the tricorn hat, and waistcoats, breeches and belts were white. Grenadiers would have worn Austrian-style bearskin caps. Officers wore waist sashes under the coat; these were silver, with narrow red and black stripes. The Swabian region also provided the Fuerstenberg Dragoons with light blue coat and waistcoat, dark green facings, yellow buttons, black belts and breeches.

The Middle Rhine Region contributed the Heidelberg Dragoons with red coat, black facings edged in yellow, yellow buttons, white belts, waistcoat and breeches.

The Electorate of Mainz provided infantry in white coats, linings, waistcoats, breeches and belts. The Upper Rhine Regional Infantry Company wore a dark blue coat with red facings, white buttons, waistcoat, breeches and belts.

Regimental Distinctions: Imperial Contingents

Title	Coat	Facings	Buttons	Hat tassels
Kürassier Regiments				
Treskow	buff	red	yellow	red within white
Hohenzollern	white	red	white	red within white
	buff waistcoat and breeches			
Dragoon Regiments				
Anspach	white	light blue	white	light blue within white
Württemberg	light blue	black	yellow	yellow and light blue
	light blue lining; buff waistcoat and breeches			
Infantry Regiments				
Kerpen	dark blue	white	yellow	light blue within white
	red lining			
Schertel	dark blue	yellow	white	yellow and dark blue
	lined red			
Hohenlohe	dark blue	red	yellow	red and dark blue
Wolfegg	white	red	white	red and white
Fugger	white	red	yellow	red and dark blue
Baden-Durlach	dark blue	red	yellow	red and dark blue
Württemberg	dark blue	yellow	yellow	yellow and light blue
Artillery Corps				
Schlemilch	dark blue	red	yellow	

In 1801, following the Peace of Luneville, the Electorates of Cologne, Mainz and Trier were dissolved; most of their territories fell to France and the regiments were disbanded. The mini-army was intended mainly to mark the status of the Prince Elector and supply a mounted guard at his palace; their weapons were old, they did no live firing. Only the hussars and the *Jägers* were competent soldiers. The uniform worn exhibited much Austrian influence. From 1792 to 1796 these troops fought alongside the Prussians and Austrians against the army of Revolutionary France.

By 1797 France had overrun all territory on the left bank of the Rhine. The Treaty of Campo Formio of 17 October 1797 recognized this new arrangement. The imperial contingents were soon to be abolished or found themselves absorbed by those German states that sided with Napoleon.

▼ TROOPER, WÜRTTEMBERG DRAGOONS, 1792 *A Swabian regiment, this was one of the few cavalry units fielded by small German states ever cautious about military expenditure. Note the buff leather gauntlets and heavy cavalry boots.*

▼ PRIVATE, WOLFEGG INFANTRY REGIMENT, 1792 *Another Swabian regiment. This infantryman wears more practical footwear and his uniform is Prussian in style.*

▲ GRENADIER CORPORAL, ELECTORATE OF MAINZ, 1794 *Part of the Middle Rhine Region, the tiny army of the Electorate of Mainz consisted in 1795 of four weak regiments of infantry, a corps of* Jägers, *a company of hussars (employed as police), a company of engineers and a company of artillery.*

The Electorate of Trier provided a regiment of infantry (named Wenz), wearing white with red facings, and a two-company corps of *Jägers*. There was also a company of mounted Life Guards (*Leibgarde zu Pferde*) for ceremonial guard duty, but most of the men had no horses.

RUSSIA

With a population of almost 50 million people at the opening of the nineteenth century, Russia possessed almost unlimited manpower. Half the male population were agricultural labourers – serfs or slaves – and owned by the czar. But brutal discipline, and miserable living conditions, failed to rob the Russian soldier of his patriotism and devotion to his ruler. Tough and resilient, the Russian *moujik* was perhaps the perfect martial material. Terms of military service were for life; if a man survived to retirement, or became incapacitated, he would be transferred to a veteran unit in some garrison town. If still fit for limited duties, he would be called upon to stand guard or patrol the town as a type of police force. The performance of the Russian soldier in 1812 proved what progress had been made in military efficiency in this vast realm. On one occasion, the entire 27th Infantry Division retired before French cavalry, maintaining good order under fire.

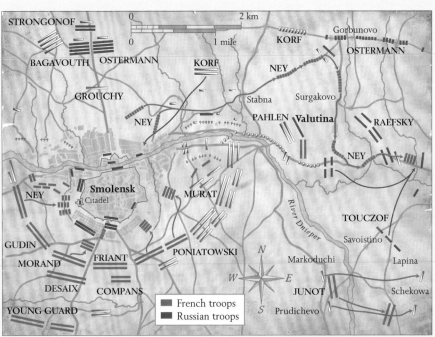

▲ *Napoleon assaulted the city of Smolensk on 17 August 1812 as he pushed deeper into the Russian Empire. After a stubborn battle, and with the city in flames, the Russians withdrew, their infantry, which displayed its traditional zeal, fighting a string of rearguard battles and drawing the French eastward towards Moscow.*

◄ *Napoleon and Czar Alexander of Russia sign the Treaty of Tilsit, 7 July 1807. Following the signing of the peace, there was much mutual entertainment. Here Alexander shows Napoleon some of his more exotic Asian warriors.*

THE CZAR AND THE ARMY

A major factor in the Russian Army's development following the Seven Years' War (1756–63), had been the improvements of Potemkin, Catherine II's adjutant-general and ex-lover. His autocratic reforms were often introduced without imperial approval, but were, in the main, practical and beneficial to the army. But, even so, Russia's forces remained underfunded.

In 1765 Catherine II showed great interest in the Military Academy, in which the sons of the aristocracy were prepared for leadership. Ages ranged from 5 years to 21 years, and the boys were trained in an extraordinarily broad range of subjects, including: basic literacy, arithmetic, geography, chronology, history, mythology, Slavonic language, military and civil engineering, book-keeping, etiquette and the responsibilities of the landed gentry. In the final class, sciences were emphasized: justice, political science, international laws, physics, chemistry, ballistics, navigation and astronomy. Despite this, the level of the education of Russian officers remained below that of other European armies.

Meanwhile, the grand duke and heir apparent, Paul Petrovitch, devoted himself to recreating the army of Prussia's Frederick the Great. In 1782 he founded the Gatschina army detachment to guard his palaces at Pavlovsk and the island of Kameny-Ostrov, near St Petersburg. By 1796, when Paul succeeded to the throne, this corps had grown to 1,750 men and included a battalion of grenadiers, four of musketeers, a company of *Jägers*, a regiment each of cuirassiers, dragoons, hussars and Cossacks, and a battalion of artillery, both horse and foot. As soon as he was installed on the throne, Paul ordered the army to scrap Potemkin's practical uniforms and revert to the style worn in 1762.

Paul inherited an army of the officer cadet academy, Imperial Guard (three grenadier regiments, four of cavalry), 12 grenadier and 55 musketeer regiments, 20 field battalions, 40 *Jäger* battalions, five cuirassier regiments, 16 carabineer regiments, a mounted grenadier regiment, 11 dragoon regiments, two of hussars, 11 of light cavalry and four regiments of mounted rifles. The foot artillery had the artillery school, the bombardier regiment, two cannonier and two fusilier regiments and three bombardier battalions. The horse artillery had six companies. The engineers consisted of the engineer school, four companies of engineers and one each of miners and pioneers. There were also 110 battalions of garrison troops, while Cossacks formed

▲ *Catherine II, of Russia. A talented woman who deserved her epithet of Great.*

the armies of Astrakhan, the Black Sea, the Don, Jekaterinoslaw, Orenburg, Siberia and the Urals. There were also nine regiments of regular Cossacks and five of Kalmucks. Including minor formations, it totalled 507,538 men.

Before ascending the throne, Paul had spent much time preparing a whole raft of reforms directed at the military. In 1796 he reorganized the army into 12 geographical divisions, based on the peacetime locations of the troops. Each division contained grenadier, musketeer and garrison infantry regiments plus cavalry regiments. These were later called "Inspectorates". *Jäger* battalions appeared only in the 5th, 6th, 8th, 9th, 10th and 12th Divisions. In case of war, *ad hoc* tactical formations were to be formed from these units and grouped into operational armies.

In 1798 Paul established two army orphanages: one for the orphans of officers, one for those of other ranks. He also raised the number of Soldiers' Schools to 66, teaching 64,000 pupils.

◄ *Paul I, his wife Maria Feodorovna and their children, shortly before Paul's murder.*

But plots against Paul's life brewed amid the alienated nobility, led – it is thought – by Count Pahlen, head of the Secret Police. On the night of 12 March 1801, Pahlen, Count Bennigsen and the brothers Nikolai and Platon Zubov entered the Mikhailovski Palace and murdered the czar. Some suspect that his son, Alexander, was implicated in the plot, but as Pahlen destroyed any incriminating evidence, we will never know. At any rate, Alexander I succeeded to the Russian throne on 12 March 1801. He abandoned Paul's neutrality and his claim to the island of Malta, recognizing England's control of the seas. As a civil and military reformer he, too, was extremely active. He established 17 schools for the sons of the aristocracy, who were also invited to contribute financially to the running of these institutions. Each school was to send 16 graduates to the St Petersburg Cadet Corps and eight to the university there each year.

The Staff

In 1772, Potemkin had formalized and introduced the first general staff organization to the Russian Army. It consisted of a Quartermaster General (QMG), a Lieutenant QMG in the rank of brigadier general, a 2nd Lieutenant QMG in rank a colonel, two Over-QMs (lieutenant colonels), eight Over-QMs (majors), 12 Divisional QMs (captains), 12 Divisional QMs (lieutenants), 10 Column Leaders (sergeants), 50 Column Leaders (corporals) and eight clerks.

From 1766 a War Rations Commissariat of 104 officers and men was established to manage the provision of rations for the army in peace and in war. The Supply Commissariat managed the procurement, storage and provision of cloth, leather, and so on, for the manufacture of uniforms. Strangely enough, in 1796, Czar Paul disbanded the general staff corps: an inexplicable act of great disservice to the army.

On his accession in 1801, Alexander reinstated the existence of the "Quartermaster's Department of His Imperial Majesty's Suite".

▲ *Alexander I, dressed in military splendour, at the height of his success in 1814. An enlightened ruler, his resolve was instrumental in defeating Napoleon.*

Recruitment

Army recruits were levied by periodic imperial decrees, as need dictated. Each locality would be told how many men to produce. Married men and skilled tradesmen were exempt from military service, and the rich were permitted to buy others to serve for them: so it was mainly unskilled serfs who went into the military.

In 1812 the Russian Army had 17,139 officers, of whom 89 per cent were from the aristocracy. Despite this, a commission could be earned by suitable applicants from all walks of life and even by foreigners. As well as graduating from the Military Academy,

there was another way in which an aspirant could become an officer. To do this, he would have to serve as an NCO for 12 years (except for sons of Russian nobles and foreigners, who were required to serve four years only).

In 1812 the ages of a sample of 1,315 officers ranged from 16 to 65, with 88 per cent lying in the 20 to 45 years of age bracket. The academic abilities of these individuals is also of interest: 65 per cent of officers could read and write, 10 per cent could calculate mathematically, 25 per cent knew a foreign language.

Foreigners in the Army

The Russian Army welcomed foreign officers into its ranks; but in November 1797, the Count of Condé's entire corps of *émigré* Frenchmen (five regiments and two companies of artillery) was taken into service. It formed its own inspectorate, but in February 1800 left Russian service to fight under the British flag.

In 1812 about 1.3 per cent – or some 200 – of the officers serving in the Russian Army were foreigners. Of these, most were from German states – mainly Prussia and Württemberg – but there were some French *émigrés* as well. If they had no knowledge of the Russian language when they were accepted, they were allowed one year on full pay to learn it. By recruiting well-qualified officers from western Europe, Alexander hoped to improve the combat effectiveness of his troops.

Most prominent among these foreign officers were Langeron, von Phull, St Priest and Wintzingerode. Of these, Karl von Phull had the czar's ear on military matters and it was he who suggested the building of the armed camp at Drissa, on the River Dvina in 1812, which was to stop Napoleon's invasion. It was a costly folly, which just consumed scarce funds and had to be abandoned. Many of these foreigners were capable soldiers, who gained promotion on transfer and were granted favours and awarded honours by the czar. Competent or not, most of them were cordially hated by their Russian fellow officers.

RUSSIA'S CONFLICT WITH NAPOLEON

Historically, Russia had been outside Europe, looking in. Trade went on between east and west, particularly the importation of timber for the ship-building industries of western Europe. Russia had been involved in the Great Northern War (in a coalition with Prussia) with Charles XII's Sweden from 1700 to 1721. By the end of that conflict Russia had supplanted Sweden as the dominant power in the Baltic, and further expansion west came during the Seven Years' War (1756–63). Russia was allied with Sweden against Prussia in this conflict and invaded Pomerania and East Prussia. Frederick the Great was hard put to retain his throne, but was saved by the death of Czarina Elisabeth, one of his worst enemies, for her successor, Czar Peter III, was an ardent admirer of the Prussian king, who promptly offered peace and withdrew his armies from Prussian territory.

But the Russian Army and aristocracy were incensed at Peter's policy and plotted the czar's downfall. Prince Grigori Orlov – lover to the czar's wife Catherine – and his brother

Alexei murdered Peter. Thus, Catherine (later to be titled "The Great") came to the throne. Although German by birth, Catherine threw herself into understanding her new realm with a will. By dint of hard work and iron determination, she reformed the entire government and state.

For expertise, Catherine turned to England. Admiral Knowles was brought in to advise on the building of warships and the setting up of dockyards. All the czarina's governor generals were ordered to map their provinces, conduct censuses, construct or repair roads and bridges, and set up policing and fire services. A massive public education programme was begun, and hospitals were built, staffed and equipped. Meanwhile, technicians from the foundries at Tula were sent to England to learn how to manufacture mathematical instruments, and to absorb the latest steel-making processes. Textile factories were set up outside Moscow, and Germans were invited to settle in the Volga River region to improve agricultural methods. Trade blossomed, with

Catherine exporting timber, hemp, flax, leather and steel to Europe, and by 1765 the massive debts the czarina had inherited had been converted into a surplus.

Catherine died in November 1796, to be succeeded (briefly) by her son Paul, who, as discussed, was assassinated in 1801 and succeeded by his son, Alexander I. Following Napoleon's victory over Russia and Austria at Austerlitz on 2 December 1805, and over Russia and Prussia at the Battle of Friedland on 14 June 1807, Czar Alexander made peace with France via the Treaty of Tilsit. In so-doing, he agreed to implement Napoleon's Continental System of trade barriers against Britain.

It was the French emperor's aim to combat British trade by locking all goods made in Britain, or carried on British merchantmen, out of the markets of mainland Europe. Unable to compete with the Royal Navy since

▼ *Skirmishing was a frequent event, whether here in 1807, where the 5th Chasseurs à Cheval fight Cossacks, or in 1812 in Russia.*

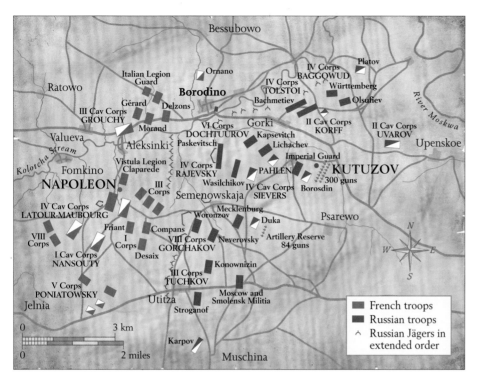

The Battle of Bordino in September 1812, showing troop positions at the start of the battle. During the course of the day, the Russians moved troops from the north to the south to counter Napoleon's main assaults.

its resounding victory over the Franco-Spanish fleets at Trafalgar on 21 October 1805, or mount an invasion of Britain to achieve a military victory over his hated foe, Napoleon hoped to ruin the "nation of shopkeepers" by devastating its financial infrastructure. But a trade boycott is a double-edged weapon: Napoleon's plan would succeed only if he – and all his allies and satellites – could survive a lack of imports longer than Britain could survive a lack of exports.

By skilfully tweaking the customs barriers between France and her allies, and by banning many of his satellite states from producing things such as silk, the emperor had skewed the playing table in France's favour. Thus, while France was cushioned from the worst effects of the new order, there was much hardship and industrial stagnation in the Confederation of the Rhine and Italy in the later years of Napoleon's reign.

Widespread smuggling of contraband colonial goods from Britain into Europe forced the emperor into annexing ever-larger sections of the coastline into France and employing an ever-increasing army of customs officers to combat the flourishing trade. Holland fell in 1810, much of the Baltic coastline and that of the Adriatic followed.

With Russia suddenly denied access to her considerable trade with England, her economy started to suffer too. Discontent grew among the merchant classes, while the nobles began to make their concerns known to Alexander. The czar, well aware of the fate of rulers who trod on too many aristocratic toes, soon took heed.

By 1810 Alexander had opened his Baltic ports to British imports, many of which then flowed into western Europe at increased prices. The universal public taste for coffee, tea, spices and silks was too avid to be stilled by Napoleon's absolute decrees. For his part, Alexander had no stomach for conflict with his own subjects on the matter. Britain's economy did suffer under the Continental System, but her borrowing capacity was so much greater than Napoleon's that it was clear she would outlast him.

By 1810 it dawned on Napoleon that he had to move against Russia and force her to adhere to the blockade of British trade or his entire empire would become an open laughing stock. But Alexander was quietly adamant that domestic trade was his business alone and refused to step into line. In 1812, Napoleon chose to settle the matter with force: in fact, he had no alternative – by this time the invasion of Russia was inevitable.

▼ *First sight of Moscow. The French reached Moscow after Borodino but rejoicing was shortlived when the city went up in flames.*

THE IMPERIAL GUARD

There were three regiments of Foot Guards in 1792: the Preobrazhenski, Siemenovski and Ismailovski regiments. In 1800 the latter two were increased to three grenadier battalions, each of five companies, and a wing company. The Preobrazhenski Regiment was increased to four grenadier battalions, each of five companies, and two wing companies. There were also three mounted regiments and a squadron of Cossacks. A battalion of *Jägers* was raised in 1796. In 1800 the Guard numbered 13,361 men – the equivalent of more than a division.

The Foot Guards

The Guard regiments were more than palace troops and saw frequent field service, as in 1805, 1807 and 1812–14.

The conversion of the regimental structure of the Guard in October 1810 followed that of the line infantry; rather than the old pattern of one grenadier and two fusilier/musketeer battalions, a regiment was now to have three fusilier/musketeer battalions and each battalion was to have one grenadier company and three of fusiliers/musketeers. Each company had two platoons; in the grenadier companies the 1st Platoon was the grenadiers and formed on the right of the battalion, the 2nd Platoon was the sharpshooters and formed on the left. This was a direct copy of the French system. On 10 May 1805 the Guards *Jäger* Regiment was raised from the old *Jäger* Battalion; it had two battalions.

◀ **OFFICER OF GRENADIERS, SIEMENOVSKI REGIMENT, 1796** *Czar Paul was a great admirer of the uniforms of the Prussian Army of Frederick the Great and from 1796 to 1801 he lavished much attention and money to dress his troops in this type of archaic costume. As a grenadier officer, this man wears a gilt mitre cap, lavishly decorated with feathers for parades. The officer's silver gorget bears the double-eagle on trophies of arms, with the peripheral inscription "1700 NO. 19." awarded to this regiment and the Preobrazhenski Foot Guards for their heroism in the Russian defeat at Sweden's King Charles XII's hands on 19 November 1700.*

▶ **MUSKETEER NCO, ISMAILOVSKI GUARDS INFANTRY REGIMENT, 1796** *This regiment was raised in 1730 from Ukrainian militia units, but the officers came mainly from the Baltic territories. This is a much simpler costume but still appears relatively archaic. Czar Alexander would modernize the army's uniform and organization.*

On 12 December 1806 the first militia battalion was raised and on 19 October 1811 it was converted to the Finland Life Guard Regiment. On 7 November the Lithuanian Life Guard Regiment was formed from a battalion of the Preobrazhenski Foot Guards and other selected personnel. The infantry of the Guard were now organized into three brigades, in their own division.

Infantry Uniform

The Guard did not adopt the Potemkin uniforms when these were introduced for the rest of the army in 1786, but retained their old costumes. As all three regiments

Foot Guard Uniforms

The Preobrazhenski Foot Guards
Raised 1683 by Peter I.
Red facings and brass buttons.

Mitre cap colours

Battalion	Band	Backing
1st	brass	crimson
2nd	brass	orange
3rd	dark blue	red
4th	yellow	red
5th	dark blue	red

The Siemenovski Foot Guards
Also raised in 1683 by Peter I.
Light blue collars and shoulder
straps, red cuffs and turnbacks,
brass buttons.

Mitre cap colours

Battalion	Band	Backing
1st	brass	light blue
2nd	red	light blue
3rd	white	light blue

The Ismailovski Foot Guards
Raised in 1730.
Dark green collars and shoulder
straps, red cuffs and turnbacks,
white buttons 1796; brass by 1800.

Mitre cap colours

Battalion	Band	Backing
1st	brass	white
2nd	red	white
3rd	black	white

were grenadiers, they wore the brass-
fronted mitre caps with different
coloured headbands and backing for
each regiment, or the fusilier caps in
the same colour scheme.

In 1803 the shako began to be
issued to the Guard infantry; it was of
the same design as that worn by the
line infantry, but had a strip of the
Guards' braid – as worn on the collar
and cuffs – around the top.

The front was decorated with a brass
grenade and instead of the pompon,
there was a black horsehair plume,
18 in (49 cm) high and 9 in (20 cm)
in diameter. NCOs wore braid in the
button colour around the top of the
shako and their plumes had a white
tip, with a vertical orange stripe down
the centre. Drummers and other

musicians wore red plumes. Shakos
were worn only for everyday duties, the
old mitre caps being worn for parades
and guard duty.

On 13 February 1805 the mitre caps
of the grenadiers and fusiliers were
ordered to be withdrawn from service
and to be replaced by the shako, but
these were without the Guards' lace
around the top. The fusiliers had no
brass grenade badge.

In April 1808 the *kiwer* (bell-
topped hat with the "scooped out"
top) of the line infantry pattern
replaced the Guards' shako. The front
badge was the crowned double-eagle
and the cords were mixed red and
yellow. The huge old plumes were
replaced with tall, narrow models. The
Guard *Jägers* had no plumes.

Officers' cords were of silver, mixed
with black and orange threads; their
plumes of cock feathers gave way to
horsehair plumes and the chinstrap
was replaced by a gilt chain. They
still wore the bicorn off duty.

▶ **MUSKETEER NCO, SIEMENOVSKI FOOT
GUARDS, 1797** *This regiment was raised
by Peter the Great in 1683, at the time
of the foundation of the Russian
standing army. Although this costume
seems ceremonial, the unit played an
important role in all of Russia's
Napoleonic campaigns. The gilt mitre
cap was worn on campaign and
officers wore the silver gorget with
double-headed eagle.*

▼ **GRENADIER CAP PLATE, 1800** *This
shows the double-headed eagle and
cyrillic "P" for Paul. Such mitre plates
were standard issue for line grenadiers
between 1796 and 1801.*

The newly raised Lithuanian Foot
Guards received the same uniform as
that of the Preobrazhenski Regiment,
but with red lapels. The officers had
simple gold loops to collar and cuffs
rather than the complex embroidery of
the older regiments.

The Mounted Guards
The Guard had originally consisted of
infantry, mounted regiments only
being added in the 1720s. In 1803 it
was ordered that each regiment would
form a depot half-squadron, which
stayed in the peacetime location
and trained new recruits and
remounts.

THE LIFE GUARDS. This regiment
was raised in 1721 and was
soon recognized as being
the social elite of the
entire army. It was
more than a highly
placed club for
young aristocrats,
however, and took
to the field on various
occasions, as at
Austerlitz in 1805,
where it took its
share of casualties.

The regiment wore a uniform of white tunic with red facings and silver lace. THE CHEVALIER GUARD. Originally raised in 1724, this regiment was disbanded in 1796 by Czar Paul and re-raised in 1800 by Alexander at five squadrons. The uniform was a white tunic with red facings, silver lace; rather similar to that of the mounted Life Guards.

THE LIFE GUARD HUSSARS. This regiment was raised fairly late, in 1775. The uniform consisted of the typical hussar-style costume, with a brown fur colpack, light blue dolman and pelisse with gold lace and buttons; white fur trim for officers, black for the men. They wore white breeches. Red belts and bandoliers were worn, with red and gold barrel sashes for officers, but red and white for the men. The sabretasche was red with gold edging and bore the decoration of the crowned imperial cipher.

THE LIFE GUARD COSSACK SQUADRON. This corps was raised in 1775 at the strength of a squadron; the simple Cossack uniform consisted of a brown colpack with red bag, a dark blue kaftan and a red tunic with silver cartridge pouches on the chest. It was increased to a regiment of five squadrons in 1800.

LIFE GUARD LANCERS AND LIFE GUARD DRAGOONS. In December 1809 the Grand Duke Constantine Lancers was split to begin to form these regiments.

The Artillery

Initially each of the Guard foot regiments had an artillery company attached to it. On 6 November 1796, however, all the artillery companies were amalgamated as one, and reorganized to form the new Artillery Regiment of the Gatschina Army Detachment. This unit later became the Life Guards Artillery Regiment.

◀ GRENADIER SERGEANT, ISMAILOVSKI FOOT GUARDS, 1800 *The old mitre cap with the crest around the top was uncomfortably heavy and in October 1804 was ordered to be replaced by the stove-pipe shako. It is similar in style to the Prussian Army's grenadier cap of the 1806 campaign. It seems that these mitre caps were worn at the Battle of Austerlitz. The light blue headband and white backing indicate the 1st Battalion. The front of the later shako was decorated by a black-within-orange cockade over a grenade. Note the cane, a badge of office.*

▲ MITRE CAP, GRENADIER SERGEANT, ISMAILOVSKI FOOT GUARDS, 1800 *This ornate Guards' grenadier mitre cap had a pierced copper plate and a surrounding rim of black sheepskin or fur.*

▼ OFFICER, HORSE LIFE GUARDS, 1796–1801 *This regiment was raised in March 1721. The officer's cuirass was decorated in gold, and the badge on the chest was crowned with the double-eagle, within a crowned cartouche, surrounded by trophies of arms. The hat cockade was black silk ribbon, with four double stripes of orange along it. The cavalry boots and the straight-bladed sword denote that the unit was heavy cavalry.*

Training Units

The Guards had the pick of trained officer material drawn from a number of schools and academies.

THE ARMY CADET TRAINING CORPS. Raised in 1731 by Czarina Anna. The uniform was a dark green tunic and cuff flaps, red facings, brass buttons, buff waistcoat and breeches, white belts, plain bicorn with white tassels.

THE MOSCOW CADET CORPS. Raised in December 1752 by Czarina Elisabeth I as a naval officers' training college. The uniform was dark green tunics with white collar, cuffs, lapels, turnbacks, waistcoat, breeches, buttons and belts. Plain bicorns.

THE ARTILLERY AND ENGINEER CADET CORPS. Raised in 1762.

The Engineer School had been founded in 1712, the Artillery School in 1719. Uniform: as for the Army Cadets, but without cuff flaps.

Guard Equipage

On 16 February 1810 the Guard Equipage was formed of naval personnel, at a strength of four companies of naval infantry and an artillery unit. They served regularly as part of the mobilized army and were by no means ceremonial soldiers. Their performance at Borodino was impressive and costly. They also fought at Leipzeig, and had the honour of marching into Paris in 1814.

▲ TROOPER, LIFE GUARD DRAGOONS, 1812
This was one of the youngest regiments of the entire Russian Army, being raised in December 1809 from men of the Guard Lancers. In 1812 they fought at Borodino. On the helmet front plate and on the horse furniture was the eight-pointed star of the Order of St Andrew. The grey overalls were standard and very practical campaign wear.

▶ OFFICER, LIFE GUARD HUSSARS, PARADE UNIFORM, 1802 *The pomp of the Russian Imperial Guard may be imagined as we regard this officer, complete with leopardskin pelisse. The mirliton with plume is unusual, while the elaborate parade harness is amazing. This regiment was raised on 19 February 1775 by Catherine the Great.*

THE LINE INFANTRY AND *JÄGERS*

Russian line infantry were originally organized into musketeer and grenadier regiments. These were supported by *Jäger* detachments, then, later, *Jäger* regiments. In Czar Paul's army reforms of 1796, the independent infantry field battalions were reorganized into six new musketeer regiments. The wing companies of the grenadier regiments and the grenadier companies of the musketeer regiments were, in case of war, to be taken from their parent regiments and formed into combined grenadier battalions, each made up of four companies.

In 1798 six new musketeer regiments were raised and named after their colonels-in-chief; in 1800 the old regional names were restored to all infantry and cavalry regiments. The revised titles of these six regiments are shown in brackets behind the original names: Berg (Baklanovski then Ukraine), Brandt (Kaschkin then Olonetz), Leitner (Nessvetajev then Saratov), Marklovski (Anikejev then Poltava), Mueller I (Kolywan), Pavluzki (Runitsch then Tenginsk). In 1800 the Senate's Regiment was raised, later becoming the Uschakov Regiment, then the Lithuanian.

Uniform Developments

It was in 1803 that the shako appeared in the Russian Army and it was the musketeer regiments that were first to

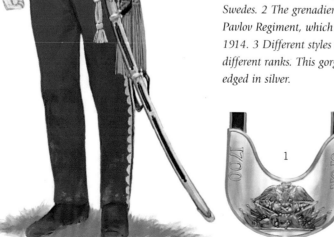

◀ **OFFICER, KIEV LINE GRENADIER REGIMENT, 1786–96** *In 1799 this old regiment had scarlet facings and in 1805, as part of the Ukrainian Inspectorate, it had pink collars and cuffs, white shoulder straps and the pikes of the regiment were painted white. In 1812 the regiment was in the 2nd Grenadier Division of General Prince Karl of Mecklenburg, in Borodin's VIII Corps of the 2nd Army of the West.*

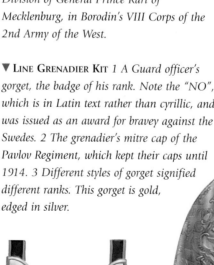

▲ **GENERAL OF INFANTRY, 1800** *It was the custom in the Russian Army of this date that generals who were also colonels-in-chief of regiments wore the uniform of their regiment. This figure is from the Musketeer Regiment Muromsk, a regiment raised in 1708 as a grenadier regiment, converted to musketeers in 1725. The hat's white feather trim distinguishes the wearer's rank.*

▼ **LINE GRENADIER KIT** 1 *A Guard officer's gorget, the badge of his rank. Note the "NO", which is in Latin text rather than cyrillic, and was issued as an award for bravey against the Swedes.* 2 *The grenadier's mitre cap of the Pavlov Regiment, which kept their caps until 1914.* 3 *Different styles of gorget signified different ranks. This gorget is gold, edged in silver.*

Facings and buttons, *Jäger* battalions: 1797

No.	Facings	Buttons
1	bright yellow	yellow
2	bright red	yellow
3	black	white
4	brick red	yellow
5	purple	yellow
6	orange	yellow
7	dark orange	yellow
8	white	yellow
9	dark brown	white
10	orange	white
11	light brown	yellow
12	black	white
13	bright blue	yellow
14	pale crimson	yellow
15	light blue	white
16	light blue	white
17	pink	yellow
18	dark blue	yellow
19	black	white
20	crimson	yellow

be equipped with it. The artillery, garrison troops and grenadiers followed. This first shako was sensibly designed, far removed from the grotesque things that they became in so many armies in the later decades. It had a leather peak and chinstrap and the front was decorated with a cockade under a tuft or pompon. There were two cloth flaps inside, which were designed to protect the ears and cheeks from frost damage in winter. NCOs' shakos had a band in the button colour around the top.

Officers retained the old bicorn, but the embroidered brooch was replaced by a simple loop in the button colour. The plume was raised in height, a great disadvantage on active service, particularly in the Caucasus, where the native marksmen quickly learned to home in on the Russian commanders. It was ordered on 23 December 1805 that officers in combat should wear the same shakos as the men.

Jäger Organization pre-1806

The first *Jägers* appeared in the Russian Army in 1765 as detachments of 60 men, armed with rifles, with each of the 25 infantry regiments of the heavily forested Baltic provinces. By 1769 they had proved their worth so well, that they were attached to all infantry regiments. They were trained in open order combat, marksmanship and in fighting in snow-shoes in winter. In Czar Paul's army reforms of 1797, the *Jäger* Corps was reorganized into 20 *Jäger* battalions; in 1800 the *Jäger* regiments surfaced again, being numbered 1–19, the old 1st having been disbanded.

Jäger Uniforms

The grass green tunic was as for the line infantry but without lapels; the waistcoats and shoulder straps were also grass green. The front of the coat bore six pairs of buttons and all ranks wore a yellow/gold aiguillette on the right shoulder. No pompons were worn on the hats. Breeches were white, belts black; all ranks wore below-knee boots and buff gauntlets. The old bicorns were replaced by a type of top hat, with a brim all around it. This was the forerunner of the shako.

The Inspectorate System of 1801

The Army was organized into 14 regional inspectorates, which had significance only in times of peace. When mobilized, the tactical grouping had nothing in common with the inspectorates. As far as costumes were concerned, in 1802 the hair style was much simplified and shortened, and new uniform regulations for the artillery were issued.

▶ **DRUMMER AND PRIVATE, LINE INFANTRY, 1786–96** *In 1786 Catherine the Great introduced this uniform for most regiments. It was designed by her favourite, Prince Gregory Potemkin, and was eminently practical. The strips of cloth at the back of the cap could be used to protect the ears in winter. No other army's costumes were anything like as good. All infantry regiments wore red facings and were only distinguished by shoulder knots, worn on the left shoulder. Note the drummer's leather apron and the private's canteen.*

The new regulations were to serve as a test-bed for the entire army. All regiments wore dark green tunics with red turnbacks (joined by a regimental button) and two rows of buttons on the chest (with or without lapels); cuffs were usually plain, with two buttons with distinctive regimental lace, (with or without tassels) above each. The horizontal pocket flaps on the hips had two buttons each, just under the flap. Waistcoats and breeches could be white, buff or dark buff.

Grenadier and fusilier cap plates were in the button colour, backed in the facing colour, with headbands of various colours, mostly dark green. The headbands were decorated with metal grenades in the button colour on the sides and at the back. Belts were white with brass fittings. Only the Life Grenadiers wore white gaiters; other regiments wore black.

Under the new system, regiments' collars and cuffs and skirt turnbacks would be coloured according to the inspectorate to which they were allocated. Each regiment had differently coloured shoulder straps, small clothes and loops of lace above each cuff. This produced an incredibly complicated "system" of uniform distinctions, which was maintained until 1807, when all infantry facings were ordered to be red.

BREST INSPECTORATE (straw yellow facings): Apscheron, Azov, Old Ingermannland, Pensa, Podolsk, Riaschk, Vyborg and Vilna Musketeers, 8th Jägers.

CAUCASIAN INSPECTORATE (mid-blue facings): Caucasus Grenadiers, Kabardinsk, Kazan, Susdal, Tiflis and Vologda Musketeers, 16th and 17th Jägers.

CRIMEAN INSPECTORATE (buff facings): Bielev, Sevastopol, Troitsk and Vitebsk Musketeers, 14th and 15th Jägers.

DNIESTROVSK INSPECTORATE (dark green facings): Cherson and Siberian Grenadiers, Alexopol, Crimean, Koslov, Ladoga, New Ingermannland, Nischegorod, Vladimir and Yaroslav Musketeers, 9th, 10th, 11th, 12th and 13th Jägers.

FINNISH INSPECTORATE (yellow facings): The Nievski, Riasan and Veliki-Luki Musketeers, 1st and 2nd Jägers.

KIEV INSPECTORATE (raspberry facings): Butirsk, Kolivansk (ex-Mueller I), Moscow, Narva, Novgorod, Poltava (ex-Marklovski) and Viazma Musketeers.

LITHUANIAN INSPECTORATE (light green facings): Yekaterinoslav Grenadiers,

▼ INFANTRY REGIMENTAL SHOULDER KNOTS, 1762–96 *(left to right). Top row: Kurinsk 1777, Kurinsk pre-1777, Kurinsk post-1777, Siberia, Uglitch, Ladoga, Keksholm, Butyrsk (field officers). Middle row: Rostov, Kiev, Nishegorod, Uglitch 1777, Butyrsk (junior officers), Butyrsk (other ranks), Vyborg (officers), Vyborg (other ranks). Bottom row: St Petersburg (other ranks), St Petersburg (junior officers), St Petersburg (field officers), Perm (junior officers), Jaroslavl, Nizovsk (pre 1770), Nizovsk (1770 other ranks), Nizovsk (junior officers).*

Archangel, Muromsk, Nizov, Pskov, Rostov, Tula and Volhynian Musketeers, 5th, 6th and 7th Jägers.

LIVONIAN INSPECTORATE (turquoise facings): St Petersburg and Tauride Grenadiers, Dniepr, Koporsk, Reval, Sievsk, Sofia, Tchernigov and Tobolsk Musketeers, 3rd and 4th Jägers.

MOSCOW INSPECTORATE (orange facings):

Astrakhan Grenadiers, Brandt (ex-Olonetz), Nascheburg, Navaginsk (ex-Pavlutzki), Orlov, Saratov, Schlüsselburg, Staroi-Okolsk, Tambov and Ukrain (ex-Berg) Musketeers.

ORENBURG INSPECTORATE (buff facings): Ekaterinburg, Riga, Rilsk, Schirwan and Ufimsk Musketeers, 18th and 19th Jägers.

ST PETERSBURG INSPECTORATE (red facings): The Life and Pavlov Grenadiers, the Bielosersk, Kexholm, Lithuanian, Pernov and Tenginsk and Yeletz Musketeers.

SIBERIAN INSPECTORATE (grey facings): Chirwansk, Selenginsk and Tomsk Musketeers.

▼ NCO, 7TH JÄGERS, 1799 *The no-nonsense uniforms introduced by Potemkin in 1786 saw the Jäger regiments dressed in light green, with similar collars and cuffs. According to surviving garments, they wore no skirt turnbacks. Due to the slow rate of fire of their rifles (about one shot every two minutes), the Jägers also carried a pistol on the waist belt.*

▼ FUSILIER, GRENADIER REGIMENT YEKATERINOSLAV 1799 *The outdated Prussian flavour of this uniform is apparent in this figure. The fusilier cap plate was only about two-thirds of the height of that of a grenadier. The archaic powdered hairstyle was to be abolished in 1803. Note the many gaiter buttons, which might be artistic licence.*

▼ PRIVATE, MUSKETEER REGIMENT SCHLÜSSELBURG, 1799 *This regiment was raised in 1700. The costume is that worn by the Russians in northern Italy in 1799 and in Switzerland in 1800. The Swedish cuffs and turnbacks are in the regimental facing colour and turnbacks were red. White gaiters were worn in summer, black in winter.*

▲ INFANTRY REGIMENTAL SHOULDER KNOTS,
1762–96 *(left to right). Top row: Perm (field
officers), Apsheron (other ranks), Apsheron
(junior officers), Apsheron (field officers),
Nizovsk (field officers), Susdal (other ranks),
Susdal (officers), Susdal (parade). Middle
row: Smolensk 1767, Smolensk post-1767
(other ranks), Smolensk post-1767 (officers),
Velikiluki, Naresk post-1766, Tobolsk,
Voronesch (other ranks), Voronesch (officers).
Bottom row: Vologda, Nasheburg up to 1770,
Nasheburg post-1770, Naresk up to 1776,
Astrakhan, Bielosersk, Muromsk, Troitsk.*

SMOLENSK INSPECTORATE (white facings):
Fanagoria and Moscow Grenadiers,
Kursk, Perm, Polotzk, Uglitch and
Voronesch Musketeers.
UKRAINIAN INSPECTORATE (pink facings):
Kiev and Little Russia Grenadiers,
Briansk, Galitz and Smolensk
Musketeers.

In the reforms of 1802 seven new
infantry regiments were raised:
Crimean, Galitz, Koporje, Petrovsk,
Podolia, Volhynia and Vologda.

On 12 August 1803 the three
combined garrison battalions, which
had distinguished themselves in the
defence of Danzig, went to form the
Bialistok Musketeers. In August 1805 it
was decided to raise another seven new
regiments of musketeers; these were
the Estland, Kaluga, Kostroma,
Mohilev, Odessa, Pensa and Vilna. In
July and August 1806 the following
musketeer regiments were raised: Brest,
Yakutsk, Kamtschatka, Krementschug,
Mingrelian, Minsk, Neuschlot,
Ochotsk, Pernau, Tambov and
Wilmannstrand.

Infantry Reforms from 1806

On 4 March 1806, 11 of the 14
inspectorates were reorganized into 13
divisions, while the troops stationed in
the Caucasus, Orenburg and Siberia
retained their old titles. These divisions
were the tactical formations in which
the regiments would fight in war time.

On 14 June 1806 the 14th Division
was formed, ten days later four more

were formed, the 15th from regiments
that previously had not belonged to a
division, the 16th, 17th and 18th from
newly raised regiments. The garrison
infantry regiments were all ordered to
wear yellow collars and cuffs and red
shoulder straps bearing their
regimental numbers (1–72) in yellow.

In 1807 the troops in the Caucasian
Inspectorate were formed into the 19th
and 20th Divisions; the 21st was
formed of the Libau Regiment and
units from the old 1st Division.
Various other divisions contributed
units to form the 22nd Division. In
February 1808 the Orenburg
Inspectorate became the 23rd Division,
the Siberian Inspectorate the 24th. At
the same time, the Rostov Musketeer
Regiment's title changed to
"Araktschejev", the name of their
colonel-in-chief. The need for
competent NCOs led to the
establishment at this point of the
Grenadier Training Battalion. In 1809,
24 recruit training depots were set up,

one for each division, where the new recruits were given eight months preparatory training. In 1811 two more were set up. In this year, the 24th, 25th and 26th Divisions were also established by taking regiments from the stronger divisions. Each division was divided into three brigades, each of two regiments.

Visible attempts were being made already to standardize the internal structure and composition of these divisions, so that each would have equal tactical value. Regimental organization of the line infantry and the *Jägers* was changed in October 1810: rather than the old pattern of

one grenadier and two fusilier/ musketeer battalions, a regiment was to have three fusilier/musketeer battalions and each battalion was to have one grenadier company and three of fusiliers/musketeers. Each company had two platoons: in the grenadier companies the 1st Platoon was the grenadiers and formed on the right of the battalion, the 2nd Platoon was the sharpshooters and formed on the left. This was a direct copy of the French system. At the time of mobilization the 2nd Battalion of each regiment (less the grenadier company) stayed in the regimental depot to train new recruits. The grenadier companies of these 2nd Battalions formed two combined grenadier battalions within each division. They could be combined into grenadier brigades and divisions.

Fourteen musketeer regiments (Lithuanian, Vilna, Sofia, Podolian, Voronesch, Galitz, Briansk, Odessa, Orel, Estonia, Novgorod, Veliki-Luki, Pensa and Saratov) were converted to the 33rd–46th Jägers in October 1810. On 26 October the Napoleonic corps system was adopted by divisions in the Western Russian region.

The I Corps had the 5th and 14th Divisions; the II Corps had the 16th, 17th and 21st Divisions; the III Corps

◄ **GRENADIER, MUSKETEER REGIMENT YAROSLAV, 1799** *The design of the cap plate has a "union jack" of the cross of St Andrew on that of St George at the bottom centre. Regiments having a member of the ruling family as their colonel-in-chief had this field painted in red, the St George's cross in white and the St Andrew's in black, outlined in white. It was common for these caps to be held on with ribbons under the pigtail.*

► **NCO, PAVLOVSKI GRENADIER REGIMENT, 1800** *This was the youngest grenadier regiment, having been raised in November 1796. It was awarded the right to retain the mitre cap in 1807, for its bravery in the 1807 campaign. By 1812 the headband and cords of the mitre cap were white, the cloth backing red. All other grenadier regiments had been ordered to adopt the shako in 1805. The lace edging to collar and cuffs denotes an NCO.*

had the 2nd, 3rd and 4th Divisions; the IV Corps had the 7th and 8th Divisions and the 2nd Battalions of the 9th, 10th and 18th Divisions; the V Corps remained vacant; the VI Corps had the 19th and 20th Divisions.

Fourteen divisions remained uncommitted. In November 1810 the 25th Division became the 24th and the regiments of the old 24th were uncommitted. The new 25th Division was formed of the troops in the Orenburg Line; the 26th Division was formed from those in the Siberian Line. The invalided soldiers were organized into 570

companies in various towns and used for guard duties if they were fit enough. Also, in January 1811 the Musketeer Regiment Count Araktschejev was converted to a grenadier regiment. In February the Caucasian Grenadiers were renamed the Georgian (Grusinski) Grenadiers. From the same month musketeer regiments were retitled infantry regiments. The 49th Jägers became the Sofia Infantry Regiment. The three naval infantry regiments were taken into the 25th Infantry Division and the 19th and 20th Divisions became the Georgian Corps – the basis for the Army of the Caucasus.

Before the end of the year, four new regiments were formed: Odessa, Simbirsk, Vilna and Zhitomir.

They went to form the 27th Division, with the 49th and 50th Jägers. There were now 14 grenadier, 96 infantry and three naval infantry regiments. From the 52 remaining garrison infantry companies, 12 were used to form three garrison battalions and the rest were distributed in 40 towns around the state, where, with locally raised security companies, they now comprised the "Home Guard" of some 17,000 men. The aim of this force was to maintain peace and security throughout the realm and it was placed under command of the Ministry of War.

Infantry Uniforms post-1806

Following the reforms of 1806, the hated pigtails were cut off and the hair cut short. In March 1807 officers were ordered to discard their spontoons and canes and all officers, except those of the hussars, were now to wear epaulettes. On 7 November 1807 the mad system of trying to distinguish each regiment with its own facings and buttons was abandoned and all regiments were ordered to wear red facings and brass buttons.

The inspectorates were abolished and the regiments organized into divisions of unequal strengths. Within each division, the first regiment would

◀ OFFICER, ST PETERSBURG GRENADIER REGIMENT, 1805 *As part of the Livonian Inspectorate, this regiment wore turquoise collars and cuffs and red shoulder straps and pompon centres. The gilt eagle badges on the sides of officers' shakos were copied by the Prussian Army after 1806. It is possible that some officers retained the bicorn. Grey overalls add a practical appearance to the uniform.*

▶ GRENADIER NCO, UFIMSK INFANTRY REGIMENT, 1805–06 *At this stage the Russian infantry regiments were each distinguished by their own facings and buttons. This changed by the Order of 7 November 1807, by which the facings were red and the buttons yellow for all infantry regiments. The huge, horsehair plume was retained until February 1811, when the narrow model was introduced. In July 1808, all grenadier regiments adopted the three-flamed grenade as their cap and cartridge box badges.*

have red shoulder straps, the second white, the third yellow, the fourth dark green edged red, the fifth light blue. The divisional number was embroidered on the shoulder strap in red for the white and yellow straps, in yellow on the others. For officers these numerals were in gold thread.

At this time also, the sabre waist belt was replaced by a bandolier over the right shoulder. The old Prussian-pattern sabres were replaced by straight-bladed swords. The tops of the shakos were now of leather, which extended down the edges of the sides. This trim was added to the shako bottom, and two reinforcing

◄ **DRUMMER, VYBORG INFANTRY REGIMENT, 1807** *This regiment was part of the Brest Inspectorate, hence the straw coloured collar and cuffs and the yellow shoulder straps. This regiment was raised in June 1700 in Novgorod. The sabre strap tassel identified the company of the wearer.*

straps ran from each chinstrap boss up to the top in a V shape. In December 1807, new trousers were introduced; in winter the men wore Potemkin-style, loose trousers, of white cloth, with black leather bottom sections. In summer they wore close-fitting, white linen gaiter-trousers, with white buttons on the lower parts. In July 1808 the cockade on the front of the shako was replaced by a brass grenade (as on the cartridge pouch), for musketeers it had a single flame, grenadiers' grenades had three flames. Meanwhile, the cylindrical, black

► **INFANTRY KIT**
1. The epaulette of an infantry officer belonging to the 12th Division. 2 An officer's cockade complete with the imperial cipher of Czar Alexander I.

► **OFFICER, JÄGERS, 1807** *This is a simple uniform and relatively practical. Unlike their counterparts in the line infantry, Jäger officers did not wear gorgets. The number of regiments of light infantry was raised to 50 in 1812, showing the growing emphasis being placed on open order skirmishing. The shoulder strap carries the battalion number.*

leather packs were changed to rectangular models, worn on the back on two white straps. It was ordered that officers should wear packs whenever the men did.

At the same time, the officers' gorgets were reduced in size and rank was shown as follows: ensign – all silver; second lieutenant – gilt edged; lieutenant – a gilt eagle; staff captain – gilt eagle and rim; captain – gold with silver eagle. All field officers wore gilt gorgets. The white feather trim of generals' bicorns was abolished in July 1809, but the loop was replaced by a four-fold gold bullion braid brooch. Musketeer privates wore the same grenadier's badges on *kiwer* and pouch but with a single flame.

▼ **INFANTRY KIT** *1 The standard 1796 pattern Russian musket with brass metal parts. Guard muskets were made from wood from walnut trees and were of a higher quality. 2 A Russian Jäger rifle, which was extremely slow to load but more accurate than the musket, with sword bayonet. 3 The steel lock plate, showing the place of manufacture (the Tula arsenal) and the date. 4 Cartridge pouches: on the left a grenadier's pouch, on the right a guard's.*

◀ NCO DRUMMER, 21ST JÄGERS REGIMENT, 1807 *Here we see the Jäger "top hat" from the front. It has the gold top band, indicating the rank of the wearer. It was replaced in 1807 by the line infantry shako. The 21st Jäger Regiment was one of the three raised in 1805 and had red facings piped in white.*

▶ NCO HORNIST 1ST BATTALION, 11TH Jägers, 1807 *Hornists were the preferred way for light infantry units and light infantrymen to signal to one another. This regiment fought in the wars against the Turks in present day Romania and Bulgaria through much of the period. The hornist wears the unusual "top hat" introduced in 1802.*

in the Combined Grenadier Division would have worn the numerals of their parent divisions.

On 17 January 1811 it was ordered that all officers' *kiwer* cords should be of silver thread; those of NCOs should be as for the men but with black-white-orange flounders and tassels. In 1812 the 1st–14th home guard infantry regiments were raised, as were the Kurland Rifles and the Militia Battalion of the Grand Duchess Catherine Pavlova.

In July 1812 the czar issued a proclamation calling all able-bodied men to arms to defend their homeland. The response was amazing: over 220,000 men came forward to volunteer to join the *Landwehr*.

During the course of the war of 1812, a Russo-German Legion was raised from German prisoners of war. It consisted of seven battalions of infantry, a company of rifles, two regiments of hussars, one foot and two horse batteries and an artillery park company. They dressed in Russian uniforms, the 1st Infantry Brigade and the *Jägers* with red facings and yellow buttons, the 2nd with light blue collars and yellow shoulder straps. The 1st Hussars had dark green dolmans, pelisses, white fur, red facings, yellow lace and buttons; the 2nd were all in black with light blue facings and sash and brown fur. The artillery were as for the Russian artillery. These regiments fought in northern Germany in 1813 and went into Prussian service in

Pompon colours were as follows: 1st Battalion – green within white; 2nd – white within green; 3rd – white within sky blue. The headbands of the forage caps also identified the battalion of the wearer: 1st – all red; 2nd – red piped green; 3rd – red piped sky blue. The front of the headband showed the company initials in yellow: "1. P" (1st company). The sabre straps were in the company colours; all straps and tassels were white; details of the bodies, crowns and wreaths varied with the company. We know the infantry regiments wore their divisional numbers on their shoulder straps, while the *Jägers* wore them on their pouch lids. For the grenadier regiments the numerals would have been "1. G" and "2. G" in Cyrillic script. The units

March 1815. The Greek Division had been disbanded in 1799; the men, Greeks and Albanians, were used to form the Greek Battalion of three companies in Odessa.

Jäger Organization

The 20th *Jägers* was raised in 18 May 1802. When the new shakos were introduced for the line infantry and foot guards in 1805, the *Jägers* retained their old models until September 1807. The 21st and 22nd Jägers were raised in November 1805, and in 1806 10 new *Jäger* Regiments (23–32) were raised. In January 1811 the 47th, 48th and 49th Jägers were raised from men of the garrison regiments. This latter regiment was converted to the Sofia

▲ GRENADIER, LITTLE RUSSIA GRENADIERS, **1805** *This figure wears the uniform used at Austerlitz in December of that year.*

Infantry Regiment. The 49th and 50th Jägers were raised in November 1811 and went into the 27th Division.

Jäger Uniform

The 1807 uniform was subdued in its colour scheme and included a sensible hat; all cuffs became red. For the *Jägers*, collars were now white, piped in red. In November 1807 it was ordered that the coats and breeches were to be changed from light to dark green. In December 1807 the old cartridge

Musketeer regiments converted to the *Jägers*, October 1810	
Musketeer regiment	***Jäger* regiment**
Lithuanian	33rd
Vilna	34th
Sophia	35th
Podolian	36th
Voronesch	37th
Galitsch	38th
Briansk	39th
Odessa	40th
Orel	41st
Estonian	42nd
Novgorod	43rd
Veliki-Luki	44th
Pensa	45th
Saratov	46th

pouches on the waist belts were abolished in favour of line infantry pouches on black bandoliers. The lids were plain. At this time, the grass green tunics started to be replaced by dark green. The collars remained as before, but the first regiment in a division had red shoulder straps, whilst the second had light blue.

In August 1808 it was ordered that all *Jäger* regiments should have white collars edged red, red cuffs and red piping down the outer seam of the trousers. In mid-1809 the white collars were again replaced by dark green, piped red, and the regimental number was worn on the cartridge pouch lid in brass. By this time the *Jägers* were almost all equipped with muskets just

▶ CARABINEER NCO, 13TH JÄGERS, 1812
Here we see the very unusual kiwer shako, introduced during the 1812 campaign. In 1806, all Jäger NCOs and the 12 best shots of each company had been armed with rifles, but by 1812, most regiments were equipped with the standard smoothbore musket, which had a much faster rate of fire. The elite companies in Jäger regiments equated to grenadier companies in line infantry regiments and wore the same distinguishing badges.

as for the line infantry. In this year *Jäger* officers adopted the gorget as for the line. In late 1810 it was ruled that the first regiment in each brigade was to wear yellow shoulder straps, the second light blue. They were to bear the divisional number in red. In the September of this year, gold epaulettes, of the same design as those of officers of line infantry were introduced; they were worn on backing in the same colour as the shoulder straps of the men of their regiment.

Before 1807 was out, the number of the division in which the regiment served was added to the epaulette strap. In November 1807, the colour of the *Jäger* uniforms changed from light green to dark. The gaiter-breeches were of white linen in summer; in winter they were of heavier white cloth, with black leather cuffs on the bottoms. In 1811 it was ordered that the 1805 model shako should be replaced by the concave-topped *kiwer*, but it was probably not issued in time for the French invasion of 1812.

THE CUIRASSIERS AND DRAGOONS

In 1763 the cavalry was divided into heavy and light for the first time. The former consisted of the six cuirassier and 19 carabineer regiments, the latter of seven regiments of dragoons. In the whirlwind of change introduced by the new Czar Paul in 1796, nine of the carabineer regiments were converted to cuirassiers (of which there were now 16), the other six were converted to dragoons, of which there were now also 16. Each regiment had five squadrons. In 1798 six new cavalry regiments were raised; in 1800 all but

two (Zorn Cuirassiers and Schreiders Dragoons) were disbanded again. Schreiders Dragoons later became the Dragoon Regiment Mueller II. That same year six dragoon regiments were combined into three, each with 10 squadrons: Vladimir and Taganrog, which became Obrjewskov (later Schepelev); Narva and Nischegorod, which came Puschkin (later Portnjagin); and Irkutsk and Siberian, which became Sacken II (later Skalon).

In 1800 the Yamburg, Riazan, Nieschin and Sofia cuirassiers and the Rostov and Astrakhan dragoons were disbanded: and in 1801 the old regimental titles were reinstated; Zorn Cuirassiers became Tver and the Mueller II Dragoons became Kinburn.

Cuirassier Uniforms before 1803

All regiments wore plain bicorns, white plumes, yellow, black and orange cockade, red-within-white hat tassels, white tunics, waistcoats, breeches, gauntlets and belts. Facings were shown on collars, cuffs, the edging to the front of the tunic, and edgings to the waistcoat and the white skirt turnbacks, as well as the sabretasche. The sabretasche was

◄ **REGIMENTAL TRUMPETER, MOSCOW DRAGOONS, 1812** *The Moscow Dragoons were raised in 1700 as the Preobrazhenski Dragoons, assuming their present title in 1706. Russian dragoons had black harnessing with brass fittings.*

▶ **STANDARD BEARER, EKATERINBURG CUIRASSIERS, 1797–1801** *This is a distinctly Prussian-style uniform, as befits a member of Czar Paul's army. Only the front plate of the cuirass was worn. Green cuffs are worn under the leather gauntlets.*

edged in the button colour.

KHARKOV CUIRASSIERS. In 1796 they converted to cuirassiers. Black facings, white buttons and lace.

KIEV CUIRASSIERS. Converted to cuirassiers in 1784. Orange facings, white buttons.

TCHERNIGOV CUIRASSIERS. In 1784 it became the Tchernigov Carabineers. Present title since 1796. Pink facings, white buttons.

KAZAN CUIRASSIERS. Present title since 1756. Crimson facings, white buttons.

HIS MAJESTY'S LIFE CUIRASSIERS. In 1733 it became the Bevernski Cuirassiers; present title since November 1796. Light blue facings, white buttons; they wore the eight-pointed star of the

▲ REGIMENTAL TRUMPETER, KAZAN CUIRASSIERS, 1786-96 *Here we see the cavalry version of the Potemkin uniform. Dragoon regiments also wore these colours and were distinguished only by the shoulder piece on the left shoulder. No cuirasses were worn until 1796 when the bicorn replaced this helmet.*

Order of St George on helmet and saddle cloth.

HER MAJESTY'S LIFE CUIRASSIERS. In 1733 known as the Life Cuirassiers. Present title since November 1796. Crimson facings, yellow buttons. They wore the eight-pointed star of the Order of St George on helmet and saddle cloth.

RIAZAN CUIRASSIERS. A carabineer regiment in 1763. Present title since November 1796. Royal blue facings, yellow buttons.

YAMBURG CUIRASSIERS. Present title since November 1796. Light blue facings, yellow buttons.

EKATERINOSLAV CUIRASSIERS. From 1789 its title was the Potemkin Cuirassiers. Present title since November 1796. Orange facings, white buttons.

RIGA CUIRASSIERS. In 1763 it became a carabineer regiment. Present title since November 1796. Red facings, yellow buttons.

MILITARY ORDER CUIRASSIERS. In 1774 known as the Georgian Military Order Dragoons. Present title since November 1796. Black facings, yellow buttons. Trumpeters wore the lace of the Order of St George rather than the usual trumpeters' lace.

GLUCHOV CUIRASSIERS. Raised in 1783 from Kazaks in Little Russia as the Gluchov Light Horse; in 1784 it converted to carabineers. Present title since November 1796. Bright blue facings, white buttons.

NIEZHINSKI CUIRASSIERS. Raised from Kazaks as above, forming the Niezhinski Cavalry; in 1784 it converted to carabineers.

Present title since November 1796.

SOFIA CUIRASSIERS. Raised in 1783 from Kazaks, forming the Sophia Cavalry; converted to carabineers in 1784. Present title since November 1796. Facings pink, buttons yellow.

STARODUB CUIRASSIERS. Raised from Kazaks as above, forming the Starodub Cavalry; in 1784 it converted to carabineers. Present title since November 1796. Facings dull red, buttons white.

LITTLE RUSSIAN CUIRASSIERS. Raised in 1785 by Grand Duke Potemkin in the Little Russian region as the 10th Horse Grenadiers; in 1790 their title changed to the Horse Grenadiers of the Military Order. Present title since November 1796. Facing orange, buttons yellow.

◄ STANDARD BEARER, LIFE CUIRASSIER REGIMENT OF HIS MAJESTY, 1812 *This young officer carries the white, sovereign's standard of the regiment. The rolled blanket on the saddle offers some extra protection to this heavily armed and formidable cavalryman.*

Cuirassier Organization

In 1803 it was ordered that each regiment would form a depot half-squadron, which stayed in the peacetime location on mobilization and trained new recruits and remounts. As the invasion of Russia developed during 1812, the reserve squadrons of the cuirassier divisions were formed into a reserve division. In November 1810 some of the cavalry regiments in western Russia were organized into brigades and divisions, and were permanently attached to the newly formed infantry corps.

A major step forward in the standardization of firearms took place in 1810, when it was decided to arm all cuirassier, dragoon and hussar regiments with new carbines and pistols of the same calibre as the infantry musket ("7 lines").

Cuirassier Uniforms

In October 1803 it was decided to replace the bicorns of the cuirassiers and dragoons with black, lacquered leather helmets. These were topped with a black leather comb, on top of which sat a mighty caterpillar crest. This was black for troopers, red for musicians, black with a white front with a vertical orange stripe for NCOs. Officers in the field wore crests of the same dimensions, but white, with a black tip, separated from the white body by an orange ring. Off duty, all ranks wore the bicorn, with simple loop and button. In 1808 the ridiculously huge crests were replaced by short, straight items of horsehair.

Dragoon Uniforms

In 1796 the uniform was a bicorn with white plume, yellow, black and orange cockade, red and white hat tassels, long-skirted, dark green tunic, with facings shown on collar, cuffs, shoulder straps, lapels (if worn), white lining and buff turnbacks. Buff waistcoats, white breeches and belts, high, cuffed boots. Officers wore an aiguillette on the right shoulder in the button colour, and two

▲ OFFICER, CUIRASSIER REGIMENT EKATERINOSLAV, 1809 *A sausage crest on the helmet was short-lived, being replaced by this bristly crest. The cuirasses too were now much simpler than before. The regiment bore the crowned cipher "A" over "I" in the button colour on their horse furniture, which was in the facing colour, edged white.*

buttonholes in the button colour on each side of the tunic, below the lapels. The square shabraque and holster covers were in the facing colour, edged in the button colour. Harness was black.

SIEVERSK DRAGOONS. In 1779 named the Sieversk Little Russian Light Horse; converted to carabineers in 1784. Present title in 1796. Facings orange, buttons yellow.

MOSCOW DRAGOONS. Converted from dragoons to carabineers in 1763. Present title in 1796. Facings crimson (no lapels), buttons yellow.

ASTRAKHAN DRAGOONS. Horse grenadiers

◄ TRUMPETER, CUIRASSIER REGIMENT OF THE MILITARY ORDER, 1812 *Rather than the usual musicians' lace decoration, trumpeters in this regiment wore the ribbon of the Order of St George. They also wore the star of that order on their helmets and horse furniture.*

Mounted Rifle Regiments 1813–15

No.	Title	Facings
1	Arsamas	purple
2	Dorpat	lilac
3	Lithuania	crimson
4	Nezhinsk	light blue
5	Pereslav	raspberry
6	Sieversk	red
7	Tiraspol*	deep yellow
8	Tchernigov	dark purple

*newly raised.

in 1756; in 1763 converted to carabineers. Present title in 1786. Facings orange, buttons yellow.

VLADIMIR DRAGOONS. Facings bright blue, buttons yellow.

PSKOV DRAGOONS. Carabineers in 1763. Present title in 1788. Facings pink (no lapels), buttons white.

NIZHEGOROD DRAGOONS. Carabineers in 1763. Present title in 1775. Facings black (no lapels), buttons white.

INGERMANNLAND DRAGOONS. Carabineers in 1763. Present title in 1796. Facings crimson, buttons yellow.

NARVSKI DRAGOONS. Carabineers in 1763. Present title in 1796. Facings light blue, buttons yellow.

ROSTOV DRAGOONS. Carabineers in 1763. Present title in 1796. Facings bright red, buttons yellow.

KARGOPOL DRAGOONS. Carabineers in 1763. Present title in 1796. Facings bright red, buttons white.

ST PETERSBURG DRAGOONS. Carabineers in 1765. Present title in 1775. Facings bright red (no lapels), buttons yellow.

SMOLENSK DRAGOONS. Formed in 1765 from the Smolensk Militia. Present title in 1775. Facings orange, buttons white.

TAGANROG DRAGOONS. Raised in 1775 from the Perm and Viatska Carabineer Regiments with the present title. Facings light orange, buttons yellow.

▶ TROOPER, NEZHINSK MOUNTED RIFLES, **1813** *The regiment was converted from dragoons to mounted rifles in 1813; the conversion involved changes to the uniform and the adoption of light cavalry weapons and tactics. The scooped-out* kiwer *shako replaced the dragoon helmet.*

SIBERIAN DRAGOONS. Raised in 1775 as the Siberian Dragoon Corps. Present title in 1777. Facings white (no lapels), buttons yellow.

IRKUTSK DRAGOONS. Raised in 1784 from part of the Siberian Dragoons. Present title in 1796. Facings white (no lapels), white buttons.

ORENBURG DRAGOONS. Raised in 1784 from the Orenburg and Yadrinsk field battalions under the present title. Facings black, buttons white.

In 1798 four new dragoon regiments were raised: Kurland, New Russian, Borissoglebsk and Pejeraslav. In August 1805 two more were raised; the Zhitomir and Livland. In June 1806 the Finland and Mittau dragoons were raised, and in August the regiments Arsamass, Jamburg, Libau, Nezhinsk, Serpuchov, Tiraspol and Dorpat. In late December 1812 several regiments of dragoons were converted to mounted rifles or lancers.

The dragoon helmet issued in 1803 had peaks to front and rear and was surmounted with a leather comb. This was topped with a black leather comb, on top of which sat a mighty, horsehair crest. This was black for troopers, red for musicians, and black with a white front, having a vertical orange stripe, for NCOs. Officers in the field wore white crests with a black tip, separated from the white body by an orange ring. The front was covered with a brass plate bearing the crowned double-eagle badge. In December 1807 the light green tunic began to be replaced by dark

green and in 1808 the balloon plumes were replaced by short, straight items of horsehair, black for all ranks, except trumpeters, who wore red. In 1809 the tunic skirts were shortened to the length worn by cuirassiers.

Mounted Rifles

In late December 1812 the following regiments of dragoons were converted to mounted rifles: Arsamass, Dorpat, Lithuania, Nezhinsk, Pereslav, Sieversk Tchernigov. Others were converted to lancers to raise the numbers of light cavalry units. These new mounted rifle regiments were equipped as for hussars, with Bock saddles, curved sabres and hussar-style harness in black leather. They wore the *kiwer*, with hussar-

▶ DRAGOON OFFICER KIT: *1 The straight, heavy cavalry sword with white buffalo leather swordbelt. 2 bandolier with a ring for the carbine (4). 3 Cartridge pouch bearing the double-headed eagle. 5 A dragoon musket, which could have been fitted with a bayonet. 6 A swordknot.*

style cockade, button and loop, white cords and plumes, with the usual colour coding for officers, NCOs and trumpeters. All regiments wore dark green tunics and breeches. The collars were also dark green, the buttons were white, as were the belts. Facing colours were worn on the piping to top and front of the collar, the shoulder straps, the pointed cuffs and the stripes down the trouser legs. The troops were equipped as light cavalry and used for scouting and skirmishing.

◀ CAVALRY STANDARD
Russian dragoons carried standards rather than swallow-tailed guidons. The colours bore no relation to the regimental facings.

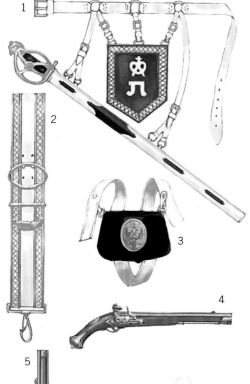

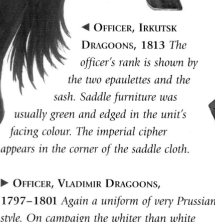

◀ OFFICER, IRKUTSK DRAGOONS, 1813 *The officer's rank is shown by the two epaulettes and the sash. Saddle furniture was usually green and edged in the unit's facing colour. The imperial cipher appears in the corner of the saddle cloth.*

▶ OFFICER, VLADIMIR DRAGOONS, 1797–1801 *Again a uniform of very Prussian style. On campaign the whiter than white breeches would be replaced by grey overalls buttoned down the side.*

THE HUSSARS AND LANCERS

Each hussar regiment had two battalions of five squadrons. In 1800 the Moscow Hussar Squadron merged with the Achtyrsk Hussars, and in 1803 two new hussar regiments (Odessa and Bielorussian) were raised; the latter converted to lancers that year.

Uniforms of the Hussars

By 1797 hussars wore a black fur colpack with bag in the regimental dolman colour, white plume and cords. The dolman bore regimental facings on collar and cuffs and the buttons and lace were in the regimental colour; the pelisse was edged in fur, which was the same colour for officers and men. The lace and buttons on it matched those on the dolman. The barrel sash was in the regimental colours; breeches and belts were usually white. In the October of 1803, the infantry-style shako was issued surmounted by huge, white horsehair plumes and fitted with red and white mixed cords. On the front was the cockade. In 1809 the white breeches were replaced by items in the dolman colour.

SSUMSKI HUSSARS. In 1796 titled the Hussars of General of Cavalry Shevitz; 1799 – Hussars of Likochina; April 1800 – Hussars of Major General Kologrivova; October 1800 – Hussars of Colonel Grebova; December 1800 – Hussars of Lieutenant General Count Zubov; 1801 – Hussars of Major General Count Pahlen III; in that same month it became the Ssumski Hussars. In 1797 the uniform was a yellow dolman, white lace and buttons, light blue facings and pelisse, black fur, light blue and white sash. Light blue sabretasche, white edging, and embroidery. This was changed into grey dolman, pelisse, shabraque; crimson facings, breeches and vandyking to the shabraque; white lace and buttons, crimson and grey sash. Officers had black fur, the men white. They were later awarded St George's trumpets in

◀ **OFFICER, ISUM HUSSARS 1797–1801** *The present title was bestowed in 1801. The elaborate "Polish" harness and the jagged edging to the saddle cloth were favourites of all European hussars. There is little that is Russian about this uniform.*

▲ TRUMPETER, BIELORUSSIAN HUSSARS, 1803
This was a new regiment. Trumpeters either wore additional lace or reversed colours in most European armies to distinguish them on the battlefield. Unusually the pelisse also has swallows' nest lace on the shoulders.

April 1813 for distinguished service during the 1812 campaign, and *kiwer* plaques in April 1814 for the campaign of that year.

ACHTYRSK HUSSARS. In 1796 titled the Hussars of Lieutenant General Lindener; 1800 – Hussars of Colonel Barchugova; present title in 1801. In 1796 the uniform was a medium brown dolman and pelisse, white lace and buttons, yellow facings, white fur,

Lancer Regiments in 1813

Regt	Facings	Buttons/ Epaulettes	*Czapka* top	*Czapka* cords	Lance fanions
Life Guards	red	yellow	dark blue	yellow	red/white
Polish	raspberry	white	dark blue	white	dark blue/raspberry
Tartars	raspberry	white	raspberry	white	raspberry/white
Lithuanian	raspberry	white	white	white	white/dark blue
Wolhyinian	raspberry	yellow	dark blue	yellow	yellow/raspberry
Tchuguchev	red	white	red	white	red/dark blue
Yamburg	raspberry	yellow	white	red	white/raspberry
Orenburg	raspberry	yellow	raspberry	yellow	dark blue/raspberry
Zhitomir	red	white	dark blue	white	yellow/dark blue
Siberian	red	white	white	red	yellow/white
Vladimir	red	yellow	dark blue	yellow	yellow/dark blue
Taganrog	red	yellow	white	red	yellow/red
Serpuchov	red	yellow	red	yellow	dark blue/red

▲ HUSSARS OFFICER KIT *1 The curved steel-hilted light cavalry sabre and steel scabbard. 2 and 3 A scabbard and straight-bladed sword with brass hilt. 4 and 5 A cavalry carbine, sometimes painted black. 6 A barrelled sash. 7 A sabretasche bearing the cipher of Czar Paul I and sword belts with sabre.*

◄ OFFICER, PAVLOGRAD HUSSARS, 1807 *This regiment was raised in 1783 as a regiment of light horse. They were later awarded a kiwer plaque for distinguished conduct. This officer has short hair – traditionally hussars wore plaits and a pigtail but these were abolished in 1806.*

red and yellow sash. Brown sabretasche, yellow edging and embroidery. This was changed to a brown dolman and pelisse. Yellow lace and buttons, brown and yellow sash, white fur, royal blue breeches, sabretasche and horse furniture with yellow decoration. The Achtyrsk Hussars were awarded silver trumpets in April 1813 for distinguished service during the 1812 campaign, and a *kiwer* plaque in May 1814 for that campaign.

ISUM HUSSARS. In 1796 became the Hussars of Major General Zoritsa. In the following year it became the Hussars of Major General Annekova; in 1798 the title changed to Major General Bovria. In 1800 it became Major General Graf Pahlen. Red dolman was worn with white lace and buttons, mid-blue facings and pelisse, white fur, blue and white sash. Red sabretasche, white edging and embroidery. Later, dark blue breeches and saddle furniture were adopted.

MARIUPOL HUSSARS. In 1796 the Hussars of Major General Borovski; in 1797 – Major General Prince Bagration; in 1798 – Major General Prince Kekuatov; in 1799 – Major General Count

yellow facings, lace and buttons, a yellow and blue sash, yellow decorations to horse furniture.

They were awarded silver trumpets in April 1813 for distinguished service during the 1812 campaign, and a *kiwer* plaque in September 1814 for the campaign of that year.

PAVLOGRAD HUSSARS. Present title awarded in 1801. Original uniform: light blue dolman and pelisse, white lace and buttons, white fur, light blue and white sash. White sabretasche, light blue edging and embroidery. By 1805 this was a dark green dolman, red lace, yellow buttons, light blue collar and cuffs; red and light blue sash; light blue pelisse with white fur; dark green breeches, saddle cloth and sabretasche with red embroidery.

ELISABETHGRAD HUSSARS. In 1796 became the Hussars of General of Cavalry Dunina; in 1798 it was the Hussars of Major General Voropansko and next year the title changed to Major General Sucharev. In 1800 it was Major General Sacken then it adopted the present title. In 1796 they wore yellow dolman, white lace and buttons, red facings, yellow pelisse, white fur, red and white sash. The sabretasche was yellow with white edging and embroidery.

They were awarded silver trumpets in April 1813 for distinguished service during the 1812 campaign, and a *kiwer* plaque in November 1814 for the campaign of that year.

OLVIOPOL HUSSARS. In 1796 known as the Hussars of General of Cavalry Baron Schitza; in 1800 – Hussars of Colonel Miloradovitch, then Colonel Tschaplitz. In 1801 the present title was adopted. In 1796 they

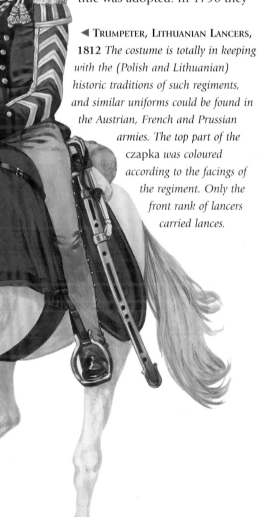

◀ TRUMPETER, LITHUANIAN LANCERS, **1812** *The costume is totally in keeping with the (Polish and Lithuanian) historic traditions of such regiments, and similar uniforms could be found in the Austrian, French and Prussian armies. The top part of the czapka was coloured according to the facings of the regiment. Only the front rank of lancers carried lances.*

▲ OFFICER, ACHTYRSK HUSSARS, 1812 *This splendid uniform was worn from 1812 onward. For this brutal campaign it was awarded a commemorative shako plaque in 1813. The officer's plume has an orange and black base. Note also the Hungarian knots on the breeches.*

Wittgenstein; 1801– Major General Melissino, then Mariupol Hussars. In 1797 the uniform was white dolman, yellow lace and buttons, yellow facings, dark blue pelisse, white fur, red and yellow sash, yellow sabretasche, white edging and embroidery. Some time after 1802 and before 1812 it became dark blue dolman, pelisse, breeches, sabretasche and shabraque, wore black dolman and pelisse, white lace and buttons, white fur, red and white sash, black sabretasche, white edging and embroidery. By 1809 their uniform was a dark blue dolman and pelisse, red facings, breeches and decoration to the dark blue sabretasche and shabraque, a red and yellow sash, yellow lace and buttons.

ALEXANDRIA HUSSARS. In 1796 known as the Hussars of Major General Godlevski. Uniform at that time was: black dolman and pelisse, white lace and buttons, red facings, black fur for officers, white for the men, red and white sash. Black sabretasche, red edging and embroidery. In 1797 the title was Major General Guzhitsko; in 1798 – Major General Nikoritz; in 1799 – Major General Telepniev. In 1800 it was Colonel Kischinski, and in 1801 it assumed its present title. The sash became black and red.

They were awarded silver trumpets in April 1813 for distinguished conduct in the 1812 campaign and a *kiwer* plaque in 1 May 1814

BIELORUSSIAN HUSSARS. Raised in 1803 from men of the Alexandria, Elisabethgrad, Olviopol and Pavlograd Hussars. Dark blue dolman, breeches, sabretasche and shabraque, white buttons, lace and vandyking, red facings and dolman, white fur, red and white belt.

GRODNO HUSSARS. Raised in 1806 in the Pskov region at five squadrons from men of the Isum, Olviopol and Ssumski Hussars. All uniform items were dark blue, facings and decoration light blue, white buttons and lace, white fur, light blue and white sash.

LUBNY HUSSARS. Raised in 1807 in the areas of Schklove and Mogilev. The uniform and saddle furniture were all dark blue, facings yellow, buttons, lace, fur and decorations white. After the 1814 campaign they were awarded a *kiwer* plaque for

distinguished service.

IRKUTZK HUSSARS. Raised in December 1812 from men of the Irkutzk Dragoons and Moscow Hussars of Count Soltikov. Brown dolman with crimson facings and yellow buttons and lace, yellow and white sash, brown pelisse, black fur; crimson breeches and sabretasche with yellow trim, brown shabraque with crimson vandyking and yellow lace.

Lancers

The Odessa Hussars were converted into lancers (*ulans*) in 1803. It later became the Life Guard Lancers. The Czesaravitsch Lancers were issued with lances in 1806. The Volhynian Cavalry Regiment was raised in April 1807 and in the following November became a lancer regiment, together with the Polish, Lithuanian and Tartar cavalry regiments. In August 1808 the Tschugujev Cossack Regiment was converted to lancers. Lancers had 10 field squadrons and a depot squadron.

In late December 1812 four regiments of dragoons were converted to lancers: Serpuchov, Siberia, Taganrog and Vladimir. All lancer regiments wore the Polish slate blue *kurtka* and the square-topped *czapka*. In general, facings were worn on lapels, cuffs, piping, the waist sash and the double trouser stripes, as well as on the edging and crowned cipher on the saddle cloth. Lance fanions, in two colours, were placed on the horizontally split, swallow-tailed cloth. Life Guards wore the double-headed eagle on the *czapka* front; *czapkas* of the line regiments were plain. In 1808 the thick plumes of the Lancer regiments were replaced by thin, white ones.

◀ GENERAL OF HUSSARS, 1812 *This figure is dressed in the unusual and flamboyant uniform of General Kulniev, a colonel-in-chief of the Grodno Hussars. Kulniev distinguished himself in the early stages of the 1812 Campaign, and designed himself an extravagant uniform, which demonstrated his lavish tastes, and incorporated just about all the elements of traditional hussar dress.*

THE ARTILLERY AND ENGINEERS

Russian technical troops struggled from years of comparative neglect. Yet sensible artillery reform led to an efficient branch of service. Engineers and specialists were always lacking.

Artillery Uniform

Traditionally, artillery wore red coats faced black, and red breeches. In 1796 they wore the bicorn and their black facings were replaced by dark green, piped red until 1801, when black was reintroduced.

In 1803 the pioneers and foot artillery were issued with the shako. Horse artillery were issued with the dragoon-style black leather helmet. It had peaks to front and rear and

was surmounted with a leather comb on top of which sat a mighty, horsehair crest. This was black for troopers, red for musicians, black with a white front, having a vertical orange stripe for NCOs. Officers in the field wore crests of the same dimensions, but white, with a black tip, separated from the white body by an orange ring. The front was covered with a brass plate bearing the crowned double-eagle badge. Off duty, officers wore the bicorn, with simple loop and button.

In August 1808 all brigades were ordered to wear red shoulder straps, with the brigade number in yellow. The kiwer was adopted by the foot artillery, with crossed cannon barrels and grenade badge and red cords.

In August 1805 it was decided to raise the 10th and 11th Artillery Regiments. In 1806 the two pioneer regiments were each increased to three battalions. In 1809 all artillery officers were to wear red piping to the front and bottom of the collar; this became known as the "educated edge" and was later extended to all technical troops.

Engineers

These too had been reorganized by Potemkin in 1763 and their strength then stood at 1,147 officers and men.

◀ **OFFICER OF ENGINEERS, 1799** *The engineers were skilled officers, trained in construction and bridging techniques and also cartography. This uniform's style dates from the time of the Seven Years' War.*

▶ **SERGEANT OF FOOT ARTILLERY, 1800** *Traditionally, the Russian artillery wore black facings, but under Paul I (1796–1801) the collar and cuffs were in the coat colour, piped in red. The two long pickers were for piercing the bagged charge on the gun, through the touch-hole, so that ignition could be achieved. The hat pompon, corner tassels and the sabre knot show the black-white-orange combination that distinguished NCOs. The buttons were of copper.*

There was a company each of miners and sappers. In 1796 the Engineer Corps had 1,147 men. By July 1802 the pioneers had been increased to a regiment of two battalions. A second such regiment was raised in 1802.

In 1809 the Engineer School was increased in size and courses were introduced for officers. The corps was distributed round Russia's fortresses, mapping staying with the field army.

The *Pontonniers*

The *pontonniers*, or bridging specialists of the army, were brought into the artillery in 1796 and were increased to eight companies; later joined by the pioneer regiment of two battalions.

THE COSSACKS, KALMUCKS AND BASCHKIRS

For many years the Russian state had been successfully subduing the tribes of nomadic horsemen on their eastern and southern borders, then settling them into permanent colonies. In 1792 the old Zaporozha Cossacks became the Army of the Cossacks of the Black Sea. In 1793 the 1st–3rd Tschugujev Cossack Regiments were organized. In the reforms of 1796, the 3rd Tschugujev Regiment was disbanded. In 1796 the Jekaterinoslav Cossack Army was disbanded (it was re-raised in October 1801) and in 1797 two companies of horse artillery were attached to the Army of the Don Cossacks. A second regiment of Teptjars was raised in 1798, and in 1800 the two Tschugujev regiments were reduced to one.

▶ BASCHKIR, 1813 *Among the Asiatic troops in Russian service were mounted archers from the central and southern Urals. The French nicknamed them "cupids". They were Muslims and were mounted on small, tough and wiry ponies. Their combat effectiveness was limited, but they were good for scouting, raiding and escorting prisoners. This man wears chain mail on his shoulders.*

Cossacks

In 1803 there was a flurry of reorganizational activity in this section of the army. The 1st–3rd Bug Cossacks were raised from the settlers along the lower reaches of that river; they included many Bulgars. The Jekaterinoslav Cossack Regiment, which was settled along the line of the Caucasus mountains, was retitled the Caucasian Regiment.

The Orenburg Cossack Army, raised in 1798, was divided into five cantons, and the Orenburg Cossack Regiment was raised. In 1803 the Ural Cossack Army was raised to ten regiments, each composed of five squadrons (*sotnia*). In August 1808 the Tschugujev Cossack Regiment was converted to a lancer regiment.

The irregular Cossacks along the Caucasian Line were given two Cossack horse artillery batteries.

An army of irregular Siberian Cossacks was also formed in 1808; it too had two batteries of horse artillery.

In 1812 four regiments of Ukrainian Cossacks, each of eight squadrons, were raised. Apart from these regular troops, when the czar issued his *Landwehr* proclamation in July 1812, among the scores of volunteer formations that sprang up were

▲ **Officer, Don Cossacks, 1802** *There were 36 Pulks or regiments of Cossacks from the Don serving with the Russian Army in 1812 and Cossacks were an integral part of Russia's armed forces. Under Czar Paul tough men such as this on hardy little ponies were prepared for a proposed expedition against the British forces in India. They excelled in scouting and skirmishing and were the eyes and ears of any formation.*

the following: a Lubny Cossack Regiment, 24 Cossack regiments from Orenburg province and a regiment of Cossacks in Lithuania.

Kalmucks

In 1803 the Kalmuk Regiment was formed from Kalmucks of the Stavropol Army. In April 1812 these

▲ **Officer, Ataman's Cossack Regiment, 1812** *Count Matvei Ivanovich Platov was Ataman (commander) of the Host of the Don Cossacks and colonel-in-chief of this regiment, which served in the 1st Army of the West. Again, note the black leather belt and its elaborate decoration.*

became the 1st, 2nd and Stavropol Kalmuck Regiments.

Baschkirs

In April 1811 the government of the province of Orenburg raised the 1st and 2nd Baschkir regiments from the tribesmen of the area.

▶ **Officer, Don Cossacks Kit** *Two examples of Cossack cartridge pouches, each having belts with elaborate silver ornamentation.*

▲ **NCO, 1st Kalmucks, 1812** *Both regiments of Kalmucks served in General Count Lambert's Corps in General Tormassov's 3rd Army of the West in 1812. The square-topped czapka indicates the same ethnic origins as the lancers in the south-eastern regions of Europe. They were light cavalry, similar to the Cossacks, and they fought predominantly with the lance.*

PRUSSIA

Under its indecisive, opportunistic king, Frederic William III, Prussia managed to avoid war with France from 1795 until 1806. But in 1806, with incredibly poor timing, Prussia chose to challenge Napoleon. In the whirlwind campaign of October 1806, the Prussian Army – pride of Frederick the Great – was almost completely destroyed in one day at the twin battles of Jena and Auerstädt. Although crushed, and humiliated for years, Prussia managed to rise from the ashes like a phoenix, army and state dramatically reformed, in 1813. It was a major contributor to the ejection of Napoleon from Germany in this year and spearheaded the invasion of France on New Year's Day in 1814. The spring campaign of that year saw Napoleon at his best; every Allied error was ruthlessly exploited, but eventually, their restored co-operation saw his defeat and first abdication. In 1815 Prussia joined the Anglo-Dutch-Hanoverian army to defeat Napoleon for the last time, at Waterloo.

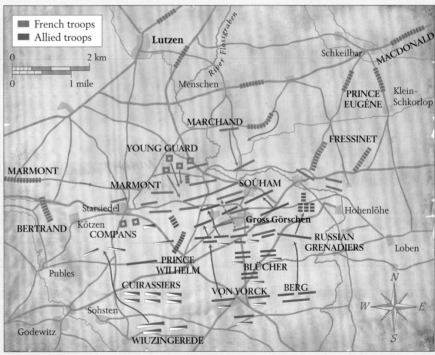

▲ *The Battle of Lützen was the first major action of the 1813 campaign. Russian Count Wittgenstein commanded the Russo-Prussian army, and although the French achieved a victory, their lack of cavalry meant that they were unable to exploit it.*

◄ *At the Battle of Eylau, 7–8 February 1807, the Prussian General l'Estocq's small corps was caught up in the mainly Russian defeat.*

THE PRUSSIAN STATE

As France descended into revolution the extensive kingdom of Prussia was apparently powerful and cohesive and boasted a military force that had an impressive reputation for efficiency and a tradition of excellence.

The King

In 1792 Prussia was ruled by King Frederick William II (1786–97), a nephew of Frederick the Great. He was a popular monarch, intent on improving the lot of his people by reducing taxation levels and encouraging schools and universities. He also opened the Prussian Academy to German writers, something forbidden by Frederick the Great, who was enthralled by the French language. But Frederick William II was less interested in military matters; abandoning the practical approach of his predecessors, he left management

▼ *Napoleon receives Queen Louise of Prussia, wife of Frederick William III, referred to by Napoleon as his "beautiful enemy".*

of the army to the Duke of Brunswick and General von Möllendorf. His foreign policy was also unfocused and cost his treasury dearly.

Although he led the nation into the wars of the First Coalition in 1792, he had a clear set of national priorities and quit the alliance in 1794 to participate in the final dismemberment of Poland. This brought him the new provinces of South Prussia and New East Prussia, but lost him the support of the other European monarchs.

At the time of Frederick William II's death in 1797, his confused realm was close to bankruptcy and his army was led by an ossified general staff, no longer fit to compete on the battlefield with the vigorous young bloods in the armies of the French Revolution.

He was succeeded by his son, Frederick William III, whose queen, Louise Augusta, took an active and positive role in ruling Prussia and soon came to regard Napoleon as her most dangerous enemy. She repeatedly urged Frederick William to join in the Allied

▲ *King Frederick William II of Prussia, nephew of Frederick the Great, left his country's finances in ruins. He concluded a peace with France in 1795.*

coalitions against France, but he resisted and kept Prussia neutral until 1806. Louise was beautiful, and popular with the Prussian people. Napoleon called her his "beautiful enemy" and – after having humbled the Prussian Army in October 1806 – "the only man in Prussia". She died of an unidentified illness on 17 July 1810.

Even so, Louise succeeded in having the king sign the secret Treaty of Potsdam on 3 November 1805, with Austria and Russia, by which a Prussian military contingent was to join the Austro-Russian army in Bohemia. Less than a month later, Napoleon was to destroy that army before the Prussian soldiers had even left their barracks.

The State

Prussia was a typical European absolute monarchy in 1792, with a feudal, agrarian, society. The great exception to this rule was the coal-rich province of Silesia, which Frederick the Great had taken from Maria Theresa in the Silesian and Seven Years' Wars.

Two groups in Prussia at this time owed services to landlords: those who owned property but had legal obligations to landlords and could move away only under forfeiture of that property, and those peasants who owned no property at all. The second group was often likely to work for landlords without pay. The numbers liable to this imposition were highest in the east of the kingdom and reduced the farther west one came. From 1713, Prussian kings tried to minimize or eradicate serfdom. When Prussia won Silesia in 1743 after the First Silesian War, the feudal rights of landowners were abolished, but an attempt to do the same in Pomerania in 1763 (after the Seven Years' War) failed in the face of the united resistance of the local nobility, who managed to convince the king that the entire economy of the province would collapse if his reforms were introduced.

The last vestiges of such feudal conditions were, however, swept away in Prussia by the Landrecht Act of 1794, which reformed the ownership

▲ *Prussian Field Marshal von Blücher, Napoleon's most implacable enemy, had an amazing ability to inspire the officers and men that he led to achieve great things.*

of the lands. This still left the state struggling to flourish under the most bureaucratic and inflexible of administrative systems. This resulted in a climate of almost universal political apathy, with slight traces of patriotism.

Before the disasters of 1806 there were reformers in Prussia – social, political and military. Prince Karl August von Hardenberg, a Hanoverian by birth, had been in Prussian service since 1792 and was one of the leading political reformers. He was foreign minister from 1804 to 1806; following Napoleon's defeat of Prussia, he was forced from office. In 1810, however, Hardenberg was appointed chancellor and continued his reform programme. He abolished restrictions on internal trade, introduced a uniform system of taxation, granted equality of status to the Jews and further eased the burdens of the peasants. He also proposed a consultative national political assembly, but the Prussian nobility defeated this effort. Hardenberg formed the alliance with Russia in 1813 and represented Prussia at the Congress of Vienna.

The Army

From 1807 to 1812, the remnants of the Prussian Army (and the state) were examined and probed, purged of outdated commanders, tactics, policies and practices, and rebuilt to a dramatically modernized format. Researchers of Prussian history prior to 1806 may well be surprised at the number of the colonels-in-chief of regiments who "died in post". This was the logical outcome of a state in which most of the landed aristocracy (from whom alone officers of the army could be drawn) were without adequate alternative income to military service and were forbidden to sell their land or to practise a trade. This produced a true caste system as rigid as that of the Hindu religion. This was aggravated by the practice of officers "owning" units down to company level, paring expenses on things such as clothing, equipment and training, to maximize their own personal profits.

This was a common feature of many military systems of the time and went on until its evils became too obvious to overlook. Continuing in military service until a ripe old age was the only way for many of these veteran officers to survive economically. This led to the disasters of 1806, when Napoleon and his able young senior commanders wrecked the Prussian Army, led largely as it was by physically – sometimes also mentally – infirm geriatrics. The average age of senior Prussian commanders in October 1806 was $58^3/_4$ years; that of Napoleon's team was $40^1/_2$ years.

Promotion in the Prussian Army prior to the catastrophe of 1806 was literally a matter of stepping into dead men's boots. It was only when pensions were introduced that older officers could afford to retire and the average age of the Prussian officer corps was significantly cut. Perhaps the greatest exception that proved the rule of ensuring that older officers should retire was Field Marshal von Blücher. Although aged 73 in 1815, he stood up well to campaigning and was inspired with a hatred of Napoleon and everything he stood for.

THE CATASTROPHE OF 1806

After discovering the secret Austro-Russo-Prussian treaty, Napoleon demanded that Prussia sign a draconian peace treaty. Queen Louise persuaded Frederick William to reject it, which provoked Napoleon into sending a harsher deal in February 1806; Frederick William signed. Then, perhaps goaded forward by his fiery consort, he seemed to recant and gave Napoleon an ultimatum to withdraw his troops from Germany by 8 October. His sense of timing was less than perfect. Having dithered on the sidelines of European affairs for nine years, and having just seen the great powers of Austria and Russia humbled at Austerlitz, he chose the summer of 1806 to challenge the military genius of the era – Napoleon Bonaparte.

Disaster

Napoleon's response was another convincing demonstration of the supremacy of his army. One of Frederick William's sons, Prince Louis Ferdinand, was killed at the opening of the campaign on 10 October at Saalfeld, commanding a combined Prussian-Saxon force as it resisted the advance of Marshal Lannes' V Corps. Four days later, Napoleon, with 54,000 men, rushed upon the lesser half of the still-divided Prussian Army (some 45,000 men) at Jena, defeating it in short order. That same day, some 12¼ miles (20 km) away to the north at the tiny village of Auerstädt, Marshal Davout's isolated III Corps, some 29,000 men, bumped into the 52,000 troops of the Prussian Army's main body. Nevertheless, Davout inflicted a crushing defeat on the Prussians, killing and wounding 10,000 and capturing a further 3,000 for the loss of about 7,000 of his own men.

The beaten Prussians fled the field, their brittle morale shattered, and most of the staff and commanders rendered useless with panic. Brigades and regiments just fell apart, all military cohesion was lost. The fugitives streamed away to the north and east, obsessed with saving their own skins.

Over the next few weeks there was a dramatic series of unprecedented and utterly shameful capitulations of numerous Prussian fortresses, such as Plassenburg, Spandau, Prenzlau, Pasewalk, Stettin, Magdeburg, Erfurt, Hamlin and Glogau.

Only Gebhart Leberecht von Blücher kept his nerve. With his corps of some 20,000 men he bravely fought his way north up to Lübeck, where he was cornered – out of ammunition and supplies – and forced to capitulate to Marshal Bernadotte's I Corps on 7 November at Ratkau.

The king and his court retreated eastward to Königsberg, determined to carry on the fight together with Czar Alexander's army. One Prussian corps, that of General von L'Estocq, had survived in East Prussia and took the field with the Russian Army under General Bennigsen. This war dragged on through the bitter Polish winter, ending with the Allied defeat at Friedland on 14 June 1807. Prussia was reduced to a third-rate power.

▲ *The humiliating surrender of the mighty Prussian fortress at Erfurt, 16 October 1806.*

Learning Lessons

Following the treaties of Tilsit (9 July 1807) and Paris (8 September 1808), Prussia was humbled, crushed, her shattered army limited to 42,000 men, the state crippled by the imposition of massive fines, her cities occupied by French troops, the cost of which had to be borne by Prussia. Napoleon ensured that all activities of the Prussian government were closely monitored by the army of spies with which he infested the country. He interfered with royal appointments and ensured that officials hostile to France were replaced by neutral figures.

The Electorate of Saxony had been raised to the status of a kingdom by Napoleon and granted nominal rule over the Grand Duchy of Warsaw. As these two states were separated by Prussian territory, the Saxons were granted the right to use a military road across it to communicate with Warsaw.

Although not allowed to attend most of the negotiations leading up to the Treaty of Tilsit, Frederick William

III was bound by their outcome. Prussia lost about half its pre-war population and area. The only fortresses remaining in Prussian hands were Colberg, Cosel, Glatz, Graudenz, Pillau and Silberberg. The gains of 1795 were lost as were all lands west of the River Elbe.

Military Reform

The king was outraged that his senior officers had failed him so dramatically. The commanders of those fortresses, formations and regiments that had been tainted by shameful capitulations were placed before courts-martial, and several were sentenced to death, but the king usually relented and commuted the sentences to imprisonment. The legendary Prussian Army had crumbled in one day. It had performed well in 1792–94 and did seem to be in reasonable order before 13 October, but something under the surface had been wrong with it.

It was vital, for the survival of the kingdom, that the king found out what was wrong and rectified it as soon as possible. So, on 15 July 1807, he invited Scharnhorst and Graf von Lottum to investigate the causes of the debacle and to present plans for the reform of the army. The body given that task was entitled the Army Reorganization Commission (*Militair-Reorganisations-Kommission des Heeres*). The king proposed: the identification and punishment of all officers guilty of dishonourable conduct in 1806 (208 from a total of 6,915 serving officers); the opening up of careers as officers to all candidates; improvements in uniforms and supply systems; a revised set of Articles of War and improved tactical regulations; the abolition of the practice of allowing soldiers to buy freedom from guard duty and the custom of entering young nobles into the regimental records when they were only 12 years old.

Other reforms were introduced, including a certain degree of social mobility. Foundations were also laid for a *Landwehr*, or home guard. Flogging as a military punishment was abolished and a more liberal code of military justice was introduced. All able-bodied male citizens of a particular age group were theoretically liable for military service. Exemptions were minimized and the recruitment of foreigners was forbidden.

Birth and status were no longer the only keys to entry into the officer class, because literacy was a prerequisite for a commission. As literacy was still limited, however, it did not dramatically widen the potential pool of new officers. Officer candidates now had to serve for three months as privates before being commissioned. On 10 March 1809 the king asserted the right to appoint commanders on the basis of merit.

The *Kanton* and *Krümper* had survived the storms of the Napoleonic era and were of critical importance for the great struggles of the Wars of Liberation of 1813–15. Each regiment was allotted an area (*Kanton*) in which to recruit; this produced regiments with strong local ties, in which many of the men knew one another from childhood. Under the *Krümper* system, a number of men surplus to the military establishment would be called forward for military training, and when this was completed, they would be discharged back into civilian life. Thus the number of soldiers remained within permitted limits, but a growing pool of trained civilians was created for future service. On 6 August 1808 the king ordered that the system should make a start in that each company was to rotate from three to five men in that year. The recruits were to be drilled for one month then released. They were subsequently drilled on Sundays and holidays by officers and NCOs sent out into the towns. Gradually, these rotation quotas were increased. The reports of October 1812 show that 33,337 *Krümper* were trained and fit for duty in the field and that a further 3,087 were fit and capable of performing garrison duty.

This system was popular with the farmers because conscripted men were absent only for short periods. Army officers were less enthusiastic about the brevity of the training. As of 1809, the units of each brigade were billeted in garrisons and this gave the opportunity for all-arms training to be carried out for the first time.

▼ *Napoleon's victory over the Russians on 14 June 1807, at Friedland, ensured Prussia's relegation to a minor power until 1813.*

THE PRUSSIAN ARMY AND THE CAMPAIGNS OF 1812–15

Years of reform produced the desired effect. By 1812 Prussia, to all intents and purposes, could boast a new, modernized army.

Napoleon's Invasion of Russia

In February 1812 France and Prussia entered into a military alliance in which Prussia was committed to providing almost 21,000 men for Napoleon's projected invasion of Russia. This theoretically left 22,000 soldiers in Prussia according to the terms of the Treaty of Paris. In reality, there were some 38,300 when the trained *Krümper* were included.

The Prussian corps was to be attached to Marshal Macdonald's X Corps and commanded by General von Yorck. Macdonald was directed to take the Baltic port of Riga. Early in the campaign, the 2nd Combined Hussar Regiment and the Combined Lancer Regiment were taken from the Prussian corps at Napoleon's express order and added to the I and II Cavalry Corps respectively. They thus fought at Borodino and the remnants were destroyed during the retreat. The bulk of the Prussian contingent experienced a low-key campaign in Latvia, and suffered little in comparison to

Napoleon's main body. By mid-December, Macdonald was falling back on Tilsit, the Russians following carefully. On 30 December, General von Yorck concluded the Convention of Tauroggen with General von Diebitsch of the Russian general staff, whereby the Prussian corps was given neutral status and allowed to withdraw into Prussia. Yorck's action catapulted his monarch on to the horns of a dilemma. A studied silence was maintained for some weeks, but in March 1813, as the tide of war crept slowly westward, Frederick William bowed to the growing murmurings of Prussian patriotism and declared his alliance with Russia.

The whole nation swung behind the mobilization and rearmament programme. The *Krümper* were recalled, new recruits were enrolled, equipped and drilled. Arsenals were set up, clothing factories poured out new uniforms and patriotic women gave their gold to aid the national cause.

The War of Liberation 1813

Napoleon raised a new army out of the ground in an amazingly short time and advanced back into Germany. The first major action was at Lützen (Gross-

Görschen) on 2 May; Napoleon won, but without cavalry could not exploit it. He won again at Bautzen and Würschen on 20–21 May, though unconvincingly. The Allies nevertheless proposed an armistice and the emperor agreed. Both sides worked furiously to repair and improve their armies, but soon Napoleon felt himself to be stronger and his demands at the negotiating table grew harsher; he rejected Allied peace proposals. Austria had initially acted as a neutral broker between the opposing camps, but in August it joined the Allies against France. In Prussia the military expansion took off only in July, when many new regular regiments were formed, but the *Landwehr* had already been pouring into the front lines before that.

The armistice ended; the Allies attacked Dresden, but by wasting a whole day, they gave Napoleon time to come up and were again defeated. Over the next few days, however, they won victories at Hagelberg, Plagwitz, the Katzbach, Kulm and Dennewitz.

The campaign climaxed with the Battle of the Nations at Leipzig on 16–19 October, in which Napoleon was soundly beaten. He had no option but to flee back to France, while the Allies advanced to his borders.

The Invasion of France 1814

On New Year's Day, Blücher's Army of Silesia crossed the Rhine at Kaub and entered France unopposed. The other Allied armies, those of Bohemia and the North, followed suit. The 1814 campaign showed Napoleon at his best whenever the Allies were rash enough to lower their guard. His victories at Brienne, Champaubert, Montmirail,

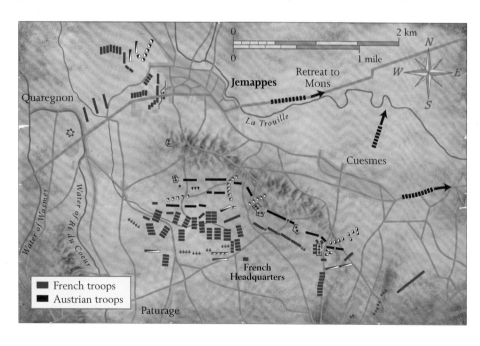

◀ *The Battle of Jemappes, 6 November 1792. Although it was purely an Austrian force that was defeated here, as a result the Prussians were also forced to scrap their plans for the invasion of France.*

Château-Thierry, Vauchamps, Nangis and Montereau in late January and early February rocked them on their heels. But the Prussian Army was so robust and battle-hardened that it weathered all these storms and was still an effective weapon, right through to final victory at Paris on 30 March.

The Waterloo Campaign 1815

Napoleon's exile to the island of Elba was brief; in the spring of 1815 he returned to Paris and seized power once more. The Allies all agreed to act against him. The Prussian Army was still in the field, in eastern Belgium and around Cologne. Together with the Duke of Wellington's army of Germans, Netherlanders and British to their west, it was the force most readily available to counter the French.

In the early hours of 15 June a strong force of French cavalry fell upon General von Zieten's extended I Prussian Corps at Fleurus and pushed them back to the north-east. Napoleon's plan was to strike between Blücher and Wellington, divide them and destroy each in detail. The Allies were alert to this threat and had agreed to try to counter it by sticking together. On 16 June there occurred the twin battles of Ligny and Quatre Bras. Marshal Ney failed to break Allied

resistance at Quatre Bras, so the first phase of Napoleon's plan had failed.

Due to the poor tactical deployment of the Prussians at Ligny, they lost over 12,000 casualties and were forced to withdraw, initially northwards. But the second step of Napoleon's plan fell apart. Rather than falling back along their lines of communication, the Prussians shook off Marshal Grouchy, who headed the French pursuit, and turned west.

Wellingon's army took a battering at Waterloo on 18 June, as Napoleon sought to destroy him. By afternoon, however, troops began to appear on

▲ Prince Schwarzenberg announces victory over the French to the Allied kings at the Battle of Leipzig, on 19 October 1813.

the eastern edge of the battlefield. It was the battered, but combat-worthy Prussian Army, longing to get at their foes. The defeat of the Imperial Guard and Prussian pressure on the French won the day. The French began to disintegrate and the Prussians pursued them. Napoleon had been thwarted; Jena and Auerstädt were avenged.

▼ Wellington and Blücher meet at the end of the Battle of Waterloo.

THE INFANTRY BEFORE 1806

The Prussian infantry of 1806 were beaten by a more mobile and flexible enemy. Their dress and organization were eighteenth-century in style.

The Fusilier Battalions

Fusiliers were raised specifically as light infantry in the 1780s. There had been light infantry in the Prussian Army under Frederick the Great but such units had been disbanded. The fusiliers had shorter muskets than the line infantry, were four companies strong and had ten sharpshooters in each company armed with rifles. They were trained to skirmish in open order. In 1806 there were 24 such fusilier battalions but, after 1807, the new-style infantry regiments each had a

fusilier battalion attached to it on a permanent basis.

Fusiliers wore infantry bicorns, dark green tunics, white breeches, short black gaiters and black leatherwork. The bicorn was originally worn but would soon be replaced by a peaked felt shako with eagle badge. In 1798 the twenty-four fusilier battalions were formed into nine brigades on a regional basis, mostly with three battalions, some with only two.

Each brigade had its common facing and button colour; within each brigade every battalion had its own arrangement of facings on the jackets. In all cases, the shoulder straps and the edging to the green turnbacks of the coats were in the brigade facing colour. Belts were black. The eagles on the hats were in the brigade button colour.
KURMARK BRIGADE. 1st Battalion "Wedel". Crimson collar and cuffs, yellow buttons, lapels in the coat colour. Red pompon on the shako in 1801. 2nd Battalion "von Bila". Crimson collar, lapels and cuffs, yellow buttons. White pompon on the shako in 1801. 5th Battalion "Graf Wedel". Crimson lapels, yellow buttons; green collar and cuffs. Yellow pompon

◀ DRUMMER, INFANTRY REGIMENT GRAF KUNHEIM No. 1, 1795 *NCOs in this regiment wore the usual black and white pompons and sword knots, as well as silver lace edging to the lapels, cuffs and cuff flaps.*

▶ MUSKETEERS, INFANTRY REGIMENT PRINZ VON ORANIEN No. 19, 1806 *The brass pouch badge bears the royal cipher "FWR" amid trophies of arms. The sabre knot tassels indicate the wearer's company: 1st Grenadier. red; 2nd Grenadier, black; Life, white; 1st Musketeer, red; 2nd, yellow; 3rd, pink; 4th, orange; 5th, light blue; 6th, purple; 7th, cobalt blue; 8th, green; 9th, blue.*

on the shako in 1801.
MAGDEBURG BRIGADE. 18th Battalion "Holtzschuher". Crimson lapels, the collar and cuffs were green; white buttons. The pompon on the shako in 1801 was red. 19th Battalion "Ernest". Crimson collar, lapels and cuffs, white buttons. The pompon an the shako in

Infantry Regimental Distinctions: 1806

No./Title	Facings	Buttons	Lace (*no tassels)	Small clothes
1 Kunheim	poppy red	white	white*	white
2 Rüchel	light brick red	yellow	crimson	buff
3 Renouard	poppy red	yellow	black & white	white
4 Kalckreuth	orange	yellow	white & light blue lines	buff
5 Kleist	pale buff	yellow	orange	white
6 Grenadier Guard	scarlet	yellow	red & gold	white
7 Owstein	pink	white		white
8 Ruits	scarlet	yellow	white & 2 blue lines*	white
9 Schenk	scarlet	yellow	yellow*	white
10 Wedell	light blue	white	white & 6 red lines	white
11 Prince Heinrich	crimson	white	white & red & blue lines	white
12 Duke Frederick of Brunswick	brick red	yellow	white	white
13 Arnim	white	white	white	white
14 Besser	brick red	yellow	white & 2 red lines	white
15 Foot Guards	red	white	white*	white
16 Diericke	red	yellow	white with red & black lines	white
17 Treskow	white	yellow	white & 6 red lines	white
18 The King's	pink	white	white	white
19 Orange	orange	white	white	white
20 Prince Louis	scarlet	yellow	white & 3 blue lines	white
21 Duke Carl Brunswick	scarlet	white	white & 2 red lines	white
22 Pirch	poppy red	yellow	white & red dicing lines*	white
23 Winning	pink	white	white & 6 blue lines	white
24 Zenge	poppy red	yellow	white & red lines/worm*	white
25 Möllendorf	scarlet	yellow	white & 6 blue lines*	white
26 Old Larisch	brick red	yellow	yellow & 6 red lines*	white
27 Tschammer	poppy red	yellow	yellow	white
28 Malschitzky	buff	white		white
29 Treuenfels	crimson	yellow	white with 4 red & 4 blue lines*	white
30 Borcke	buff	yellow	white with 2 red & 4 blue lines*	white
31 Kropff	pink	yellow		white
32 Hohenlohe	buff	yellow		white
33 Alvensleben	white	yellow		white
34 Prince Ferdinand	poppy red	white	white	white
35 Prince Henry	sulphur yellow	white	white	white
36 Puttkammer	white	white		white
37 Tschepe	crimson	white		white
38 Pelchrzim	scarlet	yellow		white
39 Zastrow	buff	yellow		white
40 Schimonsky	pink	white		white
41 Lettow	raspberry	yellow	yellow*	white
42 Plötz	orange	yellow		white

▶

1801 was white. 20th Battalion "Borke". Crimson collar and cuffs, green lapels. The pompon on the shako in 1801 was yellow.

1ST EAST PRUSSIAN BRIGADE. 3rd Battalion "Wakenitz". Violet lapels, yellow buttons; green collar and cuffs. The pompon on the shako in 1801 was yellow. 6th Battalion "Rembow". Violet collars, cuffs and lapels, yellow buttons. White pompon on the shako in 1801. 11th Battalion "Eichler". Violet collar and cuffs, green lapels. Red pompon on the shako in 1801.

2ND EAST PRUSSIAN BRIGADE. 21st Battalion. "Stutterheim". Violet lapels, collar and cuffs, white buttons. White pompon on the shako in 1801. 23rd Battalion "Yorck". Violet collar and

▼ HORNIST, INFANTRY REGIMENT VON PUTTKAMMER NO. 36, 1806 *Signals for light troops were given on hunting horns instead of drums, the latter being too bulky for troops skirmishing in open order. This regiment was raised in 1740.*

cuffs, white buttons. Red pompon on the shako in 1801. 24th Battalion, "Bülow". Violet lapels, green cuffs and collar, white buttons. Yellow pompon on the shako in 1801.

SOUTH PRUSSIAN BRIGADE. 7th Battalion "Schultz". Light blue collar, lapels and cuffs, white buttons. Red pompon on the shako in 1801. 8th Battalion "Kloch". Light blue lapels, green collar and cuffs, white buttons. The pompon on the shako in 1801 was white.

1ST WARSAW BRIGADE. 9th Battalion "Ledebur" Light green lapels, collar and cuffs, white buttons. The pompon on the shako in 1801 was red. 12th Battalion "Eiche". Light green collar and cuffs, white buttons. The pompon on the shako in 1801 was yellow. 17th Battalion "Hinrichs". Light green collar, cuffs and lapels, white buttons. The pompon on the

No/Title(1806)	Facings	Buttons	Lace (*no tassels)	Small Clothes
43 Strachwitz	light orange	white		white
44 Hagken	buff	yellow	white & 6 blue lines	white
45 Zweiffel	lemon yellow	yellow	white & 3 red lines	white
46 Thile	scarlet	yellow		white
47 Grawert	light orange	white		white
48 Hessen-Kassel	white	yellow	white red tassels	white
49 Müffling	white	white	white with 3 light blue lines	white
50 Sanitz	blossom pink	white	white*	white
51 Kauffberg	sulphur yellow	white	white	white
52 Reinhart	scarlet	white		white
53 Jung Larisch	buff	yellow		white
54 Natzmer	buff	white		white
55 Manstein	crimson	yellow	yellow	white
56 Tauentzien	scarlet	white		white
57 Grevenitz	pink	yellow	white & 3 pink lines	white
58 L'Homme de Courbiere	bright yellow	white	white*	white
59 Wartensleben	white	yellow		white
60 Chlebowsky	lemon yellow	yellow		white

shako in 1801 was white.

2ND WARSAW BRIGADE. 4th Battalion "Greiffenberg". Light green collar, lapels and cuffs, yellow buttons. The pompon on the shako in 1801 was red. 16th Battalion "Oswald". Light green lapels, green collar and cuffs. Yellow pompon on the shako in 1801.

UPPER SILESIAN BRIGADE. 10th Battalion "Anhalt". Black collar, lapels and cuffs, white buttons. White pompon on the shako in 1801. 22nd Battalion "Puttlitz". Black lapels, green collar and cuffs. The pompon on the shako in 1801 was yellow.

LOWER SILESIAN BRIGADE. 14th Battalion "Pelet". Black collar, lapels and cuffs, yellow buttons. White pompon on the shako in 1801. 15th Battalion "Rühle". Black lapels, green collar and cuffs, white buttons. Red pompon on the shako in 1801. 13th Battalion "Rabenau". Black lapels, green collar and cuffs, white buttons. The pompon on the shako in 1801 was yellow.

◀ GENERAL OFFICER OF INFANTRY, 1806
Generals wore dark blue coats with red collars and cuffs, with gold embroidery, and a gold aiguillette on the right shoulder. The uniform was to be simplified in the reforms of 1807.

The Field *Jägers*

These were first raised in 1740. All uniform details were as for the fusiliers of line infantry except as noted below. The shako had no top band and was decorated with dark green cords and a black plume for parades. The uniform was as follows: canary green coat, buff leather breeches, boots; white waistcoat, poppy red cuffs and collar, gold aiguillette. Officers had black and silver cords. Dark green tunic and turnbacks, red collar, shoulder straps, Swedish cuffs and piping to turnbacks, yellow buttons. Grey breeches, short, black gaiters, and black leatherwork. Officers wore eight embroidered gold loops to each lapel, two on each cuff, two on the pocket flap; four in the small of the back. A wide, scalloped gold hat edging. *Jägers'* plain hats had plumes, white over black; green and silver hat cords and fist straps.

Prussian infantry uniforms had changed little since the days of the Seven Years' War. Largely due to Prussian successes in that war, modernization, which might include improvements in dress and equipment, was deemed largely unnecessary. Any changes were largely superficial. The

▲ OFFICER, 1ST WARSAW FUSILIER BRIGADE, 1806 *This unit was originally the Fusilier Battalion No. 9. The dark green coats and simple style of decoration were to complement the light infantry role of these troops. Grey overalls were becoming popular by this time for wear in the field. This officer wears a bicorn with his hair bound in the regulation pigtail, which was abolished in 1808.*

▲ OFFICER, FIELD JÄGERS, 1806 *Jägers, trained to act as skirmishers and adept at using the terrain, universally adopted uniforms that would, relatively speaking, allow them to remain hidden. Feldjaegers were also to be used for skirmishing, and their dark green coats aided camouflage. Their uniforms were copied by many other German states in the eighteenth century.*

cap was covered in cloth of the facing colour, edged in the button colour. The back of the leather front plate was painted in the facing colour; light blue for those regiments with white facings. Grenadier officers wore no items to distinguish them from musketeer officers. The national cockade, worn on the bicorn, was black within white.

Drummers and musicians of the

▼ HORNIST, FUSILIER BATTALION VON REMBOW NO. 6, 1792 *Hornists were distinguished by the regimental braid to the collars, cuffs, lapels and by the swallows' nests at their shoulders. This unit was raised in 1787 from garrison regiments and became the 1st East Prussian Fusilier Brigade in 1798. In 1806–07 it was in East Prussia and it fought in L'Estocq's corps at Königsberg on 14 June 1807. Prussia's uniforms had, on the surface, changed little since the time of Frederick the Great.*

bicorns and the grenadiers' mitre caps were then replaced by the *Kasket* in 1787. The front of the *Kasket* was decorated with metal badges in the button colour: a flaming grenade for grenadiers, the cipher "FWR" for Musketeers. The 24 fusilier battalions raised at the end of the eighteenth century had the Prussian eagle badge on their *Kaskets*. In 1799 the *Kasket* was superseded by the old-style bicorn for

musketeers and fusiliers, and a new model cap for grenadiers. This new grenadier cap had a black leather front plate and peak. The peak was edged in brass, the front plate bore a brass bottom band with the Prussian eagle in black and over this was a brass flaming grenade. The edges of the front plate were trimmed with a worsted roll, a white plume was worn on the left-hand side. The head band of the

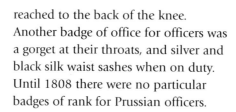

Prussian Army in the late eighteenth century were distinguished by a special braid decoration to sleeves, cuffs, lapels and buttonholes. This lace varied from regiment to regiment in design and was also worn on the swallows' nests at the top of each sleeve. Drummers and musicians carried no firearms but did wear a short sabre. Officers' coats were longer and more finely made than those of the enlisted men, and their skirts reached to the back of the knee. Another badge of office for officers was a gorget at their throats, and silver and black silk waist sashes when on duty. Until 1808 there were no particular badges of rank for Prussian officers.

The Grenadier Battalions

As with most armies of this era, in time of war, the Prussians took the grenadier companies away from their parent regiments and combined them

▼ OFFICER, INFANTRY REGIMENT VON ARNIM NO. 13, PARADE DRESS, 1806 *Officers did not carry spontoons in the field anymore, but they were retained for parades.*

▼ GRENADIER NCO, INFANTRY REGIMENT VON KROPFF NO. 31, 1806 *A single grenade was worn on the* Kasket *by Prussia's grenadiers, the cipher "FWR" by musketeers, and the triple-flamed grenade by the artillery. The hat badges were in the regimental button colour. This NCO carries a lethal-looking spontoon. Each regiment wore its own style of lace buttonholes, differing for the men, the NCOs and the officers. There was no standard system of badges of rank for NCOs.*

▲ GRENADIER FIFER, INFANTRY REGIMENT VON THILE NO. 46, 1803 *This musician sports swallows' nests on his shoulders, a shoulder decoration that was distinctive to regimental musicians across Europe.*

into elite battalions, which were used as a reserve on the battlefield. By the Order of 28 February 1799 (effective on 1 June) the grenadier companies were to be formed into standing grenadier battalions. The grenadier companies of the following regiments were excluded from this scheme and stayed with their parent regiments: Nos. 3, 5, 18, 22, 36 and 46. The wing grenadier (*Flügelgrenadier*) companies of the four Guards battalions were together only in peacetime. If mobilized for war, they were to return to their parent regiments.

THE CUIRASSIERS BEFORE 1806

Prussia's cuirassiers (*Kürassiers*) had been used by Frederick the Great as shock troops: heavily armed men on heavy horses employed to punch through enemy formations. From early times (1688), the coat worn by these regiments of heavy horse was usually a buff leather *Kollet*, which had excellent protective properties against sword cuts and was light and flexible. From about 1720 a two-piece metal cuirass was worn, but from 1735 the back plate was discarded and the front plate held in place by straps. The cuirass was polished for the Body Guard, blackened for the other regiments. These breastplates were abandoned under King Frederick William II. The cuirasses of officers were edged in gilt metal and their shoulder straps were covered in gilt plates. On the top centre of the breastplate they wore the crowned Prussian crest in trophies of arms, all gilt. A waist sash in the facing colour was worn over the tunic. Facings were worn on the collar, the Swedish cuffs and on the narrow shoulder straps. The short turnbacks were in the coat colour. Apart from the colour of the facings and buttons, each regiment was distinguished by a braid edging to the front of the coat, the cuffs, turnbacks, waistcoats and carbine bandoliers. The skirts of officers' tunics were to the knee; those of the men were cut short so that they just covered the buttocks. Breeches were in buff leather; white gauntlets and knee cuffs were worn, and stiff, high-jacked boots.

Headgear was a large bicorn with national cockade, black loop and regimental button. Under the bicorn

▶ **NCO Trumpeter, Cuirassier Regiment von Quitzow No. 6, 1806** *Each regiment had its own particular lace for its musicians. As an NCO, the trumpeter had gold lace to the cuff, carried a cane and had a red tip to his plume and a black and white tassel to his sword strap. Prussian cuirassier regiments had abandoned their armour by the 1790s.*

an iron skull cap was worn when in action. White plumes were worn for parades from 1762 onward. For NCOs the plume tip was black, for officers the base was black. From about 1735 onward, the leather tunics were replaced with white cloth items, only Regiment No. 2 retained the yellow colour and were then known as "the yellow riders".

Waistcoats were originally in the coat colour, but in 1735 they were changed to be

▼ **NCO, Cuirassier Regiment von Wagenfeld No. 4, 1806** *This rear view shows just how brief the coat-tails were in 1806. Note how the sabretasche was worn high up on the left hip. NCO status is shown by the black tip to the plume, the black and white hat tassels, the gold lace to the shoulder strap, the cuff, the bandolier and pouch lid and the black and white tassel to the sword strap. The regiment was in L'Estocq's reserve corps in 1806, thus avoiding destruction. In 1807 they became the new Cuirassier Regiment No. 1.*

Henkel von
Donnersmark No. 1

Von Beeren No. 2

Life Regiment No. 3

Von Wagenfeld No. 4

Von Balliodz No. 5

Von Quitzow No. 6

Von Reitzenstein No. 7

Von Heising No. 8

Von Holzendorf No. 9

Gendarmes No. 10

Life Carabinieers
No. 11

Von Bunting No. 12

Gardes du Corps No. 13

in the regimental facing colour. Only the Regiment Gendarmes No. 10 retained them in blue as before. After the 1st Silesian War (1741–42) the facings of some regiments changed, then remained the same until 1806.

Leatherwork was white. Weapons were a brace of pistols and a heavy, straight-bladed sword. A pouch (much like the sabretasche of the hussars) was carried from the waist belt and sat high up on the left hip. It was in the facing colour, edged with the regimental lace and bore various designs. The harness was black with steel fittings. Holster covers and the square shabraques were in either the facing colour or the colour of the coat and were edged in the regimental lace. The designs on the holster covers and in the rear corners of the shabraque varied from regiment to regiment.

As well as the daily uniform, officers also had a white state uniform with lapels, Swedish cuffs and collar in the colour of their waistcoats. On each lapel were six embroidered lace loops, two under them, two on the cuff, two on each pocket flap and four in the small of the back. The small clothes were buff. The lids of officers' cartouches were in the facing colour, edged in the regimental braid, usually enclosing trophies of arms and the crowned royal cipher. Officers' cartouche lids of regiments Nos. 7, 8, 9, 11 and 12 bore the crowned black Prussian eagle on trophies of arms. Officers of each regiment wore gold or silver lace decorations to their buttonholes that were unique to their regiment. Those of NCOs were in the facing colour, edged in braid in the button colour, bearing a crowned round plate showing the royal cipher. The badges of rank for NCOs varied from regiment to regiment. Troopers had black pouch lids with a round brass plate bearing the Prussian eagle. NCOs' cuffs were decorated with gold or silver lace, the pattern varying from regiment to regiment. Standard bearers had standard bandoliers in the facing

◀ *NCOs' badges of rank in cuirassier regiments in 1806.*

colour, edged and fringed in the button colour. The finial of the pike was in the form of a lance.

Regimental Distinctions of the Cuirassiers 1806

All regiments had white tunics and breeches except Regiment No. 2, which had lemon yellow tunics.

1 HENKEL VON DONNERSMARK. Facings: poppy red, lace: white with three red stripes. Officers' lace: silver. Holster covers and shabraque: crowned royal cipher within braid edging. Troopers' sabretasches: white crown, cipher and edging on poppy red ground.

2 VON BEEREN. Facings: crimson, lace: crimson (white on the waistcoat). Officers' lace: silver. Holster covers and the shabraque: crowned royal cipher within braid edging.

3 LIFE REGIMENT. Facings: dark blue, lace: dark blue velvet with wide central white stripe. Officers' lace: gold. Holster covers and shabraque: crowned royal cipher within braid edging. Troopers' sabretasches: white crown, cipher and edging, dark blue ground and stripes

4 VON WAGENFELD. Facings: black, lace: white braid with three lines of dark blue squares. Officers' lace: gold. Holster covers and shabraque: crowned shield bearing the crowned Prussian eagle within braid edging.

5 VON BALLIODZ. Facings: sky blue, lace: white and sky blue diced braid. Officers' lace: gold. Holster covers and shabraque: crowned shield bearing the crowned Prussian eagle within braid edging. Troopers' sabretasches: white crown, cipher and edging, light blue ground.

6 VON QUITZOW. Facings: light brick red, lace: white braid with a light brick red pattern. Officers' lace: gold. Holster covers and shabraque: crowned royal cipher within braid edging.

7 VON REITZENSTEIN. Facings: lemon, lace: white braid with three lemon stripes. Officers' lace: silver. Holster covers and shabraque: a crowned royal cipher with braid edging.

8 VON HEISING. Facings: dark blue, lace: white braid with two wide, dark blue stripes and narrow dark blue edge

piping. Officers' lace: silver. Holster covers and shabraque: crowned shield bearing the crowned Prussian eagle within braid edging.

9 VON HOLZENDORF. Facings: crimson, lace: white braid with three crimson stripes. Officers' lace: gold. Holster covers and shabraque: crowned shield bearing the crowned Prussian eagle within braid edging. Troopers' sabretasches: white crown,

cipher and edging, crimson ground.
10 GENDARMES. Facings: red, lace: red braid with a golden stripe. Officers' lace: gold. Officers' holster covers and shabraque: crowned, eight-pointed star within braid edging. Troopers' sabretasches: yellow crown, cipher and edging, red ground.
11 LIFE CARABINEERS. Facings: light blue, lace: white braid with a light blue central, diamond pattern between two light blue stripes. Officers' lace: silver. Holster covers and shabraque: crowned royal cipher within braid edging.

12 VON BUNTING. Facings: dark orange, lace: white braid with two wide orange stripes. Officers' lace: gold. Holster covers and shabraque: crowned shield bearing the crowned Prussian eagle within braid edging.
13 GARDES DU CORPS. Facings: red (blue waistcoats), lace: red braid with silver stripes. Officers' lace: silver. Officers' holster covers and shabraque: crowned, eight-pointed star, also on cartouche lids within braid edging. Troopers' sabretasches: white crown, cipher and edging, red ground.

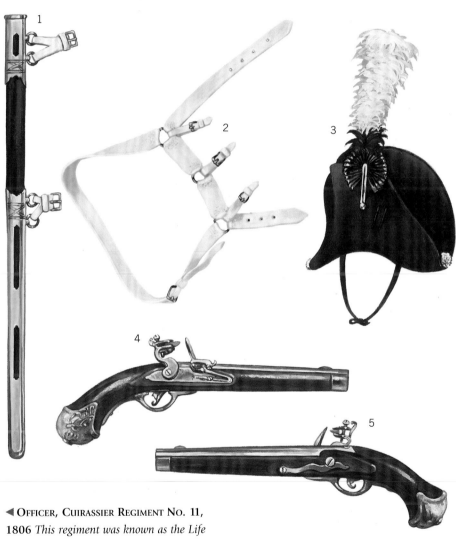

◄ OFFICER, CUIRASSIER REGIMENT NO. 11, 1806 *This regiment was known as the Life Carabineers and was raised in 1692, initially as a dragoon regiment. It was converted to a cuirassier regiment in 1718. The officer's tunic hooked together down the front. The silver waist belt had taken the place of the heavy, wide silver sash worn by infantry officers. The regiment surrendered at Pasewalk on 29 October, where they lost their five regimental standards. They were not re-raised after the war.*

▲ *The equipment carried by Prussia's heavy cavalrymen before the disaster of 1806: 1 Trooper's sheath made in black leather with steel fittings. 2 Trooper's white leather waist belt. 3 Squadron officer's undress bicorn complete with the black cockade worn by all Prussian troops. 4 and 5 Heavy cavalry pistols, probably manufactured at Potsdam, with brass fittings and decorated butts.*

THE DRAGOONS BEFORE 1806

Prussia's dragoons were organized and equipped, to all intents and purposes, as heavy cavalry. Indeed, originally, the dragoons wore the same bicorns, breeches, boots, gauntlets, waistcoats and buff leather tunics as the cuirassiers; their cuffs were usually light blue. Under Frederick William I red facings were also to be seen, and light blue woollen coats of infantry style were introduced; all cuffs were of Swedish style, and there was a distinctive aiguillette on the right shoulder strap in the button colour. Facings were worn on the collar, cuffs, lapels and turnbacks. Officers' parade uniform coats were decorated with embroidered lace loops in the button colour, six on and two under each lapel, two on the cuff, two on each pocket flap and four in the small of the back. Dragoons wore high black, heavy cavalry boots in the same style as those worn by the cuirassiers.

Leatherwork was white and the cartridge pouch was worn on the carbine bandolier. The brass-hilted long, straight sword (*Pallasch*) was carried in a brown leather sheath. It had a basket pattern guard and an eagle's head for the pommel. The dragoons bore swallow-tailed guidons instead of the square cavalry standards of the cuirassiers. The harness was black, heavy cavalry style with steel fittings. The holster covers and shabraques were usually in the facing colour and bore lace edging and ciphers or eagles as with the cuirassiers. Some regiments had square-ended shabraques, others had rounded ends.

The table opposite shows the uniforms of the dragoons as they were at the time of the death of Frederick the Great (1786).

In the period from 1784 to 1792, the turnbacks came to be in the coat colour, edged in the facing colour; the waistcoat was abandoned and in 1797

◀ NCO, QUEEN'S DRAGOONS NO. 5, 1806
The NCO's silver bandolier was edged in the regimental tape; the silver edging to his cuffs can also just be seen. As well as the black tip to the plume, his rank badges include the black and white hat tassels, silver shoulder straps and aiguillette and the black and white tassel to the brown leather sabre strap. This regiment was raised in 1717; in 1806 it fought on the left wing at Auerstädt on 14 October and most of the regiment fought their way out east to Danzig. They participated in the 1807 campaign and after the war were renumbered the Dragoon Regiment No. 1.

▲ TROOPER, DRAGOON REGIMENT KING OF BAVARIA NO. 1, 1806 *This rear view shows to good effect the regulation pigtail common to all of Prussia's soldiers. It also shows that the cartouche now has its own bandolier, having previously been worn on that of the carbine. The small cartridge pouch is decorated with a round plate bearing the Prussian eagle. Note the extremely short tails to the tunic and the white cuffs around his knees to protect them in a clash with enemy cavalry. Note also the carbine hook and bandolier and the shoulder cord or aiguilette on his right shoulder.*

the cartouche received its own narrow bandolier, which was worn over the right shoulder. The relatively complicated system of distinguishing NCOs and officers from troopers followed that used by the cuirassiers, badges of rank, and plumes, etc., being identical to those used by their heavy cavalry counterparts.

▼ CUIRASSIER SADDLE FURNITURE; REGIMENT VON QUITZOW NO. 6, 1806. *Prussian heavy cavalry used the so-called English saddle. The saddle cloth and holsters were in the regimental facing colour (here light brick red) and edged with a double strip of the regimental lace. The crowns are yellow, the ciphers are white. Cuirassier sabretasches 1806: top line, left to right: von Balliodz; Life Regiment; Henkel von Donnersmark. Bottom line, left to right: von Holtzendorff; Gendarmes; Gardes du Corps.*

No./Title	Collar & cuffs	Lapels	Turnbacks	Buttons
Dragoon Regimental Distinctions before 1806				
1 Graf Lottum	black	white	black	yellow
2 Mahlen	white	pink	white	yellow
3 Thun	pink	buff	pink	white
4 Götzen	buff	dark red	buff	white
5 Anspach–Bayreuth	dark red	white	dark red	white
6 Rohr then von Auer	white	none	white	white
7 Borcke	scarlet	scarlet	scarlet	yellow
8 Esebeck	scarlet	none*	scarlet	white
9 Herzberg	light blue	none*	blue	white
10 Manstein	orange	none	orange	white
11 Voss	yellow	yellow	yellow	white
12 Brüsewitz	black	black	black	white
13 Roquette	crimson	crimson	light blue	yellow
Raised 1802				
14 Wobese	buff	buff	light blue	yellow
Raised 1803				

*white laces to the buttonholes on the chest.

▶ SHARPSHOOTER, DRAGOON REGIMENT VON GILSA NO. 3, 1792 *The three black sections in the white plume denote these marksmen, who were armed with rifled carbines. This image provides an excellent view of the aiguillette worn on the right shoulder, a distinctive feature of the dragoons. In 1806 (then known as "von Irwing") the regiment fought at Auerstädt. Some surrendered in Erfurth, but most joined von Blücher's corps, which fought its way up to Lübeck before being captured. The regiment was not re-raised.*

◀ CUIRASSIER SADDLE *The "English" saddle, shabraque and holster covers decorated with regimental lace. The holster covers are removed to show the black leather holsters.*

THE HUSSARS BEFORE 1806

There were 11 regiments of Prussian hussars, although Regiment No. 9 was something of a special case, being a unit of lancers, armed and equipped in a "Polish" manner. The other regiments of hussars wore the traditional Hungarian costume of a richly laced dolman and pelisse,

▼ HUSSARS KIT

1 A hussar's wooden Bock saddle. This kind of saddle was copied from Hungarian light cavalry. It had originated with Mongolian nomadic horsemen and the raised ends gave the rider a very secure seat in the saddle.
2 Leather cushion for the Bock saddle.
3 NCO's black and white sabre strap.
4 A special sabre strap for troopers who were distinguished in the 1806 campaign.
5 Light cavalry officers' leather sabre strap, considerably more decorative than those worn by troopers. 6 Dragoon sword hilt complete with Prussian royal eagle.

coloured barrel sash, leather breeches and short boots with the top front cut out in a "V" shape with a tassel. The pelisse was lined with fur in the regimental colour and this was worn slung over the left shoulder. NCOs and trumpeters often wore fox fur edging. The original headgear was the fur-trimmed cap; in 1756 this had given way to the *mirliton* (that of Regiment No. 5 was originally decorated on the front with a white skeleton; by 1791 this had been reduced to a skull and crossbones) and by 1786 the brown fur colpack was being worn. By 1806 the artist Knötel shows them wearing black felt shakos with a leather peak. They were armed with a carbine, curved sabre and a pair of pistols. Harness was black, Hungarian-style with steel fittings. They used the Mongolian-style Bock saddle made on a birch-wood frame.

In 1976 the *Deutsche Gesellschaft für Heereskunde* published a hitherto unknown collection of watercolours of the Prussian hussar regiments (the *Preussische Husarenbilder um 1791*) of 1791 (1792 in the case of Regiment No. 11), which threw much new light on the uniforms of this arm. They were painted by an artist with much detailed knowledge of his subject: where the details of

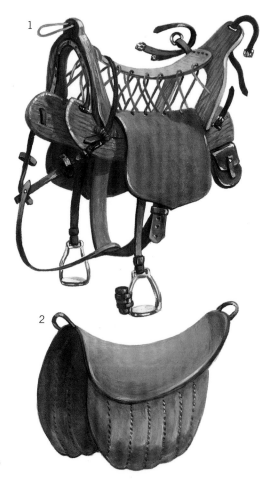

these plates conflict with other sources, these are mentioned separately. Interestingly enough, regiments 1–4, 9 and 10 of this watercolour series are shown wearing brown fur busbies, with bags in the colour of the dolman. Number 9, the Bosniaken, wear black Astrakhan caps in one plate and brown fur colpacks in the other, Regiments 5–8 wear *mirlitons*, or winged caps. Officers' parade harness is shown as being elaborately decorated with white cowrie shells.

Regimental Distinctions of the Hussars in 1806

The hussars' breeches were white except for regiments Nos. 6 and 11, which were light blue, and 10, which were dark blue. Other distinctions were as follows:

1 VON GETTKANDT. Dolman: light green, pelisse: dark green, facings: red, buttons and lace: white, sash: red and white. Sabretasche: light green with white crowned royal crest and edging. Shabraque: dark green with light green wolf's tooth edging and white piping.

2 LIFE HUSSAR REGIMENT VON RUDORFF. Dolman: scarlet, pelisse: dark blue, facings: dark blue, buttons and lace: white, sash: blue and white. Sabretasche: scarlet with white crowned cipher and white edging. Shabraque: dark blue with scarlet wolf's tooth edging and white piping.

◀ **OFFICER, HUSSAR REGIMENT NO. 8, VON BLÜCHER, 1806** *The headgear of the Prussian hussars is a complex subject but this regiment would seem to have worn the* mirliton *at this time. Also known as a winged cap, it was popular with hussars throughout Europe. Each Prussian regiment wore its own colours on the barrel sash (here blue and white), and the designs on the lids of the sabretasches of the officers were different for each regiment. In October 1806, the Hussars No. 8 fought at Auerstädt, then withdrew with the rest of General von Blücher's corps to Lübeck, where they were cornered by the French and forced to capitulate due to lack of ammunition on 7 November. All members of the regiment then escaped to East Prussia to rejoin the army. In recognition of this, they would become the new Hussars No. 5.*

3 VON PLETZ. Dolman: dark blue, pelisse: dark blue, facings: yellow, buttons and lace: yellow, sash: yellow and white. Sabretasche: yellow with white crowned royal cipher and edging Shabraque: dark blue with white wolf's tooth edging and white piping.

4 PRINZ EUGEN VON WÜRTTEMBERG. Dolman: light blue, pelisse: light blue, facings: red, buttons and lace: white/blue and white, sash: yellow and white. Sabretasche: white with light blue crowned royal cipher and edging. Shabraque: light blue with white wolf's tooth edging and blue piping.

5 VON PRITTWITZ. Dolman: black, pelisse: black with black trim (white for officers), facings: scarlet, buttons and lace: white, sash: red and white. Sabretasche: black. Shabraque: black with red wolf's tooth edging and with blue piping.

6 SCHIMMELPFENNIG VON DER OEYE. Dolman: dark brown, pelisse: dark brown, facings: yellow, buttons and lace: yellow, sash: yellow and white. Sabretasche: brown with yellow crowned royal cipher and edging. Shabraque: brown with yellow wolf's tooth edging and yellow piping.

7 VON KÖHLER. Dolman: lemon yellow, pelisse: light blue, facings: light blue, buttons and lace: white, sash: light blue and white. Sabretasche: light blue with yellow crowned royal cipher and edging. Shabraque: light blue with yellow wolf's tooth edging and piping.

8 VON BLÜCHER. Dolman: crimson, pelisse: crimson, facings: black, buttons and lace: white, sash: red and white. Sabretasche: black. Shabraque: black.

9 (SEE LANCERS)

10 USEDOM. Dolman: dark blue, pelisse: dark blue, facings: sulphur yellow, buttons and lace: white, sash: dark blue and crimson. Sabretasche: black. Shabraque: black.

11 VON BILA. Dolman: dark green, pelisse: dark green, facings: scarlet, buttons and lace: yellow, sash: red and white. Sabretasche: red with yellow crowned royal cipher and edging. Shabraque: dark green with red wolf's tooth edging and yellow piping.

▲ **OFFICER, HUSSAR REGIMENT NO. 2 VON RUDORFF, 1806** *The officers' uniform was similar to that of the men, but more elaborate, and used materials of a higher quality. For example, officers' pelisses were often edged with the white fur from the throats of foxes. It was around about 1806 when the* mirliton *began to be replaced in hussar regiments by the more practical shako. This trend was observed among all armies, but the French seem to have led the way; while Prussia lagged behind. The Hussars No. 2 fought with Blucher's corps and surrendered at Ratkau on 7 November 1806. They then became the 3rd Hussars.*

The Lancers (Ulans) 1745–1806

Officially, Hussars No. 9 were a hussar regiment, but they were armed as lancers. Known as the Bosniaken or, by 1806, von L'Estocq, initially they received no uniforms, but clothed themselves in red tunics and wide, red Turkish trousers, black frock coats (*Katanken*), red fez and white turban. In 1787 they were given a new uniform: the frock coat became dark blue and the Turkish trousers gave way to white leather breeches. The sabretasche was of plain black leather, belts were black and the

▲ *Prussia was smashed at Jena, 14 October 1806, even though a number of individual units fought well, including the hussars.*

shabraque was red with white lace piping. The turban was replaced by black Astrakhan caps. The short red tunic had dark blue collar and cuffs. In 1799 the Bosniaken were disbanded and a corps of *Towarczys* (Comrades) was raised in the new provinces taken from Poland. There were 15 squadrons, split into a

◀ **LIFE HUSSARS NO. 1, 1807**
These were the old Hussars von Prittwitz No. 5, often referred to as "Der Ganze Todt" ("The Whole Death") on account of their distinctive death's head cap badge. In 1806 the Life Hussars were in L'Estocq's reserve corps, they escaped Prussia's twin disasters of Jena and Auerstädt and fought in the 1807 campaign. In December 1808 the regiment split into the Life Hussar Regiments Nos. 1 and 2. Two squadrons went to Russia in 1812, fighting with Napoleon's troops.

regiment of ten and a battalion of five. The regiment had yellow buttons, the battalion white. The 5th Squadron of the battalion was composed of native Tartars. The front rank of the *Towarczys* were armed with a lance, a sabre and a brace of pistols. The second rank had carbines, sabres and pistols.

Each squadron had its own colour code worn as a cockade on the hat, in the cap lines and on the lance pennants. The first and third colours were the central part of the cockade and the upper half of the lance pennant; the second was the central ring of the cockade and the lower half of the pennant. In the regiment these colours were: 1st Squadron–white; 2nd–black; 3rd–red; 4th–vermillion; 5th–green; 6th–green, white, green; 7th–green and red; 8th–white and red; 9th–black, yellow, black; 10th–orange. In the battalion the squadron colours were repeats of the first five squadrons of the regiment.

The lance pennants of NCOs bore the sun in the black upper half and the eagle and "NON SOLI CEDIT" in the white lower half.

THE ARTILLERY AND TECHNICAL TROOPS BEFORE 1806

Although Prussia's artillery had weathered the storms of eighteenth-century wars, the disasters of 1806 would necessitate a root and branch reform of this key branch of service.

The transformation of the artillery from a civilian guild into a military organization had begun under Frederick William I. He reclassified field guns into four main categories: 3, 6, 12, and 24-pounders from 1715. A similar scheme was imposed on the mortars: there were to be bronze pieces at 10, 25, 50 and 75 pounds the light, wrought-iron Coehorn weapon and a few heavy, stone items. Howitzers came into general use early on, but in about 1740 the 18-pounder became the standard piece. General von Linger recorded in 1722 that the Prussian Army then had 722 bronze cannon, 1,425 iron cannon, 171 bronze mortars, 128 iron mortars, 28 bronze howitzers and 27 of iron. When Frederick II came to the throne, the Prussian artillery was at much the same state of evolution as that of any other European nation.

The Artillery
The artillery was regarded historically as more of a technical guild than as an integral part of the army. During the Silesian and Seven Years' Wars, the superiority of the Austrian artillery became painfully evident and made reform essential. The train of artillery drivers were taken from civilian contractors and militarized and the design of the guns and vehicles was considerably improved, lightened and standardized.

The Foot Artillery
From 1785 there were four field artillery regiments wearing the following uniform: a dark blue tunic of line infantry cut, with black facings, red turnbacks, yellow buttons, Brandenburg cuffs, white small clothes and belts and a red stock. Privates wore

no lace decoration; NCOs wore 22 gold lace buttonholes. Until 1757 bombardiers of this corps wore fusilier caps, brass fronted, with black headband and cap head piece. It seems doubtful that this headgear was ever in general use, although it seems that bombardiers wore it. When the *Kasket* was introduced in 1787, it bore a brass grenade badge having three flames. It was worn until 1798. On the body of the grenade was the cipher "FWR". The same badge was worn on the pouch lid. The pompon was yellow over red over black. Prior to and after the *Kasket*, the men's tricorns were decorated with a button and a black loop. The artillery carried straight-bladed swords.

The *Pontonniers*
This corps of bridge-builders was part of the artillery with a uniform of infantry cut, dark blue coat, dark blue lapels, red collar, Prussian cuffs, shoulder strap and turnbacks, yellow buttons, white belts and small clothes. The bicorn was decorated with a button, black loop and light blue over red over yellow pompon. The *Kasket* bore the royal cipher "FWR" in brass.

Foot Artillery and Supply Train
The men entrusted with supplying the needs of the artillery and armies wore blue, single-breasted, long-skirted coats, with dark blue collars, red cuffs, yellow buttons, red turnbacks, buff breeches and high boots. The bicorn was decorated with a button and black loop. Members of the supply train

▶ GUNNER, FOOT ARTILLERY, 1806 *The hat pompons reflect the traditional artillery colours: black, red and yellow. Due to the dirty environment in which they fought, the uniform colours were rather sombre. The long, brass pickers were for piercing the painted canvas bags containing the explosive charge in the gun barrel, through the touch hole. The side arm is straight, with a short blade.*

wore the same uniform but with white buttons and light blue collars.

The Horse Artillery
Frederick the Great raised the first units of this arm in 1759. In 1796 the Horse Artillery Regiment achieved independence as a distinct unit under Oberst Heinrich Ernst von Hüser. By 1805 there were ten companies. Crews were all mounted on horses instead of marching behind the guns. Uniforms were as for the foot artillery but the coat was light blue and of dragoon cut. The bicorn was decorated with a button and yellow loop; white plumes were worn. The light blue

◄ **OFFICER, ENGINEERS, 1806** *Since 1792 the lace decoration to the coats of officers and NCOs of the Prussian Army had been much simplified. Even today, officers of engineers in the German Army wear black velvet facings, keeping up a tradition centuries old and one reasonably practical.*

civilians, recruited only when war threatened. They wore dark blue, single-breasted, dragoon-style tunics with yellow buttons and red turnbacks, buff breeches and high boots. The bicorn was decorated with a button, black loop and cockade and a white plume.

The Garrison Artillery

These men manned the guns in the fortresses; they did not go into the field in time of war. Their uniforms were as for the foot artillery but with black stocks.

The Engineers

This was an all-officer corps. In 1787 there were three brigades in this corps, increasing to four in 1800.

Uniforms consisted of a dark blue coat of line infantry cut, black facings, red turnbacks, white buttons, Swedish cuffs, no lace decoration, buff small clothes. The bicorn was decorated with a silver brooch, button and black and silver cockade.

The Miners

It was the task of this corps to carry out the physical tasks of digging mines under enemy fortresses, erecting field defences, removing obstacles and similar tasks.

In 1758 the miners, or pioneers, became a separate corps and initially they wore a low, skullcap – like a headdress – with a silver front plate, orange headband and cap, white tape and pompon. To each side was a silver flame, and at the back was the three-flamed grenade in silver. In 1791 there was one company each in the fortresses of Glatz, Graudenz and Schweidnitz. Uniform was of infantry cut, dark blue coat, dark blue lapels, red collar, Prussian cuffs, shoulder strap and turnbacks, yellow buttons, white belts

and small clothes. The bicorn was decorated with a button, black loop and light blue over red over yellow pompon; the *Kasket* bore the royal cipher "FWR" in brass. In 1798 the Miners received the same uniform as the artillery.

▼ **NCO, HORSE ARTILLERY, 1806** *King Frederick the Great raised the first horse artillery battery in 1759; by 1796 there were seven such companies (batteries) in the Artillery Regiment No. 4. Some batteries of artillery had been issued with shakos before the war of 1806; the brass badge was the old triple-flamed grenade as previously worn on the Kasket.*

turnbacks of the men's tunics were edged in wide black lace, piped red on both sides. Light cavalry sabres in black leather sheaths with brass fittings were carried. The saddlecloth was light blue, edged with a wide black lace piped yellow. The rear corner bore the crowned royal cipher. In 1806 some companies received the new shako, with white top band and cords, black and white cockade and an impressive three-flamed grenade badge.

The Horse Artillery Train

This organization provided the horses and drivers to move the guns and vehicles used by the gunners. Until the late eighteenth century they were

THE INFANTRY AFTER 1806

The disaster of 1806, and the near-total collapse of the Prussian Army, necessitated a series of extremely thorough reforms. The resulting transformation prepared Prussia for revenge in 1813.

Reorganization

The only infantry regiments to survive the catastrophe of 1806 intact were: Rüchel No. 2; Rüts No. 8; Schöning No. 11; Besser No. 14; Diericke No. 16; Plötz No. 42 (minus its 3rd Musketeer Battalion); Hamberger No. 52; and de Courbiere No. 58.

During the war the following new formations, reserve battalions, had been raised from escaped prisoners of war, recruits and volunteers: six in East Prussia, six in West Prussia, three each in Pomerania and the New Mark, one in Silesia. Several Free Corps (in reality private armies) outside the state's military establishment) were also raised from volunteers in besieged cities such as Danzig.

Each infantry regiment now had a depot company, two grenadier companies, two musketeer battalions and a fusilier (or light) battalion each of four companies. The fusilier battalions were now combined into the new regiments as their light battalions. Compared with the 1806 uniforms, the new costumes were of the utmost simplicity.

The Musketeers

The uniform for musketeers was a black felt shako with white top band and black-within-white pompon; black leather chinstrap. The front was decorated with the uncrowned royal cipher "FWR" in brass. The Foot Guards had an eight-pointed star. For parades, white cords and thin, black plumes were worn. The double-breasted dark blue coat had two rows of brass buttons, dark blue cuff flaps with three buttons and two buttons in the small of the back. The turnbacks were red and plain. Collars and cuffs

were in the provincial colour: East Prussia–brick red, West Prussia–crimson, Pomerania–white, Brandenburg–poppy red, Silesia–white. The Colberg Regiment had white facings. The shoulder straps of the first regiment in each province were white, red for the second, yellow for the third and light blue for the fourth. The buttons on the shoulder straps bore the company number in Arabic numerals. The shoulder straps themselves were coloured in order of seniority of the battalions within each regiment: 1st–white; 2nd–red; 3rd–yellow. Breeches were grey, the short, black gaiters had black leather buttons. Belts were white with brass buckles; the cartridge pouch had a round brass plate with the eagle on it. The brass-hilted sabre was borne in a brown leather sheath on the waist belt. The sabre strap and tassel were white for all companies; the 1st Battalion also had white crowns and bodies to the tassel. Company identity was shown by the colour of the wreath: 1st–white; 2nd–yellow; 3rd–light blue; 4th–red. In the 2nd Battalion the crown and wreath were in the company colours as shown below: 1st–green; 2nd–yellow; 3rd–light blue; 4th–red. The fusilier battalion had the same colours as the 2nd Battalion, but the body of the tassel was also in the company colour. Musketeer NCOs had gold top band to shako, gold braid to the top of the cuffs and to the front and bottom of the collar, white gloves and a black and white sabre strap and tassel. Their black plumes had a white tip.

Musketeer drummers and musicians had swallows' nests in the provincial facing colour with white lace. Drums were brass, with red and white hoops and black sticks. On the body of the drum was the crowned royal cipher within trophies of arms. Company officers wore the shako in finer construction and materials. At each side was a small Prussian eagle in

▼ **PRIVATE OF GRENADIERS, FOOT GUARDS, 1813–15** *On 9 November 1808 this unit was given the title of The Foot Guards, later to become the 1st Foot Guards. The uniforms of the Russian and Prussian armies were often similar and that is repeated here, particularly with the enormous plume and the lace to collar and cuffs. The star on the shako bears the black Prussian eagle. The infantry officer's sword hilt and strap is shown in detail together with the black leather and steel scabbard.*

gilt metal. The cords, cockade and pompon were silver and black, as were their waist sashes. Their coat tails reached to the back of the knee, and there were horizontal, false pocket flaps on the hips, each with two buttons. They carried swords in brown sheaths on white slings with gilt hilts and silver and black sword strap and tassel. In October 1808, rank badges

▼ NCO, FUSILIERS OF THE GUARD, 1813–15
The NCO carries a carbine as opposed to a standard infantry musket and is further distinguished by the white base to his immense plume, silver lace to collar and cuffs and the black and white sabre strap.

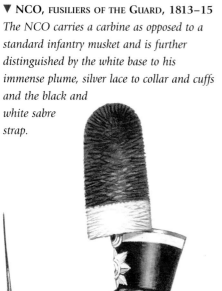

were introduced for officers in the form of shoulder straps in the facing colour edged in red. A lieutenant had a single black and silver lace along the centre of the strap, a captain had one lace at either side, and a major's strap was edged around with the same lace.

Grenadiers, Fusiliers and The Guard

As for the musketeers except that the shako had a brass Prussian eagle plate; the shoulder strap buttons bore the company number in Roman numerals. Black and white sabre strap tassels.

Fusiliers were as for the musketeers except that instead of the "FWR" badge they wore a black-within-white cockade, with regimental button and loop. For NCOs this loop was of brass. Belts were black and worn crossed. Those armed with rifles had sword-bayonets. The Guard regiments were distinguished by simple lace loops, in the button colour, to cuffs and collar.

The War of Liberation

Due to the upsurge of patriotism in Prussia in 1813, most regiments had "Volunteer *Jäger* Detachments" attached to them. These were formed by intellectuals, professionals and the well-off, who volunteered to serve for the duration of hostilities and bought their own equipment. All such units wore dark green uniforms with the facings of the regiments with which they served. If they were with a *Jäger* battalion, they had white shoulder straps. A plethora of new units were raised in the enthusiasm of 1813, resulting in a thorough overall of Prussian infantry units, as follows.

2 FOOT GUARDS. Raised on 19 June 1813. The 1st Battalion came from a unit raised in 1811 from men from all existing infantry regiments. The 2nd Battalion came from the Colberg Regiment, raised in August 1808. The Fusilier Battalion came from von Schill's Free Corps, raised in December 1806.

1 GRENADIER REGIMENT. This unit was raised on 14 October 1814 from the following units: Life Grenadier Battalion (raised on 27 December 1806 in Colberg) and 1st East Prussian Grenadier Battalion. In 1806 this had been the Grenadier Battalion von Schlichting or von Below, "2nd East Prussian Grenadier Battalion" (in 1806 this was the Grenadier Battalion von Fabieckij) and from two companies each of the 14th and 16th. On 19 October 1814 it became the Grenadier Regiment Kaiser Alexander No. 1.

2 GRENADIER REGIMENT. Raised 14 October 1814, the 1st Battalion coming from the Pomeranian Grenadier Battalion (raised on 7 November 1801 from the Grenadier Battalion von Massow) from two grenadier companies each of Infantry Regiments No. 8 and No. 42 and from the Grenadier Battalion von Jung-Braun. The 2nd Battalion was raised from the West Prussian Grenadier Battalion (raised 21 January 1803), from the Grenadier Battalion von Brauschitz and two companies each from the Infantry Regiments No. 52 and No. 58. The Fusilier Battalion was raised from the Silesian Grenadier Battalion, the Grenadier Battalion von Losthin, the 4th and 5th Battalions of Regiment No. 33 and the 3rd and 4th Battalions of Regiment No. 47. All these battalions had been raised in 1807. On 25 December 1814 this became Kaiser Franz Guard Grenadier Regiment No. 2.

1 GRENADIER REGIMENT CROWN PRINCE (1ST EAST PRUSSIAN). Raised from the Infantry Regiment No. 2 on 7 September 1808, this became the 1 East Prussian Infantry Regiment. It provided both musketeer battalions of the new regiment. The old Fusilier Battalion No. 11 became the Fusilier Battalion Crown Prince in January 1808; in 1814 it became the fusilier battalion of this new regiment.

3 EAST PRUSSIAN INFANTRY REGIMENT NO. 4, raised from the old Infantry Regiment No. 14.

4 EAST PRUSSIAN INFANTRY REGIMENT NO. 5, raised from the old Infantry Regiment No. 16, this regiment became the Grenadier Regiment König Friedrich I in 1814.

1 WEST PRUSSIAN INFANTRY REGIMENT NO. 6. Raised from the old Regiment No. 52, it assumed the title of Grenadier Regiment Graf Kleist von Nollendorf (1st West Prussian) No. 6 in 1814.

2 WEST PRUSSIAN INFANTRY REGIMENT (VON COURBIERE) NO. 7. Raised from the Infantry Regiment No. 58. On 20 November 1807 it absorbed men from the disbanded regiments 29, 37, 40, 43, 54 and 55. In 1814 it became the Grenadier Regiment King William I (2nd West Prussian No. 7).

8 LIFE INFANTRY REGIMENT. In 1808 it had been the 1 Brandenburg Infantry Regiment No. 9, and on 14 September 1808 the title changed again to the Life Infantry Regiment No. 9, but in July 1813 the number changed to 8.

COLBERG INFANTY REGIMENT NO. 10. In 1814 it became the Colberg Grenadier Regiment Graf Gneisenau (2nd Pomeranian) No. 9.

1ST SILESIAN INFANTRY REGIMENT NO. 11. On 1 July 1813 the title became the 1st Silesian Infantry Regiment No. 10, in 1814 Grenadier Regiment King Frederick William II (1st Silesian) No. 10.

2ND SILESIAN INFANTRY REGIMENT NO. 12. On 1 July 1813 the title changed to: Silesian Infantry Regiment No. 11, and in 1814 it changed to 12 Grenadier Regiment King Frederick III (2nd Silesian) No. 11.

BRANDENBURG INFANTRY REGIMENT NO. 12. This regiment was raised on 1 July 1813 from the Life Infantry Regiment. The Fusilier Battalion was raised from the 3rd Musketeer Battalion of the 1 West Prussian Infantry Regiment.

INFANTRY REGIMENT HERWARTH VON BITTENFELD (1ST WESTPHALIAN) NO. 13. Raised on 1 July 1813.

INFANTRY REGIMENT COUNT SCHWERIN (3RD POMERANIAN) NO. 14. Raised on 1 July 1813 from the 1st Pomeranian Infantry Regiment, which was raised itself on 6 July 1811.

3 RESERVE INFANTRY REGIMENT. This regiment was raised on 1 July 1813 from men of the 2nd East Prussian Infantry Regiment. On 25 March 1815 it became the Infantry Regiment No. 15 (4th Silesian); on 11 July 1815, the title changed to the Infantry Regiment Count Bülow of Dennewitz No. 15. Later that year it became the Infantry Regiment Prince Henry of the Netherlands (2nd Westphalian) No.15.

4 RESERVE INFANTRY REGIMENT. Raised on 1 July 1813 from men of the 3rd East Prussian Infantry Regiment, on 25 March 1815 it became the Infantry Regiment No. 16.

5 RESERVE INFANTRY REGIMENT. Raised on 1 July 1813 from men of the 4th East Prussian Infantry Regiment, on 25 March 1815 it became the Infantry Regiment No. 17.

6 RESERVE INFANTRY REGIMENT. Raised on 1 July 1813 from men of the 1st West Prussian and 1st Silesian Infantry Regiments, on 25 March 1815 it became the Infantry Regiment No. 18 (1st Westphalian).

7 RESERVE INFANTRY REGIMENT. Raised on 1 July 1813 from men of the 2nd West Prussian Infantry Regiment. on 25 March 1815 it became the Infantry Regiment No. 19.

▼ OFFICER, 1ST EAST PRUSSIAN INFANTRY REGIMENT NO. 1, 1812 *Stringent economy ruled that Prussian uniforms of this era were plain and simple. Musketeers wore the royal cipher "FWR" on their shakos, fusiliers wore the black-within-white cockade, and grenadiers wore the eagle. All officers wore the cockade on their shakos. As a junior officer, this man wears the universal red shoulder strap with one line of black and silver lace along it.*

▼ OFFICER, JÄGERS OF THE GUARD, 1813 *The Field Jägers were incorporated into the Guard on 14 November 1808. The colours of their uniforms were preserved. This officer carries a light cavalry sabre as most light infantry officers did.*

▲ DRUMMER, COLBERG INFANTRY REGIMENT, **1812** *A light blue label bearing COLBERG in gold, was borne on their colours.*

8 RESERVE INFANTRY REGIMENT. Raised on 1 July 1813, on 25 March 1815 it became the Infantry Regiment No. 20.
9 RESERVE INFANTRY REGIMENT. Raised on 1 July 1813, on 25 March 1815 it became Infantry Regiment No. 21.
10 RESERVE INFANTRY REGIMENT. Raised on 1 July 1813, on 25 March 1815 it became the Infantry Regiment No. 22.
11 RESERVE INFANTRY REGIMENT. Raised on 1 July 1813, on 25 March 1815 it became the Infantry Regiment No. 23.
12 RESERVE INFANTRY REGIMENT. Raised on 1 July 1813, on 25 March 1815 it became the Infantry Regiment No. 24.
13 RESERVE INFANTRY REGIMENT. Raised on 18 February 1813, in March 1815 it became Infantry Regiment No. 25.

26 INFANTRY REGIMENT. Raised on 12 March 1813 as Reuss's Foreign Battalion, on 5 July 1813 its title was the Elbe Infantry Regiment and on 25 March 1815 it became the Infantry Regiment No. 26.
27 INFANTRY REGIMENT. Raised on 7 March 1815.
28 INFANTRY REGIMENT. Raised on 5 December 1813 from men of the old 1st Infantry Regiment of the ex-Grand Duchy of Berg.
29 INFANTRY REGIMENT. Raised on 5 December 1813 from men of the 2nd Infantry Regiment of the ex-Grand Duchy of Berg.
30 INFANTRY REGIMENT. Raised in 1815 from the Russo–German Legion.
31 INFANTRY REGIMENT. Raised in 1815 from men of the Russo–German Legion, the 3rd and 4th Regiments of the Confederation of the Rhine and the Saxon Prince Max Regiment.
32 INFANTRY REGIMENT. Raised on 7 March 1815 from men of the Elbe Infantry Regiment, Westphalian and Saxon *Landwehr.*
33 INFANTRY REGIMENT. Raised on 1 October 1815 from the ex-Swedish Royal, Queen's and Engelbrechten Infantry Regiments.

The Free Corps
In early 1813 there was a distinct upsurge of patriotic spirit in Prussia, which was harnessed by the following:
VON LÜTZOW'S ROYAL PRUSSIAN FREE CORPS. Raised on 18 February 1813. The volunteers were mostly foreigners. The infantry uniform was a shako with black, drooping horsehair plume and cords, brass "loop" and button. The plain black coat was in the *Litewka* style, a double-breasted frock coat with red piping to collar, shoulder straps and Polish cuffs. Trousers, gaiters, belts were also black, buttons yellow.
VON REUSS'S FOREIGN BATTALION. Raised in Berlin 21 March 1813 from deserters from foreign armies.
VON REICHE'S FOREIGN JÄGER BATTALION. Raised in Berlin on 10 March 1813, mainly from Westphalians. Uniform was a Prussian shako with brass chin scales, green *Litewka* with two rows of yellow buttons, red collar and cuffs,

▲ NCO, RUSSO–GERMAN LEGION, 1813
These uniforms were at first in standard Russian style, as shown here, the only difference being light blue facings and yellow shoulder straps piped in red.

light green shoulder straps piped red, grey breeches in boots; black belts.
VON HELLWIG'S FREE CORPS. Infantry uniform was a shako with tin chin scales, green tunic with black collar, cuffs, shoulder straps and belts; white buttons, white or grey trousers.
SCHILL'S CORPS. In March 1813 Major von Schill of the 2nd Silesian Hussars took 100 men of his regiment to recruit a corps of infantry and cavalry.
LAUSITZ VOLUNTEER JÄGER CORPS. In 1813 this unit was raised by a certain Captain von Lyncker.
SCHIVELBEIN'S CORPS. Of such dubious quality it was very quickly disbanded.

THE CUIRASSIERS AFTER 1806

The 1806 campaign decimated Prussia's cavalry. Really only the cuirassier regiments No. 4 and 13 had survived. Four regiments of cuirassiers were subsequently recreated, the No. 3 being given the distinction Gardes du Corps. On 25 March 1815 this regiment lost their number in the line cavalry and were raised to Guard status; the Regiment (Brandenburg) No. 4 became the Cuirassiers No. 3.

With the reorganization of 1808, the following uniform, similar to that of the Russian cuirassiers, was adopted. A black leather helmet with leather comb and stiff, black horsehair crest (red for trumpeters), with brass chin scales,

▶ EMBROIDERED BUTTONHOLES TO CUIRASSIER OFFICERS' TUNICS (ABOVE RIGHT)
1 2nd and 3rd Battalions, No. 15;
2 1st Battalion, No. 15;
3 No. 9; 4 No. 18.

▼ *The humiliating climax to the 1806 campaign saw Napoleon triumph over the Prussians at the Battles of Jena and Auerstadt. Here the defeated Prussians pledge the Oath of the Sassoni to the Emperor.*

▶ NCO TRUMPETER, EAST PRUSSIAN CUIRASSIER REGIMENT NO. 2, 1813
Trumpeters were distinguished by their swallows' nests, which were in the facing colour and covered by wide gold lace. He has the NCO's gold braid to collar and cuffs and the black and white tassel to his sword strap. The red horsehair crest was normally only worn for parades; for daily and field service they wore black.

front to comb and edging to the front peak. A large brass front plate bore the double-headed Prussian eagle, except for the Garde du Corps, who wore an eight-pointed star instead Underneath the left-hand chinstrap boss of the

▶ **CUIRASSIER ARMS** *1 and 2 An 1809 rifle; shorter than the musket, the barrel was 33 in (82.5 cm) long with eight grooves with a calibre of 0,56 Rheinisch inches. It had a rear and fore-sight (calibrated to 150 and 300 paces). 3 and 4 An 1809 musket, the barrel was 37¹/₂ in (93.5) cm long. The calibre was 0,72 Rheinisch inches, and it weighed over 11 pounds (5 kg).*

helmet they wore the black-within-white national cockade.

The double-breasted white tunic had two rows of eight buttons on the front, Swedish cuffs and a standing collar in the facing colour; the white turnbacks and the bottom of the lapels were edged in the facing colour. Initially the shoulder straps were in the facing colour, but this rapidly became white with piping in the facing colour. The white knee breeches were now covered in grey overalls, with side piping and regimental buttons down the outside of the leg. The inside of the leg and the bottoms of the overalls were trimmed with black leather. The sword fist strap for rank and file was of red leather with a tassel in the

▶ **OFFICER, SILESIAN CUIRASSIER REGIMENT NO. 1, 1813** *This regiment was raised on 16 October 1807 and on 7 September 1808 it became the Cuirassier Regiment No. 1. Cavalry officers wore the same sashes as their infantry counterparts, but usually had the black leather and silver chain fist strap for field service.*

◀ **NCO, BRANDENBURG CUIRASSIERS NO. 4, 1813** *Raised in 1691, this was one of the few regiments to survive the war of 1806, having fought at Auerstädt. There is some confusion over the exact shade of blue of the facings of this regiment: the regulations of May 1810 stipulated dark blue, but the king then verbally granted them cornflower blue.*

Cuirassier Regimental Distinctions		
No./Title	Facings & buttons	Shabraque
1 Silesian	black	yellow
2 East Prussian	light blue	white
3 Garde du Corps	red	white
4 Brandenburg	dark blue	yellow

occasions. In April 1814 the Prussians took French-pattern cuirassier swords from Versailles to replace their own. Officers of the Guards wore a small Guards' star on the hilt of their swords. Their sashes were worn under the cuirass, except by adjutants who wore them bandolier fashion.

squadron colour: 1st–white; 2nd–yellow; 3rd–light blue; 4th–red. The tassel of honour for good conduct in the war of 1806–07 was as for the infantry. NCOs had black and white tassels as for the infantry. Since 1789 the sergeants (*Wachtmeisters*) had worn officers' *portépées* (sabre fist straps) in black leather and silver thread. In 1807, NCO's lace went along the front and bottom of the open collar and along the top and back of the cuff; in 1814 the collar was shorter, worn closed and their lace now ran along top and front of the collar.

Until August 1812 officers wore shoulder straps showing their ranks with silver and black lace of infantry pattern. These were then replaced by metal scale epaulettes in the button colour. In 1813 these were replaced by a common model. The strap was white and the lining edging of the strap and the silver cross piece were red for all regiments until 1834. The metal half-moons at the shoulders were of the button colour; majors and above wore fringes to the half-moons also in the button colour. Trumpeters wore swallows' nests in the facing colour, laced in the button colour. Standard bandoliers were in the facing colour in velvet, edged in gold or silver according to the button colour.

Cuirasses had been withdrawn by King Friedrich Wilhelm II; they were re-introduced in April 1814, when the four regiments then in existence were equipped with items taken from the arsenal in Versailles. The Garde du Corps and the

Brandenburg regiments added brass sheeting to theirs. The shoulder scales and the rivets on all cuirasses were brass. They were edged in red. In 1814 Czar Alexander presented the Gardes du Corps with black, Russian-style cuirasses edged in red; these were worn on special

◀ **OFFICER, GARDE DU CORPS, 1813–15**
This was raised from the old Cuirassier Regiment No. 13, which fought at Auerstädt in October 1806, then escaped to East Prussia to fight with L'Estocq's corps. In 1808 it was given the number 3, but lost this in 1813 and was known just by its title. Once again, Russian influence can be seen in the helmet and the lace decoration to the collar and cuffs.

THE DRAGOONS AND HUSSARS AFTER 1806

Prussia's medium and light cavalry were thoroughly reformed after 1806 with many units being disbanded or merged into new units.

Dragoon Uniforms

Prussia reduced its dragoon regiments to six in 1808. The shako was reinforced with leather at the top and bottom and to the sides. The cap badge was a brass Prussian eagle and white plumes and cords were worn for parades. NCOs plumes had a black tip, those of officers had a black base. Trumpeters wore red plumes. Brass chin scales were worn on campaign. The light blue, double-breasted tunic had two rows of eight buttons down the front; collar, shoulder straps, Swedish cuffs and edging to the light blue turnbacks in the regimental colour. Grey overalls with buttoned sides. White belts. Facings and buttons were as follows:

1 KÖNIGIN DRAGOONS. Facings: crimson, buttons: white. In September 1808 this unit became the 1 West Prussian Dragoons.

2 LITHUANIAN DRAGOONS. Facings: white, buttons: white.

3. Facings: red, buttons: yellow.

2 WEST PRUSSIAN DRAGOONS AND No. 4. Facings: red, buttons: white.

5 BRANDENBURG DRAGOONS .Facings: black, buttons: yellow.

6 NEUMARK DRAGOONS. Facings: light red, buttons: white.

The Guards Dragoon Regiment No. 1 was raised on 21 February 1815. A 7th regiment was formed in 1815 with white facings, yellow buttons. An 8th regiment was also raised with yellow facings, white buttons.

Swords had red leather fist straps with tassels in the squadron colour: 1st–white; 2nd–yellow; 3rd–light blue; 4th–red. On 27 August, 1813 officers were ordered to

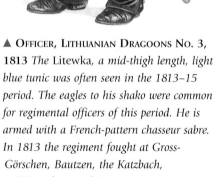

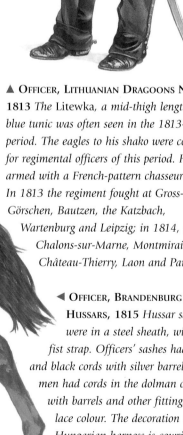

▲ OFFICER, LITHUANIAN DRAGOONS No. 3, 1813 *The Litewka, a mid-thigh length, light blue tunic was often seen in the 1813–15 period. The eagles to his shako were common for regimental officers of this period. He is armed with a French-pattern chasseur sabre. In 1813 the regiment fought at Gross-Görschen, Bautzen, the Katzbach, Wartenburg and Leipzig; in 1814, at Chalons-sur-Marne, Montmirail, Château-Thierry, Laon and Paris.*

◄ OFFICER, BRANDENBURG HUSSARS, 1815 *Hussar sabres were in a steel sheath, with black fist strap. Officers' sashes had silver and black cords with silver barrels, the men had cords in the dolman collar with barrels and other fittings in the lace colour. The decoration on the Hungarian harness is cowrie shells. Overalls protect the expensive breeches and hussar boots.*

Hussar Regimental Distinctions after 1806

No./Title	Dolman & Pelisse	Collar & Cuffs	Buttons & lace	Sash
1 Life*	black	red	white	red & white
2 Life*	black	red	white	red & white
1 Brandenburg	dark blue	red	white	red & white
2 Brandenburg	dark blue	red	yellow	red & white
Pomeranian (Blücher's)	light blue	black	yellow	blue & yellow
Upper Silesian	brown	yellow	yellow	white & yellow
Lower Silesian	green	red	white	white & green

* Split into two regiments in December 1808, No. 1 receiving white shoulder straps, No. 2 red.

wear the same scale epaulettes as the cuirassiers; the field was in the facing colour, the lining, edging and cross strap were red. The dragoons now wore the long-skirted, light blue, double-breasted tunic. The Normal Dragoon Squadron had red facings and yellow buttons and two lace loops to each side of the collar and on he cuffs. Their shako badge was the Guard's eight-pointed star. Officers did not wear cartouches until 1808; those of the line bore the crowned royal cipher; the Guard and Normal Squadron wore silver and enamelled stars. In the Wars of Liberation, the Brandenburg Dragoons captured many French cuirassiers' swords, which they used instead of the issued items.

The volunteer *Jäger* detachments attached to each regiment wore green coats, brass epaulettes and regimental facings.

Hussar Uniforms Post 1806

Few hussar regiments survived the catastrophe of 1806 intact. Shakos as for the dragoons, with cockade, loop and button, white cords and plumes as before. The cords of NCOs were white with black and white flounders and tassels; officers' cords were silver and black. The two Life Hussar regiments wore white silver skull and crossbones badges to their shakos. The dolman had 15 rows of lace on the chest and three rows of buttons; the collar and cuffs were in the regimental colour as were the lace and buttons. Privates of

all line regiments wore white fur trim to the pelisse; NCOs and officers had black fur trim. The sabretasche was red with crowned royal cipher and edging in the button colour, except for the two Life Hussar regiments and the Pomeranians, which had plain black leather lids. Carbines were carried on black bandoliers; the best shots had rifled weapons. The shabraque was in the dolman colour, with wolf's tooth edging in the collar colour and lace in the regimental colour. Harness was black with fittings in the regimental button colour and of Hungarian style.

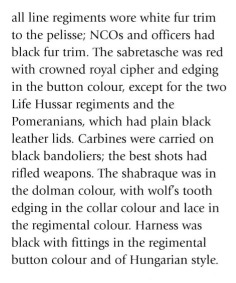

▼ TRUMPETER, POMERANIAN HUSSARS, 1813 *Hussar trumpeters, in addition to all the standard hussar decoration, also had swallows nests in the collar colour. The Pomeranian Hussars were at Ligny and Waterloo in 1815 and were ambushed at Versailles by General Exelmans' 9th Cavalry Division on 1 July of that year, suffering heavy losses.*

▼ OFFICER, 2ND BRANDENBURG HUSSARS 1809 *This officer wears the winter field uniform of the Hussars No. 2 and the cross of the Pour le Merite hanging over his red and gold trimmed bandolier. This was Ferdinand von Schill's regiment,, which accompanied him to his attack on Stralsund.*

THE LANCERS, *LANDWEHR* AND CAVALRY REGIMENTS AFTER 1806

Prussia's cavalry was considerably augmented for the Wars of Liberation. New regiments, many of them made up of volunteers, supplemented the regiments that had survived 1806.

The Lancers

In March 1809 a Life Lancers Squadron was raised. This became the Guard Lancers Squadron. A Normal Lancers Squadron was created in March 1811. These units wore dark blue lancer costume with red collar, cuffs, piping and edging, yellow buttons, and were differentiated by their shoulder straps. There were also the following units:

1 (WEST PRUSSIAN) LANCERS. White shoulder straps, yellow buttons. Raised from the depots and men of Dragoon regiments 8, 9 and 10.

2 (SILESIAN) LANCERS. Red shoulder straps; yellow buttons. Raised on 23 November 1808 from men of the old Hussars No. 1 and two squadrons of the Lancers No. 1. On 31 May 1809 their title became the Silesian Lancers.

3 (BRANDENBURG) LANCERS. Yellow shoulder straps, yellow buttons. Raised on 16 May 1809 from the remnants of the 2nd Brandenburg Hussars and from one squadron each of the Lancers No. 1 and No. 2.

4 (POMERANIAN) LANCERS. Light blue shoulder straps. Yellow buttons. Raised in March 1815. The 1st Squadron was drawn from the Lancers No. 1; the 2nd from the East Prussian National Cavalry Regiment No. 1 and the 3rd came from the Pomeranian National

▼ CAVALRY LIEUTENANT, VON LÜTZOW'S ROYAL PRUSSIAN FREE CORPS, 1813 *The uniform was based on the* Litewka, *the skirted, double-breasted coat; the black colour was taken from the duke of Brunswick's Black Band of 1809. They became Lancer Regiment No. 6 but retained this uniform.*

▼ OFFICER, 2ND (SILESIAN) LANCERS, 1813 *Apart from the cuirassiers, all Prussian cavalry regiments wore the shako at this time. Officers' shakos were decorated with the Prussian eagle. The arrangement of the silver and black cap lines was rather complex. The pennants of the lances were red over dark blue.*

▼ TROOPER, POMERANIAN NATIONAL CAVALRY REGIMENT, 1813 *This volunteer wears the brass scale epaulettes, which mark him out as a member of the elite squadron of the regiment, whose other squadrons wore white shoulder straps.*

from Schill's Streifkorps. Wore their old uniforms.

8 LANCERS. Raised March 1815 from the 1st and 2nd Hussars of the Russo–German legion. Wore their old uniforms.

The *Landwehr*

Uniforms were basic. They wore the shako in black wax cloth cover, having the white "iron cross" painted on the front, blue *Litewka* with collar and cuffs in the provincial colour: East Prussia–red, West Prussia–black, Pomerania–white, Silesia–yellow, Brandenburg–poppy red. Black belts, grey overalls with red side seam, black sheepskin saddle cloth with red edging. They were armed with sabres and lances with fanions in white and the provincial colour.

The National Cavalry Regiments

These units were formed by rich patriots in early 1813.

EAST PRUSSIAN NATIONAL CAVALRY REGIMENT. Shako, dark blue *Litewka* with yellow buttons and hussar-style lace on the chest, red collar and cuffs,

yellow epaulettes, white shoulder straps. The elite squadron had busbies and red bags, dark blue overalls with red stripe, red and yellow sash, black belts, sabretasche and shabraque with red edging.

ELBE NATIONAL CAVALRY REGIMENT. The uniform consisted of a green dolman and pelisse, blue collar and cuffs, yellow buttons and lace, white and green sash.

POMERANIAN NATIONAL CAVALRY REGIMENT. The uniform was a shako in black waxed cover, green tunic, white collar and cuffs and shoulder straps, yellow buttons, light green waist sash edged red, grey overalls, black belts, green shabraque edged white. The elite squadron wore brass scale epaulettes.

SILESIAN NATIONAL CAVALRY REGIMENT. Their uniform was a black shako, black dolman and pelisse with red collar, cuffs, shoulder straps and lace. They had white buttons and a black and white sash.

▲ TROMPETER, 1ST WEST PRUSSIAN ULAN REGIMENT *As the senior lancer regiment, they wore white shoulder straps to the traditional Polish jacket, with the square-topped* czapka. *Due to the extremely difficult supply situation, uniformity of dress within a regiment was almost impossible to achieve. Many lancers wore normal shakos, some even wore items of hussar costume.*

Cavalry Regiments.

5 LANCERS. Raised on 7 March 1815. The 1st Squadron came from the Silesian Lancers; the 2nd from the Brandenburg Lancers and the 3rd from the ex-Hussars of Berg.

6 LANCERS. Raised on 23 March 1815 from men of the cavalry regiment of the Royal Prussian Free Corps (Lützow's). Wore their old uniforms.

7 LANCERS. Raised in 1815 from the 1st and 2nd Squadrons ex-Hellwig's Streifkorps; the 3rd Squadron came

▶ TROOPER, 1ST SQUADRON, LANCER REGIMENT NO. 7, 1815 *Although it had been stated which lancer regiments were to wear the infantry shako, this man served in von Hellwig's Free Corps, which bent the rules and adopted the square-topped, traditional Polish* czapka, *together with British-supplied hussar dolman, pelisse (not worn) and sabretasche.*

THE ARTILLERY AND TECHNICAL TROOPS AFTER 1806

Prussia learned a good many lessons from the disaster of 1806 and also lost a good deal of equipment. Subsequent years therefore saw a complete overhaul of Prussia's technical troops.

The Foot Artillery and *Pontonniers*

Foot artillery was now formed into three brigades. Uniforms were as for musketeers except as noted below.

▼ **DRUMMER, 1ST (PRUSSIAN) BRIGADE OF FOOT ARTILLERY, 1813** *As the senior brigade, the shoulder straps were white. The drum was of standard infantry pattern, but the bandolier was of black leather. For parades a red plume was probably worn.*

Yellow top band to shako, brass, three-flamed grenade badge to shako and pouch; black collars and cuffs edged red, yellow buttons. Officers wore the black and silver cockade instead of the grenade, and white with a black base. The shoulder buttons bore the company numbers 1–12. Shoulder

▼ **OFFICER, HORSE ARTILLERY, 1813** *Officers of horse artillery wore the black and white cockade on the front of the shako instead of the three-flamed grenade. They also wore the side eagles as for dragoon officers. The metal shoulder scales were on black backing, with black fields. This man wears the black leather and silver sabre strap.*

straps in the provincial, or brigade, colour: Prussia (1st)–white, Brandenburg (2nd)–red, Silesia (3rd)–yellow. They wore black belts. Drummers' swallows' nests were black, decorated with eight vertical bands of yellow lace. Drummers of the Guard wore the three-flamed brass grenade on their drum bandoliers. During 1808–14, four companies of artillery were raised for the Guards; they all wore foot artillery uniform, but all with Swedish cuffs. On their collars and cuffs were two old Prussian laces in yellow with pointed ends. Those on the cuffs had buttons. All guard artillery companies had red shoulder straps. Officers of the Guard wore a golden aiguillette on the right shoulder instead of the shoulder strap. Shakos of the Guard had orange top bands and a brass star rather than a three-flamed grenade. Their feather plumes were black with a white tip. Trumpeters of the Guard had black and yellow cords to their trumpets. The *pontonniers'* uniform was as for the foot artillery.

Artillery and Supply Train

The foot artillery train wore dark blue, single-breasted coats, with dark blue collars, red cuffs, yellow buttons, red turnbacks, buff breeches, high boots. The bicorn was decorated with a button and black loop.

The horse artillery train had dark blue, single-breasted, dragoon-style tunics with yellow buttons and red turnbacks, buff breeches, high boots. The bicorn was decorated with a button, black loop and cockade and a white plume.

Members of the supply train wore the same uniform but with white buttons and light blue collars.

The Horse Artillery

Their uniform was as for the foot artillery but with dragoon shako, white plumes, yellow cords, brass

chin scales. Yellow shako cords for the men, black and white for NCOs and trumpeters. The yellow shoulder buttons were smooth. Dark blue turnbacks edged in red-black-red lace. Dragoon boots were worn. Officers wore a golden aiguillette on the right shoulder instead of the shoulder strap.

The Miners and Engineers

There were seven companies of miners in 1813. Their work was hard and often dangerous, as it involved digging

fortifications in the front line, often under direct enemy fire. Their French counterparts had adopted heavy helmets and body armour for these duties, but it seems that the Prussians did not. Their uniform was very similar to that of the foot artillery, with black leather equipment and no added protective clothing.

After 1808 the engineers dressed as for the artillery with black velvet facings, white buttons, and black shoulder straps edged red.

▼ GUNNER, SILESIAN FOOT ARTILLERY BRIGADE, 1815 *The shoulder strap buttons bore the company number; the three-flamed grenade was also worn on the cartridge pouch lid. As the third brigade, the Silesians wore yellow shoulder straps to their infantry-style tunics.*

▼ PRIVATE, ENGINEERS, 1813 *Instead of the usual infantry cuff, the engineers wore the simpler, "Swedish" pattern. The pouch badge was the royal cipher "FWR". The sword had a toothed back and doubled as a saw.*

▲ OFFICER, FOOT ARTILLERY OF THE GUARD, 1813–15 *As with Napoleon's Imperial Guard and the Russian Imperial Guard, the Prussian equivalent was to become a miniature army, containing infantry, cavalry, artillery and engineers. This man is in parade dress, hence the rather ridiculous plume. The decoration of the sides of the shako with small Prussian eagles is a detail often overlooked in modern publications. Prussian and Russian uniforms of this era were often very similar.*

THE USA AND OTHER NATIONS

The United States of America played no great part in the Napoleonic Wars. It did, however, get caught in the crossfire of economic warfare between Britain and France. This led directly to the Anglo–American conflict of 1812. Fighting on the ground in north America in 1812–15 was fairly limited; In January 1815 British Major-General Sir Edward Packenham (Wellington's brother-in-law) led a force of some 12,000 men against the city of New Orleans, which was defended by the resourceful, energetic General Andrew Jackson with 6,000 men. Jackson became a national hero and went on to become the seventh president of the United States in 1824.

Nations such as Portugal and Spain, however, were in the thick of the Continental fighting, as the battlegrounds of the hard-fought Peninsular War. Meanwhile, tiny states such as Bavaria, Saxony, Württemberg and the Grand Duchy of Warsaw made a huge contribution to Napoleon's war-effort, providing some of the emperor's best troops.

▲ *During the period 1805–10 France expanded along the North Sea coast by annexing Holland, Bremen, Hamburg, Luebeck and, later, Oldenburg. The states in the area covered by modern Germany were then part of the Confederation of the Rhine. The Grand Duchy of Warsaw was created by taking territory from Prussia following her defeat of 1806.*

◀ *General Andrew Jackson of the US, at the Battle of New Orleans, 8 Jan 1815, in which the British squandered 2,000 men. Under Jackson the Americans lost some 20 men.*

THE FEDERAL FORCES OF THE USA

The United States emerged victorious from its War of Independence but had virtually disbanded its regular army, relying heavily on militias. Experience against Native American Indians demonstrated the unreliability of this system and, following a series of reforms, a small force of regulars formed the core of America's defences.

The United States was involved in campaigns against Native Americans in 1790 (suffering defeat), 1794 (when it was successful) and 1811. There were also the Creek Wars of 1813 and 1814, and the naval wars against Algerian pirates and French privateers. But the key test of the period was the War of 1812 fought against the British in Canada. The US Regular Army was unprepared, small and comparatively ineffective, but it was supplemented by a host of militias and volunteers and knew that Britain was now fighting in two theatres of war.

The War of 1812

At the request of President James Madison, Congress declared war on Britain on 18 June 1812. The apparent cause was the impressments of American nationals into service in the Royal Navy. Articles of Peace were signed on 24 December 1814. This was approved in Great Britain on 28 December 1814 and in the USA on 17 February 1815, taking effect on 18 February 1815. The United States had not achieved any of its stated war aims; neither did it achieve many of its implied war aims either, for example the conquest of Canada.

But the War of 1812 hastened the end of the war against the Native Americans of the old north-west, which had been spluttering on since about 1786, and had been pushed forward by USA victories in 1794 and 1811. The same results were being achieved in the south-east.

Apart from Britain's aim of successfully defending its territory, no other great gains were made. It failed to achieve a better boundary between New Brunswick and the District of

◀ **INFANTRY OFFICER, 1792** *Officer status was shown by the crimson silk waist sash, the epaulettes and the much higher quality of the clothing. It seems the gold and crimson sword strap was not always worn as a plain white leather, or leather strap with gold tassel were often to be seen. General Andrew Jackson (originally commander of the Tennessee militia) soon proved to be one of the most able commanders in the American Army, as was shown by his victory in the Battle of New Orleans on 8 January 1815. Here, with 6,000 men in a clever defensive position, he defeated an assault by 6000 British troops under General Lord Packenham, brother-in-law of the Duke of Wellington. Six thousand other British troops were present but were not deployed.*

▶ **TROOPER, LIGHT DRAGOONS 1812** *The crested helmet was reminiscent of the "Rumford Kasket" worn by the Bavarian Army in the 1790s. There were few large-scale cavalry actions in this war; most actions were small scale, but bitterly contested for all that. There were just two American cavalry regiments and they were mostly used for scouting and patrolling duties. The light role of this unit is reflected in the hussar-style frogging on the chest and the light cavalry sabre.*

▲ Private, 1st Infantry Regiment, 1812
This shows the ideally dressed and equipped
American soldier – a total rarity in the real
world. The colour and quality of the clothing
varied from state to state and over time. Most
regiments had brass belt plates bearing the
regimental name. Some of these were oval,
some octagonal. The blue-painted canvas pack
bore various designs on the flap; these varied
from "US" in white, within a white oval, to
the regimental title on scrolls of various
colours, to large ovals bearing the spread eagle
and the regimental name underneath. Most
tin shako plates bore the spread eagle; some
carried the regimental name. The musket is a
copy of the French M 1777, made in
Springfield and other places.

Maine or to create a Native American
State to act as a buffer between Canada
and the United States.

At the war's end, however, the
British held Fort Niagara on the
American side of the
border, much of the
District of Maine, Fort
Bowyer in Alabama, Fort
Michilimackinac, Prairie du
Chien in Wisconsin and Fort
Astoria, Oregon Territory.

Neither side held the western
territory in Ontario: a dead zone
existed between Detroit, in Michigan,
and Burlington Heights (Hamilton), in
Ontario. But the British had
maintained different outposts, with
detachments of regulars, at such places
as Delaware, London, Long Point and
Turkey Point, Ontario.

At the start of the war the United
States was divided militarily into the
Northern Department and the
Southern Department, but in March
1813 it was reorganized into ten
districts: 1 Massachusetts and New
Hampshire; 2 Rhode Island and
Connecticut; 3 New York to the
Highlands and part of New Jersey; 4
part of New Jersey, all of Pennsylvania
and Delaware; 5 Maryland and Virginia
(reorganized 2 July 1814); 6 North
Carolina, South Carolina and Georgia;
7 Louisiana, Tennessee and Mississippi;
8 Kentucky, Ohio and the Northwest
Territory; 9 New York north of the
Highlands and Vermont; 10 parts of
Maryland and Pennsylvania,
Washington DC and Northern Virginia
(formed 2 July 1814).

Units of the Regular American Army

Many of the Federal American
Volunteer Regiments were organized
from militia volunteers and are called
"militia" in the history books, thus it is
sometimes difficult to separate them
from militia units that were called up
for service. For instance, at Fort Detroit
in 1812 the three Ohio regiments were
called militia, but in fact they were
Federal Volunteer Regiments, organized
from militia volunteers and numbered
1st, 2nd and 3rd. Two of their

▲ Senior Officer, Light Artillery, 1812
The similarity with British Army uniforms
and badges of rank is marked. The shako was
largely the same model that had been in use
in 1792. The light artillery cap plate bore a
spread eagle holding a scroll. Other cap plates
featured a pile of cannon balls and the unit
designation or a cannon.

regimental colonels were Ohio Militia
Brigadier Generals.

The Regiment of Artillerists (i.e. 1st
Regiment of five battalions, each of
four companies) existed from 1 April
1802 to 12 May 1814. A regiment of
light artillery of ten companies was
raised on 12 April 1808. The 2nd and

3rd regiments of artillery were raised on 11 January 1812; on 12 May 1814 these were re-formed as one regiment of 12 battalions of 48 companies.

Cavalry

A regiment of light dragoons was raised on 12 April 1808; this later became the 1st and 2nd regiments from 11 January 1812 to 12 May 1814.

Infantry

The 1st Infantry Regiment was raised on 29 September 1789; the 2nd on 3 March 1791. The 3rd–7th were raised in January 1812. All had two battalions; in June that year they were strengthened and reorganized into single battalion regiments, thus creating the 8th–17th. The 18th–25th were raised on 29 January 1813 and the 26th–44th were ordered to be raised on 30 March 1814. The 45th, 46th, 47th, 48th Regiments existed at least on paper.

Six companies of rangers were raised from 2 January 1812 to 25 February 1813. This was increased to 16 companies on 25 February 1813. A regiment of riflemen was organized on 12 April 1808; the 2nd–4th on 10 February 1814.

The Sea Fencibles, of 10 companies, was raised on 26 July 1813. Each regiment was assigned a recruiting area

▲ CORPORAL, 25TH INFANTRY REGIMENT PIONEERS *These men were tasked with field works and with the construction and destruction of defensive works. Few battles involved earthworks, but the Battle of New Orleans saw the Americans construct defensive lines and repel an attack of British redcoats under General Packenham.*

▶ INFANTRY REGIMENT KIT *1 Infantry stovepipe shako, 1812. 2 Early pattern, tin shako plate, 15th Regiment. 3 Brass shako plate, 4th Rifle Regiment. 4 Brass shako plate, 2nd Artillery Regiment.*

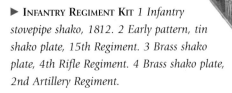

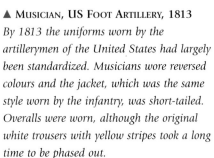

▲ MUSICIAN, US FOOT ARTILLERY, 1813 *By 1813 the uniforms worn by the artillerymen of the United States had largely been standardized. Musicians wore reversed colours and the jacket, which was the same style worn by the infantry, was short-tailed. Overalls were worn, although the original white trousers with yellow stripes took a long time to be phased out.*

as follows: New Jersey: 1st and 15th; Louisiana: 2nd and 44th; Mississippi: 3rd; New Hampshire: 4th; Pennsylvania: 5th, 16th, 22nd; New York: 6th, 13th, 23rd, 27th, 29th, 41st and 46th; Kentucky: 7th, 17th and 28th; Georgia: 8th; Massachusetts: 9th, 21st, 33rd, 34th, 40th and 45th; North Carolina: 10th and 43rd; Vermont: 11th, 26th, 30th and 31st; Virginia: 12th, 20th and 35th; Maryland: 14th and 38th; South Carolina: 18th; Ohio: 19th; Tennessee: 24th and 39th; Connecticut: 25th and 37th;

Delaware–Pennsylvania: 32nd;
Maryland–Virginia: 36th;
Pennsylvania–New York: 42nd.

Although exact figures are hard to
confirm and official sources not that
reliable, it is estimated that the total
number of American troops engaged
was 57,000 regulars, 10,000 volunteers
and 3,000 rangers. There were 20,000
more men in the navy and marines.
Upwards of 410,603 militiamen were
available to be called out during the
war, the majority for coastal defence.

Uniforms

US infantry were originally uniformed
in beaver hats, dark blue coats with red
facings and white small clothes.

By 1812 the infantry wore a
stovepipe shako about 7 in (18 cm)
tall, with a pewter front plate bearing
the eagle, the service and the
regimental number. The shako carried
a black cockade on the top left-hand
side and white cords across the front.
The tunic was supposed to be dark
blue, faced in red, lined in white, with
pewter buttons, but cloth supplies were
short and many variations arose. The
8th Regiment had a mixture of black
and brown coats, the 10th blue and
brown, and the 16th had black; other
regiments had three different colours
of coats. Breeches and gaiters were
similarly mixed. Belts were white. The
designs of the buttons were equally
diverse; many bore just "US", others
had elaborate designs of scrolled
initials over numerals.

Corporals wore one white, worsted
epaulette on the right shoulder;
sergeants had two and a crimson waist
sash. Officers had silver lace to the
collar and crimson silk waist sashes. A
lieutenant wore a silver epaulette on
the left shoulder, a captain one on the
right; field officers wore two epaulettes.

In 1813 a version of the high-
fronted British Belgic shako was
adopted, but the old plates continued
in use. Generally the generals wore a
large bicorn, a dark blue double-
breasted coat with buff facings, gold
buttons, buff small clothes and short
boots. In 1813 the coat was single-
breasted with black lace.

▲ *At the Battle of Lake Erie, 10 September
1813, US Commodore Oliver Hazard Perry
defeated the British, taking six of their ships.
This secured the northern frontier, opened up
supply lines and raised American morale.*

The Light Dragoons

Light dragoons wore a black leather
helmet, with front peak and leather
comb, from which hung a white,
horsehair crest. On the left side was a
blue-over-white plume. The front bore
a pewter plate with the figure of a
horseman galloping on it. White metal
chin scales covered the chinstrap. The
dark blue tunic was plain, single-
breasted and decorated with hussar-
style frogging to the chest. The collar
was edged in white, with two white
lace loops to each side. There were four
white chevrons on each lower sleeve.
Turnbacks, belts and breeches were
white. The troopers were armed with
steel-hilted sabres in steel sheaths.

These were light cavalry regiments,
and the United States did not raise
heavy cavalry in the European style.

Artillery

Originally the artillery had worn the
stovepipe shako although the 1st
Artillery had retained the bicorn until
1813. By 1813 all the artillery were
issued with the new-style shako with
rectangular brass plates bearing the
regimental name and a pyramid of six
cannon balls. A red-over-white plume
was worn on the left. The coat was
dark blue with a black collar and
yellow buttons. Breeches were dark
blue, belts white.

The light artillery, which essentially
served as horse artillery, was dressed in
a short-tailed lapelled jacket, blue
pantaloons and a black shako with
yellow cords, white plume with red tip.

There was also a Corps of Artificers
in dark green, with red facings and
yellow buttons.

The Engineer Corps had been
established in 1802 but was largely
restricted to coastal defence,
engineering as such being the task of
those pioneers attached to each
infantry company.

A Corps of Topographical Engineers
was also raised in 1813, but it
numbered just 16 officers.

Militia

America relied heavily on its militias
for military activity, both mounted
men, and artillery and foot soldiers.
They were dressed in all manners of
style, being uniformed and equipped
by their local authorities. Some carried
rifles, but the majority used rather out-
of-date muskets.

THE KINGDOMS OF DENMARK AND SWEDEN

Until 1814, Norway belonged to Denmark, then to Sweden. Finland had been Swedish territory but was lost to Russia after Sweden's defeat in 1809. Britain's high-handed actions against Denmark in 1801 and 1807 drove her into Napoleon's arms and made British naval operations in the Baltic more difficult, but not impossible. Napoleon permitted Denmark to keep her sovereignty in return for help in trying to keep the British out of the Baltic.

Sweden remained neutral until 1808, when Russia defeated her. Marshal Bernadotte had fallen from Napoleon's favour in 1809; on 21 August 1810 he was chosen by the Swedish government to become Crown Prince of that country, as the king – Charles XIII – had no heir. In 1812, Napoleon seized Swedish

Danish Infantry Regimental Distinctions: 1792–1815			
Title	**Facings**	**Piping**	**Buttons**
Guard	light blue	none	white
Danish Life Regiment	light yellow	none	white
Norwegian Life Regiment	light yellow	white	white
Koenig	light blue	none	white
Koenigin	light blue	none	yellow
Kronprinz	light blue	white	white
Erbprinz Friedrich	green	none	white
Fuenen	white	none	white
Seeland	green	white	white
1st Jutland	black	none	yellow
2nd Jutland	white	white	white
Oldenburg	green	none	white
Schleswig	light blue	white	yellow
Holstein	green	white	yellow

Pomerania and Bernadotte joined the Allies in the Sixth Coalition against his former comrade in 1813. For this he was awarded Norway, which until then had belonged to Denmark.

Danish Uniforms

The infantry wore black top hats with the extended left brim turned up and held by regimental loop and buttons, red tunics in the Russian "Potemkin" style of 1792, white lining, small clothes, gaiters and belts. The guard had bearskins and no lapels. In 1813 the line regiments adopted the shako with white cords. The Jägers wore green coats of line infantry cut and black facings. Elite companies were armed with rifles.

Denmark had a regiment of guard cavalry as well as heavy cavalry and various light regiments. The Life Guard til Hest wore the British-style tarleton helmet with black fur crest, red and silver turban and white plume with red

◄ OFFICER, DANISH LIFE GUARD TIL HEST, **1806** *The Guard cavalry wore helmets very like the British tarleton and wore a distinctive bright yellow coat. They carried light cavalry equipment but wore high boots similar to that worn by the heavy cavalry.*

tip on the left side. Their single-breasted tunics had red collars and cuffs edged with silver. They wore high boots, black belts, red sabretasche edged silver, with the crowned silver cipher "C7" (Christian VII).

Heavy line cavalry wore bicorns with white plumes, red tunics of infantry cut, with yellow lining, buff breeches, white belts. Facings were worn on collar, cuffs and lapels. All buttons were white, the facings of the Holstein Regiment were piped in yellow. Light dragoons wore the tarleton, red tunics, yellow lining, white buttons, gauntlets, belts and breeches, hussar-style boots. Hussars wore the *mirliton*, light blue dolmans, red pelisses with black fur, white lace, buff leather breeches and hussar-style boots. There was also a regiment of Bosniaks. Artillery were uniformed as for the line infantry but with dark blue facings and breeches.

Swedish unifoms

There is much confusion regarding Swedish uniforms of this era. In 1792 most Swedish infantry regiments wore blue coats with yellow facings. From 1807 to 1810 all regiments wore single-breasted grey uniforms with dark blue facings and turnbacks; in 1810 dark

buttons and white lace. From 1807 they wore the *kusket*, a crested version of the top hat. The crest ran from rear left to front right and a large brass front band bore the Swedish crest.

There was a guards regiment, dragoon regiments, hussars and Mounted *Jägers*. Most wore the *kusket* until after 1812 and, from then on, a shako, the guards had white coats until 1807, then blue like the rest. The Skanska Hussars were the exception,

▼ **TROOPER, SWEDISH MOERNER HUSSARS, 1813** *This was one of the few Swedish regiments that came into action in 1813 when they approached the fringes of the Battle of Leipzig on 18 October. He wears the traditional Swedish colours of blue and yellow and a shako that owes a lot to the shako then in use by the Austrians.*

wearing buff rather than blue coats. Facings were predominantly yellow, although the Skanska Hussars adopted dark blue. Most regiments carried sabretasches in dark blue, edged in yellow and bearing three yellow crowns. Saddle furniture was the same. Artillery seem to have worn the top hat or *kusket*, dark blue coats and breeches, yellow lace and buttons.

▼ **SWEDISH LINE INFANTRY MAJOR 1813** *Most Swedish regiments were part-time militia. Permanent officers and NCOs maintained the regimental equipment, while the men worked at their civilian occupations and came together for parades or national emergency. This individual still wears the top hat, but the kiwer, a Russian-style shako, was introduced that year and worn until the end of the Napoleonic conflict.*

▲ **PRIVATE, DANISH LIVJÄGERS, 1809** *The dark green costume and black leatherwork is classic for this corps of marksmen. The British raid on Copenhagen in 1807 drove the Danes into Napoleon's arms until 1814. Their rifle had a calibre of 19,1mm.*

blue tunics, with yellow turnbacks were reintroduced. All coats were dark blue, except for the *Jägers*, who wore dark green. Initially the troops wore blue-within-yellow cockades, but in 1807 each infantry regiment adopted its own cockade, bearing a Maltese cross in various colours. The line wore top hats in 1792, although the style was changed in 1807. The Russian Kiwer shako was introduced in late 1812.

The Life Guard infantry (Konungens Svea Lif Garde) had a dark blue coat, yellow facings and

THE KINGDOM OF BAVARIA

Bavaria had a close relationship with France, reinforced by her wary attitude towards her larger neighbour, Austria.

Line Infantry

In 1792 the Bavarian infantry wore the "Rumford casket", a low-crowned, black leather helmet, with leather comb, brass front plate and drooping horsehair crest, white for grenadiers, black for fusiliers. The white tunic was short-skirted, with facings on collar,

▼ CAPTAIN, 5TH FUSILIER REGIMENT VON WAHL, 1792–99 *Rank was shown by the five buttons and buttonholes on the lapel; field officers' buttonholes were embroidered in gold or silver. This uniform was designed for economy, the coat and waistcoat were one garment, as were the trouser-gaiters.*

Bavarian Infantry Regimental Distinctions: 1792

No./Title	Facings	Buttons
1st Grenadiers Life Regiment	light blue	white
2nd Grenadiers Kurprinz	light blue	yellow
3rd Grenadiers Graf Ysenburg	dark blue	white
4th Grenadiers Baaden	dark blue	yellow
1st Fusiliers Zweibruecken	red	white
2nd Fusiliers Birkenfeld	red	yellow
3rd Fusiliers Rodenhausen	brick red	white
4th Fusiliers de la Motte	brick red	yellow
5th Fusiliers Wahl	yellow	white
6th Fusiliers Pfalzgraf Max	yellow	yellow
7th Fusiliers Zedtwitz	green	white
8th Fusiliers Rambaldi	green	yellow
9th Fusiliers Weichs	peach/red	white
10th Fusiliers Hohenhausen	peach/red	yellow
11th Fusiliers Preysing	crimson	white
12th Fusiliers Belderbusch	crimson	yellow
13th Fusiliers Isenburg	black	white
14th Fusiliers Kling	black	yellow

lapels, cuffs and turnbacks. Breeches were grey, with black, hussar-style gaiters. Belts were white. In 1799 this uniform was replaced by the black leather helmet (*Raupenhelm*) with large black, caterpillar crest, brass front band and oval plate. Until 1805 all officers kept the cocked hat, thence company officers also wore the *Raupenhelm*. The coat became cornflower blue and facings were now as shown below. Turnbacks were red for all regiments.

In 1814 new 12th and 14th Regiments were raised as was the Guard Grenadiers. The latter wore bearskins with brass plates, white cords, red top patch with white cross. Coats as for the line, but with white buttonholes to the white lapel buttons. The 1st and 2nd Regiments lost their buttonhole decoration at this point. Officers wore silver silk waist sashes with light-blue stripes until April 1812, when they adopted the gilt gorget.

Light infantry

Up to 1799 there were two Field Jäger regiments with light green coats and black helmet crests; the 1st Schweicheldt had black facings and white buttons, the 2nd Ysenburg with black and yellow. In 1799 both regiments adopted the same uniforms as the line, but in the light green and black colour scheme; in 1809 the coats became dark green and facings were piped in red. Breeches were grey.

In 1801 six light infantry battalions were raised, facings and buttons were as follows: 1st, red facings, yellow buttons; 2nd, red facings, white buttons; 3rd, black facings, white buttons; 4th, black facings, yellow buttons.

In 1803 the 5th (crimson, white until 1806, when facings changed to black) and 6th (crimson, yellow until 1806, when the collar changed to lemon-yellow and the cuffs to black, piped in red) were raised.

In 1807 the Tyroler Jäger Battalion was raised with a dark green tunic with light blue collar and cuffs and white buttons. The 7th Battalion was raised in 1808, with light blue facings edged in red and white buttons.

Artillery and Engineers

In 1792 the artillery wore black crests to the helmet, dark blue coat, black facings, yellow buttons. The artillery train had grey tunics, light blue facings, white buttons and black belts. Black facings were later piped in red. Engineers wore the same uniforms.

▼ TROOPER, 1ST DRAGOONS, MINUCCI, 1806
In Russia in 1812 the Bavarian cavalry was taken from its parent corps by Napoleon and attached to Grouchy's III Cavalry Corps; they fought at Borodino and melted away to nothing in the retreat. Of note is the distinctive Bavarian Raupenhelm *which was generally worn from 1805 onwards.*

No./Title	Lapels & cuffs	Collar	Buttons
Bavarian Infantry Regimental Distinctions: 1811			
1 Konig	red*	red*	white
2 Kronprinz	red	red	yellow
3 Prinz Karl	red**	red**	yellow
4 Sachsen-Hildburghausen	yellow***	yellow***	white
5 Preysing	pink	pink	white
6 Herzog Wilhelm	red**	red**	white
7 Lowenstein-Wertheim	pink	pink	yellow
8 Herzog Pius	yellow***	yellow***	yellow
9 Ysenburg	yellow***	red	yellow
10 Junker	yellow***	red	white
11 Kinkel	black***	red	white
12 (no title)	black***	red	yellow

*with white lace buttonholes, **edged white, ***edged red

Cavalry

The 1792 uniforms of the Bavarian cavalry were of infantry cut, with white helmet crests. Collars were in the coat colour; white for cuirassiers and dragoons, light green for Chevau-Légèrs. White belts.

In 1804 the cavalry uniforms and changes were as follows: the 1st Cuirassiers (scarlet, white) became the 1st Dragoons and in 1811 it converted to the 1st Chevau-Légèrs. The 2nd Cuirassiers (scarlet, yellow) became the 4th Chevau-Légèrs. The 1st Dragoons (black, white) was disbanded in 1803.

The 2nd Dragoons (black, yellow) became the 2nd Chevau-Légèrs in 1811. The 1st Chevau-Légèrs (black, white until 1811 thence red, yellow) of 1792 became the 4th in 1804, then the 3rd; in 1811 it became the 5th. The 2nd Chevau-Légèrs of 1792 (black, yellow) became the 3rd in 1799 and was disbanded in 1801. The 3rd Chevau-Légèrs of 1792 (apple green, white) became the 2nd in 1799, the 1st in 1804 and the 3rd in 1811, when facings were black, buttons yellow. The 4th Chevau-Légèrs was raised in 1803 (black, white) and was renumbered the 6th in 1811.

▶ PRIVATE, 4TH LIGHT INFANTRY BATTALION, 1812 *This battalion was in General von Wrede's 2nd Division in the suppression of the Tyrolean revolt in 1809. The unit was destroyed in Russia in 1812. This figure wears a uniform adopted in 1809.*

SAXONY AND WESTPHALIA

Saxony benefited territorially from the alliance with France. Westphalia was a new state that emerged from the reorganization of Germany.

SAXONY

A French ally from 1807 to 1813 Saxony was then substantially reduced by the victorious Allies.

The Guard

The Grenadier Life Guard Regiment wore a bearskin bonnet with brass plate with the crowned royal cipher "FA" within laurels. It had a yellow top patch with white cross and cords, red coat, yellow facings and white buttons.

Saxony Line Infantry Regimental Distinctions: 1792–1815

No./Title in 1809	Facings	Buttons
1st Koenig	red	yellow
2nd Cerrini*	red	white
3rd Prinz Anton	dark blue	white
4th Prinz Clemens**	dark blue	yellow
5th Prinz Max	yellow	yellow
6th Burgsdorff*	yellow	white
7th Prinz Friedrich August	light green	yellow
8th Loew**	light green	white
9th Oebschelwitz*	light blue	yellow
10th Dyherrn*	light blue	white
11th Niesemueschel	purple	white
12th Rechten**	purple	yellow

*Disbanded 1810 **Disbanded 1813

▼ DRUMMER, INFANTRY REGIMENT PRINZ FRIEDRICH AUGUST, 1812 *Saxon troops fought with the French in Russia and escaped largely unscathed. This was the 7th regiment of the line. Drummers did not wear reversed colours but had swallows' wings and extra lace.*

Line and Light Infantry

Initially the line infantry wore the bicorn, but from 1809 the shako with crowned shield with the cipher, French rank badges and intercompany distinctions were worn. White coats, belts and small clothes. Officers' shakos had gold top bands.

LIGHT INFANTRY. The 1st and 2nd Schützen Battalions wore dark green tunic and small clothes, black facings and belts, yellow buttons; green plume and cords to shako. The Jäger Battalion wore the same but with brass hunting horn badge on the shako, white cords, red piping to the black facings, dark green collar with black front patches.

Cavalry

HEAVY CAVALRY. Until 1810 the heavy cavalry wore the bicorn, thence the brass helmet with comb, caterpillar crest, brown fur turban (circled with gold oak leaves for officers) and white plume to left side. Only the front plate of the cuirass was worn; it was black with red edging. Officers wore the crowned cipher in gold on it. Buff, single-breasted *kollets* edged in the regimental lace, white breeches and belts, brass-hilted sword in brown leather sheath. Saddle furniture in the facing colour, edged in the

▶ GRENADIER OFFICER, INFANTRY REGIMENT KURFÜRST, 1806 *This man wears the distinctive white coat of the Saxons and has a bearskin, a distinction of grenadier officers. The elaborate gorget with crimson background was worn by all infantry officers until the introduction of French badges of rank. In 1806 Saxony was a Prussian ally and shared in her defeat.*

button colour. Black and steel harness.

CHEVAU-LÉGÈRS. Bicorns until 1810 thence shakos. Red coats with yellow buttons, buff waistcoats, white breeches and belts.

HUSSARS. White dolman and pelisse until 1806, light blue collar and cuffs, white buttons and lace. Light blue sabretasche and shabraque edged and decorated with the crowned cipher in white. From 1806 light blue dolman, black facings, white buttons and lace.

Artillery and Engineers

FOOT ARTILLERY. Uniforms of infantry cut; initially with the bicorn then the shako in 1809 with a black plume. The dark green coat had red facings and yellow buttons. Waistcoat and breeches were buff; they wore white belts.

HORSE ARTILLERY AND TRAIN. The uniform of the horse artillery was as for the foot, but with white breeches and hussar boots. The artillery train wore light blue coats with black facings edged red and white buttons.

ENGINEERS They were the bicorn with silver edging, a dark green coat with red facings, white buttons and red small clothes.

WESTPHALIA

Napoleon created the kingdom of Westphalia in November 1807 from the old Electorates of Hanover and Hessen-Kassel and the Duchy of Brunswick. Badges of rank and distinctions were as for the French.

The Guard

GARDE DU CORPS. Steel helmets with brass trim, comb and black crest. On the front plate was the crowned cipher "JN". White tunic, belts and breeches, royal blue collar, lapels and cuffs piped red, with gold lace buttonholes; gold buttons, contre epaulettes.

GUARD CHEVAU-LÉGÈRS. Black helmet with brass comb, chin scales and

fittings; black fur crest, red plume. Short, dark green tunic, red collar, cuffs and turnbacks, yellow trefoil epaulettes and buttonholes to collar, chest and cuffs. Green breeches with yellow thigh knots and side seams, hussar boots with yellow tassels.

GUARD HUSSARS. Red shako with yellow top band cords, chin scales and crowned shield bearing "JN", white plume, black peak. Red dolman, dark blue pelisse and breeches, yellow buttons and lace, red and white sash, white belts, black sabretasche with brass crowned "JN".

GUARD GRENADIERS. Bearskin with red top patch, yellow grenade badge, cords and plume. White tunic, belts, breeches and gaiters, red collar, lapels, cuffs and turnbacks with yellow grenades. Gold buttons and buttonholes.

GUARD JÄGERS. Shako with white eagle plate, white cords, plume

and chin scales. Dark green coat and breeches, lemon yellow collar, cuffs and piping to dark green lapels. White buttons and lace to collar, cuffs and lapels. Green epaulettes, white Hungarian thigh knots. Black, hussar-topped gaiters trimmed white. White hunting horn pouch badge. Green sabre knot.

JÄGER CARABINEER BATTALION Shako with red-tipped green plume, red cords, yellow eagle plate. Plain dark green tunic and breeches, red piping to collar, cuffs, turnbacks and front of tunic. Yellow buttons. Red thigh knots and side seams; red trim and tassel to black gaiters, black belts.

GUARD FUSILIERS. As for the line infantry but with white buttonholes to collar, lapels and cuff flaps.

ARTILLERY OF THE GUARD. Shako with red plume, cords and pompon, brass rhombic plate with a crown over crossed gun barrels, brass chin scales. Dark blue coat with red collar, cuffs, turnbacks and epaulettes. Seven red lace bars on the chest, yellow buttons. Dark blue breeches with red thigh knots and side stripe, hussar boots trimmed red, buff belts and gauntlets.

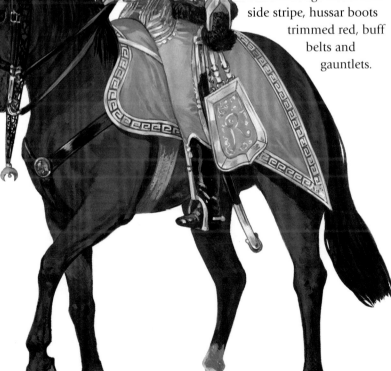

▶ OFFICER, SAXON HUSSARS, 1813 *The single regiment of hussars was uniformed and equipped in the French manner. The shako had only been introduced in 1810 and it bore the "FA" cipher under a crown. This regiment was at full strength of 10 squadrons in 1813.*

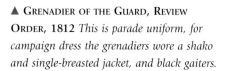

▲ Grenadier of the Guard, Review Order, 1812 *This is parade uniform, for campaign dress the grenadiers wore a shako and single-breasted jacket, and black gaiters.*

▲ Officer, Light Infantry, 1812 *In 1807 the French system of organization, badges and intercompany distinctions was adopted. The curved sabre was a favourite of officers.*

▲ Officer, Foot Artillery, 1812 *A very French-style uniform. Only the shako badge and variations in insignia differentiate him from his French counterpart.*

Infantry

Shako with brass rhombic plate bearing the crowned Westphalian eagle or the crowned "JN" over the number. White tunics, breeches and belts, black gaiters, brass buttons. From 1807 to 1810, facings were worn on collar, lapels, cuffs and turnbacks: 1st and 2nd Regiments dark blue, 3rd and 4th light blue, 5th and 6th yellow. In 1810 all facings became dark blue and regimental identity was shown only on the buttons. In 1812 the fusilier companies adopted dark blue epaulettes with white crescents in place of the previous white shoulder straps edged in dark blue. There were three battalions of light infantry. By 1809 the coat was dark green, faced light blue. They wore dark green breeches, black belts and gaiters. Shako with white eagle plate and chin scales.

Line Cavalry and Artillery

Cuirassiers. French cuirassier helmets, brass front plate with the crowned "JN". The 1st Regiment had a white tunic (blue from 1812), buttons and breeches, crimson collar, cuffs, lapels and turnbacks. Officers had black bandoliers trimmed in silver. Brass-hilted swords in steel sheaths. 2nd Regiment: dark blue coat faced orange. Chevau-Légers. Their helmet was as for the Chevau-Légers of the Guard, but with white metal fittings. Dark green, single-breasted tunic with, for the 1st Regiment, orange collar, pointed cuffs, turnbacks and piping down the front of the coat, white buttons. Buff facings

for the 2nd Regiment raised in 1812. Dark green breeches with silver thigh knots and side stripes, hussar boots with silver trim. Sabres in steel sheaths. Hussars. The 1st: shako with white eagle plate, cords and chin scales, green plume. Green dolman, pelisse, breeches, collar and cuffs, white buttons and lace, black fur, red and white barrel sash. Black sabretasche with white metal "1". The 2nd: white plume, light blue dolman, pelisse and breeches, red collar and cuffs; white metal "2" on the sabretasche.

The artillery wore a shako with brass rhombic plate with crowned, crossed guns, brass chin scales, red cords, plume and pompon. Dark blue coat, breeches and lapels (with red piping), red collar, cuffs and turnbacks.

THE KINGDOM OF WÜRTTEMBERG

This south German kingdom was another of Napoleon's creations and a staunch supporter until 1813, when it deserted to the Allies. Until 1799 uniforms and badges were as for Prussia. In 1806 the line infantry uniform was a black leather helmet with front plate in the button colour, black comb and "sausage" crest. The cockade was red-within-black-within-yellow. Officers wore a silver silk waist sash with red stripes, epaulettes in the button colour and a silver and red sword knot. Dark blue tunics and lapels, with facings on collar, cuffs, shoulder straps and turnbacks. White small clothes and belts, black gaiters.

The two light infantry battalions wore shakos with brass rhombic plates, dark green coats, light blue facings, white piping and brass buttons, buff belts. The 1st and 2nd Fussjägers wore the same uniforms, but with black belts and facings, green plumes, white buttons. In 1812 the infantry helmet was replaced by a bell-topped shako the brass rhombic plate bearing the crowned cipher "FR".

Cavalry

Troopers wore a crested, black leather helmet, with a yellow-over-green crest, crowned, oval plate bearing the Württemberg crest over the motto "Fearless and Faithful" and chin scales. Officers had the high-crowned, Bavarian-style caterpillar-crested helmet, with a front plate and supporters. Their tunic was dark blue, with dark blue half lapels, facings (shown on the collar), cuffs, lapel piping and turnbacks. Shoulder scales were in the button colour, backed in the facing colour.

Artillery

The foot artillery wore Bavarian-style crested, black leather helmets, brass buttons, light blue tunics, lapels and breeches, black collar, cuffs and turnbacks, tin buttons and shoulder scales, white belts. Horse artillery had yellow turnbacks with wide black braid edging, hussar boots.

▼ **OFFICER, INFANTRY REGIMENT PRINZ FRIEDRICH, 1808** *These distinctive helmets were retained until the adoption of shakos after the campaign in Russia.*

◄ **PRIVATE OF JÄGERS, 1813** *The light infantry had adopted shakos in 1807. There was only one battalion of Jägers in 1801 and they acted as specialist sharpshooters.*

► **GUNNER, HORSE ARTILLERY, 1812** *The Württembergers formed part of III Corps in Russia in 1812. The 1st Battery of Horse Artillery had Guard status and, generally, this branch of service was something of an elite.*

THE GRAND DUCHY OF WARSAW

The rump state of Poland had been partitioned among Prussia, Austria and Russia in 1795. In 1807, Napoleon created the Grand Duchy as a bolster against these states. In 1813 it was overrun by Russia, which founded the new Kingdom of Poland.

Lithuanian Units

In the summer of 1812, as Napoleon's army advanced into Russia, a number of Lithuanian units were raised and served with the duchy's forces. Their uniforms were very similar but the troops wore a

◀ OFFICER, 15TH POLISH LANCERS, 1812
This officer represents one of the many anomalies of the period, in that he is wearing trousers in the facing colour, instead of slate blue with crimson side stripes. This sort of thing was common in the chaos that followed 1813.

mounted warrior badge rather than an eagle. There were five lancer regiments, three line infantry regiments and a regiment of light infantry. Various gendarme units were also raised, as well as civic militias. These were almost entirely destroyed in the retreat from Moscow.

Line Infantry

There were 17 infantry regiments until 1812, when the 18th–21st were raised in Lithuania. Each regiment had three battalions, each of six companies on the French model. In 1807 all wore the square-topped Polish *czapka* with white cockade, brass, sunburst plate, rapidly replaced by the crowned Polish eagle over a Greek shield bearing the regimental number. There was a company pompon and plume, and brass chin scales. Grenadiers had a red top band to the *czapka*, the light company had yellow. The chinstrap bosses bore the company emblem: a five-pointed star, a grenade and the hunting horn. The *kurtka* was dark-blue, with regimental numbers on the buttons. Initially facings were allocated by the division in which the regiment served. The 1st Division had red collars and cuffs and yellow lapels; the 2nd, crimson facings and tin buttons; 3rd, white faces and brass buttons.

In 1810 grenadiers adopted the bearskin cap with red top and white cross, red cords. Some regiments had brass front plates with the Polish eagle between grenades, others did not. Grenadiers wore red epaulettes, voltigeurs green with yellow crescents; they also had yellow collars.

Drummers wore a wide variety of costume, the uniforms being dictated by the regimental colonel. The 13th Regiment wore white uniforms with light blue facings and white buttons; all others now had white half-lapels, dark blue collar edged red, red piping to tunic edges, white turnbacks piped red. Officers wore gilt gorgets with silver Polish eagles.

Three regiments of line infantry (the 4th, 7th and 9th) served with distinction with the French in Spain. They should not be confused with the Vistula Legion, which also fought in Spain. They seem to have almost entirely adopted French uniform and badges of rank, even wearing tricolour cockades rather than the tradtional white version.

Foot Artillery

They wore a shako with brass front band with a grenade over crossed gun barrels all under a white, crowned eagle, red pompon, plume and cords. The dark green *kurtka* had black collar, cuffs, lapels and turnbacks all piped red, yellow buttons, white breeches and belts.

Horse Artillery

As for the foot artillery, but with fur colpack, red pompon, plume and cords. Brass scale epaulettes with red fringes and crescents, single-breasted dark green tunic with yellow grenade collar badges, black facings, yellow badges in the turnbacks, dark green breeches with red thigh knots and side seams, hussar boots with yellow trim. Trumpeters wore white colpacks with red cords, dark green over red plume, dark-green bag. White tunic faced black, piped red, red epaulettes, waistcoats and breeches all laced yellow; red trumpet cords. Dark green shabraque with black edging piped red. In the rear corners the grenade over crossed gun barrels in yellow. Black harness with brass fittings.

Artillery Train and Engineers

They wore a dark-blue *czapka*, white cockade and eagle plate, brass chin scales. Dark blue, single-breasted tunic with yellow collar and plain cuffs, yellow piping to front of tunic and to the dark blue shoulder straps and turnbacks, white buttons. Dark blue breeches with yellow side stripes. White belts. On the upper left arm an oval brass plate with the Polish eagle and the number of the division and the vehicle. The baggage train was as for the artillery train but with a grey *kurtka* and breeches.

Engineeers were dressed as for the foot artillery, but with gold grenades on the collars and trophies of arms on the buttons.

Cavalry

CHASSEURS À CHEVAL (Regiments 1, 4 and 5). They wore the shako with a white cockade, eagle plate or white loop and button, dark green over red plume. The elite companies wore colpacks with red tops, cords and plumes and brass scale epaulettes with red fringes. They had the dark-green, single-breasted tunic, with collar, cuffs, piping and turnback edging in the facing colour: 1st, red, 4th, crimson, 5th, orange. Non-elite companies wore brass scale epaulettes with white fringes. Brass buttons, dark green breeches with a double side stripe in the facing colour; white belts, hussar sabre and a carbine. Their horses had dark green saddle cloths edged in the facing colour.

LANCERS (Regiments 2, 3, 6, 7, 8, 9, 11, 12, 15, 16, 17, 18, 19, 20, 21, the last five being raised in Lithuania). Black *czapka* with white eagle over a Greek shield plate bearing the regimental number, also a brass, semicircular, rayed plate with crowned eagle. Dark blue *kurtka*, with dark blue lapels and turnbacks piped in the facing colour, except the 11th and 15th Regiments, which had crimson lapels. Facings were worn on collar and pointed cuffs. The colour of the twin side stripes of the breeches had no relation to the facings Elite companies possibly wore colpacks rather than *czapkas*.

◀ **GRENADIER, 13TH LINE INFANTRY REGIMENT, 1812** *The 13th were unique in that they wore white coats, perhaps harking back to their origin as a Galician regiment (Galicia had been an Austrian province until 1809). This regiment survived the 1812 campaign. Here the shako with red plume has replaced the square-topped czapka.*

HUSSARS (10th and 13th Regiments). Both wore the same uniforms, the 10th with yellow lace and buttons, the 13th with white. Light blue shako with white plume with black base, white loop and cockade, white cords and chin scales crimson dolman and pelisse, light blue collar, cuffs and breeches, crimson shabraque edged in the button colour, crimson sabretasche with silver border and Polish eagle with gold crown. Black harness with steel fittings. The elite companies would seem to have worn a fox fur colpack. They had crimson breeches for the 10th and had a crimson dolman, light blue breeches and red boots for the 13th.

CUIRASSIERS (14th Regiment). Their uniform was as for the French cuirassiers; dark blue tunic, red facings, yellow buttons. Trumpeters had red crests, white plume and a tunic faced red, with red and yellow lace bars on the chest. They wore no cuirass. They fought at Borodino in 1812 but were largely destroyed in the retreat from Moscow. Indeed the Poles suffered enormous losses.

KRAKUS. These so-called Polish cossacks were light cavalry and dressed in a traditional Polish uniform of square-topped *Konfederatka* and a loose-fitting dark blue coat (or *Litewka*). They carried lances and proved useful as scouts in 1813.

▼ **GRENADIER AND LANCER HEADGEAR** *There were several variations in cap badges, eagles and in the method of indicating NCO`s rank during the period. 1 Grenadier NCO of a line infantry regiment, note the gold braid top band. 2 Grenadier NCO, 2nd Line Infantry Regiment. 3 Czapka of an officer, 11th Lancers.*

THE KINGDOMS OF ITALY AND NAPLES

Following Napoleon's victories of 1796 a rash of republics bloomed over the Italian peninsula. In 1805, Napoleon created the kingdom of Italy, which included the old Italian Republic, Venice, Dalmatia and the Ionian Isles. In the south the Kingdom of Naples was formed from the old Kingdom of the Two Sicilies.

ITALY

All badges of rank and intercompany distinctions were as in the French Army. The Italian cockade was green-within-red-within-white.

Guard Infantry

GRENADIERS. As for the grenadiers of the French Imperial Guard, except the coat was dark green and cap plate and buttons were

◀ GRENADIER OFFICER OF 5TH ITALIAN LINE INFANTRY REGIMENT, 1809 *The uniform is French in style although in white. Infantry uniforms and facings reflected the national colours of red, white and green.`*

white. The eagle had a five-pointed star on the chest, enclosing an "N".

VÉLITE GRENADIERS. As for the grenadiers except that they had a brass front plate to bearskin, white coat with dark green collar, lapels, cuffs, French cuff flaps. The turnbacks and piping to pocket flaps were also dark green; they wore red epaulettes and yellow buttons.

CHASSEURS. As for the vélites except for red collar and cuffs; white piping to collar, lapels, turnbacks and pocket flaps. They wore the shako with white top band cords, loop and button; brass eagle front plate, green plume.

VÉLITE CHASSEURS. They wore the white coat as for the vélites; the carabineers had bearskins with red over green plumes, brass plate and buttons.

Guard Cavalry

GUARDS OF HONOUR. Their uniform was a brass helmet as for the French carabineers, but the comb was in the form of a brass eagle, they wore a steel turban with crowned "N", black peak and neck shield edged in steel, black crest, white plume, brass chin scales. Dark green tunic with company facings to collar, lapels, round cuffs, turnbacks and pocket piping. The collar and cuffs were decorated with two white lace loops; brass scale epaulettes with backing in the facing colour. White small clothes and belts, high, cuffed boots. Facings: 1st, pink, 2nd, yellow, 3rd, buff, 4th, scarlet, 5th, orange.

DRAGOONS. Uniforms were as for the dragoons of the Imperial Guard, but with white lace and buttons.

Artillery and Engineers

FOOT ARTILLERY. The wore a black bearskin with no front plate, a red top patch with white cross, red cords and

plume. They wore a dark green coat, waistcoat and breeches. The coat had a black collar and lapels piped red, red cuffs and French cuff flaps, red epaulettes and turnbacks with green grenade badges. They had white belts and wore short, below-the-knee boots.

GENDARMERIE OF THE GUARD. Uniforms were as for the French unit, but with the Italian cockade.

HORSE ARTILLERY. As for that of the horse artillery of the Imperial Guard.

ARTILLERY TRAIN. They wore a black, Polish *czapka* with a brass badge of crossed gun barrels under the Iron Crown on the upper front left side, red pompon and plume, brass chin scales and the cockade. They wore a grey coat with dark green collar, Polish cuffs, epaulettes and turnbacks, the latter with white grenade badges. There were five dark-green bars across the chest.

Line Infantry

Before 1807 they wore the bicorn with regimental button and loop, Italian cockade and company pompon. This was then replaced by the shako with lozenge plate in the button colour, cockade, loop and button, and company pompon. Until 1806, coats were dark green, thence white. The regiment of Istrian Chasseurs wore a dark green uniform of French light infantry cut, with light blue facings and white buttons. The Dalmatian Infantry Regiment wore a brass lozenge shako plate with "RDI" under the Iron Crown. The uniform was a dark-green coat and breeches with red facings and yellow buttons. White belts were worn.

ENGINEERS. They wore a uniform similar to that of the foot artillery, but with French shakos, red pompon and epaulettes, and black, pointed cuffs piped in red.

Line Cavalry

1ST AND 2ND DRAGOONS. As for the French dragoons. The helmet had a black fur turban, green plume on the

Italian Line Infantry Regimental Distinctions

No.	Collar	Lapels	Cuffs	Cuff flaps	Turnbacks	Buttons
1	green*	red*	red*	green*	red*	yellow
2	white**	red*	white**	red*	white**	yellow
3	red*	red*	red*	red*	red*	yellow
4	red*	white***	white***	green*	white***	white
5	red*	green*	green*	red*	white***	white
6	white***	green*	white***	green*	white***	yellow
7	green*	white***	red*	none	white***	white

*piped white, **piped red,
***piped green

left. They wore dark green coats and shoulder straps with white buttons, belts and small clothes. Facings were pink for the 1st, crimson for the 2nd.

1ST–4TH CHASSEURS À CHEVAL. They wore the shako with cockade, loop and button, white chin scales and a dark green plume with the tip in the facing colour. The uniform was completed

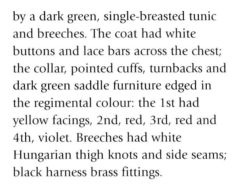

by a dark green, single-breasted tunic and breeches. The coat had white buttons and lace bars across the chest; the collar, pointed cuffs, turnbacks and dark green saddle furniture edged in the regimental colour: the 1st had yellow facings, 2nd, red, 3rd, red and 4th, violet. Breeches had white Hungarian thigh knots and side seams; black harness brass fittings.

THE KINGDOM OF NAPLES

Napoleon formed this kingdom in 1807 from the mainland part of the Kingdom of the Two Sicilies. All badges of rank and intercompany distinctions were as for the French. The cockade was crimson-within-white.

Guard Infantry

THE GRENADIERS. They wore a bearskin, red cords and plume, crimson top patch with yellow grenade. Dark blue coat with light crimson collar, lapels, cuffs, French cuff flaps and turnbacks, all but the latter piped white. The coat had yellow buttons and two tasselled buttonholes to the collar, two to each

◀ OFFICER, ITALIAN GUARD OF HONOUR, 1812 *This unit was formed from the sons of wealthy Italian families and was very much an elite within an elite. The elaborate helmet was both heavy and expensive; off duty the men wore a round fatigue cap.*

▶ SARDININA GRENADIER 1795 *A classic grenadier uniform of the early revolutionary period, with moustache, bearskin bonnet, redundant brass match case on the bandolier and sabre. Note the picker and cleaning brush for the musket hanging from the buttonhole.*

cuff and seven to each lapel. Red epaulettes and sabre knots were worn. Small clothes and belts were white, they wore black gaiters. Drummers wore reversed colours.

1ST VÉLITES. Their uniforms were as for those of the grenadiers, but with green cords to the bearskin and with a green plume with a red tip. White tunic, small clothes and belts; crimson collar, pointed cuffs and lapels all piped white, crimson turnbacks, yellow buttons and buttonholes as for the grenadiers. Officers had gold bearskin cords, epaulettes, gorget, sword knot and trim to hussar-style boots. Drummers wore crimson and white striped lace edging to facings, crimson swallows nests and seven such striped chevrons on each sleeve. The 2nd Vélites' uniforms was as for the 1st, but the plume was all green.

BATTALION OF MARINES. They wore a shako with shield-shaped brass plate bearing the crowned "JN", a cockade, red pompon and

ords, brass chin scales. They had a dark-blue coat and breeches, with red collar, cuffs, lapels and turnbacks, yellow buttons, red epaulettes with white crescents, buff belts edged white.

Guard Cavalry

GUARDS OF HONOUR. Black colpack with a red bag and yellow braid trim, tassel and cords. White dolman, with red collar and cuffs, yellow lace and buttons, crimson and yellow sash, red pelisse, black fur, yellow lace and buttons. Light green breeches with yellow trim, and yellow trim to hussar boots. Light green shabraque edged red and piped yellow. This unit was later converted to the Garde du Corps.

GARDE DU CORPS. The uniform of this new unit consisted of a bicorn with a white loop, button and plume. A red, single-breasted tunic with yellow collar, cuffs and turnbacks, red cuff flaps, yellow piping to vertical pocket flaps. A white epaulette and aiguillette on the right shoulder, white

breeches, heavy cavalry boots. Blue saddle furniture with white edging and red piping, white crowned "JN" in the rear corner, square blue portmanteau.

VÉLITES À CHEVAL. They wore a shako with gold top band and cords, chin scales and sunburst plate with the crowned "JN" cipher, white plume. Dark blue Polish *kurtka* with yellow facings and buttons. Double yellow side stripes to dark-blue breeches. The dark blue saddle furniture had yellow edging and cipher. Trumpeters wore reversed colour.

HUSSARS. Raised from the Vélites à Cheval in 1814. Sky blue dolman, crimson facings, white buttons and lace. Crimson pelisse, white buttons and lace, and black fur. Crimson and white barrel sash. The sky blue breeches had white thigh knots, side stripes and belt. Black shako with brass fittings, white top band and cords. The saddle furniture was sky-blue, edged in white and with the crowned cipher "JN" in the pointed rear corner. The black harness had brass fittings.

Guard Artillery

FOOT GUARD ARTILLERY. As for Imperial Guard, but pale purple facings and "JN" cipher.

GUARD HORSE ARTILLERY. As for Imperial Guard horse artllery, but pale purple facings and "JN" cipher.

ARTILLERY TRAIN. As for the foot artillery above, but light blue tunics and breeches and white buttons.

Line Infantry

French-style shako with shield-shaped plate bearing the crowned "JN", cockade and pompon. White tunics, small clothes, belts and shoulder straps and brass buttons. Facings were shown on the collar, lapels, cuffs, French cuff

◄ DRUMMER, 1ST NEAPOLITAN LIGHT INFANTRY REGIMENT, 1809 *Neapolitan troops fought in Spain from 1809 to 1814. The 1st Light was one of the unlucky regiments sent to Spain, serving in the east of the country. It was largely destroyed through desertion and guerrilla warfare. As a member of a light infantry regiment, this drummer wears a blue jacket with distinctive lace.*

flaps and turnbacks. Black gaiters were worn. Drummers' uniforms were as for those of the Vélites.

The Light Infantry

As for the line, but with white metalwork. A medium blue coat, lapels and breeches of French light infantry style, with yellow collars and facings shown on cuff flaps and on piping to the cuffs and lapels. Green pompons, white hunting horn badges on the blue turnbacks. Green epaulettes with yellow crescents, green sabre straps. The Carabineer companies wore bearskins with red cords, plume and top patch with a white grenade. Collars in the facing colour: 1st, black, 2nd, yellow, 3rd, red, 4th, orange.

The Line Cavalry

1ST CHEVAU-LÉGÈRS. French-style shako with white sunburst plate, with brass centre bearing the crowned cipher "JN", white top band, crimson-within-white pompon. Light blue, double-breasted tunic, collar, lapels, shoulder straps and pointed cuffs, all edged crimson; white buttons, belts and lace. The crimson turnbacks were decorated with white hunting horn badges. Light blue breeches with double crimson side stripes, white trim to hussar boots. Trumpeters wore reversed colours; the elite company wore colpacks with red trim, red epaulettes and sabre straps. The light blue saddle furniture was edged in crimson with the white cipher "JN" in the rear corner.

1ST CHASSEURS À CHEVAL. Shako with cockade, brass lozenge plate bearing the "1", brass chin scales, white top band cords, loop and button. Dark green tunic with red turnbacks and piping to dark green collar, lapels, pointed cuffs and shoulder straps; white buttons, belts and hunting horn badges in the turnbacks. Red breeches with twin, dark green side stripes, hussar boots with white trim. Dark green saddle furniture edged red with white crowned cipher "JN". Black harness with brass fittings. The 2nd's uniform was as for that of the 1st. Infantry uniform was dark blue with red facings.

THE KINGDOMS OF SPAIN AND PORTUGAL

Spain was ruled by the Bourbons until Napoleon placed his brother Joseph on the throne. The result was the Peninsular War, which lasted until 1814. Portugal was traditionally a British ally and, although its royal family fled in 1807, it fought alongside Britain until 1814.

THE KINGDOM OF SPAIN

Between 1808 and 1814 Spain's army was to suffer repeated, heavy defeats in the field against the French, largely because of bungling generals and poor cavalry. But time and again, the shattered fragments came together again to fight again. Given the chaotic internal situation in Spain during 1809–14, it is unlikely much attention was paid to uniforms.

Line Infantry

This nation wore a red cockade in its hats. There were only palace guards; no field units. Fusiliers wore the bicorn with cockade, loop and button;

▼ OFFICER OF ENGINEERS, 1808 *There were many sieges during the Peninsular War. The Spanish had 174 engineer officers in 1808. They had a silver castle badge on their collar.*

Spanish Infantry Regimental Distinctions: 1808

Title	Collar	Cuffs & Flaps	Lapels	Buttons
Rey	violet	violet	violet	yellow
Reyna	violet	violet	violet	white
Principe	white	violet	violet	yellow
Soria	white	violet	violet	white
La Princesa	violet	violet	white	white
Saboya	black	black	black	yellow
La Corona	black	black	black	white
Africa	white	black	black	yellow
Zamora	white	black	black	white
Sevilla	black	black	white	white
Granada	light blue	light blue	light blue	yellow
Valencia	light blue	light blue	light blue	white
Toledo	white	light blue	light blue	yellow
Murcia	white	light blue	light blue	white
Cantabria	light blue	light blue	white	white
Cordova	red	red	red	yellow
Guadalaxara	red	red	red	white
Malorca	white	red	red	yellow
Leon	white	red	red	white
Aragon	red	red	white	white
Zaragoza	green	green	green	yellow
España	green	green	green	white
Burgos	white	green	green	yellow
Asturia	white	green	green	white
Fixo de Cueta	green	green	white	white
Navarra	dark blue	dark blue	dark blue	yellow
America	dark blue	dark blue	dark blue	white
Malaga	white	dark blue	dark blue	yellow
Jaen	white	dark blue	dark blue	white
Ordenes Militares	dark blue	dark blue	white	white
Estremadura	crimson	crimson	crimson	yellow
Voluntarios de Castille	crimson	crimson	crimson	white
Voluntarios de Estado	white	crimson	crimson	yellow
Voluntarios de Corona	white	crimson	crimson	white
Voluntarios de Borbon	crimson	crimson	white	white
Irlanda*	yellow	yellow	yellow	yellow
Hibernia*	light blue	yellow	yellow	white
Ultonia*	yellow	yellow	light blue	yellow
Neapolis*	yellow	yellow	yellow	white

* these foreign regiments wore light blue tunics.

Spanish Cavalry Regimental Distinctions 1792–1815

No./Title	Collar	Cuffs	Lapels	Piping to Facings	Buttons
1 Rey	red	red	red*	white	yellow
2 Reyna	light blue	light blue	light blue**	red	white
3 Principe	red	red	red**	white	white
4 Infanta	white	white	white*	yellow	yellow
5 Borbon	red	red	red	white	white
6 Farnesio	red	red	red	yellow	white
7 Alcantara	red	red	light green	red to light green and vice versa	white
8 España	yellow	crimson	crimson	yellow	white
9 Algarbe	yellow	yellow	light blue	red	yellow
10 Calatrava	red	light blue	light blue	red	white
11 Santiago	crimson	crimson	crimson	scarlet	white
12 Montesa	crimson	crimson	white	white	white

* With yellow buttonholes. ** With white buttonholes

grenadiers had bearskin caps with no front plates, the elaborate cloth "bag" on the back being in the facing colour, embroidered in the button colour, with a different design for each regiment. Coats, small clothes and belts were white, facings being worn on the collar, cuffs, cuff flaps (with four buttons) and lapels. The short gaiters were black. All coloured parts were edged white, all white parts were piped in the facing colour. In each corner of the white turnbacks was a heart-shaped piece of cloth in the facing colour.

In 1812 stocks of uniforms from Britain began to be issued. They consisted of the conical shako, with red cockade, and brass badges. The new coats were dark blue with red collar, pointed cuffs, turnbacks and piping and brass buttons. Trousers were grey and worn over short, black gaiters, belts were white.

Light Infantry
In 1802 they wore a black Tarleton helmet, with red turban and cockade, green plume on left side and oval brass front plate, dark green dolman with

◄ OFFICER OF CAÇADORES, ESPAÑOLES HUSSARS, 1808 *The Tarleton helmet found friends in the Spanish Army as well as several others. Spain's cavalry was, by all accounts, poorly horsed and poorly officered. It could not stand up to the French in the field and was beaten again and again.*

red facings, yellow buttons and lace, red waist sash, small black pouch at the waistline, white breeches and long black gaiters. By 1806 this was replaced by uniform of line infantry style, but with dark blue tunic, white small clothes and dark brown greatcoat. Individual regiments were differentiated by facings and lace.

Artillery and Engineers
As for the the line infantry, but cut in dark blue with red facings, yellow buttons and yellow grenades on the collar. Engineers' uniform was as for the artillery, but with black facings, white buttons and piping. They wore a white castle badge on the collar.

Cavalry
Before 1800 the cavalry tunics had been white; they then changed to dark blue with red turnbacks. Headgear was a large bicorn, with red cockade, regimental button, loop and edging, long skirted coat with facings shown on collar, lapels and Swedish cuffs. On the collar were rampant lions and on the cuffs three lilies in the button colour. They wore buff small clothes, white belts, and high, cuffed boots. DRAGOONS. Hats were as for the cavalry; they wore yellow tunics and small clothes of infantry cut, white belts and breeches. In the corners of the collars were white badges of a crossed sword and palm frond; the lapels bore white

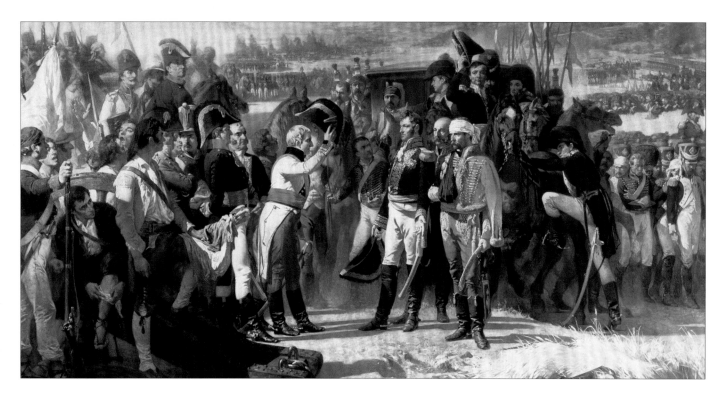

▲ *Napoleon's most embarrassing defeat to date was inflicted by Spanish General Francisco Xavier Castaños over General Dupont, at Bailen on 23 July, 1808.*

buttonholes. All facings were piped white; all buttons were white. Skirt pocket flaps were piped in the facing colour. Dragoons wore black leather gaiters and overshoes instead of boots. CHASSEURS À CHEVAL. There were two regiments of this arm in 1806; they wore shakos with red cockade and plume to the left-hand side, white top and bottom bands, white cords and front plate. Both wore a dark brown dolman with white lace and buttons, dark brown breeches and shabraque with white edging. Facings were shown on the collar, Polish cuffs, thigh knots and side stripes to breeches. The

regiment Olivença wore red facings with red and light blue barrel sash; the Volunterios de España had light blue facings and a light blue and white sash. The regiments wore the sword and palm badge in white on the collar. HUSSARS. There were two regiments in 1806. They wore uniforms as for the *chasseurs à cheval*, but with a pelisse. The regiment Maria Luisa wore a red dolman with light blue collar and cuffs, light blue pelisse with red facings, and black fur. They had a light blue and white barrel sash. There were white buttons, lace and trim to light blue breeches and to the shabraque. The regiment Españoles had a light green dolman with light blue facings, light blue pelisse faced light blue with black fur, light blue breeches, white buttons and lace; light green and white

sash. Both wore the black Tarleton helmet with brass plate and fittings, red cockade and plume.

The Army of King Joseph

This army was raised from 1809 and was in French service. Many men were recruited into this force from the prisoners captured from the old army fighting against the French; most of them just waited to be armed and equipped, then quickly deserted to the enemy. All badges of rank and intercompany distinctions as for the French Army.

The Guard infantry consisted of a regiment each of grenadiers, fusiliers and tirailleurs. Their uniform was as for the Imperial Guard, except the cockade was red and yellow. Cavalry included hussars and *chevau-légers*. There were seven line regiments, all wore a shako, dark brown coats, with facings on collar shoulder straps, lapels, Swedish cuffs and turnbacks, yellow buttons, white small clothes and belts, short black gaiters. The facings were: 1st Madrid, white; 2nd Toledo, light blue; 3rd Seville, black; 4th Soria, violet; 5th Granada, mid-blue; 6th Malaga, dark blue; 7th Cordova, red.

Light infantry wore light green pompon with red tip, green facings all

Table of Spanish Dragoon Regimental Distinctions 1792–1815

No/Title	Collar	Lapels	Cuffs and flaps
1st Rey	crimson	crimson	crimson
2nd Reyna	pink	pink	pink
3rd Almansa	light blue	light blue	light blue
4th Pavia	yellow	red	red
5th Villaviciosa	light green	light green	light green
6th Sagunto	yellow	light green	light green
7th Numantia	black	black	black
8th Lusitania	yellow	black	black

Spanish Light Infantry Regimental Distinctions: 1792–1815

No./Title	Collar	Cuffs & Flaps	Lapels	Buttons
1st Volunteers of Aragon	red	red	red	white
1st Volunteers of Cataluña	dark blue	yellow	yellow	yellow
Taragona	yellow	yellow	dark blue	yellow
Volunteers of Gerona	yellow	yellow	yellow	white
1st of Barcelona	yellow	yellow	dark blue	white
2nd of Barcelona	dark blue	red	red	yellow
Cazadores de Barbastro	red	red	dark blue	white
Volunteers of Valencia	crimson	crimson	crimson	white
Volunteers of Campo Mayor	dark blue	crimson	crimson	white
Volunteers of Navarra	crimson	crimson	crimson	yellow

The "British" uniform introduced in 1812 was as for the line, but with dark blue collar and white turnbacks.

▼ DRUM MAJOR, INFANTRY REGIMENT ZAMORA, 1809
The extra-wide bandolier was in the facing colour, embroidered in the button colour and bearing the Bourbon lily and the crest of the city of Zamorra.

edged red, brown breeches with hussar-style gaiters with red trim.

Cavalry wore uniforms as for the old Spanish cavalry, a bicorn with yellow loop, edging and button; a dark brown coat (but without the collar badges), facings to collar, lapels, Swedish cuffs and turnbacks, yellow buttons and trefoils to each shoulder, white small clothes and belts, heavy cavalry boots. Trumpeters wore red coats, faced yellow, yellow plumes with red bases, red and yellow cords. Facings were as follows: 1st, red; 2nd, white; 3rd, light blue; 4th, pink; 5th, black; 6th, green; 7th (lancers), black Chevau-Légèrs-style helmets with green crest, red plume, brass fittings. Dark brown coats were worn, with a yellow collar with red collar patches, red shoulder wings piped yellow, dark brown overalls seamed red with yellow buttons. Dark green saddle furniture edged yellow, red lance pennons with a yellow central stripe. Artillery and engineers were equipped and uniformed as for France, but with they wore a yellow and red cockade, and dark brown coat and trousers.

THE KINGDOM OF PORTUGAL

After years of neglect the Portuguese army was reorganized in 1808. A British general, William Carr Beresford, was placed in charge of a process made more difficult by the fact that the French had carried the bulk of the troops off as prisoners of war or for service in central Europe.

Infantry

The line infantry was regrouped into 24 regiments in three geographical divisions, the piping and turnbacks of the tunics reflecting the division in which the regiment was. Headgear was a shako (called a *barretina*) with raised front piece, oval brass plate bearing the Portuguese crest over a brass band pierced with the regimental number. Cords were mixed blue and the divisional colour; a white plume and the red-within-blue cockade were worn on the left side.

Grenadiers wore a brass grenade under the oval plate and wore fringes in blue and the divisional colour on their epaulettes. NCOs had blue and

Portuguese Line Infantry Regimental Distinctions 1808–1815

No./Title	Collar	Cuffs
1st or Southern Division; white piping and turnbacks		
1 Lippe's	blue	white
4 Freire's	blue	red
7 Setubal	blue	yellow
10 Lisbon	blue	sky blue
13 Peniche	white	white
16 Veira Telles	red	red
19 Cascaes	yellow	yellow
22 Serpa	sky blue	sky blue
2nd or Central Division; red piping and turnbacks		
2 Lagos	blue	white
5 1st Elvas	blue	red
8 Castello de Vide	blue	yellow
11 Penamacor	blue	sky blue
14 Tavira	white	white
17 2nd Elvas	red	red
20 Campo Major	yellow	yellow
23 Almeida	sky blue	sky blue
3rd or Northern Division; yellow piping and turnbacks		
3 1st Olivenca	blue	white
6 1st Oporto	blue	red
9 Viana	blue	yellow
12 Chaves	blue	sky blue
15 2nd Olivenca	white	white
18 2nd Oporto	red	red
21 Valenca	yellow	yellow
24 Braganca	sky blue	sky blue

their epaulettes. NCOs had blue and gold cords, officers wore gold. All buttons were brass, the coat dark blue, single-breasted, with regimental facings on collar and cuffs. Breeches and belts were white, the short gaiters were black. Drummers had lace, mixed blue and the divisional colour, to collar, cuffs and across the chest. On the cartridge pouch was the regimental number in brass.

There were six battalions of *cacadorres* (light troops), each with four companies armed with smooth-bore muskets and one – the Atiradores – with Baker rifles. They wore line infantry uniforms with green plume and shako cords, the battalion number on the shako band was within a hunting horn; a brown coat with green piping to the shoulder straps, black belts. Officers carried sabres on black slings. Buglers had lace in green and the divisional colour to collar, cuffs and across the chest. Initially each battalion had its own facings, but from July 1809 they largely adopted black.

Cavalry

Up to 1808 the Portuguese cavalry wore the conventional bicorn. The 1809 uniform was a Tarleton-style,

Portuguese Cavalry Regimental Distinctions

No./Title	Collar	Cuffs
1st or Southern Division; white piping and turnbacks		
1 Alcantara	white	white
4 Mccklcnburg	rcd	rcd
7 Caes	yellow	yellow
10 Santarem	sky blue	sky blue
2nd or Central Division; red piping and turnbacks		
2 Moira	white	white
5 Evora	red	red
8 Elvas	yellow	yellow
11 Almeida	sky blue	sky blue
3rd or Northern Division; yellow piping and turnbacks		
3 OLifeença	white	white
6 Bragança	red	red
9 Chaves	yellow	yellow
12 Miranda	sky blue	sky blue

Portuguese Light Infantry Regimental Distinctions

No/Title	Collar	Cuffs
1st or Southern Division; white piping and turnbacks		
1 Castello de Vide	brown	sky-blue
4 Beira	sky-blue	sky-blue
2nd or Central Division; red piping and turnbacks		
2 Moura	brown	red
5 Campo Major	red	red
3rd or Northern Division; yellow piping and turnbacks		
3 Tras os Montes	brown	yellow
6 Oporto	yellow	yellow

black leather helmet with black fur crest, brass oval plate and chin scales, light blue tunic with regimental and divisional trim as for the infantry, brass buttons and shoulder scales, white belts and breeches, hussar-style boots. Light blue saddle-cloths edged yellow, black harness. There were 12 cavalry regiments in all, but they were poorly mounted.

Artillery and Engineers

There were four artillery regiments in uniforms as for the line infantry, but with red collar and cuffs to the divisional piping and turnbacks, yellow buttons, white belts and breeches. The

▶ **DRUM MAJOR, 5TH PORTUGUESE CAÇADORES, 1812** *These riflemen were equipped with the Baker rifle and performed sterling service in the Peninsular War. Most of these regiments had black facings from 1809 but the 5th seems to have retained scarlet collar and cuffs. Interestingly, Portuguese units in French service also wore brown coats.*

Engineers was an all-officer corps, with dark blue coat and facings, gold buttons, and lace to collar and cuffs.

Militia

Each of Portugal's 48 districts was supposed to raise a militia regiment. Their uniforms were of poor quality in either green or blue.

▼ **COLONEL OF THE 10TH PORTUGUESE LINE REGIMENT, 1812** *As part of General Harvey's brigade, the 11th fought in Cole's 4th Division in the Battle of Albuera on 16 May 1811; this brigade lost 193 men, of which, 171 were from the Loyal Lusitanian Legion. The 11th were also at the siege and storm of Badajoz in April 1812. Note the traditional Portuguese barretina shako.*

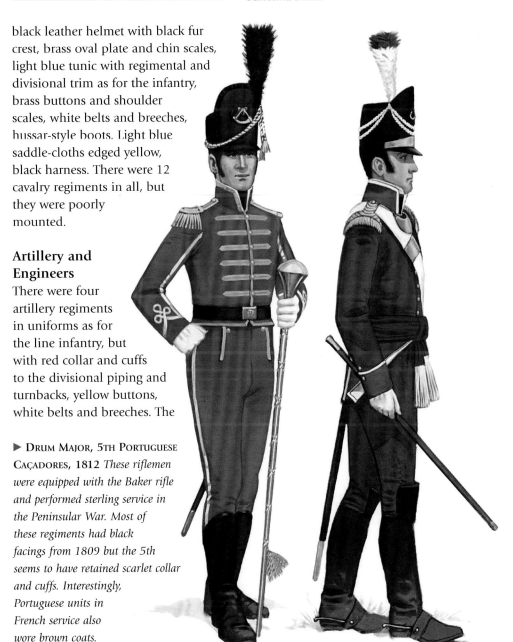

GLOSSARY

Adjutant: junior officer, assistant to a commander; not usually on the general staff. In the Prussian army the term was applied to aides-de-camp.

Aide-de-Camp: an officer of the general staff, assisting a general, by whom he was personally selected. On Napoleon's staff, these officers had considerable power.

Aiguillette: usually a gold or silver cord worn on the left or right shoulder, to denote a special status.

Army Corps: a formation of two or more divisions, usually containing infantry, cavalry and artillery.

Artillery: towed weapons, firing heavy projectiles, often explosive in nature.

Atiradores: Portuguese skirmishers.

Bandoliers: belts worn over the shoulders to carry equipment.

Bashkirs: Asian-Russian warriors, mounted and armed with bows.

Battalion: a unit of two or more companies, usually 600 men strong.

Bearskin: the fur-trimmed cap that was worn by grenadiers.

Bicorn: a round, black felt hat with the brim folded up to produce two points.

Bis: In a regimental title this signifies a second or alternate unit and is used to

▼ *The Scot's Greys ride down the French infantry at the Battle of Waterloo, 1815.*

differentiate the second of two units which share the same numerical designation.

Bock saddle: a light, wooden-framed saddle, originating in Mongolia and used by hussars and other light cavalry.

Bonnet de police: the French name for a simple cloth hat worn for fatigues.

Bosniak: light Albanian cavalry, taken into Prussian service in 1745.

Bullion: lace made of gold or silver threads.

Busby: a hussar fur cap with a coloured bag hanging to one side.

Caçadores: Portuguese light infantry armed with rifles.

Cadenettes: the little pigtails that hussars wore in front of each ear.

Cannoniers: French term for artillerymen or gunners.

Cap of Liberty: a red cloth cap worn by French revolutionaries in 1789.

Carabineer: a cavalryman, originally armed with a carbine.

Carbine: a short-barrelled musket.

Cartouche: a small pouch, filled with pistol cartridges, worn by officers.

Chasseur: French word for hunter, denoting light troops – dressed or armed for skirmishing.

Chasseur à cheval: mounted light cavalryman.

Chasseur à pied: light infantryman.

Chef d'esquadron: French cavalry squadron commander.

Chef de Bataillon: French commander of a battalion.

Chevalier-Garde: noble-born Guards, mounted on horses.

Chevau-Léger: light horse. These were light cavalrymen, mounted on smaller horses and therefore quick and nimble. Tasked with scouting and skirmishing. Also used to pursue a beaten enemy.

Cockade: a bow or rosette worn on the hat, usually in the national colours.

Colonel: an officer of senior (field) rank, below a general.

Colour: An infantry regimental flag, used as a reference and rallying point on the battlefield, highly prized as a

trophy and deemed a disgrace if lost.

Colpack: *see Busby.*

Comb: a solid vertical piece on top of a helmet, often surmounted by a crest.

Conscript: one chosen by ballot to serve in the army for a short period. Introduced by the Revolutionary government to meet the massive demands for manpower to defend the country, later adopted by other powers.

Contre-epaulette: a heavy, ornate shoulder strap with no fringes.

Corps d'Armée: *see Army Corps.*

Crest: a badge or coat of arms; a piece of fur or horsehair on a helmet.

Cuirass: armour for the upper body, consisting of a chest plate and sometimes a back plate.

Cuirassier: an armoured cavalryman mounted on a heavy horse (over 16 hands). Used for shock tactics.

Czapka: the traditional, tall, square-topped Polish hat, worn by lancer regiments of all armies of the time.

Dolman: waist-length jacket worn by hussars, heavily decorated with lace and buttons.

Dragoon: originally an infantryman, mounted to improve mobility, but equipped to fight on foot.

Eclaireurs à cheval: French term for mounted scouts.

Emigrés: French citizens who left France to escape the Terror of the Revolution from 1789 to 1800.

Engineer: a man trained in the construction of defences, bridge-building and siege warfare.

Ensign: the most junior English commissioned officer in the infantry.

Epaulettes: heavy shoulder straps with fringes to the outer ends.

Fähnrich: German term for ensign.

Fanions: small, triangular flags used to denote companies or squadrons or, in the case of lancers, used on lances to frighten enemy horses.

Farrier: a blacksmith who shod horses.

Feldmarschall: *see Field Marshal.*

Field Marshal: the senior officer's rank in an army.

Flounder: woven, flat oval-shaped patterns of cap cords, usually above the tassels at the ends of the cords.

Freiherr: German equivalent of baron.

Freikorps: Free Corps, often volunteers raised by patriotic noblemen.

Frogging: the lace bars on the chest of hussar dolmans and pelisses.

Fusil: a light musket.

Fusilier: originally soldiers armed with a fusil, first seen in France in 1640.

Gaiters: cloth or canvas coverings for the lower leg, designed to fit over the shoe to keep out dirt and stones.

Garde du Corps: bodyguard; usually a unit close to the monarch, responsible for his or her safety.

Gendarmerie: a term for military police force, French in origin but also used by other nations.

General de Brigade: an officer of general rank commanding a brigade of troops or equivalent.

General de Division: an officer of general rank commanding a division of troops or equivalent.

Gorget: a metal collar plate worn by officers on duty as a badge of office.

Grande tenue: full dress.

Greatcoat: an outer garment worn over the jacket to protect against cold and wet weather.

Grenadier: originally a man trained to ignite and throw grenades; later an elite soldier.

Grenadier à cheval: mounted grenadier.

Grenzers: Austrian border guards; regiments raised in the areas bordering the Turkish empire in the Balkans.

Gribeauval design: the field artillery pieces devised by French Jean-Baptiste-Vaquette de Gribeauval, 1715–1789, based on the Liechtenstein system that standardized and lightened French artillery and improved mobility.

Guard of Honour: a special group of soldiers assembled to honour a highly important visitor.

Guidon: swallow-tailed regimental symbol carried by dragoon regiments.

Hand: a length of 4 in (10 cm), used to measure the height of a horse.

Heavy cavalry: cavalrymen mounted on horses over 14 hands high at the shoulder used for shock action.

Horse artillery: field artillery designed to have high mobility, whose crews were all mounted on horses or artillery vehicles.

Howitzer: originally *Haufnicze*, from the Hussite Wars of 1419–36, an artillery piece designed to fire projectiles in a high trajectory, to reach targets hidden from direct view.

Hussar: originally (from 1458 to 1490) the Balkan name for light horse men raised to fight the Turks, meaning robber, freebooter or corsair.

Imperial Guard: the formation raised by Napoleon from the Consular Guard that he inherited. Russia also had an Imperial Guard, originally household troops guarding the czar's person, later an elite force of veterans.

Insurrektion: the Hungarian equivalent of a territorial defence force.

Invalides: soldiers, who by virtue of sickness, age or wounds were no longer capable of performing field duties and were accommodated in garrison towns.

Jägers: the German word for hunter, usually trained for skirmishing duties and armed with rifles. Most German states had these in their armies but they also appeared in the Russian, Swedish and Danish military.

Kalmucks: irregular Russian light cavalrymen, originally from the western Mongolian Oirat tribe, who settled in the Altai region.

Kasket: a leather helmet with peaks to front and rear, crest, and often a comb.

Katanken: black frock coat worn by many Prussian units, also known as the Litewka style

Kiwer: the trademark, Russian-style shako with a belled-out, concave top, introduced from 1810.

▲ *The British Black Watch at the Battle of Quatre Bras, 16 June, 1815.*

Kollet: a close-fitting, jacket, with short skirts, turned back at the front.

Konfederatka: a low-crowned, ornate, square-topped Polish hat, usually worn by officers.

Kurtka: the traditional, short-tailed jacket of the Polish lancer.

Kusket: Swedish version of a top hat.

Lancer: light cavalryman armed with a lance (if in the front rank of battle).

Landsturm: German name for home guard, usually boys and old men, with basic weapons and no artillery.

Landwehr: German term for territorial defence forces, lightly armed and of lower quality and less ability than regular troops; they had no artillery.

Limber: the vehicle to which a field gun trail was attached to enable the gun to be moved by a team of horses.

Light cavalry: cavalrymen mounted on smaller horses and therefore quick and agile. Tasked with scouting and skirmishing. Also used to pursue a beaten enemy. Hussars, *chasseurs*, various light horse and lancers fall into this category.

Light infantry: very mobile infantry, trained to fight in open (skirmishing) order and to operate in advance of and on the flanks of the main line of battle.

Line infantry: also heavy infantry; slower moving foot soldiers than light infantry, originally trained only to fight in lines (two, three or more ranks deep) as the main body of an army.

Litewka: full-skirted, single-breasted tunic without lapels, of Polish or Lithuanian origin.

▲ *The charge of the Britain's heavy cavalry against the French Cuirassiers at Waterloo.*

Major: the lowest rank of field officers, usually commanding a battalion.

Mamelukes: originally slaves of Turkish rulers, armed and trained to act as bodyguards for sultans and caliphs. Some were brought back to France from Egypt by Napoleon and incorporated into his Old Guard.

Marines: infantry soldiers on warships.

Marshal: *see Field Marshal.*

Middle Guard: a division of the Imperial Guard consisting of the Fusilier-Grenadiers, Fusilier-Chasseurs, Gendarmes d'Ordonnance and the Vélites of Florence and Turin.

Miner: soldier trained and equipped to dig tunnels in siege operations.

Mirliton: a peakless winged cap worn by hussars with a coloured strip of cloth wound around it, which might be worn floating freely. It was replaced by the shako from 1800 onwards.

Musket: long-barrelled, personal, flintlock firearm.

Musketeer: soldier armed with a musket acting as line infantry.

National Guard: French armed force, raised at the time of the Revolution in 1789, later a territorial defence force.

Oberst: German name for a colonel.

Old Guard: the senior division of Napoleon's Imperial Guard.

Pallasch: German straight-bladed sword of the heavy cavalry.

Pelisse: fur-lined and trimmed outer jacket of the hussar, usually worn over the left shoulder, decorated with rows of lace and buttons, as on the dolman.

Piping: a narrow cloth edging to a collar, cuff, cuff flap, lapel, shoulder strap or turnback.

Pontonniers: bridge-building troops.

Portépée: the strap attached to the hilt of a sabre or sword, originally wound around the wrist to prevent the weapon being lost in combat. By the Napoleonic era this item – in gold or silver, mixed with a national colour – was the badge of office of an officer or NCO. For privates it would show the company of the wearer by use of coloured tassels.

Portmanteau: small saddle bag or valise attached to the saddle.

Pulk: Russian for regiment.

Queue: Hair tied and bound into a pigtail at the back; sometimes this pigtail was stiffened with tar.

Regiment: a unit of two or more battalions or squadrons. Britain, having a small army, had numerous regiments of only a single battalion.

Rifle: a firearm with spiral grooves cut into the bore of the weapon, to impart spin to the projectile when fired. This made it much more accurate than conventional smoothbore firearms.

Sabretasche: decorated pouch, hung from a hussar's waist-belt, sometimes also carried by other cavalry regiments.

Sapper: troops equipped and trained to dig field defences and siege works.

Schützenverein: shooting club, a tradition in the Tyrol and Germany.

Shabraque: an ornamented saddlecloth; derived from the Turkish word *tschprak* and in European use since the seventeenth century.

Shako: a peaked cap; derived from the old Hungarian word *csako*.

Small clothes: items worn under the tunic: waistcoat, shirt and/or breeches.

Spencer tunic: French tunic introduced by Major Bardin in 1812, closed to the waist with a high, closed collar, square lapels and brief skirts turned back at front and rear. Named after Earl Spencer, who pioneered the style.

Spontoon: a weapon resembling a pike with a much shorter staff; by the Napoleonic era it was used more as a badge of office than as a weapon.

Standard: a small, square regimental flag, which served as a symbol of a cavalry regiment.

Surtout: literally "overall"; a full-skirted, single-breasted coat.

Swallows' nests: decorated arcs of cloth at the shoulders, usually worn by drummers and trumpeters. Similar shoulder decorations called wings (see below) were worn by the grenadier and light companies of the British infantry.

Tarleton helmet: a low-crowned helmet with a front peak and bearskin crest, adopted by Sir Banastre Tarleton in the War of American Independence.

Tirailleur: skirmisher or sharpshooter.

Train: the collective term for the baggage vehicles of an army.

Turnbacks: the front and back parts of the skirts of a coat, which were turned back to show the lining in a contrasting colour.

Überrock: *see Surtout.*

Uhlan or Ulan: *see Lancer.*

Vandyking: an edging to an item, which is divided from the main body of the item by a zig-zag line.

Vélites: lightly armed foot soldiers; skirmishers.

Voltigeur: literally "jumpers": agile, light infantry soldiers.

Wings: decorated arcs of cloth worn at the shoulders by members of the flank companies (grenadiers and light infantry) of British infantry battalions.

Young Guard: the junior regiments of Napoleon's Imperial Guard.

INDEX

▲ *The helmet of a Grenadier NCO, line infantry, Grand Duchy of Warsaw.*

▼ *The brass cap plate of the 43rd regiment of the French line infantry.*

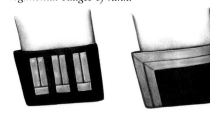

▼ *Two examples of Prussian cuirassier NCOs regimental badges of rank.*

▼ *The cap plate of the 15th regiment of the French line infantry.*

▲ *The calfskin pack and rolled blanket or greatcoat used by all French infantry.*

▶ *The hilt of the sword carried by all officers of the German and Hungarian infantry regiments.*

▲ *Russian infantry regimental shoulder knots; Nishegorod, Uglitch and Butyrsk.*

▲ *A pair of Prussian heavy cavalry pistols, with brass fittings and decorated butts.*

▲ *British royal artillery Belgic shakos, left: that of an officer, right: a private's.*

ACKNOWLEDGEMENTS

This book represents one of the most challenging projects that I have undertaken to date. Not only in the great selection of uniform plates in full colour, but the breadth of the topics covered, which range from contemporary social history, through economics, politics and tactics, to army recruiting methods, the nuts and bolts of how an army was controlled; the tactics, weapon capabilites, battle plans and results, even naval warfare. The major difference to most works of this type is that the publishers grasped the nettle and decided to include in it the relatively little-known Revolutionary period, thus presenting a rare picture of this entire dynamic era within the covers of a single volume. Great economy has had to be exercised; each colour plate has had to convey as many uniform details as possible; there has been little chance to wax eloquently, verbally, on such topics.

The many plates of items of clothing and equipment have aided this process immensely and the many elegant, well-executed colour plates of figures and items of kit and equipment form a wonderful extension to this book. The one thing which came to the fore in the preparation of this work, was that, although uniform regulations, issued at army level, may have prescribed one form for an item of clothing, it is clear that regimental commanders (who were responsible for procuring uniforms for their men in most cases) frequently ignored these instructions and ordered items of their own preferred patterns. I trust that this book will be a source of enjoyment for a very wide audience.

Digby Smith.

Picture acknowlegements
Figure and map illustrations that appear in the book are the property of Anness Publishing. Thanks to the following agencies who provided additional images:
The Art Archive
pp2, 8–9, 17 b, 19t, 20 b, 21 t, 25, 26 b, 33 b, 36–7, 53 t, 89 b, 118–19, 120 b, 122, 123, 126 t, 156–7, 158 t, 160, 188–9, 190 t, 191, 192, 193, 195 t, 229.
Peter Newark's Military Pictures
pp6 bl. 7 b, 10 both, 13 b, 15, 16, 19 b, 20 t, 22, 23 all, 29 b, 31 tr, 33 tr, 34 t, 35 b, 38 both, 39 both, 41 both, 63 l, 80–81, 82 t, 84, 125 t, 159, 248, 249, 250.
The Bridgeman Art Library pp11t, 13t, 18, 21 b, 26 t, 27 t, 28 t, 30 t, p31 tl, 51, 71 tl, 72 t, 82 b, 83, both, 85 t, 87 b, 89 t, 103 t, 132 t, 120 t, 124 both, 132 t, 158, 161 b, 190 b, 195 b, 208 t, 215 bl, 224/5, 245.

▼ *A Tartar light horseman from the Russian Army, with traditional uniform.*

▼ *A trooper of Britain's 10th light Dragoons, wearing the distinctive hussar-style coat.*